शिवपूजा

Śiva Pūjā and Advanced Yajña

By
स्वामी सत्यानन्द सरस्वती
Swami Satyananda Saraswati
and
स्वामी विट्ठलानन्द सरस्वती
Swami Vittalananda Saraswati

Published By
Devi Mandir Publications

Śiva Pūjā and Advanced Yajña,

by Devi Mandir Publications
5950 Highway 128
Napa, CA 94558 USA
Communications: Phone and Fax 1-707-966-2802
E-Mail swamiji@shreemaa.org
Please visit us on the World Wide Web at
http://www.shreemaa.org/

ISBN 1-887472-62-2
Library of Congress Catalog Card Number
CIP 98-093791

Śiva Pūjā and Advanced Yajña,
Swami Satyananda Saraswati
1. Hindu Religion. 2. Worship. 3. Spirituality.
4. Philosophy. I. Saraswati, Swami Satyananda;
Saraswati, Swami Vittalananda

Saṃskṛta and Computer Layout
by Swami Vittalananda Saraswati

Table of Contents

Introduction

There is only one God. Just as one woman is known as a mother, a daughter, a wife, a sister, or a friend, depending on the different relationships she has, in the same way the One God is called by different names by different people in different circumstances. People call Him variously Creator, Protector or Destroyer; Giver of Wisdom, Giver of Wealth, Remover of Darkness, according to the various circumstances which Life presents. People even call Him Her, and worship the Divine Mother Goddess as the Supreme Divinity.

In this world of duality, people are required to enumerate specific qualities and attitudes in order to communicate. Śiva is God's qualities of Infinite Goodness and Continual Transformation.

Conceive in your mind the ultimate goodness and when you have your picture of perfect goodness, infinite goodness, then make it better. That is the beginning of the understanding of Śiva. In this pūjā we place Śiva in our hearts, place ourselves in the presence of Śiva, and then strive to come closer and closer to this Highest Goodness, the Highest Divine Spirit. When we get to where we can't get any closer, that is when the pūjā begins. Śiva is beyond limitations. He takes us beyond the mind.

His name has an excellent meaning in Saṃskṛta:

श-कार शान्ति प्रकाश इ-पद् कारण देह ।
व-इति छिरस्ताय मिलण शिवार्थ चित्त मंगलम् ॥

śa-kāra śānti prakāśa i-pada kāraṇa deha
va-iti chirastāya milaṇa śivārtha citta maṃgalam

The letter **śa** is the illumination of Peace, the syllable **i** is the Causal Body, **va** means union with the infinite, and the definition of Śiva is the welfare of all objects of perception.

Śiva is also the Destroyer. Every moment of time has a beginning, an existence and a transformation into something else. In reality, matter is never destroyed - it only changes form. So what is called destruction is really the process of transformation from what was known into something new. Śiva is always transforming all that was into what it is becoming. He allows for the fluid motion and continual change in the ocean of existence.

All fear is of the unknown. The transitory nature of existence makes us feel insecure. We want things to stay the way they are, because we don't know what change will bring. That is why Śiva, as the Destroyer, is so frightening. What will it be like when He is done? Will He ever be done? Maybe He'll just go on changing things ad infinitum.

Until we accept the will of Śiva there will be fear. As long as we identify with the changes that are occurring, we have attachment. By saying to God, "I like the universe the way it is, please don't change it," we resist the course of nature. We create our own pain by our attachment to the way we think things should be. Śiva, as the Great Destroyer, will destroy our attachment too. That is His function as the Consciousness of Continual Transformation.

By worshiping Śiva, we cultivate the qualities of infinite consciousness, unattachment, and freedom from bondage to this world of objects and their relationships. We cultivate the attitude of perceiving the intrinsic reality, not the extrinsic appearance. We identify with that which does not change. We become the witness of the changes of nature. From this perception, we act and interact with the world. Remembering the eternal reality, we free ourselves from pain and fear. We see them as passing states of mind and accept the will of God.

Śiva is also the Lord of Saṅkalpa, the strength of will power to define and obtain our goals. Nothing deflects Śiva from His path. Śiva gives us the strength to attach ourselves to the sustaining values of life, to the values that will stay with us through eternity, which according to this tradition are called the Sanātana Dharma, the eternal ideals of perfection.

Pū means pūñya, the highest merit, and jā means jāta, to give birth. Pūjā means the actions which give birth to the highest merit. In our tradition, the highest merit is being given the privilege to sit in the presence of God. By performing pūjā, we rehearse what it would be like for God to come to our home. We shine our utensils. We decorate the altar with flowers and lights, incense and candles. We prepare good food because an honored guest is coming.

A pūjā is also a compendium of knowledge of spiritual practices. In many ways the systems of worship resemble a Table of Contents of subjects that will be of interest and benefit in the spiritual evolution of an aspirant. There are many mantras that offer a flower and obeisance to a deity or group of deities. Why we are bowing to these divine powers of the universe will be explained in other scriptures. The pūjā merely points the way to a whole other branch of learning. That is why there is no end to pūjā. There is no end to learning.

Yajña comes from the root yuj, to unite. Inside the ajña cakra the light of meditation is burning. Outside on the ceremonial fire altar is the fire, the objective measurement of how brightly our inner light is glowing. The yajña is the union between these two fires. This union is the sacrifice of all egotism and duality. The yajña fire will not burn with wood and ghee alone. The yajña fire requires devotion to the exclusion of selfishness. The purpose of the yajña is to unite the two fires so that all the thoughts become oblations to the fire, offerings of sacrifice. When we unite the fires with such devotion that there is no other thought, then we have participated in a yajña.

This advanced pūjā contains a great deal of information. It is possible that an advanced student could remain engaged in its study for several years. You are not required to learn this whole pūjā immediately. You can take bits and pieces of this pūjā and put them to work. This book includes a beginners pūjā, an intermediate pūjā, an advanced pūjā and a post-doc section. So there is more than ample material to keep you engrossed in the worship of God. Read through the pūjās and read the translations. Some mantras will call to you, something will touch your heart and illuminate an inspiration, and that is where you could begin.

Look for those mantras that say, "I belong to you, I am the echo of the vibration that is in your soul." As you practice those particular sections, other parts will call to you as well. If you don't pronounce the mantras correctly, don't worry. Put yourself in the attitude of surrender to the will of God and try to come as close as possible. Cultivate the attitude of appreciation for all the bounteous gifts of God, especially for the privilege of being able to sit in the presence of God. Cultivate the attitude of gratitude, and carry it with you throughout your daily activities. Only then will worship pervade our lives.

Worship does not mean the memorization of mantras, or even the proper placement of the flowers and other objects. Worship is an attitude of respect, of dedication, of devotion to the exclusion of selfishness, and I bow to my teacher Shree Maa, who is the greatest example that one could pray for, and I offer this work to all devotees as an expression of my appreciation for the understanding which has been entrusted to me.

Swami Satyananda Saraswati
Devi Mandir, 1998

साधनपञ्चकं

sādhana pañcakam

\- 1 -

वेदो नित्यमधीयतां तदुदितं कर्म स्वनुष्ठीयतां
तेनेशस्य विधीयतामपचितिः काम्ये मतिस्त्यज्यताम् ।
पापौघः परिभूयतां भवसुखे दोषोऽनुसन्धीयता-
मात्मेच्छा व्यवसीयतां निजगृहात्तूर्णं विनिर्गम्यताम् ॥

vedo nityamadhīyatāṃ
taduditaṃ karma svanuṣṭhīyatāṃ
teneśasya vidhīyatām
apacitiḥ kāmye matistyajyatām
pāpaughaḥ paribhūyatāṃ
bhavasukhe doṣo-nusandhīyatām-
ātmecchā vyavasīyatāṃ
nijagṛhāttūrṇaṃ vinirgamyatām

Always study words of wisdom, with all of your capacity act in accordance and perform the discipline of these words, and following the systems of worship they enumerate, make the worship of the Supreme Lord, and don't allow your consciousness to contemplate adverse desires. Wipe all the dross of sin from your mind, search for the faults in the pleasures of the world, search your own soul for true knowledge, and very quickly try to renounce the attachments to your home.

\- 2 -

सङ्गः सत्सु विधीयतां भगवतो भक्तिर्दृढा धीयतां
शान्त्यादिः परिचीयतां दृढतरं कर्माशु सन्त्यज्यताम् ।
सद्विद्वानुपसर्प्यतां प्रतिदिनं तत्पादुका सेव्यतां
ब्रह्मैकाक्षरमर्थ्यतां श्रुतिशिरोवाक्यं समाकर्ण्यताम् ॥

saṅgaḥ satsu vidhīyatāṃ
bhagavato bhaktirdṛḍhā dhīyatāṃ
śāntyādiḥ paricīyatāṃ
dṛḍhataraṃ karmāśu santyajyatām
sadvidvānupasarpyatāṃ
pratidinaṃ tatpādukā sevyatāṃ
brahmaikākṣaramarthyatāṃ
śrutiśirovākyaṃ samākarṇyatām

Maintain the association of true people, take refuge with devotion in the Supreme Divinity, and with all your capacity try to befriend the universe, and very quickly renounce the fruits of your labors. Whenever possible seek out the company of the true and knowledgeable people, and serve the sandals of their lotus feet, and ask from them even one letter of the knowledge of Brahman and listen to the great words of wisdom from the Vedas.

- 3 -

वाक्यार्थश्च विचार्यतां श्रुतिशिरः पक्षःसमाश्रीयतां
दुस्तर्कात्सुविरम्यतां श्रुतिमतस्तर्कोऽनुसन्धीयताम् ।
ब्रह्मैवास्मि विभाव्यतामहरहर्गर्वः परित्यज्यतां
देहेऽहम्मतिरुज्झ्यतां बेधजनैर्वादः परित्यज्यताम् ॥

vākyārthaśca vicāryatāṃ
śrutiśiraḥ pakṣaḥsamāśrīyatāṃ
dustarkātsuviramyatāṃ
śrutimatastarko-nusandhīyatām
brahmaivāsmi vibhāvyatām
aharahargarvaḥ parityajyatāṃ
dehe-hammatirujjhyatāṃ
bedhajanairvādaḥ parityajyatām

Always contemplate the great words of wisdom, take refuge in the great words of wisdom, and stay far away from the bondages of the soul, and search for the real inner meanings of the texts of wisdom. I am one with God, always maintain this attitude. Make renunciation of the many thoughts of the mind, and leave the egotism of your body, and don't debate idle philosophies with intellectuals.

- 4 -

क्षुद्व्याधिश्च चिकित्स्यतां प्रतिदिनं भिक्षौषधं भुज्यतां
स्वाद्वन्नं न तु याच्यतां विधिवशात्प्राप्तेन सन्तुष्यताम् ।
शीतोष्णादि विषह्यतां न तु वृथा वाक्यं समुच्चार्यता-
मौदासीन्यमभीप्स्यतां जनकृपा नैष्ठुर्यमुत्सृज्यताम् ॥

kṣudvyādhiśca cikitsyatāṃ
pratidinaṃ bhikṣauṣadhaṃ bhujyatāṃ
svādvannaṃ na tu yācyatāṃ
vidhivaśāt prāptena santuṣyatām
śītoṣṇādi viṣahyatāṃ
na tu vṛthā vākyaṃ samuccāryatām-
audāsīnyamabhīpsyatāṃ
janakṛpā naiṣṭhuryamut sṛjyatām

Take the cure for the illness of uncontrolled desire, serve your doctor as a beggar would serve a Lord, don't seek the associations of pleasure-seekers or self-centered individuals. Remain contented with whatever you receive in a divine union, that which God has consented to give. Remain the same while undergoing all the pairs of opposites like hot and cold, pleasure and pain, and don't give expression to worthless speech. Carry yourself as a great renunciate. Don't look to get grace from other men, and don't seek to obtain something from men.

\- 5 -

एकान्ते सुखमास्यतां परतरे चेतः समाधीयतां
पूर्णात्मा सुसमीक्ष्यतां जगदिदं तद्बाधितं दृश्यताम् ।
प्राक्कर्म प्रविलाप्यतां चितिबलान्नाप्युत्तरैः श्लिष्यतां
प्रारब्धं त्विह भुज्यतामथ परब्रह्मात्मना स्थीयताम् ॥

ekānte sukhamāsyatāṃ
paratare cetaḥ samādhīyatāṃ
pūrṇātmā susamīkṣyatāṃ
jagadidaṃ tadbādhitaṃ dṛśyatām
prākkarma pravilāpyatāṃ
citibalānnāpyuttaraiḥ śliṣyatāṃ
prārabdhaṃ tviha bhujyatām
atha parabrahmātmanā sthīyatām

Sit down in a quiet, conducive and comfortable environment, and contemplate the Supreme Divinity. Look into yourself with the fullness of consciousness, and see the bondage of the gross world to the soul, and reduce your necessity for action in the world. Don't allow your thoughts to be bound by karma, with the strength of wisdom free your mind from bondage. Experience the fruits of your prarabda karma, the actions performed in the past, the fruits of which are being experienced in the present, and after the past karma is complete, with an attitude of one mind, go to the realms of Union with the Highest Divinity and remain there.

\- 6 -

यः श्लोकपञ्चकमिदं पठते मनुष्यः
सञ्चिन्तयत्यनुदिनं स्थिरतामुपेत्य ।
तस्याशु संसृतिदवानलतीव्रघोर-
तापःप्रशान्तिमुपयाति चितिप्रसादात् ॥

yaḥ ślokapañcakamidaṃ paṭhate manuṣyaḥ
sañcintayatyanudinaṃ sthiratāmupetya
tasyāśu saṃsṛtidavānalatīvraghora-
tāpaḥpraśāntimupayāti citiprasādāt

Whoever will read these five verses, and with a still consciousness every day contemplate the essence of these verses, for him or her the great flames of bondage to objects and relationships and disruption to the soul's peace will be quickly eradicated.

इति श्रीमच्छङ्कराचार्यविरचितं साधनपञ्चकं सम्पूर्णम्

iti śrīmacchaṅkarācāryaviracitaṃ
sādhanapañcakaṃ sampūrṇam

Thus ends the five verses in praise of spiritual discipline written by Shankar Acharya in 700 A.D.

देवता प्रणाम्

devatā praṇām

श्रीमन्महागणाधिपतये नमः

śrīmanmahāgaṇādhipataye namaḥ

We bow to the Respected Great Lord of Wisdom.

लक्ष्मीनारायणाभ्यां नमः

lakṣmīnārāyaṇābhyāṃ namaḥ

We bow to Lakṣmī and Nārāyaṇa, The Goal of all Existence and the Perceiver of all.

उमामहेश्वराभ्यां नमः

umāmaheśvarābhyāṃ namaḥ

We bow to Umā and Maheśvara, She who protects existence, and the Great Consciousness or Seer of all.

वाणीहिरण्यगर्भाभ्यां नमः

vāṇīhiraṇyagarbhābhyāṃ namaḥ
We bow to Vāṇī and Hiraṇyagarbha, Sarasvatī and Brahmā, who create the cosmic existence.

शचीपुरन्दराभ्यां नमः

śacīpurandarābhyāṃ namaḥ
We bow to Śacī and Purandara, Indra and his wife, who preside over all that is divine.

मातापितृभ्यां नमः

mātāpitṛbhyāṃ namaḥ
We bow to the Mothers and Fathers.

इष्टदेवताभ्यो नमः

iṣṭadevatābhyo namaḥ
We bow to the chosen deity of worship.

कुलदेवताभ्यो नमः

kuladevatābhyo namaḥ
We bow to the family deity of worship.

ग्रामदेवताभ्यो नमः

grāmadevatābhyo namaḥ
We bow to the village deity of worship.

वास्तुदेवताभ्यो नमः

vāstudevatābhyo namaḥ
We bow to the particular household deity of worship.

स्थानदेवताभ्यो नमः

sthānadevatābhyo namaḥ

We bow to the established deity of worship.

सर्वेभ्यो देवेभ्यो नमः

sarvebhyo devebhyo namaḥ

We bow to all the Gods.

सर्वेभ्यो ब्राह्मणेभ्यो नमः

sarvebhyo brāhmaṇebhyo namaḥ

We bow to all the Knowers of divinity.

शिव ध्यानम्

śiva dhyānam

ॐ सदा शिवाय विद्महे सहश्राक्षाय धीमहे ।

तन्नो शम्भो प्रचोदयात् ॥

oṃ sadā śivāya vidmahe sahaśrākṣāya dhīmahe
tanno śambho pracodayāt

oṃ We meditate upon the Perfect, Full, Complete, Always Continuing, Consciousness of Infinite Goodness; contemplate He Whose Thousand Eyes see everywhere. May that Giver of Bliss grant us increase.

ॐ सद्योजातं प्रपद्यामि सद्योजातायवै नमो नमः ।

भवे भवे नाति भवे भवस्वमांभवोद्भवाय नमः ॥

oṃ sadyojātaṃ prapadyāmi
sadyojātāyavai namo namaḥ
bhave bhave nāti bhave
bhavasvamāṃ bhavodbhavāya namaḥ

oṃ I extol the Birth of Truth as Pure Existence. Again and again I bow down to the Birth of Truth as Pure Existence. In being after being, beyond all being, who Himself is all Being, from whom came all being, to That Existence I bow.

वामदेवाय नमो ज्येष्ठाय नमः श्रेष्ठाय नमो रुद्राय नमः । कालाय नमः कलविकरणाय नमो बलविकरणाय नमो बलाय नमो बलप्रमत्तनाय नमः । सर्वभूतदमनाय नमोमनोन्मनाय नमः ॥

vāmadevāya namo jyeṣṭhāya namaḥ śreṣṭhāya namo rudrāya namaḥ kālāya namaḥ kalavikaraṇāya namo balavikaraṇāya namo balāya namo balapramattanāya namaḥ sarvabhūtadamanāya namomanonmanāya namaḥ

I bow to the Beautiful God who is Beloved. I bow to the Pleasant One, to the Ultimate One; I bow to the Reliever of Sufferings. I bow to Time, I bow to the Cause of the Illumination of Darkness, I bow to the Source of Strength, I bow to the Progenitor of Strength. I bow to the Fashioner of all the elements, I bow to the Mind of all minds.

अघोरेभ्योत्तघोरेभ्योघोरघेरतरेभ्यः । सर्वेभ्यःसर्वशर्वेभ्यो नमस्तेऽस्तुरुद्ररूपेभ्यः ॥

aghorebhyottaghorebhyoghoragheratarebhyaḥ sarvebhyaḥsarvaśarvebhyo namaste-sturudrarūpebhyaḥ

I bow to He who is Free From Fear, who instills the fear of evil, who saves the righteous from fear; who is within all, the all of everything, may we give our respect to He who is the form of the Reliever of Sufferings.

ॐ तत् पुरुषाय विद्महे महादेवाय धीमहि ।
तन्नो रुद्रः प्रचोदयात् ॥

oṃ tat puruṣāya vidmahe mahādevāya dhīmahi
tanno rudraḥ pracodayāt

We meditate upon That Universal Consciousness, contemplate the Great God. May that Reliever of Sufferings grant us increase.

ईशानः सर्वविद्यानमीश्वरः सर्वभूतानाम् ।
ब्रह्माधिपतिर्ब्रह्मणोधिपतिर्ब्रह्माशिवोमेऽस्तुसदाशिवोम् ॥

īśānaḥ sarvavidyānamīśvaraḥ sarvabhūtānām
brahmādhipatirbrahmaṇodhipatirbrahmāśivome-stusadāśivom

The Seer of All, who is all Knowledge, the Lord of the Universe, who is all existence; before the Creative Consciousness, before the knowers of Consciousness, existing in eternal delight as the Consciousness of Infinite Goodness.

ॐ अग्निर्ज्योतिर्ज्योतिरग्निः स्वाहा ।
सूर्यो ज्योतिर्ज्योतिः सूर्यः स्वाहा ।
अग्निर्वर्चो ज्योतिर्वर्चः स्वाहा ।
सूर्यो वर्चो ज्योतिर्वर्चः स्वाहा ।
ज्योतिः सूर्यः सूर्यो ज्योतिः स्वाहा ॥

oṃ agnir jyotir jyotir agniḥ svāhā
sūryo jyotir jyotiḥ sūryaḥ svāhā
agnir varco jyotir varcaḥ svāhā
sūryo varco jyotir varcaḥ svāhā
jyotiḥ sūryaḥ sūryo jyotiḥ svāhā

oṃ The Divine Fire is the Light, and the Light is the Divine Fire; I am One with God! The Light of Wisdom is the Light, and the Light is the Light of Wisdom; I am One with God! The Divine Fire is the offering, and the Light is the Offering; I am One with God! The Light of Wisdom is the Offering, and the Light is the Light of Wisdom; I am One with God!

(Wave light)

ॐ अग्निर्ज्योती रविर्ज्योतिश्चन्द्रो ज्योतिस्तथैव च ।

ज्योतिषामुत्तमो देव दीपोऽयं प्रतिगृह्यताम् ॥

एष दीपः ॐ नमः शिवाय ॥

oṃ agnirjyotī ravirjyotiścandro jyotistathaiva ca
jyotiṣāmuttamo deva dīpo-yaṃ pratigṛhyatām
eṣa dīpaḥ oṃ namaḥ śivāya

oṃ The Divine Fire is the Light, the Light of Wisdom is the Light, the Light of Devotion is the Light as well. The Light of the Highest Bliss, Oh God, is in the Light which we offer, the Light which we request you to accept. With the offering of Light oṃ I bow to the Consciousness of Infinite Goodness.

(Wave incense)

ॐ वनस्पतिरसोत्पन्नो गन्धात्ययी गन्ध उत्तमः ।

आघ्रेयः सर्वदेवानां धूपोऽयं प्रतिगृह्यताम् ॥

एष धूपः ॐ नमः शिवाय ॥

oṃ vanaspatirasotpanno gandhātyayī gandha uttamaḥ
āghreyaḥ sarvadevānāṃ dhūpo-yaṃ pratigṛhyatām
eṣa dhūpaḥ oṃ namaḥ śivāya

oṃ Spirit of the Forest, from you is produced the most excellent of scents. The scent most pleasing to all the Gods, that scent we request you to accept. With the offering of fragrant scent oṃ I bow to the Consciousness of Infinite Goodness.

ārātrikam

ॐ चन्द्रादित्यौ च धरणी विद्युदग्निस्तथैव च ।

त्वमेव सर्वज्योतींषि आरात्रिकं प्रतिगृह्यताम् ॥

ॐ नमः शिवाय आरात्रिकं समर्पयामि

oṃ candrādityau ca dharaṇī vidyudagnistathaiva ca
tvameva sarvajyotīṣiṃ ārātrikaṃ pratigṛhyatām
oṃ namaḥ śivāya ārātrikaṃ samarpayāmi

All knowing as the Moon, the Sun and the Divine Fire, you alone are all light, and this light we request you to accept. With the offering of light oṃ I bow to the Consciousness of Infinite Goodness

ॐ पयः पृथिव्यां पय ओषधीषु

पयो दिव्यन्तरिक्षे पयो धाः ।

पयःस्वतीः प्रदिशः सन्तु मह्यम् ॥

oṃ payaḥ pṛthivyāṃ paya oṣadhīṣu
payo divyantarikṣe payo dhāḥ
payaḥsvatīḥ pradiśaḥ santu mahyam

oṃ Earth is a reservoir of nectar, all vegetation is a reservoir of nectar, the divine atmosphere is a reservoir of nectar, and also above. May all perceptions shine forth with the sweet taste of nectar for us.

ॐ अग्निर्देवता वातो देवता सूर्यो देवता चन्द्रमा देवता

वसवो देवता रुद्रो देवता ऽदित्या देवता मरुतो देवता विश्वे

देवा देवता बृहस्पतिर्देवतेन्द्रो देवता वरुणो देवता ॥

oṃ agnirdevatā vāto devatā sūryo devatā candramā devatā vasavo devatā rudro devatā-dityā devatā maruto devatā viśve devā devatā bṛhaspatirdevatendro devatā varuṇo devatā

oṃ The Divine Fire (Light of Purity) is the shining God, the Wind is the shining God, the Sun (Light of Wisdom) is the shining God, the Moon (Lord of Devotion) is the shining God, the Protectors of the Wealth are the shining Gods, the Relievers of Sufferings are the shining Gods, the Sons of the Light are the shining Gods; the Emancipated seers (Maruts) are the shining Gods, the Universal Shining Gods are the shining Gods, the Guru of the Gods is the shining God, the Ruler of the Gods is the shining God, the Lord of Waters is the shining God.

ॐ भूर्भुवः स्वः ।
तत् सवितुर्वरेण्यम् भर्गो देवस्य धीमहि ।
धियो यो नः प्रचोदयात् ॥

oṃ bhūr bhuvaḥ svaḥ
tat savitur vareṇyam bhargo devasya dhīmahi
dhiyo yo naḥ pracodayāt

oṃ the Infinite Beyond Conception, the gross body, the subtle body and the causal body; we meditate upon that Light of Wisdom which is the Supreme Wealth of the Gods. May it grant to us increase in our meditations.

ॐ भूः

oṃ bhūḥ

oṃ the gross body

ॐ भुवः

oṃ bhuvaḥ

oṃ the subtle body

ॐ स्वः

oṃ svaḥ

oṃ the causal body

ॐ महः

oṃ mahaḥ

oṃ the great body of existence

ॐ जनः

oṃ janaḥ

oṃ the body of knowledge

ॐ तपः

oṃ tapaḥ

oṃ the body of light

ॐ सत्यं

oṃ satyaṃ

oṃ the body of Truth

ॐ तत् सवितुर्वरेण्यम् भर्गो देवस्य धीमहि ।
धियो यो नः प्रचोदयात् ॥

oṃ tat savitur vareṇyam bhargo devasya dhīmahi
dhiyo yo naḥ pracodayāt

oṃ we meditate upon that Light of Wisdom which is the Supreme Wealth of the Gods. May it grant to us increase in our meditations.

ॐ आपो ज्योतीरसोमृतं ब्रह्म भूर्भुवस्स्वरोम् ॥

oṃ āpo jyotīrasomṛtaṃ brahma bhūrbhuvassvarom

May the divine waters luminous with the nectar of immortality of Supreme Divinity fill the earth, the atmosphere and the heavens.

ॐ मां माले महामाये सर्वशक्तिस्वरूपिणि ।

चतुर्वर्गस्त्वयि न्यस्तस्तस्मान्मे सिद्धिदा भव ॥

oṃ māṃ māle mahāmāye sarvaśaktisvarūpiṇi
catur vargas tvayi nyastas tasmān me siddhidā bhava

oṃ My Rosary, The Great Measurement of Consciousness, containing all energy within as your intrinsic nature, give to me the attainment of your Perfection, fulfilling the four objectives of life.

ॐ अविघ्नं कुरु माले त्वं गृह्णामि दक्षिणे करे ।

जपकाले च सिद्ध्यर्थं प्रसीद मम सिद्धये ॥

oṃ avighnaṃ kuru māle tvaṃ gṛhṇāmi dakṣiṇe kare
japakāle ca siddhyarthaṃ prasīda mama siddhaye

oṃ Rosary, You please remove all obstacles. I hold you in my right hand. At the time of recitation be pleased with me. Allow me to attain the Highest Perfection.

ॐ अक्षमालाधिपतये सुसिद्धिं देहि देहि

सर्वमन्त्रार्थसाधिनि साधय साधय सर्वसिद्धिं परिकल्पय

परिकल्पय मे स्वाहा ॥

oṃ akṣa mālā dhipataye susiddhiṃ dehi dehi sarva mantrārtha sādhini sādhaya sādhaya sarva siddhiṃ parikalpaya parikalpaya me svāhā
oṃ Rosary of rudrākṣa seeds, my Lord, give to me excellent attainment. Give to me, give to me. Illuminate the meanings of all mantras, illuminate, illuminate! Fashion me with all excellent attainments, fashion me! I am One with God!

एते गन्धपुष्पे ॐ गं गणपतये नमः

ete gandhapuṣpe oṃ gaṃ gaṇapataye namaḥ
With these scented flowers oṃ we bow to the Lord of Wisdom, Lord of the Multitudes.

एते गन्धपुष्पे ॐ आदित्यादिनवग्रहेभ्यो नमः

ete gandhapuṣpe oṃ ādityādi navagrahebhyo namaḥ
With these scented flowers oṃ we bow to the Sun, the Light of Wisdom, along with the nine planets.

एते गन्धपुष्पे ॐ शिवादिपञ्चदेवताभ्यो नमः

ete gandhapuṣpe oṃ śivādipañcadevatābhyo namaḥ
With these scented flowers oṃ we bow to Śiva, the Consciousness of Infinite Goodness, along with the five primary deities (Śiva, Śakti, Viṣṇu, Gaṇeśa, Sūrya).

एते गन्धपुष्पे ॐ इन्द्रादिदशदिक्पालेभ्यो नमः

ete gandhapuṣpe oṃ indrādi daśadikpālebhyo namaḥ
With these scented flowers oṃ we bow to Indra, the Ruler of the Pure, along with the Ten Protectors of the ten directions.

एते गन्धपुष्पे ॐ मत्स्यादिदशावतारेभ्यो नमः

ete gandhapuṣpe oṃ matsyādi daśāvatārebhyo namaḥ

With these scented flowers oṃ we bow to Viṣṇu, the Fish, along with the Ten Incarnations which He assumed.

एते गन्धपुष्पे ॐ प्रजापतये नमः

ete gandhapuṣpe oṃ prajāpataye namaḥ

With these scented flowers oṃ we bow to the Lord of All Created Beings.

एते गन्धपुष्पे ॐ नमो नारायणाय नमः

ete gandhapuṣpe oṃ namo nārāyaṇāya namaḥ

With these scented flowers oṃ we bow to the Perfect Perception of Consciousness.

एते गन्धपुष्पे ॐ सर्वेभ्यो देवेभ्यो नमः

ete gandhapuṣpe oṃ sarvebhyo devebhyo namaḥ

With these scented flowers oṃ we bow to All the Gods.

एते गन्धपुष्पे ॐ सर्वाभ्यो देवीभ्यो नमः

ete gandhapuṣpe oṃ sarvābhyo devībhyo namaḥ

With these scented flowers oṃ we bow to All the Goddesses.

एते गन्धपुष्पे ॐ श्री गुरवे नमः

ete gandhapuṣpe oṃ śrī gurave namaḥ

With these scented flowers oṃ we bow to the Guru.

एते गन्धपुष्पे ॐ ब्राह्मणेभ्यो नमः

ete gandhapuṣpe oṃ brāhmaṇebhyo namaḥ

With these scented flowers oṃ we bow to All Knowers of Wisdom.

Tie a piece of string around right middle finger or wrist.

ॐ कुशासने स्थितो ब्रह्मा कुशे चैव जनार्दनः ।

कुशे ह्याकाशवद् विष्णुः कुशासन नमोऽस्तु ते ॥

oṃ kuśāsane sthito brahmā kuśe caiva janārdanaḥ
kuśe hyākāśavad viṣṇuḥ kuśāsana namo-stu te

Brahmā is in the shining light (or kuśa grass), in the shining light resides Janārdana, the Lord of Beings. The Supreme all-pervading Consciousness, Viṣṇu, resides in the shining light. Oh Repository of the shining light, we bow down to you, the seat of kuśa grass.

आचमन

ācamana

ॐ केशवाय नमः स्वाहा

oṃ keśavāya namaḥ svāhā

We bow to the one of beautiful hair.

ॐ माधवाय नमः स्वाहा

oṃ mādhavāya namaḥ svāhā

We bow to the one who is always sweet.

ॐ गोविन्दाय नमः स्वाहा

oṃ govindāya namaḥ svāhā

We bow to He who is one-pointed light.

ॐ विष्णुः ॐ विष्णुः ॐ विष्णुः

oṃ viṣṇuḥ oṃ viṣṇuḥ oṃ viṣṇuḥ

oṃ Consciousness, oṃ Consciousness, oṃ Consciousness.

ॐ तत् विष्णोः परमं पदम् सदा पश्यन्ति सूरयः ।
दिवीव चक्षुराततम् ॥

oṃ tat viṣṇoḥ paramaṃ padam sadā paśyanti sūrayaḥ
divīva cakṣurā tatam

oṃ That Consciousness of the highest station, who always sees the Light of Wisdom, give us Divine Eyes.

ॐ तद् विप्र स पिपानोव जुविग्रन्सो सोमिन्द्रते ।
विष्णुः तत् परमं पदम् ॥

oṃ tad vipra sa pipānova juvigranso somindrate
viṣṇuḥ tat paramaṃ padam

oṃ That twice-born teacher who is always thirsty for accepting the nectar of devotion, Oh Consciousness, you are in that highest station.

ॐ अपवित्रः पवित्रो वा सर्वावस्थां गतोऽपि वा ।
यः स्मरेत् पुण्डरीकाक्षं स बाह्याभ्यन्तरः शुचिः ॥

oṃ apavitraḥ pavitro vā sarvāvasthāṃ gato-pi vā
yaḥ smaret puṇḍarīkākṣaṃ sa bāhyābhyantaraḥ śuciḥ

oṃ The Impure and the Pure reside within all objects. Who remembers the lotus-eyed Consciousness is conveyed to radiant beauty.

ॐ सर्वमङ्गलमाङ्गल्यम् वरेण्यम् वरदं शुभं ।
नारायणं नमस्कृत्य सर्वकर्माणि कारयेत् ॥

oṃ sarva maṅgala māṅgalyam vareṇyam varadaṃ śubhaṃ
nārāyaṇaṃ namaskṛtya sarvakarmāṇi kārayet

All the Welfare of all Welfare, the highest blessing of Purity and Illumination, with the offering of respect we bow down to the Supreme Consciousness who is the actual performer of all action.

ॐ सूर्य्यश्चमेति मन्त्रस्य ब्रह्मा ऋषिः प्रकृतिश्छन्दः आपो
देवता आचमने विनियोगः ॥

oṃ sūryyaścameti mantrasya brahmā ṛṣiḥ prakṛtiśchandaḥ āpo devatā ācamane viniyogaḥ

oṃ these are the mantras of the Light of Wisdom, the Creative Capacity is the Seer, Nature is the meter, the divine flow of waters is the deity, being applied in washing the hands and rinsing the mouth.

Draw the following yantra with some drops of water
and/or sandal paste at the front of your seat.
Place a flower on the bindu in the middle.

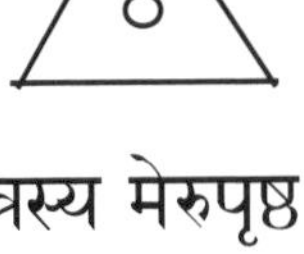

ॐ आसनस्य मन्त्रस्य मेरुपृष्ठ ऋषिः सुतलं छन्दः कूर्म्मो
देवता आसनोपवेशने विनियोगः ॥

oṃ āsanasya mantrasya merupṛṣṭha ṛṣiḥ sutalaṃ chandaḥ kūrmmo devatā āsanopaveśane viniyogaḥ

Introducing the mantras of the Purification of the seat. The Seer is He whose back is Straight, the meter is of very beautiful form, the tortoise who supports the earth is the deity. These mantras are applied to make the seat free from obstructions.

एते गन्धपुष्पे ॐ ह्रीं आधारशक्तये कमलासनाय नमः ॥

ete gandhapuṣpe oṃ hrīṃ ādhāraśaktaye kamalāsanāya namaḥ

With these scented flowers oṃ hrīṃ we bow to the Primal Energy situated in this lotus seat.

ॐ पृथ्वि त्वया धृता लोका देवि त्वं विष्णुना धृता ।
त्वञ्च धारय मां नित्यं पवित्रं कुरु चासनम् ॥

oṃ pṛthvi tvayā dhṛtā lokā devi tvaṃ viṣṇunā dhṛtā tvañca dhāraya māṃ nityaṃ pavitraṃ kuru cāsanam

oṃ Earth! You support the realms of the Goddess. You are supported by the Supreme Consciousness. Also bear me eternally and make pure this seat.

ॐ गुरुभ्यो नमः

oṃ gurubhyo namaḥ

oṃ I bow to the Guru.

ॐ परमगुरुभ्यो नमः

oṃ paramagurubhyo namaḥ

oṃ I bow to the Guru's Guru.

ॐ परापरगुरुभ्यो नमः

oṃ parāparagurubhyo namaḥ
oṃ I bow to the Gurus of the lineage.

ॐ परमेष्ठिगुरुभ्यो नमः

oṃ parameṣṭhigurubhyo namaḥ
oṃ I bow to the Supreme Gurus.

ॐ गं गणेशाय नमः

oṃ gaṃ gaṇeśāya namaḥ
oṃ I bow to the Lord of Wisdom.

ॐ अनन्ताय नमः

oṃ anantāya namaḥ
oṃ I bow to the Infinite One.

ॐ ऐं ह्रीं क्लीं चामुण्डायै विच्चे

oṃ aiṃ hrīṃ klīṃ cāmuṇḍāyai vicce
oṃ Creation, Circumstance, Transformation are known by Consciousness.

ॐ नमः शिवाय

oṃ namaḥ śivāya
oṃ I bow to the Consciousness of Infinite Goodness.

Clap hands 3 times and snap fingers in the ten directions (N S E W NE SW NW SE UP DOWN) repeating

ॐ नमः शिवाय

oṃ namaḥ śivāya
oṃ I bow to the Consciousness of Infinite Goodness.

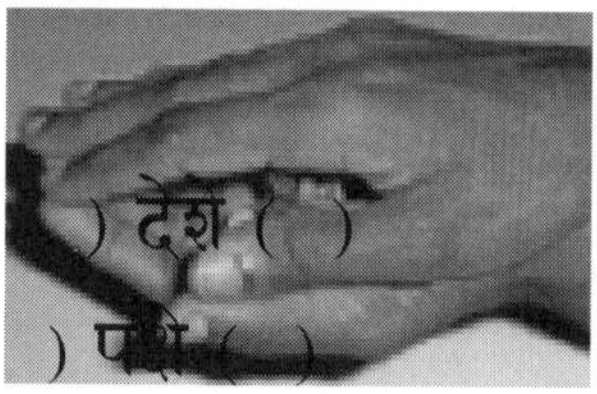

सङ्कल्प

saṅkalpa

विष्णुः ॐ तत् सत् । ॐ अद्य जम्बूद्वीपे ( ) देशे ( ) प्रदेशे ( ) नगरे ( ) मन्दिरे ( ) मासे ( ) पक्षे ( ) तिथौ ( ) गोत्र श्री ( ) कृतैतत् श्रीशिवकामः पूजाकर्माहं श्रीशिवपूजां करिष्ये ॥

viṣṇuḥ oṃ tat sat oṃ adya jambūdvīpe (Country) deśe (State) pradeśe (City) nagare (Name of house or temple) mandire (month) māse (śukla or kṛṣṇa) pakṣe (name of day) tithau (name of) gotra śrī (your name) kṛtaitat śrī śiva kāmaḥ pūjā karmāhaṃ śrī śiva pūjāṃ kariṣye

The Consciousness Which Pervades All, oṃ That is Truth. Presently, on the Planet Earth, Country of (Name), State of (Name), City of (Name), in the Temple of (Name), (Name of Month) Month, (Bright or Dark) fortnight, (Name of Day) Day, (Name of Sādhu Family), Śrī (Your Name) is performing the worship for the satisfaction of the Respected Consciousness of Infinite Goodness by reciting the Śiva Worship.

ॐ यज्जाग्रतो दूरमुदेति दैवं तदु सुप्तस्य तथैवैति ।
दूरङ्गमं ज्योतिषां ज्योतिरेकं तन्मे मनः शिवसङ्कल्पमस्तु ॥

oṃ yajjāgrato dūramudeti daivaṃ tadu suptasya tathaivaiti
dūraṅgamaṃ jyotiṣāṃ jyotirekaṃ tanme manaḥ śiva saṅkalpamastu

May our waking consciousness replace pain and suffering with divinity as also our awareness when asleep. Far extending be our radiant aura of light, filling our minds with light.

May that be the firm determination of the Consciousness of Infinite Goodness.

या गुङ्गूर्या सिनीवाली या राका या सरस्वती ।
इन्द्राणीमह्व ऊतये वरुणानीं स्वस्तये ॥

yā guṅgūryā sinīvālī yā rākā yā sarasvatī
īndrāṇīmahva ūtaye varuṇānīṃ svastaye

May that Goddess who wears the Moon of Devotion protect the children of Devotion. May that Goddess of All-Pervading Knowledge protect us. May the Energy of the Rule of the Pure rise up. Oh Energy of Equilibrium grant us the highest prosperity.

ॐ स्वस्ति न इन्द्रो वृद्धश्रवाः स्वस्ति नः पूषा विश्ववेदाः ।
स्वस्ति नस्तार्क्ष्यो अरिष्टनेमिः स्वस्ति नो बृहस्पतिर्दधातु ॥

oṃ svasti na indro vṛddhaśravāḥ
svasti naḥ pūṣā viśvavedāḥ
svasti nastārkṣyo ariṣṭanemiḥ
svasti no bṛhaspatirdadhātu

The Ultimate Prosperity to us, Oh Rule of the Pure, who perceives all that changes; the Ultimate Prosperity to us, Searchers for Truth, Knowers of the Universe; the Ultimate Prosperity to us, Oh Divine Being of Light, keep us safe; the Ultimate Prosperity to us, Oh Spirit of All-Pervading Delight, grant that to us.

ॐ गणानां त्वा गणपतिꣳ हवामहे
प्रियाणां त्वा प्रियपतिꣳ हवामहे
निधीनां त्वा निधिपतिꣳ हवामहे वसो मम ।
आहमजानि गर्भधमा त्वमजासि गर्भधम् ॥

oṃ gaṇānāṃ tvā gaṇapati guṃ havāmahe
priyāṇāṃ tvā priyapati guṃ havāmahe
nidhīnāṃ tvā nidhipati guṃ havāmahe vaso mama
āhamajāni garbbhadhamā tvamajāsi garbbhadham

We invoke you with offerings, Oh Lord of the Multitudes; we invoke you with offerings, Oh Lord of Love; we invoke you with offerings, Oh Guardian of the Treasure. Sit within me, giving birth to the realm of the Gods within me; yes, giving birth to the realm of the Gods within me.

ॐ गणानां त्वा गणपतिँ हवामहे

कविं कवीनामुपमश्रवस्तमम् ।

ज्येष्ठराजं ब्रह्मणां ब्रह्मणस्पत

आ नः शृण्वन्नूतिभिः सीद सादनम् ॥

oṃ gaṇānāṃ tvā gaṇapati guṃ havāmahe
kaviṃ kavīnāmupamaśravastamam
jyeṣṭharājaṃ brahmaṇāṃ brahmaṇaspata
ā naḥ śṛnvannūtibhiḥ sīda sādanam

We invoke you with offerings, Oh Lord of the Multitudes, Seer among Seers, of unspeakable grandeur. Oh Glorious King, Lord of the Knowers of Wisdom, come speedily hearing our supplications and graciously take your seat amidst our assembly.

ॐ अदितिर्द्यौरदितिरन्तरिक्षमदितिर्माता स पिता स

पुत्रः । विश्वे देवा अदितिः पञ्च जना

अदितिर्जातमदितिर्जनित्वम् ॥

oṃ aditir dyauraditirantarikṣamaditirmātā
sa pitā sa putraḥ
viśve devā aditiḥ pañca janā
aditirjātamaditirjanitvam

The Mother of Enlightenment pervades the heavens; the Mother of Enlightenment pervades the atmosphere; the Mother of Enlightenment pervades Mother and Father and child. All Gods of the Universe are pervaded by the Mother, the five forms of living beings, all Life. The Mother of Enlightenment, She is to be known.

ॐ त्वं स्त्रीस्त्वं पुमानसि त्वं कुमार अत वा कुमारी ।
त्वं जिर्नो दण्डेन वञ्चसि त्वं जातो भवसि विश्वतोमुखः ॥

oṃ tvaṃ strīstvaṃ pumānasi tvaṃ kumāra ata vā kumarī
tvaṃ jirno daṇḍena vañcasi tvaṃ jāto bhavasi viśvatomukhaḥ

You are Female, you are Male; you are a young boy, you are a young girl. You are the word of praise by which we are singing; you are all creation existing as the mouth of the universe.

ॐ अम्बेऽम्बिकेऽम्बालिके न मा नयति कश्चन ।
ससस्त्यश्वकः सुभद्रिकां काम्पीलवासिनीम् ॥

oṃ ambe-ambike-mbālike na mā nayati kaścana
sasastyaśvakaḥ subhadrikāṃ kāmpīlavāsinīm

Mother of the Perceivable Universe, Mother of the Conceivable Universe, Mother of the Universe of Intuitive Vision, lead me to that True Existence. As excellent crops (or grains) are harvested, so may I be taken to reside with the Infinite Consciousness.

ॐ शान्ता द्यौः शान्तापृथिवी शान्तमिदमुर्वन्तरिक्षम् ।
शान्ता उदन्वतिरापः शान्ताः नः शान्त्वोषधीः ॥

oṃ śāntā dyauḥ śāntā pṛthivī śāntam idamurvantarikṣam
śāntā udanvatirāpaḥ śāntāḥ naḥ śāntvoṣadhīḥ

Peace in the heavens, Peace on the earth, Peace upwards and permeating the atmosphere; Peace upwards, over, on all sides and further; Peace to us, Peace to all vegetation;

ॐ शान्तानि पूर्वरूपाणि शान्तं नोऽस्तु कृताकृतम् ।
शान्तं भूतं च भव्यं च सर्वमेव शमस्तु नः ॥

oṃ śāntāni pūrva rūpāṇi śāntaṃ no-stu kṛtākṛtam
śāntaṃ bhūtaṃ ca bhavyaṃ ca sarvameva śamastu naḥ

Peace to all that has form, Peace to all causes and effects; Peace to all existence, and to all intensities of reality including all and everything; Peace be to us.

ॐ पृथिवी शान्तिरन्तरिक्षं शान्तिर्द्यौः
शान्तिरापः शान्तिरोषधयः शान्तिः वनस्पतयः शान्तिर्विश्वे
मे देवाः शान्तिः सर्वे मे देवाः शान्तिर्ब्रह्म शान्तिरापः
शान्तिः सर्वं शान्तिरेधि शान्तिः शान्तिः सर्व शान्तिः सा
मा शान्तिः शान्तिभिः ॥

oṃ pṛthivī śāntir antarikṣaṃ śāntir dyauḥ
śāntir āpaḥ śāntir oṣadhayaḥ śāntiḥ vanaspatayaḥ
śāntir viśve me devāḥ śāntiḥ sarve me devāḥ śāntir
brahma śāntirāpaḥ śāntiḥ sarvaṃ śāntiredhi śāntiḥ
śāntiḥ sarva śāntiḥ sā mā śāntiḥ śāntibhiḥ

Let the earth be at Peace, the atmosphere be at Peace, the heavens be filled with Peace. Even further may Peace extend, Peace be to waters, Peace to all vegetation, Peace to All Gods of the Universe, Peace to All Gods within us, Peace to Creative Consciousness, Peace be to Brilliant Light, Peace to All, Peace to Everything, Peace, Peace, altogether Peace, equally Peace, by means of Peace.

ताभिः शान्तिभिः सर्वशान्तिभिः समया मोहं यदिह घोरं यदिह क्रूरं यदिह पापं तच्छान्तं तच्छिवं सर्वमेव समस्तु नः ॥

tābhiḥ śāntibhiḥ sarva śāntibhiḥ samayā mohaṃ yadiha ghoraṃ yadiha krūraṃ yadiha pāpaṃ tacchāntaṃ tacchivaṃ sarvameva samastu naḥ

Thus by means of Peace, altogether one with the means of Peace, Ignorance is eliminated, Violence is eradicated, Improper Conduct is eradicated, Confusion (sin) is eradicated, all that is, is at Peace, all that is perceived, each and everything, altogether for us,

ॐ शान्तिः शान्तिः शान्तिः ॥

oṃ śāntiḥ śāntiḥ śāntiḥ

oṃ Peace, Peace, Peace

शिव संकल्प स्तोत्रम्

śiva saṃkalpa stotram

- 1 -

येनेदं भूतं भुवनं भविष्यत् परि गृहीतममृतेन सर्वम् ।
येन यज्ञस्तायते सप्तहोता तन्मे मनः शिवसंकल्पमस्तु ॥

yenedaṃ bhūtaṃ bhuvanaṃ bhaviṣyat
pari gṛhītamamṛtena sarvam
yena yajñastāyate saptahotā
tanme manaḥ śivasaṃkalpamastu

By means of this all beings in the manifested worlds of the future will be able to completely accept the nectar of immortal bliss, by means of the sacrificial fire attended by seven offerings on seven levels of consciousness. May my mind be filled with that firm determination of Śiva, the Consciousness of Infinite Goodness.

- 2 -

येन कर्माण्यपसो मनीषिणो यज्ञे कृण्वन्ति विदथेषु धीराः।
यदपूर्वं यक्षमन्तःप्रजानां तन्मे मनः शिवसंकल्पमस्तु ॥

yena karmāṇyapaso manīṣiṇo
yajñe kṛṇvanti vidatheṣu dhīrāḥ
yadapūrvaṃ yakṣamantaḥprajānāṃ
tanme manaḥ śivasaṃkalpamastu

By means of the excellent actions of thinking beings, steadfastly offering their knowledge in sacrifice, that ancient means of enhancing the wealth of the people. May my mind be filled with that firm determination of Śiva, the Consciousness of Infinite Goodness.

- 3 -

यज्जाग्रतो दूरमुदैति दैवं तदु सुप्तस्य तथैवेति ।
दूरंगमं ज्योतिषां ज्योतिरेकं तन्मे मनः शिवसंकल्पमस्तु ॥

yajjāgrato dūramudaiti daivaṃ
tadu suptasya tathaiveti
dūraṃgamaṃ jyotiṣāṃ jyotirekaṃ
tanme manaḥ śivasaṃkalpamastu

May our waking consciousness replace pain and suffering with divinity as also our awareness when asleep. May our radiant aura of light be far extending, filling our minds with light. May my mind be filled with that firm determination of Śiva, the Consciousness of Infinite Goodness.

- 4 -

यत् प्रज्ञानमुत चेतो धृतिश्च यज्ज्योतिरन्तरमृतं प्रजासु ।

यस्मान्न ऋते किञ्चन कर्म क्रियते तन्मे मनः

शिवसंकल्पमस्तु ॥

yat prajñānamuta ceto dhṛtiśca
yajjyotirantaramṛtaṃ prajāsu
yasmānna ṛte kiñcana karma kriyate
tanme manaḥ śivasaṃkalpamastu

Being firm in that supreme wisdom which fills consciousness, that inner light of the nectar of bliss within all beings born, may we perform all action from that imperishable truth. May my mind be filled with that firm determination of Śiva, the Consciousness of Infinite Goodness.

- 5 -

यस्मिन्नृचः साम यजूंषि यस्मिन् प्रतिष्ठिता

रथनाभाविवाराः ।

यस्मिंश्चित्तं सर्वमोतं प्रजानां तन्मे मनः शिवसंकल्पमस्तु ॥

yasminnṛcaḥ sāma yajūṃṣi yasmin
pratiṣṭhitā rathanābhāvivārāḥ
yasmiṃścittaṃ sarvamotaṃ prajānāṃ
tanme manaḥ śivasaṃkalpamastu

From where Ṛg, Sāma and Yajūr Veda have been established, the conveyance of the great attitude; from where all the highest contemplations of all life emmanate. May my mind be filled with that firm determination of Śiva, the Consciousness of Infinite Goodness.

- 6 -

सुषारथिरश्वानिव यन्मनुष्यान्

नेनीयतेऽभीशुभिर्वाजिन इव ।

हृत्प्रतिष्ठं यदजिरं यविष्ठं तन्मे मनः शिवसंकल्पमस्तु ॥

suṣārathiraśvāniva yanmanuṣyān
nenīyate-bhīśubhirvājina iva
hṛtpratiṣṭhaṃ yadajiraṃ yaviṣṭhaṃ
tanme manaḥ śivasaṃkalpamastu

Who is the excellent charioteer of the horses of mankind, to awaken them from sloth and laziness to this renewed energy, established in delight for both the old and the young. May my mind be filled with that firm determination of Śiva, the Consciousness of Infinite Goodness.

- 7 -

ये पञ्च पञ्चाशतः शतं च सहस्रं च नियुतं चार्बुदं च ।

ते यज्ञचित्तेष्टकाटं शरीरं तन्मे मनः शिवसंकल्पमस्तु ॥

ye pañca pañcāśataḥ śataṃ ca
sahasraṃ ca niyutaṃ cārbudaṃ ca
te yajñacitteṣṭakāṭaṃ śarīraṃ
tanme manaḥ śivasaṃkalpamastu

There are five and a hundred and five, a hundred and a thousand, ten million and uncountable as well; those desired contemplations which become embodied from sacrifice. May my mind be filled with that firm determination of Śiva, the Consciousness of Infinite Goodness.

- 8 -

वेदाहमेतं पुरुषं महान्तमादित्यवर्णं तमसः परस्तात् ।

तस्य योनिं परिपश्यन्ति

धीरास्तन्मे मनः शिवसंकल्पमस्तु ॥

vedāhametaṃ puruṣaṃ mahāntam
ādityavarṇaṃ tamasaḥ parastāt
tasya yoniṃ paripaśyanti dhīrās
tanme manaḥ śivasaṃkalpamastu

The wisdom of the Vedas makes mankind great, putting an end to darkness with illumination as bright as the sun. Being nurtured in that womb touches the mind with constant energy. May my mind be filled with that firm determination of Śiva, the Consciousness of Infinite Goodness.

- 9 -

येन कर्माणि प्रचरन्ति धीरा

विप्रा वाचा मनसा कर्मणा वा ।

यत् स्वां दिशमनु संयन्ति प्राणिनस्तन्मे मनः

शिवसंकल्पमस्तु ॥

yena karmāṇi pracaranti dhīrā
viprā vācā mansā karmaṇā vā
yat svāṃ diśamanu saṃyanti prāṇinas
tanme manaḥ śivasaṃkalpamastu

By means of these actions which inspire constant energy, the twice-born speak and think and act. By this they control the directions of their own minds and all living beings. May my mind be filled with that firm determination of Śiva, the Consciousness of Infinite Goodness.

- 10 -

ये मे मनो हृदयं ये च देवा

ये अन्तरिक्षं बहुधा कल्पयन्ति ।

ये श्रोत्रं च चक्षुषी संचरन्ति तन्मे मनः शिवसंकल्पमस्तु ॥

ye me mano hṛdayaṃ ye ca devā
ye antarikṣaṃ bahudhā kalpayanti
ye śrotraṃ ca cakṣuṣī saṃcaranti
tanme manaḥ śivasaṃkalpamastu

By this means my mind and heart conceive innumerable Gods in the atmosphere, and ears and eyes all move together. May my mind be filled with that firm determination of Śiva, the Consciousness of Infinite Goodness.

- 11 -

यस्येदं धीराः पुनन्ति कवयो ब्रह्माणमेतं व्यावृणत इन्दुम् ।
स्थावरं जङ्गमं च द्यौराकाशं तन्मे मनः शिवसंकल्पमस्तु ॥

yasyedaṃ dhīrāḥ punanti kavayo
brahmāṇametaṃ vyāvṛṇata indum
sthāvaraṃ jaṅgamaṃ ca dyaurākāśaṃ
tanme manaḥ śivasaṃkalpamastu

By means of this the inspired poets are again filled with constant energy, the brahmiṇs become distinguished because of their devotion like the Moon. Established on the earth or in the atmosphere or even in the heavens. May my mind be filled with that firm determination of Śiva, the Consciousness of Infinite Goodness.

- 12 -

येन द्यौरुग्रा पृथिवी चान्तरिक्षं
येन पर्वताः प्रदिशो दिशश्च ।
येनेदं सर्वं जगद्व्याप्तं प्रजानत्
तन्मे मनः शिवसंकल्पमस्तु ॥

yena dyaurugrā pṛthivī cāntarikṣaṃ
yena parvatāḥ pradiśo diśaśca
yenedaṃ sarvaṃ jagadvyāptaṃ prajānat
tanme manaḥ śivasaṃkalpamastu

By means of which the strength of the heavens or earth and the atmosphere, by means of which the mountains show us the directions; by means of this all that is distinguished in the perceiveable universe becomes known. May my mind be filled with that firm determination of Śiva, the Consciousness of Infinite Goodness.

- 13 -

अव्यक्तं चाप्रमेयं च व्यक्ताव्यक्तपरं शिवम् ।

सूक्ष्मात् सूक्ष्मतरं ज्ञेयं तन्मे मनः शिवसंकल्पमस्तु ॥

avyaktaṃ cāprameyaṃ ca
vyaktāvyaktaparaṃ śivam
sūkṣmāt sūkṣmataraṃ jñeyaṃ
tanme manaḥ śivasaṃkalpamastu

That which cannot be divided and which is unable to be proved, above both manifest and unmanifest is Śiva. He is the most subtle of all subtle to be known. May my mind be filled with that firm determination of Śiva, the Consciousness of Infinite Goodness.

- 14 -

कैलासशिखरे रम्ये शंकरस्य गृहालयम् ।

देवतास्तत् प्रमोदन्ते तन्मे मनः शिवसंकल्पमस्तु ॥

kailāsaśikhare ramye
śaṃkarasya gṛhālayam
devatāstat pramodante
tanme manaḥ śivasaṃkalpamastu

Upon the summit of the beautiful Kailaśa is the home of the Cause of Peace. The Gods are extremely delighted. May my mind be filled with that firm determination of Śiva, the Consciousness of Infinite Goodness.

- 15 -

आदित्यवर्णं तपसा ज्वलन्तं
यत् पश्यसि गुहासु जायमानः ।
शिवरूपं शिवमुदितं शिवालयं
तन्मे मनः शिवसंकल्पमस्तु ॥

ādityavarṇaṃ tapasā jvalantaṃ
yat paśyasi guhāsu jāyamānaḥ
śivarūpaṃ śivamuditaṃ śivālayaṃ
tanme manaḥ śivasaṃkalpamastu

His austerities illuminate a light of the color of the Sun, which can be perceived in secret by the victorious mind: the form of Śiva, the delight of Śiva, the repose of Śiva. May my mind be filled with that firm determination of Śiva, the Consciousness of Infinite Goodness.

- 16 -

येनेदं सर्वं जगतो बभूव यद्देवा अपि महतो जातवेदाः ।
यदेवाग्र्यं तपसो ज्योतिरेकं तन्मे मनः शिवसंकल्पमस्तु ॥

yenedaṃ sarvaṃ jagato babhūva
yaddevā api mahato jātavedāḥ
yadevāgryaṃ tapaso jyotirekaṃ
tanme manaḥ śivasaṃkalpamastu

By means of this all comes into manifested existence, these Gods, other beings of greatness, the Knower of All (a name of the Fire, Agni), these Gods who accept the purifying austerities with one-pointed light. May my mind be filled with that firm determination of Śiva, the Consciousness of Infinite Goodness.

- 17 -

गोभिर्जुष्टो धनेन ह्यायुषा च बलेन च ।

प्रजया पशुभिः पुष्कराार्धं तन्मे मनः शिवसंकल्पमस्तु ॥

gobhirjuṣṭo dhanena
hyāyuṣā ca balena ca
prajayā paśubhiḥ puṣkarārdhaṃ
tanme manaḥ śivasaṃkalpamastu

The rays of light come as wealth granting delight and strength to all beings born, to animals and to bodies of water. May my mind be filled with that firm determination of Śiva, the Consciousness of Infinite Goodness.

- 18 -

योऽसौ सर्वेषु वेदेषु पठ्यतेऽनद ईश्वरः ।

अकार्यो निर्वणो ह्यात्मा तन्मे मनः शिवसंकल्पमस्तु ॥

yo-sau sarveṣu vedeṣu
paṭhyate-nada īśvaraḥ
akāryo nirvaṇo hyātmā
tanme manaḥ śivasaṃkalpamastu

The Lord of All resides in all the Vedas as the subtle sound which is recited. His soul is uncaused and resides in the bliss of silence. May my mind be filled with that firm determination of Śiva, the Consciousness of Infinite Goodness.

- 19 -

यो वेदादिषु गायत्री सर्वव्यापी महेश्वरः ।

तदुक्तं च यदा ज्ञेयं तन्मे मनः शिवसंकल्पमस्तु ॥

yo vedādiṣu gāyatrī
sarvavyāpī maheśvaraḥ
taduktaṃ ca yadā jñeyaṃ
tanme manaḥ śivasaṃkalpamastu

Who is known in the Vedas, etc, as Gāyatrī, and is everywhere distinguished as the Great Seer of All, and He is called as what is to be known. May my mind be filled with that firm determination of Śiva, the Consciousness of Infinite Goodness.

- 20 -

प्रयतप्राण ओंकारं प्रणवं च महेश्वरम् ।

यः सर्वं यस्य चित् सर्वं तन्मे मनः शिवसंकल्पमस्तु ॥

prayataprāṇa oṃkāraṃ
praṇavaṃ ca maheśvaram
yaḥ sarvaṃ yasya cit sarvaṃ
tanme manaḥ śivasaṃkalpamastu

Living beings who strive call Him oṃ, the Great Sound, the Great Seer of All, He who is all the Consciousness within all. May my mind be filled with that firm determination of Śiva, the Consciousness of Infinite Goodness.

- 21 -

यो वै वेद महादेवं प्रणवं पुरुषोत्तमम् ।

ओंकारं परमात्मानं तन्मे मनः शिवसंकल्पमस्तु ॥

yo vai veda mahādevaṃ
praṇavaṃ puruṣottamam
oṃkāraṃ paramātmānaṃ
tanme manaḥ śivasaṃkalpamastu

Who is known in the Vedas as the Great God, the Great Sound, the Full, Complete and Perfect Consciousness most excellent, oṃ, the Supreme Soul of All. May my mind be filled with that firm determination of Śiva, the Consciousness of Infinite Goodness.

- 22 -

ओंकारं चतुर्भुजं लोकनाथं नारायणम् ।

सर्वस्थितं सर्वगतं सर्वव्याप्तं तन्मे मनः शिवसंकल्पमस्तु ॥

oṃkāraṃ caturbhujaṃ
lokanāthaṃ nārāyaṇam
sarvasthitaṃ sarvagataṃ sarvavyāptaṃ
tanme manaḥ śivasaṃkalpamastu

He is oṃ, with four arms (Brahma), Lord of the Worlds Nārāyaṇa (Viṣṇu). All reside in Him, all move in him, all are made manifest by Him. May my mind be filled with that firm determination of Śiva, the Consciousness of Infinite Goodness.

- 23 -

तत् परात् परतो ब्रह्मा तत् परात् परतो हरिः ।

परात् परतरं ज्ञानं तन्मे मनः शिवसंकल्पमस्तु ॥

tat parāt parato brahmā
tat parāt parato hariḥ
parāt parataraṃ jñānaṃ
tanme manaḥ śivasaṃkalpamastu

That Supreme is greater than Brahma, that Supreme is greater than Viṣṇu (Hari, who dwells in the gross, subtle and causal bodies), even higher than the most superior. May my mind be filled with that firm determination of Śiva, the Consciousness of Infinite Goodness.

- 24 -

य इदं शिवसंकल्पं सदाधीयन्ति ब्राह्मणाः ।

ते परं मोक्षमाप्स्यन्ति तन्मे मनः शिवसंकल्पमस्तु ॥

ya idaṃ śivasaṃkalpaṃ
sadādhīyanti brāhmaṇāḥ
te paraṃ mokṣamāpsyanti
tanme manaḥ śivasaṃkalpamastu

This is that firm determination of Śiva, the Consciousness of Infinite Goodness which is always contemplated by knowers of divinity and those who seek for the supreme liberation. May my mind be filled with that firm determination of Śiva, the Consciousness of Infinite Goodness.

\- 25 -

अस्ति नास्ति शयित्वा सर्वमिदं
नास्ति पुनस्तथैव दृष्टं ध्रुवम् ।
अस्ति नास्ति हितं मध्यमं पदं
तन्मे मनः शिवसंकल्पमस्तु ॥

asti nāsti śayitvā sarvamidaṃ
nāsti punastathaiva dṛṣṭaṃ dhruvam
asti nāsti hitaṃ madhyamaṃ padaṃ
tanme manaḥ śivasaṃkalpamastu

Ever-present is this rest in the sleep of all, ever-present is the perception of the star which conveys blessings from the eternally young sage. Ever-present is the benefit of these harmonious tones. May my mind be filled with that firm determination of Śiva, the Consciousness of Infinite Goodness.

\- 26 -

अस्ति नास्ति विपरीतो प्रवादो
ऽस्ति नास्ति गुह्यं वा इदं सर्वम् ।
अस्ति नास्ति परात् परो यत् परं
तन्मे मनः शिवसंकल्पमस्तु ॥

asti nāsti viparīto pravādo-
sti nāsti guhyaṃ vā idaṃ sarvam
asti nāsti parāt paro yat paraṃ
tanme manaḥ śivasaṃkalpamastu

Ever-present is the world of opposites, the flickering back and forth of our inner light as though blown by the wind. Ever-present is this secret which is hidden in all. Ever-present is the Greater than the Greatest and even Greater still. May my mind be filled with that firm determination of Śiva, the Consciousness of Infinite Goodness.

गणेश पूजा

gaṇeśa pūjā

worship of gaṇeśa

gaṇeśa gāyatrī

ॐ तत् पुरुषाय विद्महे वक्रतुण्डाय धीमहि ।
तन्नो दन्ती प्रचोदयात् ॥

oṃ tat puruṣāya vidmahe vakratuṇḍāya dhīmahi
tanno dantī pracodayāt

oṃ we meditate upon that Perfect Consciousness, contemplate the One with a broken tooth. May that One with the Great Tusk grant us increase.

एते गन्धपुष्पे ॐ गं गणपतये नमः

ete gandhapuṣpe oṃ gaṃ gaṇapataye namaḥ

With these scented flowers oṃ we bow to the Lord of Wisdom, Lord of the Multitudes.

gaṇeśa dhyānam

meditation

ॐ खर्व्वं स्थूलतनुं गजेन्द्रवदनं लम्बोदरं सुन्दरं
प्रस्यन्दन्मदगन्धलुब्धमधुपव्यालोलगण्डस्थलम् ।
दन्ताघातविदारितारिरुधिरैः सिन्दूरशोभाकरं
वन्दे शैलसुतासुतं गणपतिं सिद्धिप्रदं कामदं ॥

oṃ kharvvaṃ sthūlatanuṃ gajendravadanaṃ lambodaraṃ sundaraṃ
prasyandanmadagandhalubdhamadhupavyālolagaṇḍasthalam
dantāghātavidāritārirudhiraiḥ sindūraśobhākaraṃ
vande śailasutāsutaṃ gaṇapatiṃ siddhipradaṃ kāmadaṃ

oṃ Gaṇeśa, the Lord of Wisdom, is short, of stout body, with the face of the king of elephants and a big belly and is extemely beautiful. From whom pours forth an etherial fluid, the sweet fragrance of which has captivated with love the bees who are swarming about his cheeks. With the blows of his tusks he pierces all enemies, and he is beautified by red vermillion. We bow with praise to the son of the daughter of the Mountains, Pārvatī, the daughter of Himalayas, the Lord of the Multitudes, the Giver of Perfection of all desires.

ॐ गां गणेशाय नमः

oṃ gāṃ gaṇeśāya namaḥ

oṃ We bow to Gaṇeśa, the Lord of Wisdom, Lord of the Multitudes.

kara nyāsa

establishment in the hands

ॐ गां अंगुष्ठाभ्यां नमः

oṃ gāṃ aṃguṣṭhābhyāṃ namaḥ thumb forefinger
oṃ Gaṃ in the thumb I bow.

ॐ गीं तर्जनीभ्यां स्वाहा

oṃ gīṃ tarjanībhyāṃ svāhā thumb forefinger
oṃ Gīṃ in the forefinger, I am One with God!

ॐ गूं मद्यमाभ्यां वषट्

oṃ gūṃ madyamābhyāṃ vaṣaṭ thumb middlefinger
oṃ Gūṃ in the middle finger, Purify!

ॐ गैं अनामिकाभ्यां हुं

oṃ gaiṃ anāmikābhyāṃ huṃ thumb ringfinger
oṃ Gaiṃ in the ring finger, Cut the Ego!

ॐ गौं कनिष्ठिकाभ्यां वौषट्

oṃ gauṃ kaniṣṭhikābyāṃ vauṣaṭ thumb littlefinger
oṃ Gauṃ in the little finger, Ultimate Purity!

Roll hand over hand forwards while reciting *karatala kara* and backwards while chanting *pṛṣṭhābhyāṃ*, then clap hands when chanting *astrāya phaṭ*.

ॐ गः करतल कर पृष्ठाभ्यां अस्त्राय फट्

oṃ gaḥ karatala kara pṛṣṭhābhyāṃ astrāya phaṭ
oṃ Gaḥ roll hand over hand front and back and clap with the weapon of Virtue.

ॐ गां गणेशाय नमः

oṃ gāṃ gaṇeśāya namaḥ
oṃ We bow to Gaṇeśa, the Lord of Wisdom, Lord of the Multitudes.

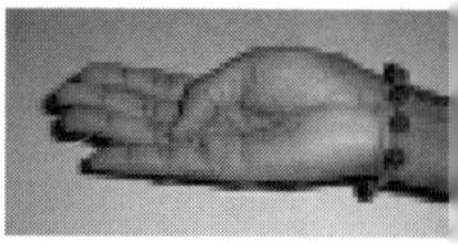

aṅga nyāsa

establishment in the body

Holding tattva mudrā, touch heart.

ॐ गां हृदयाय नमः

oṃ gāṃ hṛdayāya namaḥ touch heart
oṃ Gaṃ in the heart, I bow.

Holding tattva mudrā, touch top of head.

ॐ गीं शिरसे स्वाहा

oṃ gīṃ śirase svāhā top of head
oṃ Gīṃ on the top of the head, I am One with God!

With thumb extended, touch back of head.

ॐ गूं शिखायै वषट्

oṃ gūṃ śikhāyai vaṣaṭ back of head
oṃ Gūṃ on the back of the head, Purify!

Holding tattva mudrā, cross both arms.

ॐ गैं कवचाय हुं

oṃ gaiṃ kavacāya huṃ cross both arms
oṃ Gaiṃ crossing both arms, Cut the Ego!

Holding tattva mudrā, touch three eyes at once with three middle fingers.

ॐ गौं नेत्रत्रयाय वौषट्

oṃ gauṃ netratrayāya vauṣaṭ touch three eyes
oṃ Gauṃ in the three eyes, Ultimate Purity!

Roll hand over hand forwards while reciting *karatala kara* and backwards while chanting *pṛṣṭhābhyāṃ*, then clap hands when chanting *astrāya phaṭ*.

ॐ गः करतल कर पृष्ठाभ्यां अस्त्राय फट्

oṃ gaḥ karatala kara pṛṣṭhābhyāṃ astrāya phaṭ
oṃ Gaḥ roll hand over hand front and back and clap with the weapon of Virtue.

ॐ गां गणेशाय नमः

oṃ gāṃ gaṇeśāya namaḥ
oṃ We bow to Gaṇeśa, the Lord of Wisdom, Lord of the Multitudes.

ॐ सुमुखश्चैकदन्तश्च कपिलो गजकर्णकः ।
लम्बोदरश्च विकटो विघ्ननाशो विनायकः ॥

oṃ sumukhaścaika dantaśca kapilo gaja karṇakaḥ
lambodaraśca vikaṭo vighnanāśo vināyakaḥ
He has a beautiful face with only one tooth (or tusk), of red color with elephant ears; with a big belly and a great tooth he destroys all obstacles. He is the Remover of Obstacles.

धूम्रकेतुर्गणाध्यक्षो भालचन्द्रो गजाननः ।
द्वादशैतानि नामानि यः पठेच्छृणुयादपि ॥

dhūmraketurgaṇādhyakṣo bhāla candro gajānanaḥ
dvādaśaitāni nāmāni yaḥ paṭhecchṛṇu yādapi

With a grey banner, the living spirit of the multitudes, having the moon on his forehead, with an elephant's face; whoever will recite or listen to these twelve names

विद्यारम्भे विवाहे च प्रवेशे निर्गमे तथा ।
संग्रामे संकटे चैव विघ्नस्तस्य न जायते ॥

vidyārambhe vivāhe ca praveśe nirgame tathā
saṃgrāme saṃkate caiva vighnastasya na jāyate

at the time of commencing studies, getting married, or upon entering or leaving any place; on a battlefield of war, or in any difficulty, will overcome all obstacles.

शुक्लाम्बरधरं देवं शशिवर्णं चतुर्भुजम् ।
प्रसन्नवदनं ध्यायेत् सर्वविघ्नोपशान्तये ॥

śuklāmbaradharaṃ devaṃ śaśivarṇaṃ caturbhujam
prasannavadanaṃ dhyāyet sarvavighnopaśāntaye

Wearing a white cloth, the God has the color of the moon and four arms. That most pleasing countenance is meditated upon, who gives peace to all difficulties.

अभीप्सितार्थसिद्ध्यर्थं पूजितो यः सुरासुरैः ।
सर्वविघ्नहरस् तस्मै गणाधिपतये नमः ॥

abhīpsitārtha siddhyarthaṃ pūjito yaḥ surā suraiḥ
sarvavighna haras tasmai gaṇādhipataye namaḥ

For gaining the desired objective, or for the attainment of perfection, he is worshiped by the Forces of Union and the Forces of Division alike. He takes away all difficulties, and therefore, we bow down in reverance to the Lord of the Multitudes.

ॐ गं गणपतये नमः

oṃ gaṃ gaṇapataye namaḥ
oṃ we bow to the Lord of Wisdom, Lord of the Multitudes.

अथ गणेश्यथर्वशीर्षम् ॥

atha gaṇeśyatharvaśīrṣam

ॐ नमस्ते गणपतये ॥

oṃ namaste gaṇapataye
oṃ I bow to Gaṇapati.

त्वमेव प्रत्यक्षं तत्त्वमसि ॥

tvameva pratyakṣaṃ tattvamasi
You alone are the perceivable form of That Thou art.

त्वमेव केवलं कर्तासि ॥

tvameva kevalaṃ kartāsi
You alone are the Creator.

त्वमेव केवलं धर्तासि ।

tvameva kevalaṃ dhartāsi
You alone are the Supporter.

त्वमेव केवलं हर्तासि ॥

tvameva kevalaṃ hartāsi
You alone are the Dissolver.

त्वमेव सर्वं खल्विदं ब्रह्मासि ॥

tvaṃeva sarvaṃ khalvidaṃ brahmāsi

You alone are the entire unity of God.

- 1 -

त्वं साक्षादात्मासि नित्यं ॥

tvaṃ sākṣhādātmāsi nityaṃ

You are the actual eternal soul.

- 2 -

ऋतं वच्मि ॥ सत्यं वच्मि ॥

ṛtaṃ vacmi satyaṃ vacmi

I speak truth, I speak truth.

अव त्वं मां ॥

ava tvaṃ māṃ

Protect me.

अव वक्तारं ॥

ava vaktāraṃ

Protect my speech.

अव श्रोतारं ॥

ava śrotāraṃ

Protect my hearing.

अव दातारं ॥

ava dātāraṃ

Protect my giving.

अव धातारं ॥

ava dhātāraṃ
Protect my supporting.

अवानूचानम् ॥

ava anūcānam
Protect my learning.

अवशिष्यं ॥

ava śiṣyaṃ
Protect my disciple.

अव पश्चात्तात् ॥

ava paścāttāt
Protect me from behind.

अव पुरस्तात् ॥

ava purastāt
Protect me from the front.

अवोत्तरात्तात् ॥

avottarāttāt
Protect me from the north.

अव दक्षिणात्तात् ॥

ava dakṣiṇāttāt
Protect me from the south.

अव चोर्ध्वात्तात् ॥

ava cordhvāttāt

Protect me from above.

अवाधरात्तात् ॥

ava adharāttāt

Protect me from below.

- 3 -

सर्वतो मां पाहि पाहि समंतात् ॥

sarvato māṃ pāhi pāhi samaṃtāt

Protect me from all around on every side equally.

त्वं वङ्मयस्त्वं चिन्मयः त्वमानंदमयस्त्वं ब्रह्ममयः ॥

tvaṃ vaṅmayastvaṃ cinmayaḥ tvamānaṃdamayastvaṃ brahmamayaḥ

You are the manifestation of sound, the manifestation of consciousness, the manifestation of bliss, the manifestation of Supreme Divinity.

त्वं सच्चिदानंदाद्वितीयोऽसि ॥

tvaṃ saccidānaṃdadvitīyo-si

You are Truth, Consciousness and Bliss beyond duality.

त्वं प्रत्यक्षं ब्रह्मासि ॥

tvaṃ pratyakṣaṃ brahmāsi

You are the perceivable Brahma (Supreme Divinity).

- 4 -

त्वं ज्ञानमयो विज्ञानमयोऽसि ॥

tvaṃ jñānamayo vijñānamayo-si

You are the manifestation of wisdom and knowledge.

सर्वं जगदिदं त्वत्तो जायते ॥

sarvaṃ jagadidaṃ tvatto jāyate
All of this perceivable universe is brought forth from you.

सर्वं जगदिदं त्वत्तस्तिष्ठति ॥

sarvaṃ jagadidaṃ tvattastiṣṭhati
All of this perceivable universe has its existence in you.

सर्वं जगदिदं त्वयि लयमेष्यति ॥

sarvaṃ jagadidaṃ tvayi layameṣyati
All of this perceivable universe will dissolve its existence in you.

सर्वं जगदिदं त्वयि प्रत्येति ॥

sarvaṃ jagadidaṃ tvayi pratyeti
All of this perceivable universe will return to you.

त्वं भूमिरापोऽनलोऽनिलो नमः ॥

tvaṃ bhūmirāpo-nalo-nilo namaḥ
I bow to you as the earth, water, fire, wind.

- 5 -

त्वं चत्वारि वाक्पदानि ॥

tvaṃ catvāri vākpadāni
You are the meeting place of the syllables of speech.

त्वं गुणत्रयातीतः ॥

tvaṃ guṇatrayātītaḥ
You are beyond the three qualities.

त्वं देहत्रयातीतः ॥

tvaṃ dehatrayātītaḥ

You are beyond the three bodies (gross, subtle and causal).

त्वं कालत्रयातीतः ॥

tvaṃ kālatrayātītaḥ

You are beyond the three times.

त्वं मूलाधार स्थितोऽसि नित्यम् ॥

tvaṃ mūlādhāra stitho-si nityam

You reside eternally in the mūlādhāra cakra.

त्वं शक्तित्रयात्मकः ॥

tvaṃ śaktitrayātmakaḥ

You are the soul of the three energies.

त्वां योगिनो ध्यायंति नित्यम् ॥

tvāṃ yogino dhyāyaṃti nityam

Yogis continually meditate upon you.

- 6 -

त्वं ब्रह्मा त्वं विष्णुस्त्वं रुद्रस्त्वमिंद्रस्त्वमग्निस्त्वं वायुस्त्वं सूर्यस्त्वं चंद्रमास्त्वं ब्रह्म भूर्भुवः स्वरोम् ॥

tvaṃ brahmā tvaṃ viṣṇustvaṃ rudrastvamiṃdrastvam agnistvaṃ vāyustvaṃ sūryastvam caṃdramāstvaṃ brahma bhūr bhuvaḥ svarom

You are Brahmā, Viṣṇu, Rudra, Indra, Agni, Vāyu, Sūrya, Chandramā, the Unknowable Divinity who pervades the three worlds and beyond.

गणादिं पूर्वमुच्चार्य वर्णादिं तदनंतरम् ॥

gaṇādiṃ pūrvamuccārya varṇādiṃ tadanaṃtaram

These are the instructions for the full correct pronunciation of the letters of the Ganeśa mantras of that Supreme Soul (literally, that which is uninterrupted).

अनुस्वारः परतरः ॥

anusvāraḥ parataraḥ

Anusvāraḥ (ṃ) comes last.

अर्धेदुलसितम् ॥

ardhedulasitam

The half moon (m̐) plays

तारेण रुद्धम् ॥

tāreṇa ruddham

with the Tārā (oṃ), which it checks or restrains.

एतत्तव मनुस्वरूपम् ॥

ettattava manusvarūpam

And this is the intrinsic nature of the manifestations of mind.

गकारःपूर्वरूपम् ॥

gakāraḥ pūrvarūpam

In the beginning is the letter G.

अकारो मध्यमरूपम् ॥

akāro madhyamarūpam

In the middle is the letter a.

अनुस्वारश्चांत्यरूपम् ॥

anusvāraścāṃtyarūpam

Anusvāraḥ (ṃ) is the form at the end.

बिंदुरुत्तररूपम् ॥

biṃduruttararūpam

Bindu (ṃ) is the form above.

नादः संधानम् ॥

nādaḥ saṃdhānam

The subtle sound is joined together

संहिता संधिः ॥

saṃhitā saṃdhiḥ

according to the rules of the union of letters in literature.

सैषा गणेशविद्या ॥

saiṣā gaṇeśavidyā

This is the knowledge of the mantra of Ganeśa.

गणक ऋषिः ॥

gaṇaka ṛṣiḥ

Ganak is the Ṛṣi.

निचृद्गायत्रीच्छंदः ॥

nicṛid gāyatrīcchaṃdaḥ

Nicṛd Gāyatrī is the rhythm.

गणपतिर्देवता ॥

gaṇapatirdevatā
Gaṇapati is the devatā.

- 7 -

ॐ गं गणपतये नमः ॥

oṃ gaṃ gaṇapataye namaḥ
oṃ Gaṃ I bow to Gaṇapati.

एकदंताय विद्महे वक्रतुंडाय धीमहि ।
तन्नो दन्तिः प्रचोदयात् ॥

ekadaṃtāya vidmahe vakratuṃḍāya dhīmahi
tanno dantiḥ pracodayāt
We know He with one tooth, meditate upon He with the bent tusk. May He (of the special tooth) grant us increase.

एकदंतं चतुर्हस्तं पाशमंकुशधारिणम् ।
रदं च वरचं हस्तैर्ब्रिभ्राणं मूषकध्वजम् ॥

ekadaṃtaṃ caturhastaṃ pāśamaṃkuśadhāriṇam
radaṃ ca varacaṃ hastair bribhrāṇaṃ mūṣakadhvajam
He has one tooth and fours hands. He holds a net, a goad, an elephant's tusk and the mudrā which grants boons, bearing a banner upon which is the emblem of a mouse.

रक्तं लंबोदरं शर्पकर्णकं रक्तवाससम् ।
रक्तगंधानुलिप्तांगं रक्तपुष्पैः सुपूजितम् ॥

raktaṃ laṃbodaraṃ śarpakarṇakam raktavāsasam
raktagaṃdhānuliptāṃgaṃ raktapuṣpaiḥ supūjitam

His body is red, his belly big, his ears are like great fans and his clothing red. His body is covered with red unguents, and He is worshiped with red flowers.

भक्तानुकंपिनं देवं जगत्कारणमच्युतम् ।
आविर्भूतं च सृष्ट्यादौ प्रकृतेः पुरुषात्परम् ॥

bhaktānukaṃpinaṃ devaṃ jagatkāraṇamacyutam
āvirbhūtaṃ ca sṛistyādau prakṛteḥ puruṣātparam

He is the God who is gracious to devotees and the primary cause of perceivable existence. His presence was manifest before creation. He is beyond both Puruṣa and Prakṛti.

एवं ध्यायति यो नित्यं स योगी योगिनां वरः ॥ ८

evaṃ dhyāyati yo nityaṃ sa yogī yogināṃ varaḥ

And whoever continually meditates in this way is blessed. He becomes the Yogi of all Yogis.

नमो व्रातपतये नमो गणपतये नमः प्रमथपतये नमस्तेऽस्तु लंबोदराय एकदंताय विघ्ननाशिने शिवसुताय श्रीवरदमूर्तये नमः ॥ ९

namo vrātapataye namo gaṇapataye namaḥ pramathapataye namaste-stu lambodarāya ekadaṃtāya vighnanāśine śivasutāya śrīvaradamūrtaye namaḥ

I bow to the Lord of all Vows, to the Lord of the Multitudes, to the Lord who is foremost. I bow to the Lord with a big belly, with one tooth, who removes all obstacles, to the son of Śiva, to the Divine One who grants boons.

इदमथर्वशीर्षं योऽधीते स ब्रह्मभूयाय कल्पते ॥

idamatharvaśīrṣaṃ yo-dhīte sa brahmabhūyāya kalpate

Who studies the "Highest Meaning" conceives himself to be one with God.

स सर्वविघ्नैर्न बाध्यते ॥

sa sarvavighnairna bādhyate

No obstacle can bind him.

स सर्गतः सुखमेधते ॥

sa sargataḥ sukhamedhate

His loving intellect reflects the happiness of heaven.

स पंचमहापापात्प्रमुच्यते ॥

sa paṃcamahāpāpātpramucyate

He removes the five great kinds of sin.

सायमधीयानो दिवसकृतं पापं नाशयति ॥

sāyamadhīyāno divasakṛtaṃ pāpaṃ nāśayati

Who contemplates (this knowledge) in the night, is freed from sins committed in the day.

प्रातरधीयानो रात्रिकृतं पापं नाशयति ॥

prātaradhīyāno rātrikṛtaṃ pāpaṃ nāśayati

Who contemplates (this knowledge) in the day, is freed from sins committed in the night.

सायंप्रातः प्रयुंजानो अपापो भवति ॥

sāyaṃprātaḥ prayuṃjāno apāpo bhavati

Who contemplates (this knowledge) in the night and in the day, is freed from all sins.

सर्वत्रा धीयानोऽपविघ्नो भवति ॥

sarvatrā dhīyāno-pavighno bhavati

Who always contemplates (this knowledge), is freed from all obstacles,

धर्मार्थकाममोक्षं च विदति ॥

dharmārthakāmamokṣaṃ ca vidati

and he knows dharma (the way of truth and harmony, artha (the necessities of life), Kāma (the purification of all desires), and Mokṣa (liberation, otherwise known as self-realization).

इदमथर्वशीर्षमशिष्याय न देयम् ॥

idamatharvaśīrṣamaśiṣyāya na deyam

This "Highest Meaning" should not be given to one who is not a disciple,

यो यदि मोहाद्दात्यति स पापीयान् भवति ॥

yo yadi mohāddātyati sa pāpīyān bhavati

nor to one who is ignorant. Such giving is a sin

सहस्रावर्तनात् ॥

sahasrāvartanāt

from which extreme bad fortune arises.

यं यं काममधीते तं तमनेन साधयेत् ॥

yaṃ yaṃ kāmamadhīte taṃ tamanena sādhayet

Wherever desires are contemplated, immediately they will be fulfilled.

अनेन गणपतिमभिषिंचति स वाग्भीभवति ॥

anena gaṇapatimabhiṣiṃcati sa vāgbhībhavati

Gaṇapati will make him without fault. He will become one with knowledge and vibrations.

चतुर्थ्यामनुस्थानम् जपति स विद्यावान्भवति ॥

caturthyāmanusthānam japati sa vidyāvānbhavati

If he will recite at the fourth time of prayer, he will become full of knowledge.

इत्यथर्वण वाक्यम् ॥

ityatharvaṇa vākyam

This is the word of Atharvaṇ (a name of Śiva).

ब्रह्माद्याचरणं विद्यात् न विभेति कदाचनेति ॥

brahmādyācaraṇaṃ vidyāt na vibheti kadācaneti

He will know only divine behavior, etc., and will never act contrarily.

यो दूर्वांकुरैर्यजति स वैश्रवणोपमो भवति
यो लाजैर्यजति स यशोबान्भवति स मेधावान्भवति ॥

yo dūrvāṃkurairyajati sa vaiśravaṇopamo bhavati
yo lājairyajati sa yaśobānbhavati sa medhāvānbhavati

Whoever offers sprouts of durva grass becomes elevated in the universe. Whoever offers flattened rice becomes a repository of fame and welfare, becomes filled with loving intellect.

यो मोदकसहस्रेण यजति स वांछितफलमवाप्नोति ।
यः सत्यसमिद्भिर्यजति स सर्वं लभते स सर्वं लभते ॥

yo modakasahasreṇa yajati
sa vāṃchitaphalamavāpnoti
yaḥ satyasamidbhiryajati sa sarvaṃ labhate
sa sarvaṃ labhate

Whoever offers a thousand sweets, attains his desired objective. Whoever offers the worship with truth attains all, attains all.

अष्टो ब्राह्मणान् सम्यग्ग्राहायत्वा सूर्यवर्चस्वी भवति ।
सूर्यग्रहे महानद्यां प्रतिमासन्निधौ वा जप्वा सिद्धमंत्रो भवति ॥

aṣṭo brāhmaṇān samyagrāhāyatvā sūryavarcasvī bhavati
sūryagrahe mahānadyāṃ pratimāsannidhau vā japvā siddhamaṃtro bhavati

Whoever offers to eight Brahmaṇs for their acceptance, becomes an offeror of the Light of Wisdom. At the time of solar eclipse, on the banks of great rivers, if one recites, he becomes perfect in mantras.

महाविघ्नात्प्रमुच्यते ॥

mahāvighnātpramucyate

Great obstacles are removed.

महादोषात्प्रमुच्यते ॥

mahādoṣātpramucyate

Great faults are removed.

स सर्वविद्भवति स सर्वविद्भवति ।

य एवं वेद । इत्युपनिषद् ॥

sa sarvavidbhavati sa sarvavidbhavati
ya evaṃ veda ityupaniṣad

He becomes a knower of all. He becomes a knower of all. And this is the wisdom. Thus ends the Upaniṣad.

ॐ सह नाववतु ॥ सह नौ भुनक्तु ॥

सहवीर्यं करवावहै ॥ तेजस्वि नावधीतमस्तु ॥

मा विद्विषावहै ॥

ॐ शान्तिः । ॐ शान्तिः । ॐ शान्तिः ॥

oṃ sah nāvavatu saha nau bhunaktu
sahavīryaṃ karavāvahai tejasvi nāvadhītamastu
mā vidviṣāvahai
oṃ śāntiḥ oṃ śāntiḥ oṃ śāntiḥ

oṃ May the Lord protect us. May the Lord grant us enjoyment of all actions. May we be granted strength to work together. May our studies be thorough and faithful. May all disagreement cease.

गणेश शतनाम

one hundred eight names of gaṇeśa

- 1 -

ॐ विनायकाय नमः

oṃ vināyakāya namaḥ

Oṃ We bow to he who is the Remover of Obstacles

- 2 -

ॐ विघ्नराजाय नमः

oṃ vighnarājāya namaḥ

Oṃ We bow to he who is the King of Difficulties

- 3 -

ॐ गौरीपुत्राय नमः

oṃ gaurīputrāya namaḥ

Oṃ We bow to he who is the son of She who is Rays of Light

- 4 -

ॐ गणेश्वराय नमः

oṃ gaṇeśvarāya namaḥ

Oṃ We bow to he who is the Lord of Wisdom, Lord of the Multitudes

- 5 -

ॐ स्कन्दाग्रजाय नमः

oṃ skandāgrajāya namaḥ

Oṃ We bow to he who came before Kartikeya

- 6 -

ॐ अव्ययाय नमः

oṃ avyayāya namaḥ

Oṃ We bow to he who is the Unchangeable One

- 7 -

ॐ पूताय नमः

oṃ pūtāya namaḥ

Oṃ We bow to he who is the Son

- 8 -

ॐ दक्षाय नमः

oṃ dakṣāya namaḥ

Oṃ We bow to he who has Ability

- 9 -

ॐ अद्यक्षाय नमः

oṃ adhyakṣāya namaḥ

Oṃ We bow to he who Resides in the Now

- 10 -

ॐ द्विजप्रियाय नमः

oṃ dvijapriyāya namaḥ

Oṃ We bow to he who is the Beloved of the Twice-born

- 11 -

ॐ अग्निगर्भच्चिदे नमः

oṃ agnigarbhaccide namaḥ

Oṃ We bow to he who pierces the womb of Fire

- 12 -

ॐ इन्द्रश्रीप्रदाय नमः

oṃ indraśrīpradāya namaḥ

Oṃ We bow to he upon whom Indra bestows the highest respect

- 13 -

ॐ वाणीप्रदाय नमः

oṃ vāṇīpradāya namaḥ

Oṃ We bow to he who gives all sound

- 14 -

ॐ अव्ययाय नमः

oṃ avyayāya namaḥ

Oṃ We bow to he who is the Unchangeable One

- 15 -

ॐ सर्वसिद्धिप्रदाय नमः

oṃ sarvasiddhipradāya namaḥ

Oṃ We bow to he who bestows all attainments of Perfection

- 16 -

ॐ सर्वतनयाय नमः

oṃ sarvatanayāya namaḥ

Oṃ We bow to he whose entire body is completely reborn

- 17 -

ॐ शर्वरीप्रियाय नमः

oṃ śarvarīpriyāya namaḥ

Oṃ We bow to he who is beloved by the Star-lit Night

- 18 -

ॐ सर्वात्मकाय नमः

oṃ sarvatmakāya namaḥ

Oṃ We bow to he who is the Intrinsic Soul of All

- 19 -

ॐ स्रिष्टिकर्त्रे नमः

oṃ sriṣṭikartre namaḥ

Oṃ We bow to he who conducts Creation

- 20 -

ॐ देवाय नमः

oṃ devāya namaḥ

Oṃ We bow to he who is the Shining One, the God

- 21 -

ॐ अनेकार्चिताय नमः

oṃ anekārcitāya namaḥ

Oṃ We bow to he who gives many offerings

- 22 -

ॐ शिवाय नमः

oṃ śivāya namaḥ

Oṃ We bow to he who is the Consciousness of Infinite Goodness

- 23 -

ॐ शुद्धाय नमः

oṃ śuddhāya namaḥ

Oṃ We bow to he who is Pure

- 24 -

ॐ बुद्धिप्रियाय नमः

oṃ buddhipriyāya namaḥ

Oṃ We bow to he who is the Beloved of Intelligence

- 25 -

ॐ शान्ताय नमः

oṃ śāntāya namaḥ

Oṃ We bow to he who is Peace

- 26 -

ॐ ब्रह्मचारिणे नमः

oṃ brahmacāriṇe namaḥ

Oṃ We bow to he who Moves in Consciousness

- 27 -

ॐ गजाननाय नमः

oṃ gajānanāya namaḥ

Oṃ We bow to he who has the face of an Elephant

- 28 -

ॐ द्वैमात्रेयाय नमः

oṃ dvaimātreyāya namaḥ

Oṃ We bow to he who has two Mothers

- 29 -

ॐ मुनिस्तुत्याय नमः

oṃ munistutyāya namaḥ

Oṃ We bow to he whose praise is sung by munis

- 30 -

ॐ भक्तविघ्नविनाशनाय नमः

oṃ bhaktavighnavināśanāya namaḥ

Oṃ We bow to he who Destroys all obstacles for Devotees

- 31 -

ॐ एकदन्ताय नमः

oṃ ekadantāya namaḥ

Oṃ We bow to he who has one tooth

- 32 -

ॐ चतुर्बाहवे नमः

oṃ caturbāhave namaḥ

Oṃ We bow to he who has four arms

- 33 -

ॐ चतुराय नमः

oṃ caturāya namaḥ

Oṃ We bow to he who is the Four

- 34 -

ॐ शक्तिसम्युक्ताय नमः

oṃ śaktisamyuktāya namaḥ

Oṃ We bow to he who is United with Energy

- 35 -

ॐ लम्बोदराय नमः

oṃ lambodarāya namaḥ

Oṃ We bow to he who has a big belly

- 36 -

ॐ शूर्पकुराय नमः

oṃ śūrpakurāya namaḥ

Oṃ We bow to he whose ears are like a winnowing fan

- 37 -

ॐ हरये नमः

oṃ haraye namaḥ

Oṃ We bow to he who takes away

- 38 -

ॐ ब्रह्मविदुत्तमाय नमः

oṃ brahmaviduttamāya namaḥ

Oṃ We bow to he who is the Ambassador of Consciousness

- 39 -

ॐ कालाय नमः

oṃ kālāya namaḥ

Oṃ We bow to he who is Time

- 40 -

ॐ ग्रहपतये नमः

oṃ grahapataye namaḥ

Oṃ We bow to he who is the Lord of the Cosmos

- 41 -

ॐ कामिने नमः

oṃ kāmine namaḥ

Oṃ We bow to he who is the Embodiment of Desire

- 42 -

ॐ सोमसूर्याग्निलोचनाय नमः

oṃ somasūryāgnilocanāya namaḥ

Oṃ We bow to he whose three eyes are the Moon, the Sun and Fire

- 43 -

ॐ पाशाण्कुशधराय नमः

oṃ pāśāṇkuśadharāya namaḥ

Oṃ We bow to he who holds the net and curved sword

- 44 -

ॐ चण्डाय नमः

oṃ caṇḍāya namaḥ

Oṃ We bow to he who gets angry

- 45 -

ॐ गुणातीताय नमः

oṃ guṇātītāya namaḥ

Oṃ We bow to he who is Beyond Quality

- 46 -

ॐ निरञ्जनाय नमः

oṃ nirañjanāya namaḥ

Oṃ We bow to he who is Spotless and Pure

- 47 -

ॐ अकल्मषाय नमः

oṃ akalmaṣāya namaḥ

Oṃ We bow to he who is Spotless without stain

- 48 -

ॐ स्वयंसिद्धाय नमः

oṃ svayaṃsiddhāya namaḥ

Oṃ We bow to he who himself is perfect

- 49 -

ॐ सिद्धार्चितपदाम्बुजाय नमः

oṃ siddhārcitapadāmbujāya namaḥ

Oṃ We bow to he whose arms and legs are worshipped by Siddhas

- 50 -

ॐ बीजपूरफलासक्ताय नमः

oṃ bījapūraphalāsaktāya namaḥ

Oṃ We bow to he whose energy transforms a seed into a fully ripened fruit

- 51 -

ॐ वरदाय नमः

oṃ varadāya namaḥ

Oṃ We bow to he whose energy transforms a seed into a fully ripened fruit

- 52 -

ॐ षाश्वताय नमः

oṃ ṣāśvatāya namaḥ

Oṃ We bow to he who gives boons

- 53 -

ॐ कृतिने नमः

oṃ kṛtine namaḥ

Oṃ We bow to he who performs Karma

- 54 -

ॐ द्विजप्रियाय नमः

oṃ dvijapriyāya namaḥ

Oṃ We bow to he who is the beloved of the Twice Born

- 55 -

ॐ वीतभयाय नमः

oṃ vītabhayāya namaḥ

Oṃ We bow to he who is Free from fear

- 56 -

ॐ गदिने नमः

oṃ gadine namaḥ

Oṃ We bow to he who holds the club

- 57 -

ॐ चक्रिणे नमः

oṃ cakriṇe namaḥ

Oṃ We bow to he who holds the discus

- 58 -

ॐ इक्षुचापधृते नमः

oṃ ikṣucāpadhṛte namaḥ

Oṃ We bow to he who bends the bow of sugar cane

- 59 -

ॐ श्रीदाय नमः

oṃ śrīdāya namaḥ

Oṃ We bow to he who gives the Highest Respect

- 60 -

ॐ अजाय नमः

oṃ ajāya namaḥ

Oṃ We bow to he who is Unborn

- 61 -

ॐ उत्पलकराय नमः

oṃ utpalakarāya namaḥ

Oṃ We bow to he who is the Maker of Flowers

- 62 -

ॐ श्रीपतये नमः

oṃ śrīpataye namaḥ

Oṃ We bow to he who is the Lord of the Highest Respect

- 63 -

ॐ स्तुतिहर्षिताय नमः

oṃ stutiharṣitāya namaḥ

Oṃ We bow to he who is the Recipient of all Songs

- 64 -

ॐ कुलादिभेत्रे नमः

oṃ kulādibhetre namaḥ

Oṃ We bow to he who distinguishes different communities

- 65 -

ॐ जटिलाय नमः

oṃ jaṭilāya namaḥ

Oṃ We bow to he whose hair is matted

- 66 -

ॐ कलिकल्मषनाशनाय नमः

oṃ kalikalmaṣanāśanāya namaḥ

Oṃ We bow to he who is the Destroyer of the Darkness of Kali (the Dark Age)

- 67 -

ॐ चन्द्रचूडामणये नमः

oṃ candracūḍāmaṇaye namaḥ

Oṃ We bow to he who wears the Moon as a gem in his crown

- 68 -

ॐ कान्ताय नमः

oṃ kāntāya namaḥ

Oṃ We bow to he who is Beautiful

- 69 -

ॐ पापहारिणे नमः

oṃ pāpahāriṇe namaḥ

Oṃ We bow to he who Takes away Sin

- 70 -

ॐ समाहिताय नमः

oṃ samāhitāya namaḥ

Oṃ We bow to he who unites All

- 71 -

ॐ आश्रिताय नमः

oṃ āśritāya namaḥ

Oṃ We bow to he upon whom all are dependent

- 72 -

ॐ श्रीकराय नमः

oṃ śrīkarāya namaḥ

Oṃ We bow to he who Causes the Ultimate Prosperity

- 73 -

ॐ सौम्याय नमः

oṃ saumyāya namaḥ

Oṃ We bow to he who is Beautiful

- 74 -

ॐ भक्तवान्चितदायकाय नमः

oṃ bhaktavāncitadāyakāya namaḥ

Oṃ We bow to he who gives certainty to devotees

- 75 -

ॐ शान्ताय नमः

oṃ śāntāya namaḥ

Oṃ We bow to he who is peace

- 76 -

ॐ कैवल्यसुखदाय नमः

oṃ kaivalyasukhadāya namaḥ

Oṃ We bow to he who gives Unlimited Comfort

- 77 -

ॐ सच्चिदानन्दविग्रहाय नमः

oṃ saccidānandavigrahāya namaḥ

Oṃ We bow to he who divides the Infinite Existence-Consciousness-Bliss

- 78 -

ॐ ज्ञानिने नमः

oṃ jñānine namaḥ

Oṃ We bow to he who is the Wise One

- 79 -

ॐ दयायुताय नमः

oṃ dayāyutāya namaḥ

Oṃ We bow to he who gives Compassion

- 80 -

ॐ दान्ताय नमः

oṃ dāntāya namaḥ

Oṃ We bow to he who has great teeth

- 81 -

ॐ ब्रह्मद्वेषविवर्जिताय नमः

oṃ brahmadveṣavivarjitāya namaḥ

Oṃ We bow to he who prohibits the hatred of Supreme Divinity

- 82 -

ॐ प्रमत्तदैत्यभयदाय नमः

oṃ pramattadaityabhayadāya namaḥ

Oṃ We bow to he who gives excessive fear to the forces of duality

- 83 -

ॐ श्रीकण्ठाय नमः

oṃ śrīkaṇṭhāya namaḥ

He who has a beautiful throat

- 84 -

ॐ विभुदेश्वराय नमः

oṃ vibhudeśvarāya namaḥ

Oṃ We bow to he who is the All-Pervading Lord

- 85 -

ॐ रमार्चिताय नमः

oṃ ramārcitāya namaḥ

Oṃ We bow to he who offers with Delight

- 86 -

ॐ विधये नमः

oṃ vidhaye namaḥ

Oṃ We bow to he who is worshiped

- 87 -

ॐ नागराजयज्ञोपवीतवते नमः

oṃ nāgarājayajñopavītavate namaḥ

Oṃ We bow to he who gives the sacred thread to the King of the City

- 88 -

ॐ स्थूलकण्ठाय नमः

oṃ sthūlakaṇṭhāya namaḥ

Oṃ We bow to he who has a great throat

- 89 -

ॐ स्वयम्कर्त्रे नमः

oṃ svayamkartre namaḥ

Oṃ We bow to he who does Himself

- 90 -

ॐ सामघोषप्रियाय नमः

oṃ sāmaghoṣapriyāya namaḥ

Oṃ We bow to he who loves Songs

- 91 -

ॐ परस्मै नमः

oṃ parasmai namaḥ

Oṃ We bow to he who is Beyond

- 92 -

ॐ स्थूलतुण्डाय नमः

oṃ sthūlatuṇḍāya namaḥ

Oṃ We bow to he who has a great snout

- 93 -

ॐ अग्रण्ये नमः

oṃ agraṇye namaḥ

Oṃ We bow to he who is the Foremost

- 94 -

ॐ धीराय नमः

oṃ dhīrāya namaḥ

Oṃ We bow to he who is constant

- 95 -

ॐ वागीशाय नमः

oṃ vāgīśāya namaḥ

Oṃ We bow to he who is the Perceier of all Vibrations

- 96 -

ॐ सिद्धिदायकाय नमः

oṃ siddhidāyakāya namaḥ

Oṃ We bow to he who is the Giver of all Attainments

- 97 -

ॐ दूर्वाबिल्वप्रियाय नमः

oṃ dūrvābilvapriyāya namaḥ

Oṃ We bow to he who loves Dūrva grass and Bilva leaves

- 98 -

ॐ अव्यक्तमूर्तये नमः

oṃ avyaktamūrtaye namaḥ

Oṃ We bow to he who is Indistinguishable (Infinite) Image

- 99 -

ॐ अद्भुतमूर्तिमते नमः

oṃ adbhutamūrtimate namaḥ

Oṃ We bow to he who is the Incredible Image

- 100 -

ॐ सैलेन्द्रतनुजोत्संगखेलनोत् सुकमानसाय नमः

oṃ sailendratanujotsaṃgakhelanot sukamānasāya namaḥ

Oṃ We bow to he whose excellent thoughts are playing with the Mountain King (Lord Śiva)

- 101 -

ॐ स्वलावण्यसुधासारजितमन्म उविग्रहाय नमः

oṃ svalāvaṇyasudhāsārajitamanma uvigrahāya namaḥ

Oṃ We bow to he whose own charm extends the distribution of pure desire

- 102 -

ॐ समस्तजगदाधाराय नमः

oṃ samastajagadādhārāya namaḥ

Oṃ We bow to he who supports all the Worlds

- 103 -

ॐ मायिने नमः

oṃ māyine namaḥ

Oṃ We bow to he who Measures

- 104 -

ॐ मूषिकवाहनाय नमः

oṃ mūṣikavāhanāya namaḥ

Oṃ We bow to he who rides on a mouse

- 105 -

ॐ हृष्टाय नमः

oṃ hṛṣṭāya namaḥ

Oṃ We bow to he who is thrilled with Joy

- 106 -

ॐ तुष्टाय नमः

oṃ tuṣṭāya namaḥ

Oṃ We bow to he who is Satisfied

- 107 -

ॐ प्रसन्नात्मने नमः

oṃ prasannātmane namaḥ

Oṃ We bow to he whose soul is delighted

- 108 -

ॐ सर्वसिद्धिप्रदायकाय

oṃ sarvasiddhipradāyakāya namaḥ

Oṃ We bow to he who is the Bestower of all attainments of perfection

ॐ नमः इति

oṃ namaḥ iti

And that is the end.

वक्रतुण्ड महाकाय सूर्यकोटिसमप्रभ ।
अविघ्नं कुरु मे देव सर्वकार्येषु सर्वदा ॥

vakratuṇḍa mahākāya sūrya koṭi samaprabha
avighnaṃ kuru me deva sarva kāryeṣu sarvadā

With a broken (or bent) tusk, a great body shining like a million suns, make us free from all obstacles, Oh God. Always remain (with us) in all actions.

एकदन्तं महाकायं लम्बोदरं गजाननम् ।
विघ्ननाशकरं देवं हेरम्बं पणामाम्यहम् ॥

ekadantaṃ mahākāyaṃ lambodaraṃ gajānanam
vighnanāśakaraṃ devaṃ herambaṃ
praṇāmāmyaham

With one tooth, a great body, a big belly and an elephant's face, he is the God who destroys all obstacles to whom we are bowing down with devotion.

मल्लिकादि सुगन्धीनि मालित्यादीनि वै प्रभो ।
मयाऽहृतानि पूजार्थं पुष्पाणि प्रतिगृह्यताम् ॥

mallikādi sugandhīni mālityādīni vai prabho
mayā-hṛtāni pūjārthaṃ puṣpāṇi pratigṛhyatām

Various flowers such as mallikā and others of excellent scent, are being offered to you, Our Lord. All these flowers have come from the devotion of our hearts for your worship. Be pleased to accept them.

एते गन्धपुष्पे ॐ गं गणपतये नमः

ete gandhapuṣpe oṃ gaṃ gaṇapataye namaḥ

With these scented flowers oṃ we bow to the Lord of Wisdom, Lord of the Multitudes.

puṇyā havācana, svasti vācana

proclamation of merits and eternal blessings

ॐ शान्तिरस्तु

oṃ śāntirastu

oṃ Peace be unto you.

ॐ पुष्टिरस्तु

oṃ puṣṭirastu

oṃ Increase or Nourishment be unto you.

ॐ तुष्टिरस्तु

oṃ tuṣṭirastu

oṃ Satisfaction be unto you.

ॐ वृद्धिरस्तु

oṃ vṛddhirastu

oṃ Positive Change be unto you.

ॐ अविघ्नमस्तु

oṃ avighnamastu

oṃ Freedom from Obstacles be unto you.

ॐ आयुष्यमस्तु

oṃ āyuṣyamastu

oṃ Life be unto you.

ॐ आरोग्यमस्तु

oṃ ārogyamastu

oṃ Freedom from Disease be unto you.

ॐ शिवमस्तु

oṃ śivamastu

oṃ Consciousness of Infinite Goodness be unto you.

ॐ शिवकर्माऽस्तु

oṃ śivakarmā-stu

oṃ Consciousness of Infinite Goodness in all action be unto you.

ॐ कर्मसमृद्धिरस्तु

oṃ karmasamṛddhirastu

oṃ Progress or Increase in all action be unto you.

ॐ धर्मसमृद्धिरस्तु

oṃ dharmasamṛddhirastu

oṃ Progress and Increase in all Ways of Truth be unto you.

ॐ वेदसमृद्धिरस्तु

oṃ vedasamṛddhirastu

oṃ Progress or Increase in all Knowledge be unto you.

ॐ शास्त्रसमृद्धिरस्तु

oṃ śāstrasamṛddhirastu

oṃ Progress or Increase in Scriptures be unto you.

ॐ धन-धान्यसमृद्धिरस्तु

oṃ dhana-dhānyasamṛddhirastu

oṃ Progress or Increase in Wealth and Grains be unto you.

ॐ इष्टसम्पदस्तु

oṃ iṣṭasampadastu

oṃ May your beloved deity be your wealth.

ॐ अरिष्टनिरसनमस्तु

oṃ ariṣṭanirasanamastu

oṃ May you remain safe and secure, without any fear.

ॐ यत्पापं रोगमशुभमकल्याणं तद्दूरे प्रतिहतमस्तु

oṃ yatpāpaṃ rogamaśubhamakalyāṇaṃ taddūre pratihatamastu

oṃ May sin, sickness, impurity, and that which is not conducive unto welfare, leave from you.

ॐ ब्रह्म पुण्यमहर्यच्च सृष्ट्युत्पादनकारकम् ।
वेदवृक्षोद्भवं नित्यं तत्पुण्याहं ब्रुवन्तु नः ॥

oṃ brahma puṇyamaharyacca
sṛṣṭyutpādanakārakam
vedavṛkṣodbhavaṃ nityaṃ tatpuṇyāhaṃ bruvantu
naḥ

The Creative Capacity with the greatest merit, the Cause of the Birth of Creation, eternally has its being in the tree of Wisdom. May His blessing of merit be bestowed upon us.

भो ब्राह्मणाः ! मया क्रियमाणस्य शिवपूजनाख्यस्य कर्मणः
पुण्याहं भवन्तो ब्रुवन्तु ॥

bho brāhmaṇāḥ ! mayā kriyamāṇasya śivapūjanākhyasya karmaṇaḥ puṇyāhaṃ bhavanto bruvantu

Oh Brahmiṇs! My sincere effort is to perform the worship of Śiva. Let these activities yield merit.

ॐ पुण्याहं ॐ पुण्याहं ॐ पुण्याहं ॥

oṃ puṇyāhaṃ oṃ puṇyāhaṃ oṃ puṇyāhaṃ

oṃ Let these activities yield merit.

ॐ अस्य कर्मणः पुण्याहं भवन्तो ब्रुवन्तु ॥

oṃ asya karmaṇaḥ puṇyāhaṃ bhavanto bruvantu

oṃ Let these activities yield merit.

ॐ पुण्याहं ॐ पुण्याहं ॐ पुण्याहं ॥

oṃ puṇyāhaṃ oṃ puṇyāhaṃ oṃ puṇyāhaṃ

oṃ Let these activities yield merit (3 times).

पृथिव्यामुद्धृतायां तु यत्कल्याणं पुरा कृतम् ।
ऋषिभिः सिद्धगन्धर्वैस्तत्कल्याणं ब्रुवन्तु नः ॥

pṛthivyāmuddhṛtāyāṃ tu yatkalyāṇaṃ purā kṛtam ṛṣibhiḥ siddha gandharvaistatkalyāṇaṃ bruvantu naḥ

With the solidity of the earth, let supreme welfare be. May the Ṛṣis, the attained ones and the celestial singers bestow welfare upon us.

भो ब्राह्मणाः ! मया क्रियमाणस्य शिवपूजनाख्यस्य कर्मणः कल्याणं भवन्तो ब्रुवन्तु ॥

bho brāhmaṇāḥ ! mayā kriyamāṇasya śivapūjanākhyasya karmaṇaḥ kalyāṇaṃ bhavanto bruvantu

Oh Brahmiṇs! My sincere effort is to perform the worship of Śiva. Let these activities bestow welfare.

ॐ कल्याणं ॐ कल्याणं ॐ कल्याणं

oṃ kalyāṇaṃ oṃ kalyāṇaṃ oṃ kalyāṇaṃ

oṃ Let these activities bestow welfare (3 times).

सागरस्य तु या ऋद्धिर्महालक्ष्म्यादिभिः कृता ।
सम्पूर्णा सुप्रभावा च तामृद्धिं प्रब्रुवन्तु नः ॥

sāgarasya tu yā ṛddhirmahālakṣmyādibhiḥ kṛtā sampūrṇā suprabhāvā ca tāmṛddhiṃ prabruvantu naḥ

May the ocean yield Prosperity, as it did when the Great Goddess of True Wealth and others were produced; fully and completely giving forth excellent lustre, may Prosperity be unto us.

भो ब्राह्मणाः ! मया क्रियमाणस्य शिवपूजनाख्यस्य कर्मणः ऋद्धिं भवन्तो ब्रुवन्तु ॥

bho brāhmaṇāḥ ! mayā kriyamāṇasya śivapūjanākhyasya karmaṇaḥ ṛddhiṃ bhavanto bruvantu

Oh Brahmiṇs! My sincere effort is to perform the worship of Śiva. Let these activities bestow Prosperity.

ॐ कर्म ऋध्यताम् ॐ कर्म ऋध्यताम् ॐ कर्म ऋध्यताम्

oṃ karma ṛdhyatām oṃ karma ṛdhyatām oṃ karma ṛdhyatām

oṃ Let these activities bestow Prosperity (3 times).

स्वस्तिरस्तु याविनाशाख्या पुण्यकल्याणवृद्धिदा ।
विनायकप्रिया नित्यं तां च स्वस्तिं ब्रुवन्तु नः ॥

svastirastu yā vināśākhyā puṇya kalyāṇa vṛddhidā vināyakapriyā nityaṃ tāṃ ca svastiṃ bruvantu naḥ

Let the Eternal Blessings which grant changes of indestructible merit and welfare be with us. May the Lord who removes all obstacles be pleased and grant to us Eternal Blessings.

भो ब्राह्मणाः ! मया क्रियमाणस्य शिवपूजनाख्यस्य कर्मणः स्वस्तिं भवन्तो ब्रुवन्तु ॥

bho brāhmaṇāḥ ! mayā kriyamāṇasya śivapūjanākhyasya karmaṇaḥ svastiṃ bhavanto bruvantu

Oh Brahmiṇs! My sincere effort is to perform the worship of Śiva. Let these activities bestow Eternal Blessings.

ॐ आयुष्मते स्वस्ति ॐ आयुष्मते स्वस्ति ॐ आयुष्मते स्वस्ति

oṃ āyuṣmate svasti oṃ āyuṣmate svasti oṃ āyuṣmate svasti
oṃ May life be filled with Eternal Blessings (3 times).

ॐ स्वस्ति न इन्द्रो वृद्धश्रवाः स्वस्ति नः पूषा विश्ववेदाः ।
स्वस्ति नस्तार्क्ष्यो अरिष्टनेमिः स्वस्ति नो बृहस्पतिर्दधातु ॥
oṃ svasti na indro vṛddhaśravāḥ svasti naḥ pūṣā viśvavedāḥ
svasti nastārkṣyo ariṣṭanemiḥ svasti no bṛhaspatirdadhātu
The Eternal Blessings to us, Oh Rule of the Pure, who perceives all that changes; the Eternal Blessings to us, Searchers for Truth, Knowers of the Universe; the Eternal Blessings to us, Oh Divine Being of Light, keep us safe; the Eternal Blessings to us, Oh Spirit of All-Pervading Delight, grant that to us.

समुद्रमथनाज्ज्ञाता जगदानन्दकारिका ।
हरिप्रिया च माङ्गल्या तां श्रियं च ब्रुवन्तु नः ॥
samudramathnājjātā jagadānandakārikā
haripriyā ca māṅgalyā tāṃ śriyaṃ ca bruvantu naḥ
Who was born from the churning of the ocean, the cause of bliss to the worlds, the beloved of Viṣṇu and Welfare Herself, may Śrī, the Highest Respect, be unto us.

भो ब्राह्मणाः ! मया क्रियमाणस्य शिवपूजनाख्यस्य कर्मणः
श्रीरस्त्विति भवन्तो ब्रुवन्तु ॥
bho brāhmaṇāḥ ! mayā kriyamāṇasya śivapūjanākhyasya karmaṇaḥ śrīrastviti bhavanto bruvantu

Oh Brahmiṇs! My sincere effort is to perform the worship of Śiva. Let these activities bestow the Highest Respect.

ॐ अस्तु श्रीः ॐ अस्तु श्रीः ॐ अस्तु श्रीः

oṃ astu śrīḥ oṃ astu śrīḥ oṃ astu śrīḥ

oṃ Let these activities bestow the Highest Respect (3 times).

ॐ श्रीश्च ते लक्ष्मीश्च पत्न्यावहोरात्रे पार्श्वे नक्षत्राणि रूपमश्विनौ व्यात्तम् । इष्णन्निषाणामुं म इषाण सर्वलोकं म इषाण ॥

oṃ śrīśca te lakṣmīśca patnyāvahorātre pārśve nakṣatrāṇi rūpamaśvinau vyāttam
iṣṇanniṣāṇāmuṃ ma iṣāṇa sarvalokaṃ ma iṣāṇa

oṃ the Highest Respect to you, Goal of all Existence, wife of the full and complete night (the Unknowable One), at whose sides are the stars, and who has the form of the relentless search for Truth. Oh Supreme Divinity, Supreme Divinity, my Supreme Divinity, all existence is my Supreme Divinity.

मृकण्डसूनोरायुर्यद्ध्रुवलोमशयोस्तथा ।
आयुषा तेन संयुक्ता जीवेम शरदः शतम् ॥

mṛkaṇḍasūnorāyuryaddhruvalomaśayostathā
āyuṣā tena saṃyuktā jīvema śaradaḥ śatam

As the son of Mṛkaṇḍa, Mārkaṇḍeya, found imperishable life, may we be united with life and blessed with a hundred autumns.

शतं जीवन्तु भवन्तः

śataṃ jīvantu bhavantaḥ

May a hundred autumns be unto you.

शिवगौरीविवाहे या या श्रीरामे नृपात्मजे ।
धनदस्य गृहे या श्रीरस्माकं साऽस्तु सद्मनि ॥

śiva gaurī vivāhe yā yā śrīrāme nṛpātmaje
dhanadasya gṛhe yā śrīrasmākaṃ sā-stu sadmani

As the imperishable union of Śiva and Gaurī, as the soul of kings manifested in the respected Rāma, so may the Goddess of Respect forever be united with us and always dwell in our house.

ॐ अस्तु श्रीः ॐ अस्तु श्रीः ॐ अस्तु श्रीः

oṃ astu śrīḥ oṃ astu śrīḥ oṃ astu śrīḥ

May Respect be unto you.

प्रजापतिर्लोकपालो धाता ब्रह्मा च देवराट् ।
भगवाञ्छाश्वतो नित्यं नो वै रक्षन्तु सर्वतः ॥

prajāpatirlokapālo dhātā brahmā ca devarāṭ
bhagavāñchāśvato nityaṃ no vai rakṣantu sarvataḥ

The Lord of all beings, Protector of the worlds, Creator, Brahmā, Support of the Gods; may the Supreme Lord be gracious eternally and always protect us.

ॐ भगवान् प्रजापतिः प्रियताम्

oṃ bhagavān prajāpatiḥ priyatām

May the Supreme Lord, Lord of all beings, be pleased.

आयुष्मते स्वस्तिमते यजमानाय दाशुषे ।
श्रिये दत्ताशिषः सन्तु ऋत्विग्भिर्वेदपारगैः ॥

āyuṣmate svastimate yajamānāya dāśuṣe
śriye dattāśiṣaḥ santu ṛtvigbhirvedapāragaiḥ

May life and eternal blessings be unto those who perform this worship and to those who assist. May respect be given to the priests who impart this wisdom.

ॐ स्वस्तिवाचनसमृद्धिरस्तु

oṃ svastivācanasamṛddhirastu

oṃ May this invocation for eternal blessings find excellent prosperity.

sāmānyārghya

purification of water

Draw the following yantra on the plate or space for worship with sandal paste and/or water. Offer rice on the yantra for each of the four mantras.

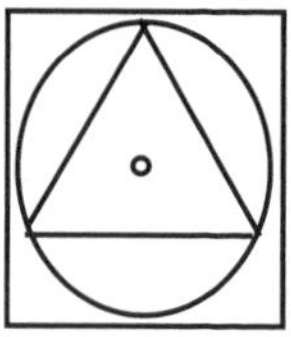

ॐ आधारशक्तये नमः

oṃ ādhāra śaktaye namaḥ

oṃ we bow to the Primal Energy

ॐ कूर्म्माय नमः

oṃ kūrmmāya namaḥ

oṃ we bow to the Support of the Earth

ॐ अनन्ताय नमः

oṃ anantāya namaḥ

oṃ we bow to Infinity

ॐ पृथिव्यै नमः

oṃ pṛthivyai namaḥ
oṃ we bow to the Earth

Place an empty water pot on the bindu in the center of the yantra when saying Phaṭ.

स्थां स्थीं स्थिरो भव फट्

sthāṃ sthīṃ sthiro bhava phaṭ
Be Still in the Gross Body! Be Still in the Subtle Body! Be Still in the Causal Body! Purify!

Fill the pot with water while chanting the mantra.

ॐ गङ्गे च जमुने चैव गोदावरि सरस्वति ।
नर्मदे सिन्धु कावेरि जलऽस्मिन् सन्निधिं कुरु ॥

oṃ gaṅge ca jamune caiva godāvari sarasvati
narmade sindhu kāveri jale-asmin sannidhiṃ kuru
oṃ the Ganges, Jamunā, Godāvarī, Sarasvatī, Narmadā, Sindhu, Kāverī, these waters are mingled together.

The Ganges is the Iḍā, Jamunā is the Piṅgalā, the other five rivers are the five senses. The land of the seven rivers is within the body as well as outside.

Offer Tulasī leaves into water

ॐ ऐं ह्रीं क्लीं श्रीं वृन्दावनवासिन्यै स्वाहा

oṃ aiṃ hrīṃ klīṃ śrīṃ vṛndāvanavāsinyai svāhā
oṃ Wisdom, Māyā, Increase, to She who resides in Vṛndāvana, I am One with God!

Offer 3 flowers into the water pot with the mantras

एते गन्धपुष्पे ॐ अं अर्कमण्डलाय द्वादशकलात्मने नमः

ete gandhapuṣpe oṃ aṃ arkamaṇḍalāya dvādaśakalātmane namaḥ

With these scented flowers oṃ "A" we bow to the twelve aspects of the realm of the sun. Tapinī, Tāpinī, Dhūmrā, Marīci, Jvālinī, Ruci, Sudhūmrā, Bhoga-dā, Viśvā, Bodhinī, Dhārinī, Kṣamā; Containing heat, Emanating heat, Smoky, Ray-producing, Burning, Lustrous, Purple or Smoky-red, Granting enjoyment, Universal, Which makes known, Productive of Consciousness, Which supports, Which forgives.

एते गन्धपुष्पे ॐ उं सोममण्डलाय षोडशकलात्मने नमः

ete gandhapuṣpe oṃ uṃ somamaṇḍalāya ṣoḍaśakalātmane namaḥ

With these scented flowers oṃ "U" we bow to the sixteen aspects of the realm of the moon. Amṛtā, Prāṇadā, Puṣā, Tuṣṭi, Puṣṭi, Rati, Dhṛti, Śaśinī, Candrikā, Kānti, Jyotsnā, Śrī, Prīti, Aṅgadā, Pūrṇā, Pūrṇāmṛtā; Nectar, Which sustains life, Which supports, Satisfying, Nourishing, Playful, Constancy, Unfailing, Producer of Joy, Beauty enhanced by love, Light, Grantor of Prosperity, Affectionate, Purifying the body, Complete, Full of Bliss.

एते गन्धपुष्पे ॐ मं वह्निमण्डलाय दशकलात्मने नमः

ete gandhapuṣpe oṃ maṃ vahnimaṇḍalāya daśakalātmane namaḥ

With these scented flowers oṃ "M" we bow to the ten aspects of the realm of fire: Dhūmrā, Arciḥ, Jvalinī, Śūkṣmā, Jvālinī, Visphuliṅginī, Suśrī, Surūpā, Kapilā, Havya-Kavya-Vahā; Smoky Red, Flaming, Shining, Subtle, Burning, Sparkling,

Beautiful, Well-formed, Tawny, The Messenger to Gods and Ancestors.

Wave hands in matsyā, dhenu and
aṅkuśa mudrās while chanting this mantra.

ॐ गङ्गे च जमुने चैव गोदावरि सरस्वति ।

नर्मदे सिन्धु कावेरि जलेऽस्मिन् सन्निधिं कुरु ॥

oṃ gaṅge ca jamune caiva godāvari sarasvati
narmade sindhu kāveri jale-asmin sannidhiṃ kuru

oṃ the Ganges, Jamunā, Godāvarī, Sarasvatī, Narmadā, Sindhu, Kāverī, these waters are mingled together.

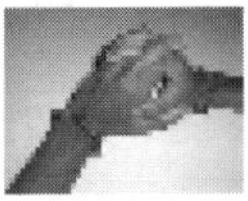

ॐ नमः शिवाय

oṃ namaḥ śivāya

oṃ I bow to the Consciousness of Infinite Goodness.

Sprinkle water over all articles to be offered,
then throw some drops of water over your
shoulders while repeating the mantra.

अमृताम् कुरु स्वाहा

amṛtām kuru svāhā

Make this immortal nectar! I am One with God!

puṣpa śuddhi

purification of flowers

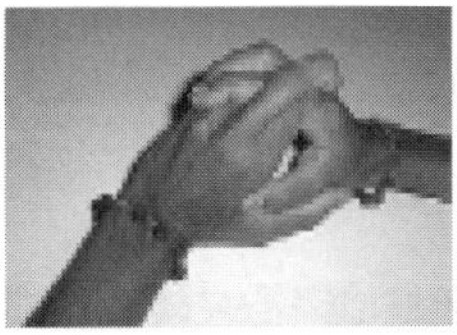

Wave hands over flowers
with prārthanā mudrā
while chanting first line and with dhenu mudrā
while chanting second line of this mantra.

ॐ पुष्प पुष्प महापुष्प सुपुष्प पुष्पसम्भवे ।

पुष्पचयावकीर्णे च हुं फट् स्वाहा ॥

oṃ puṣpa puṣpa mahāpuṣpa
supuṣpa puṣpa sambhave
puṣpa cayāvakīrṇe ca huṃ phaṭ svāhā

oṃ Flowers, flowers, Oh Great Flowers, excellent flowers; flowers in heaps and scattered about, cut the ego, purify, I am One with God!

kara śuddhi

purification of hands

ॐ ऐं रं अस्त्राय फट्

oṃ aiṃ raṃ astrāya phaṭ

oṃ Wisdom, the divine fire, with the weapon, Purify !

worship of śivā

ॐ सदा शिवाय विद्महे सहश्राक्षाय धीमहे ।

तन्नो शम्भो प्रचोदयात् ॥

oṃ sadā śivāya vidmahe sahaśrākṣāya dhīmahe
tanno śambho pracodayāt

oṃ We meditate upon the Perfect, Full, Complete, Always Continuing, Consciousness of Infinite Goodness; contemplate He Whose Thousand Eyes see everywhere. May that Giver of Bliss grant us increase.

ॐ सद्योजातं प्रपद्यामि सद्योजातायवै नमो नमः ।

भवे भवे नाति भवे भवस्वमांभवोद्भवाय नमः ॥

oṃ sadyojātaṃ prapadyāmi
sadyojātāyavai namo namaḥ
bhave bhave nāti bhave
bhavasvamāṃ bhavodbhavāya namaḥ

oṃ I extol the Birth of Truth as Pure Existence. Again and again I bow down to the Birth of Truth as Pure Existence. In being after being, beyond all being, who Himself is all Being, from whom came all being, to That Existence I bow.

वामदेवाय नमो ज्येष्ठाय नमः श्रेष्ठाय नमो रुद्राय नमः ।
कालाय नमः कलविकरणाय नमो बलविकरणाय नमो
बलाय नमो बलप्रमत्तनाय नमः ।
सर्वभूतदमनाय नमोमनोन्मनाय नमः ॥

vāmadevāya namo jyeṣṭhāya namaḥ śreṣṭhāya
namo rudrāya namaḥ kālāya namaḥ
kalavikaraṇāya namo balavikaraṇāya
namo balāya namo balapramattanāya namaḥ
sarvabhūtadamanāya namomanonmanāya namaḥ

I bow to the Beautiful God who is Beloved. I bow to the Pleasant One, to the Ultimate One; I bow to the Reliever of Sufferings. I bow to Time, I bow to the Cause of the Illumination of Darkness, I bow to the Source of Strength, I bow to the Progenitor of Strength. I bow to the Fashioner of all the elements, I bow to the Mind of all minds.

अघोरेभ्योत्तघोरेभ्योघोरघेरतरेभ्यः ।
सर्वेभ्यःसर्वशर्वेभ्यो नमस्तेऽस्तुरुद्ररूपेभ्यः ॥

aghorebhyottaghorebhyoghoragheratarebhyaḥ
sarvebhyaḥsarvaśarvebhyo namaste-
sturudrarūpebhyaḥ

I bow to He who is Free From Fear, who instills the fear of evil, who saves the righteous from fear; who is within all, the all of everything, may we give our respect to He who is the form of the Reliever of Sufferings.

ॐ तत् पुरुषाय विद्महे महादेवाय धीमहि ।
तन्नो रुद्रः प्रचोदयात् ॥

oṃ tat puruṣāya vidmahe mahādevāya dhīmahi tanno rudraḥ pracodayāt

We meditate upon That Universal Consciousness, contemplate the Great God. May that Reliever of Sufferings grant us increase.

ईशानः सर्वविद्यानमीश्वरः सर्वभूतानाम् ।
ब्रह्माधिपतिर्ब्रह्मणोधिपतिर्ब्रह्माशिवोमेऽस्तुसदाशिवोम् ॥

īśānaḥ sarvavidyānamīśvaraḥ sarvabhūtānām brahmādhipatirbrahmaṇodhipatirbrahmāśivome-stusadāśivom

The Seer of All, who is all Knowledge, the Lord of the Universe, who is all existence; before the Creative Consciousness, before the knowers of Consciousness, existing in eternal delight as the Consciousness of Infinite Goodness.

एते गन्धपुष्पे ॐ हराय नमः

ete gandhapuṣpe oṃ harāya namaḥ

With these scented flowers oṃ we bow to He who Takes Away.

एते गन्धपुष्पे ॐ महेश्वराय नमः

ete gandhapuṣpe oṃ maheśvarāya namaḥ

With these scented flowers oṃ we bow to to the Supreme Lord of All.

ॐ ध्यायेन्नित्यं महेशं रजतगिरिनिभं चारुचन्द्रावतंसं
रत्ना कल्पोज्वलांगं परशु मृगवयाभीति हस्तं प्रसन्नं ।
पद्मासीनं समन्तात् स्तुतऽममरगणैर्व्याघ्रकृत्तिं वसानं
विश्वाद्यं विश्वबीजं निखलभयहरं पञ्चवक्त्रं त्रिनेत्रं ॥

oṃ dhyāyen nityaṃ maheśaṃ
rajata girinibhaṃ cāru candrā vataṃsaṃ
ratnā kalpo jvalāṃgaṃ
paraśu mṛga vayābhīti hastaṃ prasannaṃ
padmāsīnaṃ samantāt
stuta-mama raganair vyāghra kṛtiṃ vasānaṃ
viśvādyaṃ viśva bījaṃ
nikhala bhayaharaṃ pañca vaktraṃ trinetraṃ

We always meditate on He who shines like the white mountains, ornamented by a digit of the moon on His head. His body shines like jewels. In His left hands He displays an axe and the Mṛga Mudrā (Kalpataru Mudrā, with the thumb, middle and ring fingers joined with the pointer and pinky extended up) and in His two right hands He shows mudrās granting blessings and fearlessness. He is of beautiful appearance seated in the full lotus asana. On His four sides the Gods are present singing hymns of praise. His wearing apparel is a tiger's skin. He is before the universe and the cause of the universe. He removes all fear, has five faces and three eyes.

kalaśa sthāpana

establishment of the pot

touch earth

ॐ भूरसि भूमिरस्यदितिरसि विश्वधारा विश्वस्य भुवनस्य धर्त्री ।

पृथिवीं यच्छ पृथिवीं दृंह पृथिवीं मा हिंसीः ॥

oṃ bhūrasi bhūmirasyaditirasi viśvadhārā viśvasya bhuvanasya dhartrī
pṛthivīṃ yaccha pṛthivīṃ dṛṃha pṛthivīṃ mā hiṃsīḥ

You are the object of sensory perception; you are the Goddess who distributes the forms of the earth. You are the Producer of the Universe, the Support of all existing things in the universe. Control (or sustain) the earth, firmly establish the earth, make the earth efficient in its motion.

give rice

ॐ धान्यमसि धिनुहि देवान् धिनुहि यज्ञं ।

धिनुहि यज्ञपतिं धिनुहि मां यज्ञन्यम् ॥

oṃ dhānyamasi dhinuhi devān dhinuhi yajñaṃ dhinuhi yajñapatiṃ dhinuhi māṃ yajñanyam

You are the grains which satisfy and gladden the Gods, gladden the sacrifice, gladden the Lord of Sacrifice. Bring satisfaction to us through sacrifice.

place pot

ॐ आजिग्घ्र कलशं मह्या त्वा विशन्त्विन्दवः ।

पुनरूर्ज्जा निवर्तस्व सा नः सहस्रं धुक्क्ष्वोरुधारा पयस्वती

पुनर्म्माविशताद्द्रयिः ॥

oṃ ājigghra kalaśaṃ mahyā tvā viśantvindavaḥ punarūrjjā nivartasva sā naḥ sahasraṃ dhukkṣvorudhārā payasvatīḥ punarmmāviśatāddrayiḥ

Cause the effulgent fire of perception to enter into your highly honored container for renewed nourishment. Remaining there, let it increase in thousands, so that upon removal, abounding in spotlessly pure strength, it may come flowing into us.

pour water

ॐ वरुणस्योत्तम्भनमसि वरुणस्य स्कम्भसर्ज्जनी स्थो ।
वरुणस्य ऋतसदन्नयसि । वरुणस्य ऋतसदनमसि ।
वरुणस्य ऋतसदनमासीद ॥

oṃ varuṇasyottambhanamasi varuṇasya skambhasarjjanī stho varuṇasya ṛtasadannyasi varuṇasya ṛtasadanamasi varuṇasya ṛtasadanamāsīda

You, Waters, are declared the Ultimate of waters established in all creation begotten, abiding in waters as the eternal law of truth; always abiding in waters as the eternal law of truth, and forever abiding in waters as the eternal law of truth.

place wealth

ॐ धन्वना गा धन्वनाजिं जयेम धन्वना तीव्राः समद्रो जयेम ।
धनुः शत्रोरपकामं कृणोति धन्वना सर्वाः प्रदिशो जयेम ॥

oṃ dhanvanā gā dhanvanājiṃ jayema
dhanvanā tīvrāḥ samadro jayema
dhanuḥ śatrorapakāmamaṃ kṛṇoti
dhanvanā sarvāḥ pradiśo jayema

Let wealth, even abundance, be victorious. Let wealth be sufficient as to be victorious over the severe ocean of existence. As a bow to protect us safe from the enemies of desire, let it be victorious to illuminate all.

place fruit

ॐ याः फलिनीर्याऽफलाऽअपुष्पाऽयाश्च पुष्पिणीः ।
बृहस्पतिप्रसूतास्ता नो मुञ्चन्त्वंहसः ॥

oṃ yāḥ phalinīryā-aphalā-apuṣpā-yāśca puṣpiṇīḥ
bṛhaspatiprasūtāstā no muñcantvaṃhasaḥ

That which bears fruit, and that which bears no fruit; that without flowers and that with flowers as well. To we who exist born of the Lord of the Vast, set us FREE! ALL THIS IS GOD!

red powder

ॐ सिन्धोरिव प्राध्वने शूघनासो वातप्रमियः पतयन्ति
यह्वाः । घृतस्य धारा अरुषो न वाजी काष्ठा
भिन्दन्नर्म्मिभिः पिन्वमानः ॥

oṃ sindhoriva prādhvane śūghanāso
vātapramiyaḥ patayanti yahvāḥ
ghṛtasya dhārā aruṣo na vājī kāṣṭhā
bhindannarmmibhiḥ pinvamānaḥ

The pious mark of red vermilion symbolizing the ocean of love placed prominently upon the head above the nose bursting forth, allows the vibrance of youth to fly. As the stream of ghee pours into the flames, those spirited steeds of the Divine

Fire consume the logs of wood increasing the will and self-reliance of the worshiper.

ॐ सिन्दूरमरुणाभासं जपाकुसुमसन्निभम् ।
पूजिताऽसि मया देव प्रसीद परमेश्वर ॥
ॐ नमः शिवाय सिन्दूरं समर्पयामि

oṃ sindūramaruṇābhāsaṃ japākusumasannibham
pūjitā-si mayā deva prasīda parameśvara
oṃ namaḥ śivāya sindūraṃ samarpayāmi

This red colored powder indicates Love, who drives the chariot of the Light of Wisdom, with which we are worshiping our Lord. Please be pleased, Oh Great Seer of All. With this offering of red colored powder oṃ I bow to the Consciousness of Infinite Goodness.

kuṅkum

ॐ कुङ्कुमं कान्तिदं दिव्यं कामिनीकामसम्भवम् ।
कुङ्कुमेनाऽर्चिते देव प्रसीद परमेश्वर ॥
ॐ नमः शिवाय कुङ्कुमं समर्पयामि

oṃ kuṅkumaṃ kāntidaṃ divyaṃ
kāminī kāmasambhavam
kuṅkumenā-rcite deva prasīda parameśvara
oṃ namaḥ śivāya kuṅkumaṃ samarpayāmi

You are being adorned with this divine red powder, which is made more beautiful by the love we share with you, and is so pleasing. Oh Lord, when we present this red powder be pleased, Oh Supreme Ruler of All. With this offering of red colored powder oṃ I bow to the Consciousness of Infinite Goodness.

sandal paste

ॐ श्रीखण्डचन्दनं दिव्यं गन्धाढ्यं सुमनोहरम् ।

विलेपनं च देवेश चन्दनं प्रतिगृह्यताम् ॥

ॐ नमः शिवाय चन्दनं समर्पयामि

oṃ śrīkhaṇḍacandanaṃ divyaṃ
gandhāḍhyaṃ sumano haram
vilepanaṃ ca deveśa candanaṃ pratigṛhyatām
oṃ namaḥ śivāya candanaṃ samarpayāmi

You are being adorned with this beautiful divine piece of sandal wood, ground to a paste which is so pleasing. Please accept this offering of sandal paste, Oh Supreme Sovereign of all the Gods. With the offering of sandal paste oṃ I bow to the Consciousness of Infinite Goodness.

turmeric

ॐ हरिद्रारञ्जिता देव सुख-सौभाग्यदायिनि ।

तस्मात्त्वं पूजयाम्यत्र दुःखशान्तिं प्रयच्छ मे ॥

ॐ नमः शिवाय हरिद्रां समर्पयामि

oṃ haridrārañjitā deva
sukha saubhāgyadāyini
tasmāttvaṃ pūjayāmyatra
duḥkha śāntiṃ prayaccha me
oṃ namaḥ śivāya haridrāṃ samarpayāmi

Oh Lord, you are being gratified by this turmeric, the giver of comfort and beauty. When you are worshiped like this, then you must bestow upon us the greatest peace. With the offering of turmeric oṃ I bow to the Consciousness of Infinite Goodness.

milk bath

ॐ कामधेनुसमुद्भूतं सर्वेषां जीवनं परम् ।

पावनं यज्ञहेतुश्च स्नानार्थं प्रतिगृह्यताम् ॥

ॐ नमः शिवाय पयस्नानं समर्पयामि

oṃ kāmadhenu samudbhūtaṃ
sarveṣāṃ jīvanaṃ param
pāvanaṃ yajña hetuśca snānārthaṃ pratigṛhyatām
oṃ namaḥ śivāya paya snānaṃ samarpayāmi

Coming from the ocean of being, the Fulfiller of all Desires, Grantor of Supreme Bliss to all souls. For the motive of purifying or sanctifying this holy union, we request you to accept this bath. With this offering of milk for your bath oṃ I bow to the Consciousness of Infinite Goodness.

yogurt bath

ॐ पयसस्तु समुद्भूतं मधुराम्लं शशिप्रभम् ।

दध्यानितं मया दत्तं स्नानार्थं प्रतिगृह्यताम् ॥

ॐ नमः शिवाय दधिस्नानं समर्पयामि

oṃ payasastu samudbhūtaṃ
madhurāmlaṃ śaśiprabham
dadhyānitaṃ mayā dattaṃ
snānārthaṃ pratigṛhyatām
oṃ namaḥ śivāya dadhi snānaṃ samarpayāmi

Derived from milk from the ocean of being, sweet and pleasing like the glow of the moon, let these curds eternally be our ambassador, as we request you to accept this bath. With this offering of yogurt for your bath oṃ I bow to the Consciousness of Infinite Goodness.

ghee bath

ॐ नवनीतसमुत्पन्नं सर्वसन्तोषकारकम् ।
घृतं तुभ्यं प्रदास्यामि स्नानार्थं प्रतिगृह्यताम् ॥
ॐ नमः शिवाय घृतस्नानं समर्पयामि

oṃ navanīta samutpannaṃ sarvasantoṣakārakam
ghṛtaṃ tubhyaṃ pradāsyāmi
snānārthaṃ pratigṛhyatām
oṃ namaḥ śivāya ghṛta snānaṃ samarpayāmi

Freshly prepared from the ocean of being, causing all fulfillment, we offer this delightful ghee (clarified butter) and request you to accept this bath. With this offering of ghee for your bath oṃ I bow to the Consciousness of Infinite Goodness.

honey bath

ॐ तरुपुष्पसमुद्भूतं सुस्वादु मधुरं मधु ।
तेजोपुष्टिकरं दिव्यं स्नानार्थं प्रतिगृह्यताम् ॥
ॐ नमः शिवाय मधुस्नानं समर्पयामि

oṃ tarupuṣpa samudbhūtam
susvādu madhuraṃ madhu
tejo puṣṭikaraṃ divyaṃ snānārtham pratigṛhyatām
oṃ namaḥ śivāya madhu snānaṃ samarpayāmi

Prepared from flowers of the ocean of being, enjoyable as the sweetest of the sweet, causing the fire of divine nourishment to burn swiftly, we request you to accept this bath. With this offering of honey for your bath oṃ I bow to the Consciousness of Infinite Goodness.

sugar bath

ॐ इक्षुसारसमुद्भूता शर्करा पुष्टिकारिका ।

मलापहारिका दिव्या स्नानार्थं प्रतिगृह्यताम् ॥

ॐ नमः शिवाय शर्करास्नानं समर्पयामि

oṃ ikṣusāra samudbhūtā śarkarā puṣṭikārikā
malāpahārikā divyā snānārthaṃ pratigṛhyatām
oṃ namaḥ śivāya śarkarā snānaṃ samarpayāmi

From the lake of sugar-cane, from the ocean of being, which causes the nourishment of sugar to give divine protection from all impurity, we request you to accept this bath. With this offering of sugar for your bath oṃ I bow to the Consciousness of Infinite Goodness.

five nectars bath

ॐ पयो दधि घृतं चैव मधु च शर्करायुतम् ।

पञ्चामृतं मयाऽऽनीतं स्नानार्थं प्रतिगृह्यताम् ॥

ॐ नमः शिवाय पञ्चामृतस्नानं समर्पयामि

oṃ payo dadhi ghṛtaṃ caiva
madhu ca śarkarāyutam
pañcāmṛtaṃ mayā--nītaṃ
snānārthaṃ pratigṛhyatām
oṃ namaḥ śivāya pañcāmṛta snānaṃ samarpayāmi

Milk, curd, ghee and then honey and sugar mixed together; these five nectars are our ambassador, as we request you to accept this bath. With this offering of five nectars for your bath oṃ I bow to the Consciousness of Infinite Goodness.

scented oil

ॐ नानासुगन्धिद्रव्यं च चन्दनं रजनीयुतम् ।

उद्वर्तनं मया दत्तं स्नानार्थं प्रतिगृह्यताम् ॥

ॐ नमः शिवाय उद्वर्तनस्नानं समर्पयामि

oṃ nānāsugandhidravyaṃ ca
candanaṃ rajanīyutam
udvartanaṃ mayā dattaṃ
snānārthaṃ pratigṛhyatām
oṃ namaḥ śivāya udvartana snānaṃ samarpayāmi

oṃ With various beautifully smelling ingredients, as well as the scent of sandal, we offer you this scented oil, Oh Lord. With this offering of scented oil oṃ I bow to the Consciousness of Infinite Goodness.

scent bath

गन्धद्वारां दुराधर्षां नित्यपुष्टां करीषिणीम् ।
ईश्वरीं सर्वभूतानां तामिहोपह्वये श्रियम् ॥
ॐ नमः शिवाय गन्धस्नानं समर्पयामि

gandhadvārāṃ durādharṣāṃ nityapuṣṭāṃ karīṣiṇīm
īśvarīṃ sarvabhūtānāṃ tāmihopahvaye śriyam
oṃ namaḥ śivāya gandha snānaṃ samarpayāmi

She is the cause of the scent which is the door to religious ecstasy, unconquerable (never-failing), continually nurturing for all time. May we never tire from calling that manifestation of the Highest Respect, the Supreme Goddess of all existence. With this offering of scented bath oṃ I bow to the Consciousness of Infinite Goodness.

water bath

ॐ गङ्गे च जमुने चैव गोदावरि सरस्वति ।
नर्मदे सिन्धु कावेरि स्नानार्थं प्रतिगृह्यताम् ॥
ॐ नमः शिवाय गङ्गास्नानं समर्पयामि

oṃ gaṅge ca jamune caiva godāvari sarasvati
narmade sindhu kāveri snānārthaṃ pratigṛhyatām
oṃ namaḥ śivāya gaṅgā snānaṃ samarpayāmi

Please accept the waters from the Gaṅges, the Jamunā, Godāvarī, Sarasvatī, Narmadā, Sindhu and Kāverī, which have been provided for your bath. With this offering of Ganges bath waters oṃ I bow to the Consciousness of Infinite Goodness.

cloth

ॐ शीतवातोष्णसंत्राणं लज्जायै रक्षणं परं ।

देहालंकरणं वस्त्रं अथ शान्तिं प्रयच्छ मे ॥

ॐ नमः शिवाय वस्त्रं समर्पयामि

oṃ śīta vātoṣṇa saṃ trāṇaṃ
lajjāyai rakṣaṇaṃ paraṃ
dehālaṅkaraṇaṃ vastraṃ
atha śāntiṃ prayaccha me
oṃ namaḥ śivāya vastraṃ samarpayāmi

To take away the cold and the wind and to fully protect your modesty, we adorn your body with this cloth, and thereby find the greatest Peace. With this offering of wearing apparel oṃ I bow to the Consciousness of Infinite Goodness.

sacred thread

ॐ यज्ञोपवीतं परमं पवित्रं प्रजापतेर्यत् सहजं पुरस्तात् ।

आयुष्यमग्रं प्रतिमुञ्च शुभ्रं यज्ञोपवीतं बलमस्तु तेजः ॥

oṃ yajñopavītaṃ paramaṃ pavitraṃ
prajāpateryat sahajaṃ purastāt
āyuṣyamagraṃ pratimuñca śubhraṃ
yajñopavītaṃ balamastu tejaḥ

Oṃ the sacred thread of the highest purity is given by Prajāpati, the Lord of Creation, for the greatest facility. You bring life and illuminate the greatness of liberation. Oh sacred thread, let your strength be of radiant light.

शमो दमस्तपः शौचं क्षान्तिरार्जवमेव च ।
ज्ञानं विज्ञानमास्तिक्यं ब्रह्मकर्म स्वभावजम् ॥

śamo damastapaḥ śaucaṃ kṣāntirārjavameva ca
jñānaṃ vijñānamāstikyaṃ brahmakarma svabhāvajam

Peacefulness, self-control, austerity, purity of mind and body, patience and forgiveness, sincerity and honesty, wisdom, knowledge, and self-realization, are the natural activities of a Brahmaṇa.

नवभिस्तन्तुभिर्युक्तं त्रिगुणं देवतामयं ।
उपवीतं मया दत्तं गृहाण त्वं सुरेश्वर ॥
ॐ नमः शिवाय यज्ञोपवीतं समर्पयामि

navamiṣṭantubhiryuktaṃ triguṇaṃ devatā mayaṃ
upavītaṃ mayā dattaṃ gṛhāṇa tvaṃ sureśvara
oṃ namaḥ śivāya yajñopavītaṃ samarpayāmi

With nine desirable threads all united together, exemplifying the three guṇas (or three qualities of harmony of our deity), this sacred thread will be our ambassador. Oh Ruler of the Gods, please accept. With this offering of a sacred thread oṃ I bow to the Consciousness of Infinite Goodness.

rudrākṣa

त्र्यम्बकं यजामहे सुगन्धिं पुष्टिवर्द्धनम् ।
उर्व्वारुकमिव बन्धनान्मृत्योर्म्मुक्षीयमामृतात् ॥
ॐ नमः शिवाय रुद्राक्षं समर्पयामि

tryambakaṃ yajāmahe
sugandhiṃ puṣṭivarddhanam
urvvārukamiva bandhanānmṛtyormmukṣīyamāmṛtāt
oṃ namaḥ śivāya rudrākṣaṃ samarpayāmi

We adore the Father of the three worlds, of excellent fame, Grantor of Increase. As a cucumber is released from its bondage to the stem, so may we be freed from Death to dwell in immortality. With this offering of rudrākṣa oṃ I bow to the Consciousness of Infinite Goodness.

mālā

ॐ मां माले महामाये सर्वशक्तिस्वरूपिणि ।
चतुर्वर्गस्त्वयि न्यस्तस्तस्मान्मे सिद्धिदा भव ॥
ॐ नमः शिवाय मालां समर्पयामि

oṃ māṃ māle mahāmāye sarvaśaktisvarūpiṇi
caturvargastvayi nyastastasmānme siddhidā bhava
oṃ namaḥ śivāya mālāṃ samarpayāmi

Oṃ my rosary, the Great Limitation of Consciousness, containing all energy within as your intrinsic nature, fulfilling the four desires of men, give us the attainment of your perfection. With this offering of a mālā oṃ I bow to the Consciousness of Infinite Goodness.

rice

अक्षतान् निर्मलान् शुद्धान् मुक्ताफलसमन्वितान् ।
गृहाणेमान महादेव देहि मे निर्मलां धियम् ॥
ॐ नमः शिवाय अक्षतान् समर्पयामि

akṣatān nirmalān śuddhān muktāphalasamanvitān
gṛhāṇemān mahādeva dehi me nirmalāṃ dhiyam
oṃ namaḥ śivāya akṣatān samarpayāmi

Oh Great Lord, please accept these grains of rice, spotlessly clean, bestowing the fruit of liberation, and give us a spotlessly clean mind. With the offering of grains of rice oṃ I bow to the Consciousness of Infinite Goodness.

flower garland

शङ्ख-पद्मजपुष्पादि शतपत्रैर्विचित्रताम् ।
पुष्पमालां प्रयच्छामि गृहाण त्वं सुरेश्वर ॥
ॐ नमः शिवाय पुष्पमालां समर्पयामि

śaṅkha-padma japuṣpādi śatapatrairvicitratām
puṣpamālāṃ prayacchāmi gṛhāṇa tvaṃ sureśvara
oṃ namaḥ śivāya puṣpamālāṃ samarpayāmi

We offer you this garland of flowers with spiraling lotuses, other flowers and leaves. Be pleased to accept it, Oh Ruler of All Gods. With the offering of a garland of flowers oṃ I bow to the Consciousness of Infinite Goodness.

flower

मल्लिकादि सुगन्धीनि मालित्यादीनि वै प्रभो ।
मयाऽहृतानि पूजार्थं पुष्पाणि प्रतिगृह्यताम् ॥
ॐ नमः शिवाय पुष्पम् समर्पयामि

mallikādi sugandhīni mālityādīni vai prabho
mayā-hṛtāni pūjārthaṃ puṣpāṇi pratigṛhyatām
oṃ namaḥ śivāya puṣpam samarpayāmi

Various flowers such as mallikā and others of excellent scent, are being offered to you, our Lord. All these flowers have come from the devotion of our hearts for your worship. Be pleased to accept them. With the offering of flowers oṃ I bow to the Consciousness of Infinite Goodness.

sthirī karaṇa

establishment of stillness

ॐ सर्वतीर्थमयं वारि सर्वदेवसमन्वितम् ।
इमं घटं समागच्छ तिष्ठ देवगणैः सह ॥

oṃ sarvatīrthamayaṃ vāri sarvadevasamanvitam
imaṃ ghaṭaṃ samāgaccha tiṣṭha devagaṇaiḥ saha

All the places of pilgrimage as well as all of the Gods, all are placed within this container. Oh Multitude of Gods, be established within!

lelihānā mudrā

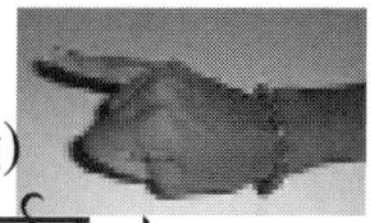

(literally, sticking out or pointing)

स्थां स्थीं स्थिरो भव विड्वङ्ग आशुर्भव वाज्यर्व्वन् ।
पृथुर्भव शुषदस्त्वमग्नेः पुरीषवाहनः ॥

sthāṃ sthīṃ sthiro bhava viḍvaṅga āśurbhava vājyarvvan
pṛthurbhava śuṣadastvamagneḥ purīṣavāhanaḥ

Be Still in the Gross Body! Be Still in the Subtle Body! Be Still in the Causal Body! Quickly taking in this energy and shining forth as the Holder of Wealth, oh Divine Fire, becoming abundant, destroy the current of rubbish from the face of this earth.

prāṇa pratiṣṭhā

establishment of life

ॐ अं आं ह्रीं क्रों यं रं लं वं शं षं सं हों हं सः

oṃ aṃ āṃ hrīṃ kroṃ yaṃ raṃ laṃ vaṃ śaṃ ṣaṃ saṃ hoṃ haṃ saḥ

oṃ The Infinite Beyond Conception, Creation (the first letter), Consciousness, Māyā, the cause of the movement of the subtle body to perfection and beyond; the path of fulfillment: control, subtle illumination, one with the earth, emancipation, the soul of peace, the soul of delight, the soul of unity (all this is I), perfection, Infinite Consciousness, this is I.

ॐ नमः शिवाय प्राणा इह प्राणाः

oṃ namaḥ śivāya prāṇā iha prāṇāḥ

oṃ I bow to the Consciousness of Infinite Goodness. You are the life of this life!

ॐ अं आं ह्रीं क्रों यं रं लं वं शं षं सं हों हं सः

oṃ aṃ āṃ hrīṃ kroṃ yaṃ raṃ laṃ vaṃ śaṃ ṣaṃ saṃ hoṃ haṃ saḥ

oṃ The Infinite Beyond Conception, Creation (the first letter), Consciousness, Māyā, the cause of the movement of the subtle body to perfection and beyond; the path of fulfillment: control, subtle illumination, one with the earth, emancipation, the soul of peace, the soul of delight, the soul of unity (all this is I), perfection, Infinite Consciousness, this is I.

ॐ नमः शिवाय जीव इह स्थितः

oṃ namaḥ śivāya jīva iha sthitaḥ

oṃ I bow to the Consciousness of Infinite Goodness. You are situated in this life (or individual consciousness).

ॐ अं आं ह्रीं क्रों यं रं लं वं शं षं सं हों हं सः

oṃ aṃ āṃ hrīṃ kroṃ yaṃ raṃ laṃ vaṃ śaṃ ṣaṃ saṃ hoṃ haṃ saḥ

oṃ The Infinite Beyond Conception, Creation (the first letter), Consciousness, Māyā, the cause of the movement of the subtle body to perfection and beyond; the path of fulfillment: control, subtle illumination, one with the earth, emancipation, the soul of peace, the soul of delight, the soul of unity (all this is I), perfection, Infinite Consciousness, this is I.

ॐ नमः शिवाय सर्वेन्द्रियाणि

oṃ namaḥ śivāya sarvendriyāṇi

oṃ I bow to the Consciousness of Infinite Goodness. You are all these organs (of action and knowledge).

ॐ अं आं ह्रीं क्रों यं रं लं वं शं षं सं हों हं सः

oṃ aṃ āṃ hrīṃ kroṃ yaṃ raṃ laṃ vaṃ śaṃ ṣaṃ saṃ hoṃ haṃ saḥ

oṃ The Infinite Beyond Conception, Creation (the first letter), Consciousness, Māyā, the cause of the movement of the subtle body to perfection and beyond; the path of fulfillment: control, subtle illumination, one with the earth, emancipation, the soul of peace, the soul of delight, the soul of unity (all this is I), perfection, Infinite Consciousness, this is I.

ॐ नमः शिवाय वाग् मनस्त्वक्चक्षुः-श्रोत्र-घ्राण-प्राणा इहागत्य सुखं चिरं तिष्ठन्तु स्वाहा

oṃ namaḥ śivāya vāg manastvakcakṣuḥ śrotra ghrāṇa prāṇā ihāgatya sukhaṃ ciraṃ tiṣṭhantu svāhā

oṃ I bow to the Consciousness of Infinite Goodness. You are all these vibrations, mind, sound, eyes, ears, tongue, nose and life force. Bring forth infinite peace and establish it forever, I am One with God!

kara nyāsa

establishment in the hands

ॐ नं अंगुष्ठाभ्यां नमः

oṃ naṃ aṅguṣṭhābhyāṃ namaḥ thumb forefinger

oṃ naṃ in the thumb I bow.

ॐ मः तर्जनीभ्यां स्वाहा

oṃ maḥ tarjanībhyāṃ svāhā thumb forefinger

oṃ maḥ in the forefinger, I am One with God!

ॐ शिं मध्यमाभ्यां वषट्

oṃ śiṃ madhyamābhyāṃ vaṣaṭ thumb middlefinger

oṃ śiṃ in the middle finger, Purify!

ॐ वां अनामिकाभ्यां हुं

oṃ vāṃ anāmikābhyāṃ huṃ thumb ringfinger

oṃ vāṃ in the ring finger, Cut the Ego!

ॐ यः कनिष्ठिकाभ्यां वौषट्

oṃ yaḥ kaniṣṭhikābhyāṃ vauṣaṭ thumb littlefinger

oṃ yaḥ in the little finger, Ultimate Purity!

Roll hand over hand forwards while reciting *karatala kara* and backwards while chanting *pṛṣṭhābhyāṃ*, then clap hands when chanting *astrāya phaṭ*.

ॐ नमः शिवाय करतल कर पृष्ठाभ्यां अस्त्राय फट् ॥

oṃ namaḥ śivāya karatala kara pṛṣṭhābhyāṃ astrāya phaṭ

oṃ I bow to the Consciousness of Infinite Goodness with the weapon of Virtue.

ॐ नमः शिवाय

oṃ namaḥ śivāya

I bow to the Consciousness of Infinite Goodness.

aṅga nyāsa

establishment in the body

Holding tattva mudrā, touch heart.

ॐ नं हृदयाय नमः

oṃ naṃ hṛdayāya namaḥ touch heart

oṃ naṃ in the heart, I bow.

Holding tattva mudrā, touch top of head.

ॐ मः शिरसे स्वाहा

oṃ maḥ śirase svāhā top of head

oṃ maḥ on the top of the head, I am One with God!

With thumb extended, touch back of head.

ॐ शिं शिखायै वषट्

oṃ śiṃ śikhāyai vaṣaṭ back of head

oṃ śiṃ on the back of the head, Purify!

Holding tattva mudrā, cross both arms.

ॐ वां कवचाय हुं

oṃ vāṃ kavacāya huṃ cross both arms

oṃ vāṃ crossing both arms, Cut the Ego!

Holding tattva mudrā, touch three eyes at once with three middle fingers.

ॐ यः नेत्रत्रयाय वौषट्

oṃ yaḥ netratrayāya vauṣaṭ touch three eyes

oṃ yaḥ in the three eyes, Ultimate Purity!

Roll hand over hand forwards while reciting *karatala kara* and backwards while chanting *pṛṣṭhābhyāṃ*, then clap hands when chanting *astrāya phaṭ*.

ॐ नमः शिवाय करतल कर पृष्ठाभ्यां अस्त्राय फट् ॥

oṃ namaḥ śivāya karatala kara pṛṣṭhābhyāṃ astrāya phaṭ

oṃ I bow to the Consciousness of Infinite Goodness with the weapon of Virtue.

ॐ नमः शिवाय

oṃ namaḥ śivāya

I bow to the Consciousness of Infinite Goodness.

ॐ नं उदीच्यै नमः

oṃ naṃ udīcyai namaḥ

oṃ I bow to naṃ in the north.

ॐ मः प्राच्यै नमः

oṃ maḥ prācyai namaḥ

oṃ I bow to maḥ in the east.

ॐ शिं दक्षिणायै नमः

oṃ śiṃ dakṣiṇāyai namaḥ
oṃ I bow to śiṃ in the south.

ॐ वां प्रतीच्यै नमः

oṃ vāṃ pratīcyai namaḥ
oṃ I bow to vāṃ in the west.

ॐ यः वायव्यै नमः

oṃ yaḥ vāyavyai namaḥ
oṃ I bow to yaḥ in the northwest.

ॐ नं ऐशान्यै नमः

oṃ naṃ aiśānyai namaḥ
oṃ I bow to naṃ in the northeast.

ॐ मः आग्नेय्यै नमः

oṃ maḥ āgneyyai namaḥ
oṃ I bow to maḥ in the southeast.

ॐ शिं नैर्ऋत्यै नमः

oṃ śiṃ nairṛtyai namaḥ
oṃ I bow to śiṃ in the southwest.

ॐ वां ऊर्ध्वायै नमः

oṃ vāṃ ūrdhvāyai namaḥ
oṃ I bow to vāṃ looking up.

ॐ यः भूम्यै नमः

oṃ yaḥ bhūmyai namaḥ
oṃ I bow to yaḥ looking down.

ॐ नमः शिवाय

oṃ namaḥ śivāya ten directions
oṃ I bow to the Consciousness of Infinite Goodness.

ॐ नं तत् पुरुषाय नमः

oṃ naṃ tat puruṣāya namaḥ thumb forefinger
oṃ naṃ I bow to That Universal Consciousness in the thumb.

ॐ मः अघोराय नमः

oṃ maḥ aghorāya namaḥ thumb forefinger
oṃ maḥ I bow to the Fearless One in the forefinger.

ॐ शिं सद्योजाताय नमः

oṃ śiṃ sadhyojātāya namaḥ thumb middlefinger
oṃ śiṃ I bow to the Birth of Truth, or True Existence in the middle finger.

ॐ वां वामदेवाय नमः

oṃ vāṃ vāmadevāya namaḥ thumb ringfinger
oṃ vāṃ I bow to the Beloved Deity in the ring finger.

ॐ यः ईशानाय नमः

oṃ yaḥ īśānāya namaḥ thumb littlefinger
oṃ yaḥ I bow to the Lord of All in the little finger.

ॐ नमः शिवाय

oṃ namaḥ śivāya

oṃ I bow to the Consciousness of Infinite Goodness.

एते गन्धपुष्पे ॐ सर्वाय क्षितिमूर्त्तये नमः

ete gandhapuṣpe oṃ sarvāya kṣiti mūrttaye namaḥ

With these scented flowers oṃ I bow to the Image of all Earth in the east.

एते गन्धपुष्पे ॐ भराय जलमूर्त्तये नमः

ete gandhapuṣpe oṃ bharāya jala mūrttaye namaḥ

With these scented flowers oṃ I bow to the Image who is full of water in the northeast.

एते गन्धपुष्पे ॐ रुद्राय अग्निमूर्त्तये नमः

ete gandhapuṣpe oṃ rudrāya agni mūrttaye namaḥ

With these scented flowers oṃ I bow to the Image of the Divine Fire, the Light of Meditation, who takes away the sufferings of all, in the north.

एते गन्धपुष्पे ॐ ऊग्राय वायुमूर्त्तये नमः

ete gandhapuṣpe oṃ ūgrāya vāyu mūrttaye namaḥ

With these scented flowers oṃ I bow to the Image of Wind who is fierce and blows as he pleases, in the northwest.

एते गन्धपुष्पे ॐ भीमाय आकाषमूर्त्तये नमः

ete gandhapuṣpe oṃ bhīmāya ākāṣa mūrttaye namaḥ

With these scented flowers oṃ I bow to the Image of Ether who is fearless, in the west.

एते गन्धपुष्पे ॐ पशुपतये यजमानमूर्त्तये नमः

ete gandhapuṣpe oṃ paśupataye yajamāna mūrttaye namaḥ

With these scented flowers oṃ I bow to the Sacrificer, the Lord of all animal life, in the southwest.

एते गन्धपुष्पे ॐ महादेवाय सोममूर्त्तये नमः

ete gandhapuṣpe oṃ mahādevāya soma mūrttaye namaḥ

With these scented flowers oṃ I bow to the Image of the Moon of Devotion, to the Great God, in the south.

एते गन्धपुष्पे ॐ ईशानाय सूर्यमूर्त्तये नमः

ete gandhapuṣpe oṃ īśānāya sūrya mūrttaye namaḥ

With these scented flowers oṃ I bow to the Image of the Sun or the Light of Wisdom, to the Lord of All, in the southeast.

ॐ नमोऽस्तु स्थाणुभूताय ज्योतिर्लिङ्गात्मने नमः ।
चतुर्मूर्त्तिवपुष्छाया भासिताङ्गाया शम्भवे ॥

oṃ namo-stu stāṇubhūtāya jyotir liṅgātmane namaḥ catur mūrttivapuṣchāyā bhāsitāṅgāyā śambhave

oṃ I bow to the Residence of All Existence, to the subtlest Consciousness of Light, I bow. The four images are His reflections, the body of the universe, Giver of Bliss.

ॐ नमः शिवाय

oṃ namaḥ śivāya

oṃ I bow to the Consciousness of Infinite Goodness.

japa
prāṇa pratiṣṭhā sūkta
hymn of the establishment of life

ॐ अस्यै प्राणाः प्रतिष्ठन्तु अस्यै प्राणाः क्षरन्तु च ।

अस्यै देवत्वमर्चायै मामहेति कश्चन ॥

oṃ asyai prāṇāḥ pratiṣṭhantu asyai prāṇāḥ kṣarantu ca

asyai devatvamārcāyai māmaheti kaścana

Thus has the life force been established in you, and thus the life force has flowed into you. Thus to you, God, offering is made, and in this way make us shine.

कलाकला हि देवानां दानवानां कलाकलाः ।

संगृह्य निर्मितो यस्मात् कलशस्तेन कथ्यते ॥

kalākalā hi devānāṃ dānavānāṃ kalākalāḥ

saṃgṛhya nirmito yasmāt kalaśastena kathyate

All the Gods are Fragments of the Cosmic Whole. Also all the asuras are Fragments of the Cosmic Whole. Thus we make a house to contain all these energies.

कलशस्य मुखे विष्णुः कण्ठे रुद्रः समाश्रितः ।

मूले त्वस्य स्थितो ब्रह्मा मध्ये मातृगणाः स्मृताः ॥

kalaśasya mukhe viṣṇuḥ kaṅṭhe rudraḥ samāśritaḥ

mūle tvasya sthito brahmā madhye mātṛgaṇāḥ smṛtāḥ

In the mouth of the pot is Viṣṇu, in the neck resides Rudra. At the base is situated Brahmā, and in the middle we remember the multitude of Mothers.

कुक्षौ तु सागराः सप्त सप्तद्वीपा च मेदिनी ।
अर्जुनी गोमती चैव चन्द्रभागा सरस्वती ॥

kukṣau tu sāgarāḥ sapta saptadvīpā ca medinī
arjunī gomatī caiva candrabhāgā sarasvatī

In the belly are the seven seas and the seven islands of the earth. The rivers Arjunī, Gomatī, Candrabhāgā, Sarasvatī;

कावेरी कृष्णवेणा च गङ्गा चैव महानदी ।
ताप्ती गोदावरी चैव माहेन्द्री नर्मदा तथा ॥

kāverī kṛṣṇaveṇā ca gaṅgā caiva mahānadī
tāptī godāvarī caiva māhendrī narmadā tathā

Kāverī, Kṛṣṇaveṇā and the Gaṅges and other great rivers; the Tāptī, Godāvarī, Māhendrī and Narmadā.

नदाश्च विविधा जाता नद्यः सर्वास्तथापराः ।
पृथिव्यां यानि तीर्थानि कलशस्थानि तानि वै ॥

nadāśca vividhā jātā nadyaḥ sarvāstathāparāḥ
pṛthivyāṃ yāni tīrthāni kalaśasthāni tāni vai

The various rivers and the greatest of beings born, and all the respected places of pilgrimage upon the earth, are established within this pot.

सर्वे समुद्राः सरितस्तीर्थानि जलदा नदाः ।
आयान्तु मम शान्त्यर्थं दुरितक्षयकारकाः ॥

sarve samudrāḥ saritastīrthāni jaladā nadāḥ
āyāntu mama śāntyarthaṃ duritakṣayakārakāḥ

All of the seas, rivers, and waters from all the respected places of pilgrimage have been brought for the peace of that which is bad or wicked.

ऋग्वेदोऽथ यजुर्वेदः सामवेदो ह्यथर्वणः ।
अङ्गैश्च सहिताः सर्वे कलशं तु समाश्रिताः ॥

ṛgvedo-tha yajurvedaḥ sāmavedo hyatharvaṇaḥ
aṅgaiśca sahitāḥ sarve kalaśaṃ tu samāśritāḥ

The Ṛg Veda, the Yajur Veda, Sāma Veda and the Atharva Veda, along with all of their limbs, are assembled together in this pot.

अत्र गायत्री सावित्री शान्तिः पुष्टिकरी तथा ।
आयान्तु मम शान्त्यर्थं दुरितक्षयकारकाः ॥

atra gāyatrī sāvitrī śāntiḥ puṣṭikarī tathā
āyāntu mama śāntyarthaṃ duritakṣayakārakāḥ

Here Gāyatrī, Sāvitrī, Peace and Increase have been brought for the peace of that which is bad or wicked.

देवदानवसंवादे मथ्यमाने महोदधौ ।
उत्पन्नोऽसि तदा कुम्भ विधृतो विष्णुना स्वयम् ॥

deva dānava saṃvāde mathyamāne mahodadhau
utpanno-si tadā kumbha vidhṛto viṣṇunā svayam

The Gods and asuras speaking together are the great givers of churning to the mind. Rise to the top of this pot to separate them from what is actually Viṣṇu, Himself.

त्वत्तोये सर्वतीर्थानि देवाः सर्वे त्वयि स्थिताः ।
त्वयि तिष्ठन्ति भूतानि त्वयि प्राणाः प्रतिष्ठिताः ॥

tvattoye sarvatīrthāni devāḥ sarve tvayi sthitāḥ
tvayi tiṣṭhanti bhūtāni tvayi prāṇāḥ pratiṣṭhitāḥ

Within you are all the pilgrimage places. All the Gods are situated within you. All existence is established within you. All life is established within you.

शिवः स्वयं त्वमेवासि विष्णुस्त्वं च प्रजापतिः ।
आदित्या वसवो रुद्रा विश्वेदेवाः सपैतृकाः ॥

śivaḥ svayaṃ tvamevāsi viṣṇustvaṃ ca prajāpatiḥ
ādityā vasavo rudrā viśvedevāḥ sapaitṛkāḥ

You alone are Śiva; you are Brahmā and Viṣṇu, the sons of Aditi, Finders of the Wealth, Rudra, the Universal Deities and the ancestors.

त्वयि तिष्ठन्ति सर्वेऽपि यतः कामफलप्रदाः ।
त्वत्प्रसादादिमं यज्ञं कर्तुमीहे जलोद्भव ।
सान्निध्यं कुरु मे देव प्रसन्नो भव सर्वदा ॥

tvayi tiṣṭhanti sarve-pi yataḥ kāmaphalapradāḥ
tvatprasādādimaṃ yajñaṃ kartumīhe jalodbhava
sānnidhyaṃ kuru me deva prasanno bhava sarvadā

All and everything has been established in you, from whence you grant the fruits of desires. From you comes the blessed fruit of the sacrifice performed with excellence. May those riches increase. Manifest your presence within us, Lord. Always be pleased.

नमो नमस्ते स्फटिकप्रभाय सुश्वेतहाराय सुमङ्गलाय ।
सुपाशहस्ताय झषासनाय जलाधिनाथाय नमो नमस्ते ॥

namo namaste sphaṭikaprabhāya suśvetahārāya sumaṅgalāya
supāśahastāya jhaṣāsanāya jalādhināthāya namo namaste

We bow, we bow to He who shines like crystal, to He who emits excellent clarity and excellent welfare. With the net of unity in his hand, who takes the form of a fish, to the Lord of all waters and that which dwells within, we bow, we bow!

पाशपाणे नमस्तुभ्यं पद्मिनीजीवनायक ।
पुण्याहवाचनं यावत् तावत्त्वं सन्निधौ भव ॥

pāśapāṇe namastubhyaṃ padminījīvanāyaka
puṇyāhavācanaṃ yāvat tāvattvaṃ sannidhau bhava

We bow to He with the net of unity in his hand, Seer of the Life of the Lotus One. With this meritorious invocation, please make your presence manifest.

viśeṣārghya

establishment of the conch shell offering

Draw the following yantra on the plate or space for worship with sandal paste and/or water. Offer rice on the yantra for each of the four mantras.

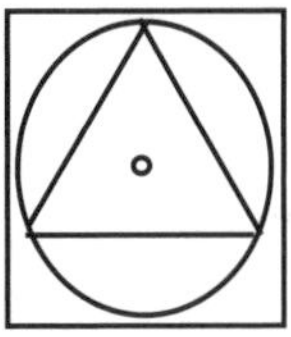

ॐ आधारशक्तये नमः

oṃ ādhāraśaktaye namaḥ

oṃ we bow to the Primal Energy

ॐ कूर्म्माय नमः

oṃ kūrmmāya namaḥ

oṃ we bow to the Support of the Earth

ॐ अनन्ताय नमः

oṃ anantāya namaḥ

oṃ we bow to Infinity

ॐ पृथिव्यै नमः

oṃ pṛthivyai namaḥ
oṃ we bow to the Earth

Place a conch shell on the bindu in the center of the yantra when saying Phaṭ.

स्थां स्थीं स्थिरो भव फट्

sthāṃ sthīṃ sthiro bhava phaṭ
Be Still in the Gross Body! Be Still in the Subtle Body! Be Still in the Causal Body! Purify!

Fill conch shell with water while chanting the mantra.

ॐ गङ्गे च जमुने चैव गोदावरि सरस्वति ।
नर्मदे सिन्धु कावेरि जलेऽस्मिन् सन्निधिं कुरु ॥

oṃ gaṅge ca jamune caiva godāvari sarasvati
narmade sindhu kāveri jale-asmin sannidhiṃ kuru
oṃ the Ganges, Jamunā, Godāvarī, Sarasvatī, Narmadā, Sindhu, Kāverī, these waters are mingled together.

Offer Tulasī leaves into water

ॐ ऐं ह्रीं क्लीं श्रीं वृन्दावनवासिन्यै स्वाहा

oṃ aiṃ hrīṃ klīṃ śrīṃ vṛndāvanavāsinyai svāhā
oṃ Wisdom, Māyā, Increase, to She who resides in Vṛndāvana, I am One with God!

Offer 3 flowers into the water pot with the mantras

एते गन्धपुष्पे ॐ अं अर्कमण्डलाय द्वादशकलात्मने नमः

ete gandhapuṣpe oṃ aṃ arkamaṇḍalāya
dvādaśakalātmane namaḥ

With these scented flowers oṃ "A" we bow to the twelve aspects of the realm of the sun. Tapinī, Tāpinī, Dhūmrā, Marīci, Jvālinī, Ruci, Sudhūmrā, Bhoga-dā, Viśvā, Bodhinī, Dhārinī, Kṣamā; Containing heat, Emanating heat, Smoky, Ray-producing, Burning, Lustrous, Purple or Smoky-red, Granting enjoyment, Universal, Which makes known, Productive of Consciousness, Which supports, Which forgives.

एते गन्धपुष्पे ॐ उं सोममण्डलाय षोडशकलात्मने नमः

ete gandhapuṣpe oṃ uṃ somamaṇḍalāya ṣoḍaśakalātmane namaḥ

With these scented flowers oṃ "U" we bow to the sixteen aspects of the realm of the moon. Amṛtā, Prāṇadā, Puṣā, Tuṣṭi, Puṣṭi, Rati, Dhṛti, Śaśinī, Caṇḍrikā, Kānti, Jyotsnā, Śrī, Prīti, Aṅgadā, Pūrṇā, Pūrṇāmṛta; Nectar, Which sustains life, Which supports, Satisfying, Nourishing, Playful, Constancy, Unfailing, Producer of Joy, Beauty enhanced by love, Light, Grantor of Prosperity, Affectionate, Purifying the body, Complete, Full of Bliss.

एते गन्धपुष्पे ॐ मं वह्निमण्डलाय दशकलात्मने नमः

ete gandhapuṣpe oṃ maṃ vahnimaṇḍalāya daśakalātmane namaḥ

With these scented flowers oṃ "M" we bow to the ten aspects of the realm of fire: Dhūmrā, Arciḥ, Jvalinī, Śūkṣmā, Jvālinī, Visphūliṅginī, Suśrī, Surūpā, Kapilā, Havya-Kavya-Vahā; Smoky Red, Flaming, Shining, Subtle, Burning, Sparkling, Beautiful, Well-formed, Tawny, The Messenger to Gods and Ancestors.

एते गन्धपुष्पे हुं

ete gandhapuṣpe huṃ

With these scented flowers huṃ

Wave hands in matsyā, dhenu and aṅkuśa mudrās while chanting this mantra.

ॐ गङ्गे च जमुने चैव गोदावरि सरस्वति ।

नर्मदे सिन्धु कावेरि जलेऽस्मिन् सन्निधिं कुरु ॥

oṃ gaṅge ca jamune caiva godāvari sarasvati
narmade sindhu kāveri jale-asmin sannidhiṃ kuru

oṃ the Ganges, Jamunā, Godāvarī, Sarasvatī, Narmadā, Sindhu, Kāverī, these waters are mingled together.

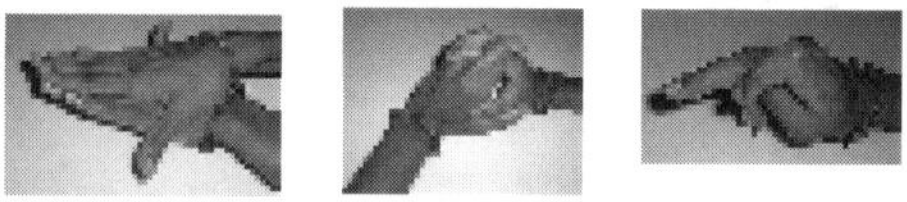

ॐ नमः शिवाय

oṃ namaḥ śivāya

oṃ I bow to the Consciousness of Infinite Goodness.

Sprinkle water over all articles to be offered, then throw some drops of water over your shoulders while repeating the mantra.

अमृतम् कुरु स्वाहा

amṛtam kuru svāhā

Make this immortal nectar! I am One with God!

bhūta śuddhi

purification of the elements

Pronounce each Bījā sixteen times in its proper location:

लं	Mulādhāra	(1st Cakra)	Laṃ	Indra	Earth
वं	Swādiṣṭhana	(2nd Cakra)	Vaṃ	Varuṇa	Water
रं	Maṇipura	(3rd Cakra)	Raṃ	Agni	Fire
यं	Anahata	(4th Cakra)	Yaṃ	Vāyu	Air
हं	Viśuddha	(5th Cakra)	Haṃ	Soma	Ether
ॐ	Āgnyā	(6th Cakra)	Oṃ	Īśvara	The Ultimate

Then move up and down the Suṣumṇa through the cakras, pronouncing each Bījā once, and feeling its presence in its proper location.

ॐ लं वं रं यं हं ॐ

oṃ laṃ vaṃ raṃ yaṃ haṃ oṃ

oṃ Earth, Water, Fire, Air, Ether, The Ultimate.

ॐ हं यं रं वं लं ॐ

oṃ haṃ yaṃ raṃ vaṃ laṃ oṃ

oṃ The Ultimate, Ether, Air, Fire, Water, Earth.

ॐ मूलशृङ्गाटाच्छिरः सुषुम्नापथेन जीवशिवं परमशिवपदे षोजयामि स्वाहा ॥

oṃ mūlaśṛṅgāṭācchiraḥ suṣumnāpathena jīvaśivaṃ paramaśivapade ṣojayāmi svāhā

Piercing the triangular junction (yantra) situated in the Mulādhāra, the center of energy between the genital and the rectum, I direct the auspicious life force upwards by way of the Suṣumna, the subtle canal which transmits nerve impulses along the spinal column, to unite in Supreme Bliss, I am One with God!

ॐ यं लिङ्गशरीरं शोषय शोषय स्वाहा ॥

oṃ yaṃ liṅgaśarīraṃ śoṣaya śoṣaya svāhā

oṃ Yaṃ (Vāyu, Air, the Spirit of Emancipation) in the subtle body, purify, purify, I am One with God!

ॐ रं सङ्कोचशरीरं दह दह स्वाहा ॥

oṃ raṃ saṅkocaśarīraṃ daha daha svāhā

oṃ Raṃ (Agni, Fire, the Purifying Light of Wisdom) in the limited body, burn, burn, I am One with God!

ॐ परमशिव सुषुम्नापथेन मूलशृङ्गाटमुल्लसोल्लस
ज्वल ज्वल प्रज्वल प्रज्वल सोऽहं हंसः स्वाहा ॥

oṃ paramaśiva suṣumnāpathena
mūlaśṛṅgāṭamullasollasa
jvala jvala prajvala prajvala so-haṃ haṃsaḥ svāhā

Oh Supreme Bliss, filling the path of the Suṣumna from the triangular junction in the Mulādhāra, dancing brilliantly, shine, shine, radiate, radiate, That is I, I am That, I am One with God!

kara śuddhi

wipe your hands with a flower

ॐ ऐं रं अस्त्राय फट्

oṃ aiṃ raṃ astrāya phaṭ

oṃ Wisdom, the Subtle Body of Light, with this weapon, Purify!

tap ground three times with fist or heel

फट् फट् फट्

phaṭ phaṭ phaṭ

Purify! Purify! Purify!

bhūtāpsāraṇa

dispersion of inimical energies

Bhūta has a number of meanings, which makes the following verses to play on the words, switching meanings even while using the same word. Its noun forms mean variously: a purified being, a good being; created thing, world; uncanny being, spirit, ghost, goblin; past, fact, reality, actual occurence; welfare; elements, especially as applied to the five gross elements of earth, water, fire, air and ether (See Bhūta Śuddhi). Here we are calling upon the friendly or the good Bhūtas to destroy obstacles created by unfriendly or bad Bhūtas.

ॐ अपसर्पन्तु ते भूता ये भूता भुवि संस्थिताः ।
ये भूता विघ्नकर्त्तारस्ते नश्यन्तु शिवज्ञया ॥

oṃ apasarpantu te bhūtā ya bhūtā bhuvi saṃsthitāḥ
ye bhūtā vighnakarttāraste naśyantu śivajñayā

We consign to you friendly spirits, friendly spirits that are situated on this earth plane, the activity of destroying any obstacles placed by unfriendly spirits, by order of the Wisdom of Infinite Goodness.

ॐ भूतप्रेतपिशाचाश्च दानवा राक्षसाश्च ये ।
शान्तिं कुर्वन्तु ते सर्वे ईमं गृह्वतु मद्बलिम् ॥

oṃ bhūtapretapiśācāśca dānavā rākṣasāśca ye
śāntiṃ kurvantu te sarve īmaṃ gṛhvatu madbalim

Hey ghosts, goblins, demons, unfriendly spirits and various forms of negativity projecting egos: you have been made entirely at peace. Please accept this offering from me.

ॐ वेतालाश्च पिशाचाश्च राक्षसाश्च सरीसुपाः ।
अपसर्पन्तु ते सर्वे नारसिंहेन ताढिताः ॥

oṃ vetālāśca piśācāśca rākṣasāśca sarīsupāḥ
apasarpantu te sarve nārasiṃhena tāḍhitāḥ

Other demons, goblins, various forms of negativity projecting egos, creeping and crawling things: I consign to you completely the striking blows of Nārasiṃha, Viṣṇu in His incarnation of man-lion.

aghamārṣaṇa

internal cleaning

Perform Jāl Neti taking water from the Samanyārghya into the left palm. Inhale it through the Iḍa or left nostril, and bring it all the way up into the Āgnyā Cakra, then expel it through the Piṅgalā or right nostril. Blow out the nasal passages so that they are clean.

ॐ ऋतमित्यस्य ऋक्त्रयस्याघमर्षण
ऋषिरनष्टुप्छन्दोभाववृत्तं देवतामश्वमेधावभृथे विनियोगः ।

oṃ ṛtamityasya ṛktrayasyāghamarṣaṇa
ṛṣiranaṣṭupchandobhāvavṛttaṃ
devatāmaśvamedhāvabhṛthe viniyogaḥ

Introducing the three Mantras which begin with "From Truth...", etc., Internal Cleaning is the Seer, Anuṣṭup is the meter (32 syllables to the verse), Who Changes the Intensity of Reality is the divinity, equal in merit to the horse sacrifice, this practice is offered in application.

ॐ ऋतं च सत्यं चाभीद्धात्तपसोऽध्यजायत ।
ततो रत्र्यजायत ततः समुद्रोऽर्णवः ॥

oṃ ṛtaṃ ca satyaṃ cābhīddhāttapaso-dhyajāyata
tato ratryajāyata tataḥ samudro-rṇavaḥ

From truth, from the Imperishable Truth, the Performers of Tapasya, or strict spiritual discipline, have come. Then came forth the night, and then the sea of objects and relationships, with the multitude of its waves.

समुद्रार्णवादधि संवत्सरो अजायत ।
अहोरात्राणिविदधदिश्वस्य भिषतो वशी ॥

samudrārṇavādadhi saṃvatsaro ajāyata
ahorātrāṇividadhadiśvasya bhiṣato vaśī

From the fluctuations of the waves on the sea, the years came forth. The night transformed into day, and the universe took birth.

सूर्या चन्द्रमसौ धाता यथापूर्वमकल्पयत् ।
दिवं च पृथिवीं चान्तरिक्षमथो स्वः ॥

sūryā candramasau dhātā yathāpūrvamakalpayat
divaṃ ca pṛthivīṃ cāntarikṣamatho svaḥ

The Sun and the Moon gave forth their lights in accordance with the command of the Creator. And the earth, the atmosphere and the heavens were His Own.

jāl netī, prāṇāyāma

cleaning of the sinuses, control of breath

bāhya mātrikā nyāsa

establishment of the letters in the external body

Every object in creation has a name to correspond to its form. There is a name which is agreed upon by the customs of language, what we may call an object; and there is a natural sound which is being emitted as a consequence of the vibrations which are taking place in the object itself, the movement of protons, nutrons, electrons, etc. Every manifested object of creation has a vibration, whether perceivable or not, and every vibration emits a sound whether audible to the physical organ of hearing or not. Every sound is expressible by a letter which symbolizes the sound that most closely approximates the vibration indicated, so that all the letters of the alphabets symbolize the total possibility of all vibrations which can be evolved or can be expressed -- the totality of creation.

This natural name is called a Bījā Mantra, often translated as Seed Mantra. These Bījās are another name for the Mātṛkās, the letters of the Saṃskṛta alphabet. In Saṃskṛta Philosophy, the microcosm is an exact replica of the macrocosm. Hence every physical body contains all the vibrations possible in the cosmos.

Bāhya Mātṛkā Nyāsa means the establishment of the letters of the Saṃskṛta Alphabet within the "Outside" or the gross body of the worshiper. Bāhya Mātṛkā Nyāsa ascribes a position in each of the centers of activity for each of the letters, so that the worshiper can understand and experience the totality of creation as existing within the physical body. By using the different Mudrās described, the worshiper begins by placing the sixteen vowels in their respective positions.

Thumb 1   Pointer 2   Middle 3   Ring 4   Pinky 5

ॐ अं नमः

oṃ aṃ namaḥ R.1.4 base top of head

ॐ आं नमः

oṃ āṃ namaḥ R.1.4 base mouth

ॐ इं नमः

oṃ iṃ namaḥ R. 4 R. eye

ॐ ईं नमः

oṃ īṃ namaḥ L. 4 L. eye

ॐ उं नमः

oṃ uṃ namaḥ R. 1 R. ear

ॐ ऊं नमः

oṃ ūṃ namaḥ L. 1 L. ear

ॐ ऋं नमः

oṃ ṛṃ namaḥ R. 1.5 R. nostril

ॐ ॠं नमः

oṃ ṝṃ namaḥ L. 1.5 L. nostril

ॐ ऌं नमः

oṃ ḷṛṃ namaḥ R. 2.3.4 R. cheek

ॐ ॡं नमः
om lṝm namaḥ L. 2.3.4 L. cheek

ॐ एं नमः
oṃ eṃ namaḥ R. 3 upper lip

ॐ ऐं नमः
oṃ aiṃ namaḥ R. 3 lower lip

ॐ ओं नमः
oṃ oṃ namaḥ R. 4 upper teeth

ॐ औं नमः
oṃ auṃ namaḥ R. 4 lower teeth

ॐ अं नमः
oṃ aṃ namaḥ R. 3.4 crown of head

ॐ अः नमः
oṃ aḥ namaḥ R. 3.4 mouth

ॐ कं नमः
oṃ kaṃ namaḥ L. 1.3.5 R. shoulder

ॐ खं नमः
oṃ khaṃ namaḥ L. 1.3.5 R. crook of elbow

ॐ गं नमः

oṃ gaṃ namaḥ L. 1.3.5 R. wrist

ॐ घं नमः

oṃ ghaṃ namaḥ L. 1.3.5 R. joint of hand

ॐ ङं नमः

oṃ ṅaṃ namaḥ L. 1.3.5 R. finger tips

ॐ चं नमः

oṃ caṃ namaḥ R. 1.3.5 L. shoulder

ॐ छं नमः

oṃ chaṃ namaḥ R. 1.3.5 L. crook of elbow

ॐ जं नमः

oṃ jaṃ namaḥ R. 1.3.5 L. wrist

ॐ झं नमः

oṃ jhaṃ namaḥ R. 1.3.5 L. joint of hand

ॐ ञं नमः

oṃ ñaṃ namaḥ R. 1.3.5 L. finger tips

ॐ टं नमः

oṃ ṭaṃ namaḥ L. 1.3.5 R. hip

ॐ ठं नमः

oṃ ṭhaṃ namaḥ L. 1.3.5 R. knees

ॐ डं नमः

oṃ ḍaṃ namaḥ L. 1.3.5 R. ankle

ॐ ढं नमः

oṃ ḍhaṃ namaḥ L. 1.3.5 R. joint of toes

ॐ णं नमः

oṃ ṇaṃ namaḥ L. 1.3.5 R. tip of toes

ॐ तं नमः

oṃ taṃ namaḥ R. 1.3.5 L. hip

ॐ थं नमः

oṃ thaṃ namaḥ R. 1.3.5 L. knees

ॐ दं नमः

oṃ daṃ namaḥ R. 1.3.5 L. ankle

ॐ धं नमः

oṃ dhaṃ namaḥ R. 1.3.5 L. joint of toes

ॐ नं नमः

oṃ naṃ namaḥ R. 1.3.5 L. tip of toes

ॐ पं नमः
oṃ paṃ namaḥ L. 1.4 base R. side

ॐ फं नमः
oṃ phaṃ namaḥ R. 1.4 base L. side

ॐ बं नमः
oṃ baṃ namaḥ R. 1.4 base Belly

ॐ भं नमः
oṃ bhaṃ namaḥ L. 1.4 base Back

ॐ मं नमः
oṃ maṃ namaḥ R. 1.2.3.4.5. flat Navel

ॐ यं नमः
oṃ yaṃ namaḥ R. 1.4 base Heart

ॐ रं नमः
oṃ raṃ namaḥ L. 1.4 base R. shoulder

ॐ लं नमः
oṃ laṃ namaḥ R. 1.4 base back of neck

ॐ वं नमः
oṃ vaṃ namaḥ R. 1.4 base L. shoulder

ॐ शं नमः

oṃ śaṃ namaḥ R. 1.4 L. shoulder to hand full

ॐ षं नमः

oṃ ṣaṃ namaḥ L. 1.4 R. shoulder to hand full

ॐ सं नमः

oṃ saṃ namaḥ L. 1.4 R. hip to leg full

ॐ हं नमः

oṃ haṃ namaḥ R. 1.4 L. hip to leg full

ॐ ळं नमः

oṃ ḷaṃ namaḥ L. 1.4 sternum to navel

ॐ क्षं नमः

oṃ kṣaṃ namaḥ R. 1.4 sternum to throat

ॐ नमः शिवाय

oṃ namaḥ śivāya
oṃ I bow to the Consciousness of Infinite Goodness.

mātṛkā nyāsa

establishment of the letters in the cakras

Following Pāṇiṇī's Grammar, which is the most authoritative on the subject, in the Bāhya Mātṛkā Nyāsa there are thirty-five consonants. Actually the number of letters varies according to different enumerations regarding differing functions, and in the Mātṛkā Nyāsa which follows, only fifty letters are to be placed.

Saṃskṛt is commonly taught with fifty letters, sixteen vowels and thirty-four consonants. Occasionally it is taught with fifty-two letters, with the addition of oṃ and hrīṃ. For the purpose of these Nyāsas, we will follow the two formats presented, as the best authorities for their accuracy agree from all the versions consulted. The explanation as to why they differ in the number of letters contained, will not be addressed here.

Mātṛkā Nyāsa places the Bījās or natural names inside the Cakras, which are the energy centers within the body. In this meditation we conceive that not only is all existence moving in My every movement, as in the former Nyāsa, but also that all the vibrations of the universe comprise the very essence of my being.

Haṃ stands for the Prāṇātman, the second ḷaṃ, for the Jīvātman, and kṣaṃ for Paramātman. In this way, Jīva puts on, so to speak, or wears the universe as a gown. All the vibrations of existence make up the cloak which covers the ever more subtle essence of consciousness, which is the Silent Witness to the Dance of Creation.

Viśuddha (5th Cakra) 16 petals

ॐ अं नमः

oṃ aṃ namaḥ

ॐ आं नमः

oṃ āṃ namaḥ

ॐ इं नमः

oṃ iṃ namaḥ

ॐ ईं नमः

oṃ īṃ namaḥ

ॐ उं नमः

oṃ uṃ namaḥ

ॐ ऊं नमः

oṃ ūṃ namaḥ

ॐ ऋं नमः

oṃ ṛṃ namaḥ

ॐ ॠं नमः

oṃ ṝṃ namaḥ

ॐ ऌं नमः

oṃ ḷṃ namaḥ

ॐ ॡं नमः

oṃ ḹṃ namaḥ

ॐ एं नमः

oṃ eṃ namaḥ

ॐ ऐं नमः

oṃ aiṃ namaḥ

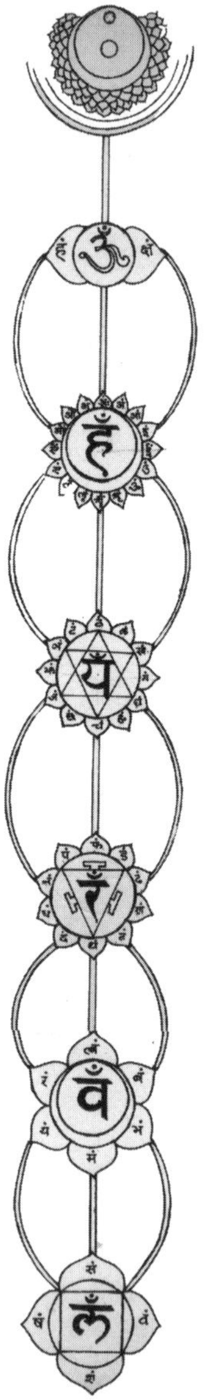

ॐ ओं नमः

oṃ oṃ namaḥ

ॐ औं नमः

oṃ auṃ namaḥ

ॐ अं नमः

oṃ aṃ namaḥ

ॐ अः नमः

oṃ aḥ namaḥ

Anahāta (4th Cakra) 12 petals

ॐ कं नमः

oṃ kaṃ namaḥ

ॐ खं नमः

oṃ khaṃ namaḥ

ॐ गं नमः

oṃ gaṃ namaḥ

ॐ घं नमः

oṃ ghaṃ namaḥ

ॐ ङं नमः

oṃ ṅaṃ namaḥ

ॐ चं नमः

oṃ caṃ namaḥ

ॐ छं नमः

oṃ chaṃ namaḥ

ॐ जं नमः

oṃ jaṃ namaḥ

ॐ झं नमः

oṃ jhaṃ namaḥ

ॐ ञं नमः

oṃ ñaṃ namaḥ

ॐ टं नमः

oṃ ṭaṃ namaḥ

ॐ ठं नमः

oṃ ṭhaṃ namaḥ

Maṇipura (3rd Cakra) 10 petals

ॐ डं नमः

oṃ ḍaṃ namaḥ

ॐ ढं नमः

oṃ ḍhaṃ namaḥ

ॐ णं नमः

oṃ ṇaṃ namaḥ

ॐ तं नमः

oṃ taṃ namaḥ

ॐ थं नमः

oṃ thaṃ namaḥ

ॐ दं नमः

oṃ daṃ namaḥ

ॐ धं नमः

oṃ dhaṃ namaḥ

ॐ नं नमः

oṃ naṃ namaḥ

ॐ पं नमः

oṃ paṃ namaḥ

ॐ फं नमः

oṃ phaṃ namaḥ

Swādiṣṭhana (2nd Cakra) 6 petals

ॐ बं नमः

oṃ baṃ namaḥ

ॐ भं नमः

oṃ bhaṃ namaḥ

ॐ मं नमः

oṃ maṃ namaḥ

ॐ यं नमः

oṃ yaṃ namaḥ

ॐ रं नमः

oṃ raṃ namaḥ

ॐ लं नमः

oṃ laṃ namaḥ

Mulādhāra (1st Cakra) 4 petals

ॐ वं नमः

oṃ vaṃ namaḥ

ॐ शं नमः

oṃ śaṃ namaḥ

ॐ षं नमः

oṃ ṣaṃ namaḥ

ॐ सं नमः

oṃ saṃ namaḥ

Āgnyā (6th Cakra) 2 petals

ॐ हं नमः

oṃ haṃ namaḥ

ॐ क्षं नमः

oṃ kṣaṃ namaḥ

ॐ नमः शिवाय

oṃ namaḥ śivāya

oṃ I bow to the Consciousness of Infinite Goodness.

Then perform Saṃhara Mātṛkā Nyāsa and
Bāhya Mātṛkā Nyāsa by repeating the processes
in reverse order from the end to the beginning.

aṅga pūjā

worship of the Divine Mother's body
Using Tattva Mudrā on both hands touch:

ॐ दुर्गायै नमः पादौ पूजयामि

oṃ durgāyai namaḥ pādau pūjayāmi feet

I bow to the Reliever of Difficulties and worship Her feet.

ॐ गिरिजायै नमः गुल्फौ पूजयामि

oṃ girijāyai namaḥ gulphau pūjayāmi ankles

I bow to the Unconquerable One from the Mountains and worship Her ankles.

ॐ अपर्णायै नमः जानुनी पूजयामि

oṃ aparṇāyai namaḥ jānunī pūjayāmi knees

I bow to the Unseverable Energy and worship Her knees.

ॐ हरिप्रियायै नमः ऊरू पूजयामि

oṃ haripriyāyai namaḥ ūrū pūjayāmi thighs

I bow to the Beloved of Consciousness and worship Her thighs.

ॐ पार्वत्यै नमः कटिं पूजयामि

oṃ pārvatyai namaḥ kaṭiṃ pūjayāmi hips

I bow to the Daughter of the Mountains and worship Her hips.

ॐ आर्यायै नमः नाभिं पूजयामि

oṃ āryāyai namaḥ nābhiṃ pūjayāmi navel

I bow to the One Purified by Knowledge and worship Her navel.

ॐ जगन्मात्रे नमः उदरं पूजयामि

oṃ jaganmātre namaḥ udaraṃ pūjayāmi stomach

I bow to the Mother of the Perceivable Universe and worship Her stomach.

ॐ मंगलायै नमः कुक्षिं पूजयामि

oṃ maṃgalāyai namaḥ kukṣiṃ pūjayāmi sternum

I bow to the Energy of Welfare and worship Her sternum.

ॐ शिवायै नमः हृदयं पूजयामि

oṃ śivāyai namaḥ hṛdayaṃ pūjayāmi heart

I bow to the Energy of Infinite Goodness and worship Her heart.

ॐ महेश्वर्यै नमः कण्ठं पूजयामि

oṃ maheśvaryai namaḥ kaṇṭhaṃ pūjayāmi throat
I bow to the Energy of the Great Seer of All and worship Her throat.

ॐ विश्ववन्द्यायै नमः स्कन्धौ पूजयामि

oṃ viśvavandyāyai namaḥ skandhau pūjayāmi
I bow to She who is Praised by the Universe and worship Her shoulders. shoulders

ॐ काल्यै नमः बाहू पूजयामि

oṃ kālyai namaḥ bāhū pūjayāmi arms
I bow to She who Takes Away Darkness and worship Her arms.

ॐ आद्यायै नमः हस्तौ पूजयामि

oṃ ādyāyai namaḥ hastau pūjayāmi hands
I bow to She who is Sacred Study and worship Her hands.

ॐ वरदायै नमः मुखं पूजयामि

oṃ varadāyai namaḥ mukhaṃ pūjayāmi mouth
I bow to She who Grants Boons and worship Her mouth.

ॐ सुवाण्यै नमः नासिकां पूजयामि

oṃ suvāṇyai namaḥ nāsikāṃ pūjayāmi nose
I bow to She of Excellent Music and worship Her nose.

ॐ कमलाक्ष्म्यै नमः नेत्रे पूजयामि

oṃ kamalākṣmyai namaḥ netre pūjayāmi three eyes
I bow to the Lotus-eyed and worship Her eyes.

ॐ अम्बिकायै नमः शिरः पूजयामि

oṃ ambikāyai namaḥ śiraḥ pūjayāmi top of head
I bow to the Mother of All and worship Her head.

ॐ देव्यै नमः सर्वाङ्ग पूजयामि

oṃ devyai namaḥ sarvāṅga pūjayāmi entire body
I bow to the Goddess and worship Her entire body.

हं रं ईं ह्रीं

haṃ raṃ īṃ hrīṃ

ॐ हकारः स्थूलदेहः स्याद्रकार सूक्ष्मदेहकः ।
ईकारः कारणात्मासौ ह्रीङ्कारोऽहं तुरीयकम् ॥

oṃ hakāraḥ sthūladehaḥ syād
rakāra sūkṣmadehakaḥ
īkāraḥ kāraṇātmāsau hrīṅkāro-haṃ turīyakam

The letter Ha indicates the Gross Body; the letter Ra is the Subtle Body. The letter Ī is the Causal Body; and as the entire letter Hrīṃ, I am beyond manifestation.

pītha nyāsa

establishment of the place of internal worship

With Tattva Mudrā place on the yantra on your chest:

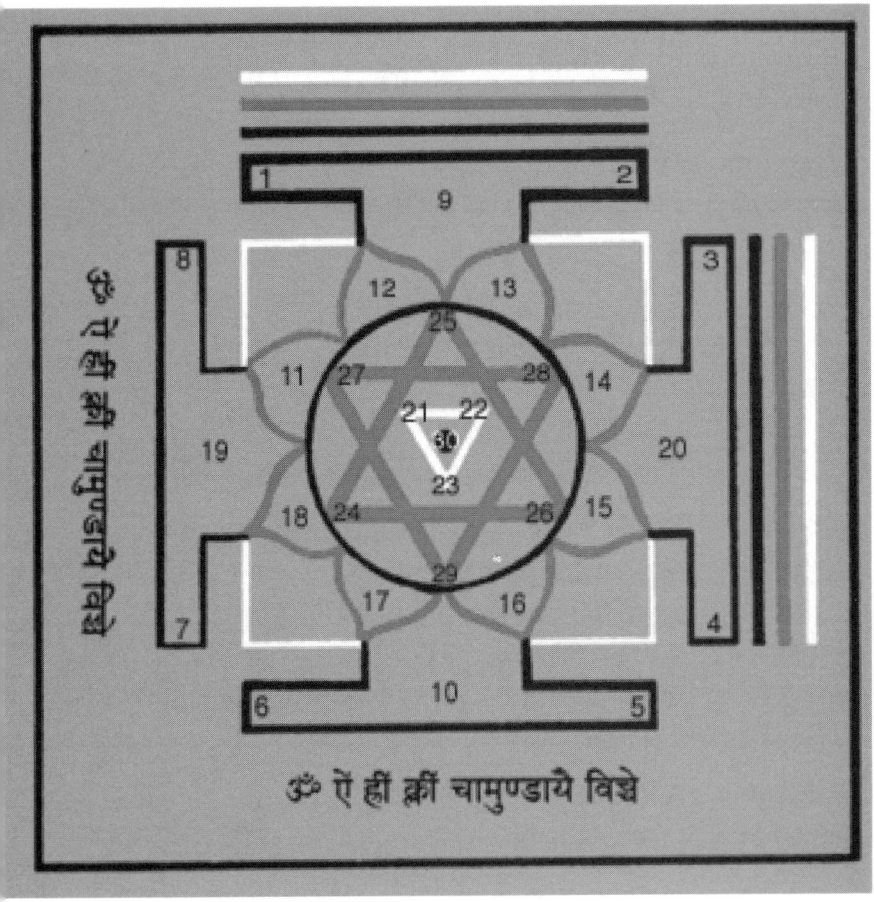

- 1 -

ॐ आधारशक्तये नमः

oṃ ādhāraśaktaye namaḥ

oṃ I bow to the primal energy which sustains existence.

- 2 -

ॐ कुर्म्माय नमः

oṃ kurmmāya namaḥ

oṃ I bow to the Tortoise which supports creation.

- 3 -

ॐ अनन्ताय नमः

oṃ anantāya namaḥ

oṃ I bow to Infinity (personified as a thousand hooded snake who holds aloft the worlds).

- 4 -

ॐ पृथिव्यै नमः

oṃ pṛthivyai namaḥ

oṃ I bow to the Earth.

- 5 -

ॐ क्षीरसमूद्राय नमः

oṃ kṣīrasamūdrāya namaḥ

oṃ I bow to the milk ocean, or ocean of nectar, the infinite expanse of existence from which all manifested.

- 6 -

ॐ श्वेतद्वीपाय नमः

oṃ śvetadvīpāya namaḥ

oṃ I bow to the Island of Purity, which is in the ocean.

- 7 -

ॐ मणिमन्दपाय नमः

oṃ maṇimandapāya namaḥ

oṃ I bow to the Palace of Gems, which is on the island, the home of the Divine Mother.

\- 8 -

ॐ कल्पवृक्षाय नमः

oṃ kalpavṛkṣāya namaḥ

oṃ I bow to the Tree of Fulfillment, which satisfies all desires, growing in the palace courtyard.

\- 9 -

ॐ मणिवेदिकायै नमः

oṃ maṇivedikāyai namaḥ

oṃ I bow to the altar containing the gems of wisdom.

\- 10 -

ॐ रत्नसिंहासनाय नमः

oṃ ratnasiṃhāsanāya namaḥ

oṃ I bow to the throne of the jewel.

\- 11 -

ॐ धर्म्माय नमः

oṃ dharmmāya namaḥ

oṃ I bow to the Way of Truth and Harmony.

\- 12 -

ॐ ज्ञानाय नमः

oṃ jñānāya namaḥ

oṃ I bow to Wisdom.

\- 13 -

ॐ वैराग्याय नमः

oṃ vairāgyāya namaḥ

oṃ I bow to Detachment.

\- 14 -

ॐ ईश्वर्ज्याय नमः

oṃ īśvarjyāya namaḥ

oṃ I bow to the Imperishable Qualities.

- 15 -

ॐ अधर्म्माय नमः

oṃ adharmmāya namaḥ
oṃ I bow to Disharmony.

- 16 -

ॐ अज्ञानाय नमः

oṃ ajñānāya namaḥ
oṃ I bow to Ignorance.

- 17 -

ॐ अवैराग्याय नमः

oṃ avairāgyāya namaḥ
oṃ I bow to Attachment.

- 18 -

ॐ अनीश्वर्ज्याय नमः

oṃ anīśvarjyāya namaḥ
oṃ I bow to the Transient.

- 19 -

ॐ अनन्ताय नमः

oṃ anantāya namaḥ
oṃ I bow to the Infinite.

- 20 -

ॐ पद्माय नमः

oṃ padmāya namaḥ
oṃ I bow to the Lotus.

- 21 -

अं अर्कमण्डलाय द्वादशकलात्मने नमः

aṃ arkamaṇḍalāya dvādaśakalātmane namaḥ
"A" we bow to the twelve aspects of the realm of the sun. Tapinī, Tāpinī, Dhūmrā, Marīci, Jvālinī, Ruci, Sudhūmrā, Bhoga-dā, Viśvā, Bodhinī, Dhārinī, Kṣamā; Containing heat,

Emanating heat, Smoky, Ray-producing, Burning, Lustrous, Purple or Smoky-red, Granting enjoyment, Universal, Which makes known, Productive of Consciousness, Which supports, Which forgives.

- 22 -

उं सोममण्डलाय षोडशकलात्मने नमः

uṃ somamaṇḍalāya ṣoḍaśakalātmane namaḥ

"U" I bow to the sixteen aspects of the realm of the moon. Amṛta, Prāṇada, Puṣā, Tuṣṭi, Puṣṭi, Rati, Dhṛti, Śaśinī, Candrikā, Kānti, Jyotsnā, Śrī, Prīti, Angadā, Pūrṇā, Pūrnāmṛta; Nectar, Which sustains life, Which supports, Satisfying, Nourishing, Playful, Constancy, Unfailing, Producer of Joy, Beauty enhanced by love, Light, Grantor of Prosperity, Affectionate, Purifying the body, Complete, Full of Bliss.

- 23 -

मं वह्निमण्डलाय दशकलात्मने नमः

maṃ vahnimaṇḍalāya daśakalātmane namaḥ

"M" we bow to the ten aspects of the realm of fire: Dhūmrā, Arciḥ, Jvalinī, Śūkṣmā, Jvālinī, Visphuliṅginī, Suśrī, Surūpā, Kapilā, Havya-Kavya-Vahā; Smoky Red, Flaming, Shining, Subtle, Burning, Sparkling, Beautiful, Well-formed, Tawny, The Messenger to Gods and Ancestors.

- 24 -

ॐ सं सत्त्वाय नमः

oṃ saṃ sattvāya namaḥ

oṃ I bow to activity, execution, light, knowledge, being.

- 25 -

ॐ रं रजसे नमः

oṃ raṃ rajase namaḥ

oṃ I bow to desire, inspiration, becoming.

- 26 -

ॐ तं तमसे नमः

oṃ taṃ tamase namaḥ

oṃ I bow to wisdom, to the darkness which exposes light, to rest.

- 27 -

ॐ आं आत्मने नमः

oṃ āṃ ātmane namaḥ

oṃ I bow to the Soul.

- 28 -

ॐ अं अन्तरात्मने नमः

oṃ aṃ antarātmane namaḥ

oṃ I bow to the Innermost Soul.

- 29 -

ॐ पं परमात्मने नमः

oṃ paṃ paramātmane namaḥ

oṃ I bow to the Universal Soul, or the Consciousness which exceeds manifestation.

- 30 -

ॐ ह्रीं ज्ञानात्मने नमः

oṃ hrīṃ jñānātmane namaḥ

oṃ I bow to the Soul of Infinite Wisdom.

शिव ध्यानम्

śiva dhyānam

वन्दे देवमुमापतिं सुरगुरुं वन्दे जगत्कारणं
वन्दे पन्नगभूषणं मृगधरं वन्दे पशूनां पतिम् ।
वन्दे सूर्यशशाङ्कवह्निनयनं वन्दे मुकुन्दप्रियं
वन्दे भक्तजनाश्रयं च वरदं वन्दे शिवं शङ्करम् ॥

vande devamumāpatiṃ suraguruṃ
vande jagatkāraṇaṃ
vande pannagabhūṣaṇaṃ mṛgadharaṃ
vande paśūnāṃ patim
vande sūryaśaśāṅkavahninayanaṃ
vande mukundapriyaṃ
vande bhaktajanāśrayaṃ ca varadaṃ
vande śivaṃ śaṅkaram

We extol the God who is the Lord of Umā, the Guru of the Gods. We extol the Cause of the perceivable universe. We extol He who has the radiance of emeralds, who shows the (mudrā) of the deer (also known as the wish-fulfilling tree). We extol He who is the Lord of all who are bound. We extol He whose three eyes are the Sun, the Moon and Fire. We extol the beloved of Viṣṇu. We extol the refuge of all devotees and the Giver of Boons. We extol the Consciousness of Infinite Goodness, the Cause of Bliss.

हे जिह्वे भज विश्वनाथ बद्रीकेदार भस्मम्बराः
भीमाशङ्करबैजनाथह्यवढे नागेशरामेश्वराः ।
ॐकारेममलेश्वरं स्मरहरं महङ्कालं मल्लिकाऽर्जुनम्
ध्यायेत् त्र्यंबकसोमनाथमनिशं एकादशे ॐ नमः ॥

he jihve bhaja viśvanātha
badrīkedāra bhasmambarāḥ
bhīmāśaṅkarabaijanātha
hyavaḍhe nāgeśarāmeśvarāḥ
oṃkāremamaleśvaraṃ smaraharaṃ
mahaṅkālaṃ mallikā-rjunam
dhyāyet tryaṃbakasomanātha
maniśaṃ ekādaśe oṃ namaḥ

Oh Tongue, sing the praises of the Lord of the Universe who dwells at Badrī-Kedārnāth and wears ashes. He stays at Bhīmāśaṅkara, Baijanātha, Nāgeśvara, Rāmeśvarā; Oṃkāreśvarā, Mamaleśvaraṃ, Mahaṅkālaṃ, Mallikārjunam, Tryaṃbaka, Somanātha, oṃ we bow and meditate on the eleven (forms of Rudra).

देवं चन्द्रकलाधरं फणिधरं ब्रह्मा कपालाधरं
गौरीवह्यधरं त्रिलोचनधरं रुद्राक्षमालागलम् ।
गङ्गारङ्गतरङ्गपिङ्गलजटाजूटं च गङ्गाधरं
नीलोग्र भज विश्वनाथसिद्धसहितं सोम शरक्षाकरम् ॥

devaṃ candrakalādharaṃ phanidharaṃ
brahmā kapālādharaṃ
gaurīvahyadharaṃ trilocanadharaṃ
rudrākṣamālāgalam
gaṅgāraṅgataraṅgapiṅgalajaṭājūṭaṃ
ca gaṅgādharaṃ
nīlogra bhaja viśvanāthasiddhasahitaṃ
soma śarakṣākaram

The God who wears the part of the Moon, wears snakes, the Supreme Divinity who wears skulls. With Gaurī on His left side, displaying three eyes and a garland of rudrākṣa. He supports Gaṅgā who is running down from His matted locks of hair. With a blue throat, the attained ones sing praises to the Lord of the Universe with full devotion, and seek His protection.

शान्तं पद्मासनस्थं शशधरमुकुटं पञ्चवक्त्रं
शूलं वज्रं च खड्गं परशुमभयदं दक्षिणाङ्गे ।

नागं पाशं च घण्टां डमरुकसहितां साङ्कुशं वामभागे
नानालङ्कारदीप्तं स्फटिकमणिनिभं पार्वतीशं नमामि ॥

śāntaṃ padmāsanasthaṃ
śaśadharamukuṭaṃ pañcavaktraṃ
śūlaṃ vajraṃ ca khaḍgaṃ
paraśumabhayadaṃ dakṣiṇāṅge
nāgaṃ pāśaṃ ca ghaṇṭāṃ
ḍamarukasahitāṃ sāṅkuśaṃ vāmabhāge
nānālaṅkāradīptaṃ sphaṭikamaṇinibhaṃ
pārvatīśaṃ namāmi

Who is filled with peace, sitting in the full lotus posture with the moon on His forehead, with five faces and three eyes, He holds the trident, thunderbolt, sword and axe and shows the mudrā which grants freedom from all fear in the (five) hands of His right side. A sword, noose, bell, a small drum and a curved sword are in those of His left side. His various ornaments are shining like gems and crystal; I bow to the husband of Pārvatī.

कर्पूरगौरं करुणावतारं संसारसारं भुजगेन्द्रहारम् ।
सदा वसन्तं हृदयारविन्दे भवं भवानीसहितं नमामि ॥

karpūragauraṃ karuṇāvatāraṃ
saṃsārasāraṃ bhujagendrahāram
sadā vasantaṃ hṛdayāravinde
bhavaṃ bhavānīsahitaṃ namāmi

Of white color like pure camphor, He is the embodiment of Compassion, Lord of the Ocean of objects and relationships, who wears the King of Snakes as a necklace. I bow to He who always resides in the lotus of the heart of all existence along with the Divine Mother of the Universe.

असितगिरिसमं स्यात्कज्जलं सिन्धुपात्रे
सुरतरुवरशाखा लेखनी पत्रमुर्वी ।
लिखति यदि गृहीत्वा शारदा सर्वकालं
तदपि तव गुणानामीश पारं न याति ॥

asitagirisamaṃ syātkajjalaṃ sindhupātre
surataruvaraśākhā lekhanī patramurvī
likhati yadi gṛhītvā śāradā sarvakālaṃ
tadapi tava guṇānāmīśa pāraṃ na yāti

When Śāradā (Sarasvati) who has performed inconceivable austerities of purification and spiritual disciplines, is unable to know or write of all your qualities, then what shall we be able to sing?

त्वमेव माता च पिता त्वमेव त्वमेव बन्धुश्चसखा त्वमेव ।
त्वमेव विद्या द्रविनं त्वमेव त्वमेव सर्वम् मम देवदेव ॥

tvameva mātā ca pitā tvameva
tvameva bandhuścā sakhā tvameva
tvameva vidyā dravinaṃ tvameva
tvameva sarvam mama devadeva

You alone are Mother and Father, you alone are friend and relative. You alone are knowledge and wealth. Oh my God of Gods, you alone are everything.

करचरणकृतं वाक्कायजं कर्मजं वा
श्रवणनयनजं वा मानसं वाऽपराधम् ।
विहितमविहितं वा सर्वमेतत्क्षमस्व
जय जय करुणाब्धे श्रीमहादेव शम्भो ॥

karacaraṇakṛtaṃ vākkāyajaṃ karmajaṃ vā
śravaṇanayanajaṃ vā mānasaṃ vā-parādham
vihitamavihitaṃ vā sarvametatkṣamasva
jaya jaya karuṇābdhe srīmahādeva śambho

Any fault committed by the actions of my hands or feet, speech or body, my eyes, ears or mind, whether authorized or unauthorized; all of that please forgive. Victory! Victory to the Ocean of Compassion, the respected Great God, Illuminator of Peace.

चन्द्रोद्भासितशेखरे स्मरहरे गङ्गाधरे शङ्करे
सर्पैर्भूषितकण्ठकर्णविवरे नेत्रोत्थवैश्वानरे ।
दन्तित्वक्कृतसुन्दराम्बरधरे त्रैलोक्यसारे हरे
मोक्षार्थं कुरु चित्तमचलामन्यैस्तु किं कर्मभिः ॥

candrodbhāsitaśekhare
smarahare gaṅgādhare śaṅkare
sarpairbhūṣitakaṇṭha
karṇavivare netrotthavaiśvānare
dantitvakkṛtasundarām
baradhare trailokyasāre hare
mokṣārthaṃ kuru cittam
acalāmanyaistu kiṃ karmabhiḥ

Upon whose head the moon resides, Destroyer of the God of Love, who supports the Gaṅgā, Cause of Peace, at whose throat the snake shines, and also as the ornaments of his ears; in whose third eye resides the fire of Universal Existence, with teeth of ivory, wearing a beautiful garment, He takes away the difficulties of the ocean of the three worlds; for the purpose of liberation, do what is necessary to stop the changes and modifications of consciousness.

ॐ तत् पुरुषाय विद्महे महादेवाय धीमहे ।

तन्नो रुद्रः प्रचोदयात् ॥

oṃ tat puruṣāya vidmahe mahādevāya dhīmahe
tanno rudraḥ pracodayāt

We meditate upon That Universal Consciousness, contemplate the Great God. May that Reliever of Sufferings grant us increase.

ब्रह्मानन्दं परमसुखदं केवलं ज्ञानमूर्तिं

द्वनद्वातीतं गगनसदृशं तत्त्वमस्यादिलक्ष्यम् ।

एकं नित्यं विमलमचलं सर्वधीसाक्षिभूतं

भावातीतं त्रिगुणरहितं सद्गुरुं तं नमामि ॥

brahmānandaṃ paramasukhadaṃ kevalaṃ jñānamūrtiṃ
dvanadvātītaṃ gaganasadṛśaṃ tattvamasyādilakṣyam
ekaṃ nityaṃ vimalamacalaṃ sarvadhīsākṣibhūtaṃ
bhāvātītaṃ triguṇarahitaṃ sadguruṃ taṃ namāmi

This bliss of Supreme Divinity, the highest pleasure, the only image of Wisdom, beyond all changes, the pure perception through the ether, the Highest Goal of all Principles. One, eternal, pure, unmovable, the Witness of the minds of all beings, beyond all attitudes, beyond the three guṇas, I bow to He who is the True Guru.

नारायणं पद्मभवं वसिष्ठं शक्तिं च तत्पुत्रपराशरं च ।

व्यासं शुकं गौडपदं महान्तं गोविन्दयोगीन्द्रमथास्य

शिष्यम् ॥

nārāyaṇaṃ padmabhavaṃ vasiṣṭhaṃ
śaktiṃ ca tatputraparāśaraṃ ca
vyāsaṃ śukaṃ gauḍapadaṃ mahāntaṃ
govindayogīndramathāsya śiṣyam

From Nārāyaṇa (Viṣṇu) to the Lotus One (Brahmā), to Vasiṣṭha, to his disciple Śakti, to his son Parāśara, to Vyāsa, to Śukadeva, to Gauḍapadācārya, to his disciple Mahānta, to the King of Yogis, Govinda, in disciplic succession;

श्रीशङ्कराचार्यमथास्य पद्मपादं च हस्तामलकं च शिष्यम् ।
तं तोटकं वार्तिककारमन्यानस्मद्गुरून्संततमानतोऽस्मि ॥

śrīśaṅkarācārya mathāsya padmapādaṃ ca
hastāmalakaṃ ca śiṣyam
taṃ toṭakaṃ vārtikakāramanyānasmad
gurūnsaṃtatamānato-smi

The Respected Śaṅkarācārya and his disciples Padmapādācārya, Hastāmalakācārya, Toṭakācārya and Sureśvarācārya, and thereafter to other gurus, always we bow the head.

अखण्डमण्डलाकारं व्याप्तं येन चराचरम् ।
तत्पदं दर्शितं येन तस्मै श्रीगुरवे नमः ॥

akhaṇḍamaṇḍalākāraṃ vyāptaṃ yena carācaram
tatpadaṃ darśitaṃ yena tasmai śrīgurave namaḥ

To He who made manifest this infinite existence, and made the individual forms which move and move not; in order to perceive His lotus feet, I bow down to the respected Guru.

गुरुर्ब्रह्मा गुरुर्विष्णुः गुरुर्देवो महेश्वरः ।
गुरुसाक्षात् परं ब्रह्मा तस्मै श्रीगुरवे नमः ॥

gururbrahmā gururviṣṇuḥ gururdevo maheśvaraḥ
gurusākṣāt paraṃ brahmā tasmai śrīgurave namaḥ
The Guru is Brahmā, Guru is Viṣṇuḥ, Guru is the Lord Maheśvaraḥ. The Guru is actually the Supreme Divinity, and therefore we bow down to the Guru.

श्रुतिस्मृतिपुरणानामालयं करुणालयम् ।
नमामि भगवत्पादं शङ्करं लोकशङ्करम् ॥

śrutismṛtipuraṇānāmālayaṃ karuṇālayam
namāmi bhagavatpādaṃ śaṅkaraṃ lokaśaṅkaram
The Repository of Compassion described in the Vedas (śruti), in the histories and commentaries (smṛti) and in the purāṇas; I bow down to the feet of that divinity, the Cause of Peace, Cause of Peace to the worlds.

शङ्करं शङ्कराचार्यं केशवं बादरायणम् ।
सूत्रभाष्यकृतौ वन्दे भगवन्तौ पुनः पुनः ॥

śaṅkaraṃ śaṅkarācāryaṃ keśavaṃ bādarāyaṇam
sūtrabhāṣyakṛtau vande bhagavantau punaḥ punaḥ
Again and again we adore with worship Śaṅkara and Keśava (Viṣṇu), along with their spokesmen and commentators Śaṅkarācārya and Vedavyāsa (Bādarāyaṇa).

ईश्वरो गुरुरात्मेति मूर्त्तिभेदविभागिने ।
व्योमवद्व्याप्तदेहाय दक्षिणामूर्त्तये नमः ॥

īśvaro gururātmeti mūrttibhedavibhāgine
vyomavadvyāptadehāya dakṣiṇāmūrttaye namaḥ
The Supreme Divinity is the soul of the guru, the image of divinity distinguished by attributes. Who is indivisible like the sky, we bow to Dakṣiṇāmūrtti, the Preferred Image.

नानासुगन्धपुष्पाणि यथाकालोद्भवानि च ।
भक्त्या दत्तानि पूजार्थं गृहाण परमेश्वर ॥

nānāsugandhapuṣpāṇi yathākālodbhavāni ca
bhaktyā dattāni pūjārthaṃ gṛhāṇa parameśvara

Various excellently scented flowers which rise in their time, your devotees are offering for your worship. Please accept, oh Supreme Lord.

सौराष्ट्रे सोमनाथं च श्रीशैले मल्लिकार्जुनम् ।
ऊज्जियन्यां महाकालमोंकारे परमेश्वरम् ॥

saurāṣṭre somanāthaṃ ca śrīśaile mallikārjunam
ūjjyinyāṃ mahākālamoṃkāre parameśvaram

In Saurāṣṭra, (He is called) Somanātha and in Śrīśaila, Mallikārjunam; in Ūjjinyāṃ, Mahākālam, in Oṃkāra, Parameśvaram;

केदारं हिमवत्पृष्ठे डाकिन्यां भीमशङ्करम् ।
वाराणस्यं च विश्वेशं त्र्यम्बकं गौतमीतटे ॥

kedāraṃ himavatpṛṣṭhe ḍākinyāṃ bhīmaśaṅkaram
vārāṇasyaṃ ca viśveśaṃ tryambakaṃ gautamītaṭe

(He is called) Kedāra on the back side of the Himalayas, and in the South, Bhīmaśaṅkaram; in Vārāṇasi, Viśveśaṃ, in Gautamī, Tryambakaṃ.

वैध्यनाथं चिताभूमौ नागेशं दारुकावने ।
सेतुबंधे च रामेशं घुश्मेशं च शिवालये ॥

vaidhyanāthaṃ citābhūmau nāgeśaṃ dārukāvane
setubaṃdhe ca rāmeśaṃ ghuśmeśaṃ ca śivālaye

In Citābhūmi, the Land of Consciousness, (He is called) Vaidhyanātha, and in the forests of Dārukā, Nāgeśaṃ. Where they made the bridge, (He is called) Rāmeśaṃ, and in the place of Śiva, Ghuśmeśaṃ.

द्वादशैतानि नामानि प्रातरुत्थाय यः पठेत् ।
सर्व पापविनिर्मुक्त सर्वसिद्धि फलं लभेत् ॥

dvādaśaitāni nāmāni prātarutthāya yaḥ paṭhet
sarva pāpavinirmukta sarvasiddhi phalaṃ labhet

Whoever will read these twelve names upon rising in the early morning, will be freed from the bondage of sin, and will attain the fruits of perfection.

ॐ नमः शिवाय

oṃ namaḥ śivāya

oṃ I bow to the Consciousness of Infinite Goodness.

āvāhaṇa

invitation

अनेकरत्न संयुक्तं नानामणि गणान्वितम् ।
कार्तस्वरमयं दिव्यमासनं प्रतिगृह्यताम् ॥
ॐ नमः शिवाय आसनं समर्पयामि

anekaratna saṃyuktaṃ nānāmaṇi gaṇānvitam
kārtasvaramayaṃ divyamāsanaṃ pratigṛhyatām
oṃ namaḥ śivāya āsanaṃ samarpayāmi

United with many gems and a multitude of various jewels, voluntarily accept my offering of a divine seat. With the offering of a seat oṃ I bow to the Consciousness of Infinite Goodness.

establishment within

āvāhaṇi mudrā (I invite you, please come.)

ॐ नमः शिवाय इहागच्छ

oṃ namaḥ śivāya ihāgaccha

oṃ I bow to the Consciousness of Infinite Goodness, I invite you, please come.

sthāpanī mudrā (I establish you within.)

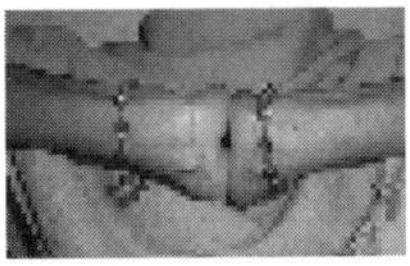

इह तिष्ठ

iha tiṣṭha

I establish you within.

sannidhāpanī mudrā (I know you have many devotees who are requesting your attention, but I request that you pay special attention to me.)

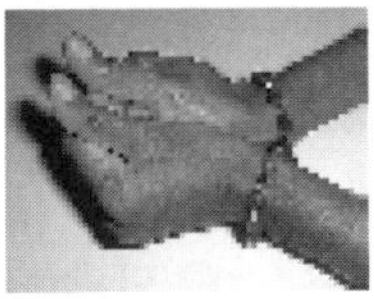

इह सन्निरुध्यस्व

iha sannirudhyasva

I am binding you to remain here.

saṃrodhanī mudrā (I am sorry for any inconvenience caused.)

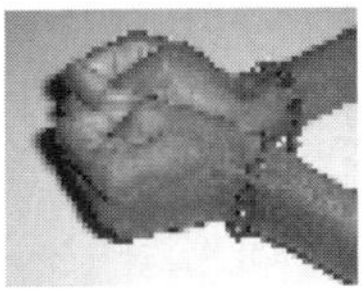

इह सनिहित भव

iha sanihita bhava

You bestow abundant wealth.

atmā samarpaṇa mudrā (I surrender my soul to you.)

अत्राधिष्ठानं कुरु

atrādhiṣṭhānaṃ kuru

I am depending upon you to forgive me in this matter.

prakṣan (I bow to you with devotion.)

देव मम पूजां गृहाण

देव बक्तशूल्वे परित्राण करायिते ।

जावोट् त्वं पूजैषामि तावोट् त्वं सुस्थिरा भव ॥

deva mama pūjāṃ gṛhāṇa
deva baktaśūlave paritrāṇa karāyite
jāvoṭ tvaṃ pūjaiṣāmi tāvoṭ tvaṃ susthirā bhava

Oh God, please accept my worship. Oh God, remove all pain from your devotees. For so long as I worship you, please remain sitting still.

prāṇa pratiṣṭhā
establishment of life

ॐ अं आं ह्रीं क्रों यं रं लं वं शं षं सं हों हं सः

oṃ aṃ āṃ hrīṃ kroṃ yaṃ raṃ laṃ vaṃ śaṃ ṣaṃ saṃ hoṃ haṃ saḥ

oṃ The Infinite Beyond Conception, Creation (the first letter), Consciousness, Māyā, the cause of the movement of the subtle body to perfection and beyond; the path of fulfillment: control, subtle illumination, one with the earth, emancipation, the soul of peace, the soul of delight, the soul of unity (all this is I), perfection, Infinite Consciousness, this is I.

ॐ नमः शिवाय प्राणा इह प्राणाः

oṃ namaḥ śivāya prāṇā iha prāṇāḥ

oṃ I bow to the Consciousness of Infinite Goodness. You are the life of this life!

ॐ अं आं ह्रीं क्रों यं रं लं वं शं षं सं हों हं सः

oṃ aṃ āṃ hrīṃ kroṃ yaṃ raṃ laṃ vaṃ śaṃ ṣaṃ saṃ hoṃ haṃ saḥ

oṃ The Infinite Beyond Conception, Creation (the first letter), Consciousness, Māyā, the cause of the movement of the subtle body to perfection and beyond; the path of fulfillment: control, subtle illumination, one with the earth, emancipation, the soul of peace, the soul of delight, the soul of unity (all this is I), perfection, Infinite Consciousness, this is I.

ॐ नमः शिवाय जीव इह स्थितः

oṃ namaḥ śivāya jīva iha sthitaḥ

oṃ I bow to the Consciousness of Infinite Goodness. You are situated in this life (or individual consciousness).

ॐ अं आं ह्रीं क्रों यं रं लं वं शं षं सं हों हं सः

oṃ aṃ āṃ hrīṃ kroṃ yaṃ raṃ laṃ vaṃ śaṃ ṣaṃ saṃ hoṃ haṃ saḥ

oṃ The Infinite Beyond Conception, Creation (the first letter), Consciousness, Māyā, the cause of the movement of the subtle body to perfection and beyond; the path of fulfillment: control, subtle illumination, one with the earth, emancipation, the soul of peace, the soul of delight, the soul of unity (all this is I), perfection, Infinite Consciousness, this is I.

ॐ नमः शिवाय सर्वेन्द्रियाणि

oṃ namaḥ śivāya sarvendriyāṇi

oṃ I bow to the Consciousness of Infinite Goodness. You are all these organs (of action and knowledge).

ॐ अं आं ह्रीं क्रों यं रं लं वं शं षं सं हों हं सः

oṃ aṃ āṃ hrīṃ kroṃ yaṃ raṃ laṃ vaṃ śaṃ ṣaṃ saṃ hoṃ haṃ saḥ

oṃ The Infinite Beyond Conception, Creation (the first letter), Consciousness, Māyā, the cause of the movement of the subtle body to perfection and beyond; the path of fulfillment: control, subtle illumination, one with the earth, emancipation, the soul of peace, the soul of delight, the soul of unity (all this is I), perfection, Infinite Consciousness, this is I.

ॐ नमः शिवाय वाग् मनस्त्वक्चक्षुः-श्रोत्र-घ्राण-प्राणा इहागत्य सुखं चिरं तिष्ठन्तु स्वाहा

oṃ namaḥ śivāya vāg manastvakcakṣuḥ śrotra ghrāṇa prāṇā ihāgatya sukhaṃ ciraṃ tiṣṭhantu svāhā

oṃ I bow to the Consciousness of Infinite Goodness. You are all these vibrations, mind, sound, eyes, ears, tongue, nose and life force. Bring forth infinite peace and establish it forever, I am One with God!

kara nyāsa

establishment in the hands

ॐ नं अंगुष्ठाभ्यां नमः

oṃ naṃ aṇguṣṭhābhyāṃ namaḥ thumb forefinger

oṃ naṃ in the thumb I bow.

ॐ मः तर्जनीभ्यां स्वाहा

oṃ maḥ tarjanībhyāṃ svāhā thumb forefinger

oṃ maḥ in the forefinger, I am One with God!

ॐ शिं मध्यमाभ्यां वषट्

oṃ śiṃ madhyamābhyāṃ vaṣaṭ thumb middlefinger
oṃ śiṃ in the middle finger, Purify!

ॐ वां अनामिकाभ्यां हुं

oṃ vāṃ anāmikābhyāṃ huṃ thumb ringfinger
oṃ vāṃ in the ring finger, Cut the Ego!

ॐ यः कनिष्ठिकाभ्यां बौषट्

oṃ yaḥ kaniṣṭhikābhyāṃ vauṣaṭ thumb littlefinger
oṃ yaḥ in the little finger, Ultimate Purity!

Roll hand over hand forwards while reciting *karatala kara* and backwards while chanting *pṛṣṭhābhyāṃ*, then clap hands when chanting *astrāya phaṭ.*

ॐ नमः शिवाय करतल कर पृष्ठाभ्यां अस्त्राय फट् ॥

oṃ namaḥ śivāya karatala kara pṛṣṭhābhyāṃ astrāya phaṭ
oṃ I bow to the Consciousness of Infinite Goodness with the weapon of Virtue.

ॐ नमः शिवाय

oṃ namaḥ śivāya
I bow to the Consciousness of Infinite Goodness.

aṅga nyāsa

establishment in the body

Holding tattva mudrā, touch heart.

ॐ नं हृदयाय नमः

oṃ naṃ hṛdayāya namaḥ touch heart

oṃ naṃ in the heart, I bow.

Holding tattva mudrā, touch top of head.

ॐ मः शिरसे स्वाहा

oṃ maḥ śirase svāhā top of head

oṃ maḥ on the top of the head, I am One with God!

With thumb extended, touch back of head.

ॐ शिं शिखायै वषट्

oṃ śiṃ śikhāyai vaṣaṭ back of head

oṃ śiṃ on the back of the head, Purify!

Holding tattva mudrā, cross both arms.

ॐ वां कवचाय हुं

oṃ vāṃ kavacāya huṃ cross both arms

oṃ vāṃ crossing both arms, Cut the Ego!

Holding tattva mudrā, touch three eyes at once with three middle fingers.

ॐ यः नेत्रत्रयाय वौषट्

oṃ yaḥ netratrayāya vauṣaṭ touch three eyes

oṃ yaḥ in the three eyes, Ultimate Purity!

Roll hand over hand forwards while reciting *karatala kara* and backwards while chanting *pṛṣṭhābhyāṃ*, then clap hands when chanting *astrāya phaṭ.*

ॐ नमः शिवाय करतल कर पृष्ठाभ्यां अस्त्राय फट् ॥

oṃ namaḥ śivāya karatala kara pṛṣṭhābhyāṃ astrāya phaṭ

oṃ I bow to the Consciousness of Infinite Goodness with the weapon of Virtue.

ॐ नमः शिवाय

oṃ namaḥ śivāya

I bow to the Consciousness of Infinite Goodness.

japa

stapana

establishment upon the altar

ॐ नमः शिवाय शान्ताय कारणत्रय हेतवे ।

निवेदयामि चात्मानं त्वं गतिः परमेश्वर ॥

oṃ namaḥ śivāya śāntāya kāraṇatraya hetave nivedayāmi cātmānaṃ tvaṃ gatiḥ parameśvara

oṃ I bow to the Consciousness of Infinite Goodness, to Peace, to the Cause of the three worlds, I offer to you the fullness of my soul, Oh Supreme Lord.

āvāhaṇi mudrā (I invite you, please come.)

ॐ नमः शिवाय इहागच्छ

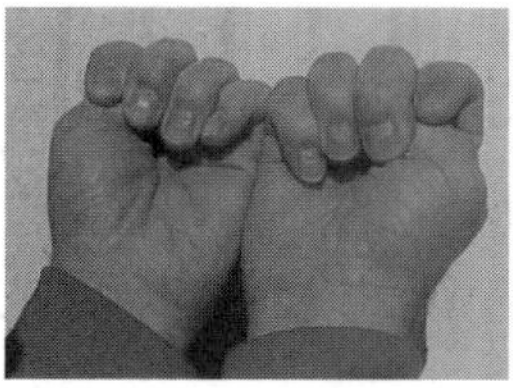

oṃ namaḥ śivāya ihāgaccha

oṃ I bow to the Consciousness of Infinite Goodness, I invite you, please come.

sthāpanī mudrā (I establish you within.)

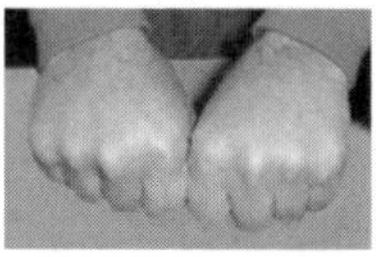

इह तिष्ठ

iha tiṣṭha

I establish you within.

sannidhāpanī mudrā (I know you have many devotees who are requesting your attention, but I request that you pay special attention to me.)

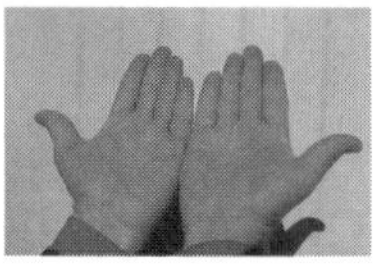

इह सन्निदेहि

iha sannidehi

I am binding you to remain here.

saṃrodhanī mudrā (I am sorry for any inconvenience caused.)

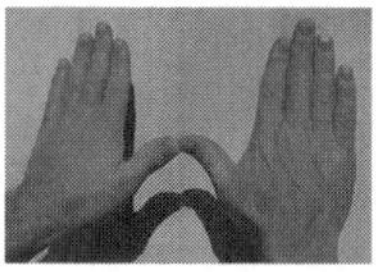

इह सनिहित भव

iha sanihita bhava

You bestow abundant wealth.

atmā samarpaṇa mudrā (I surrender my soul to you.)

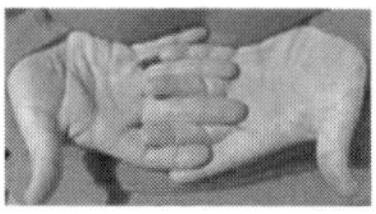

अत्राधिष्ठानं कुरु

atrādhiṣṭhānaṃ kuru

I am depending upon you to forgive me in this matter.

prakṣan (I bow to you with devotion.)

देव मम पूजां गृहाण

देव बक्तशूल्वे परित्राण करायिते ।

जावोट् त्वं पूजैषामि तावोट् त्वं सुस्थिरा भव ॥

deva mama pūjāṃ gṛhāṇa
deva baktaśūlave paritrāṇa karāyite
jāvoṭ tvaṃ pūjaiṣāmi tāvoṭ tvaṃ susthirā bhava
Oh God, please accept my worship. Oh God, remove all pain from your devotees. For so long as I worship you, please remain sitting still.

pūjā naivedya
offerings of worship
invitation

आगच्छेह महादेव ! सर्वसम्पत्प्रदायिनि ।
यावद् व्रतं समाप्येत तावत्त्वं सन्निधौ भव ॥
ॐ नमः शिवाय आवाहनं समर्पयामि

āgaccheha mahādeva ! sarvasampatpradāyini
yāvad vrataṃ samāpyeta tāvattvaṃ sannidhau bhava
oṃ namaḥ śivāya āvāhanaṃ samarpayāmi
Please come here, oh Great God, Giver of all wealth! Please remain sitting still until this vow of worship is not complete. With the offering of an invitation oṃ I bow to the Consciousness of Infinite Goodness.

seat

अनेकरत्नसंयुक्तं नानामणिगणान्वितम् ।
कार्तस्वरमयं दिव्यमासनं प्रतिगृह्यताम् ॥
ॐ नमः शिवाय आसनं समर्पयामि

anekaratna saṃyuktaṃ nānāmaṇi gaṇānvitam
kārtasvaramayaṃ divyamāsanaṃ pratigṛhyatām
oṃ namaḥ śivāya āsanaṃ samarpayāmi

United with many gems and a multitude of various jewels, voluntarily accept my offering of a divine seat. With the offering of a seat oṃ I bow to the Consciousness of Infinite Goodness.

foot bath

ॐ गङ्गादिसर्वतीर्थेभ्यो मया प्रार्थनयाहृतम् ।
तोयमेतत् सुखस्पर्शं पाद्यार्थं प्रतिगृह्यताम् ॥
ॐ नमः शिवाय पाद्यं समर्पयामि

oṃ gaṅgādi sarva tīrthebhyo mayā prārthanayāhṛtam
toyametat sukha sparśaṃ pādyārthaṃ pratigṛhyatām
oṃ namaḥ śivāya pādyaṃ samarpayāmi

The Gaṅges and other waters from all the places of pilgrimage are mingled together in this our prayer, that you please accept the comfortable touch of these waters offered to wash your lotus feet. With this offering of foot bath waters oṃ I bow to the Consciousness of Infinite Goodness.

water for washing hands and mouth

कर्पूरेण सुगन्धेन सुरभिस्वादु शीतलम् ।
तोयमाचमनीयार्थं देवदं प्रतिगृह्यताम् ॥
ॐ नमः शिवाय आचमनीयं समर्पयामि

karpūreṇa sugandhena surabhisvādu śītalam
toyamācamanīyārthaṃ devadaṃ pratigṛhyatām
oṃ namaḥ śivāya ācamanīyaṃ samarpayāmi

With camphor and excellent scent, cool with excellent taste, this water is being offered for washing, oh God, please accept. With this offering of washing waters oṃ I bow to the Consciousness of Infinite Goodness.

arghya

निधीनां सर्वदेवानां त्वमनर्घ्यगुणा ह्यसि ।

सिंहोपरिस्थिते देव ! गृहाणार्घ्यं नमोऽस्तु ते ॥

ॐ नमः शिवाय अर्घ्यं समर्पयामि

nidhīnāṃ sarvadevānāṃ tvamanarghyaguṇā hyasi
siṃhoparisthite deva ! gṛhāṇārghyaṃ namo-stu te
oṃ namaḥ śivāya arghyaṃ samarpayāmi

Presented to all the Gods, you, oh Arghya, bring an abundance of pleasure. Oh God who is seated upon the lion, accept this arghya. I bow to you. With this offering of arghya oṃ I bow to the Consciousness of Infinite Goodness.

madhuparka

दधिमधुघृतसमायुक्तं पात्रयुग्मं समन्वितम् ।

मधुपर्कं गृहाण त्वं शुभदा भव शोभने ॥

ॐ नमः शिवाय मधुपर्कं समर्पयामि

dadhi madhu ghṛtasamāyuktaṃ pātrayugmaṃ samanvitam
madhuparkaṃ gṛhāṇa tvaṃ śubhadā bhava śobhane
oṃ namaḥ śivāya madhuparkaṃ samarpayāmi

Yogurt, honey, ghee mixed together, and blended fine in a vessel; please accept this madhuparka shining with radiant purity. With this offering of madhuparka oṃ I bow to the Consciousness of Infinite Goodness.

water bath

ॐ गङ्गे च जमुने चैव गोदावरि सरस्वति ।

नर्मदे सिन्धुकावेरि स्नानार्थं प्रतिगृह्यताम् ॥

ॐ नमः शिवाय गङ्गास्नानं समर्पयामि

oṃ gaṅge ca jamune caiva godāvari sarasvati
narmade sindhu kāveri snānārthaṃ pratigṛhyatām
oṃ namaḥ śivāya gaṅgā snānaṃ samarpayāmi

Please accept the waters from the Gaṅges, the Jamunā, Godāvarī, Sarasvatī, Narmadā, Sindhu and Kāverī, which have been provided for your bath. With this offering of Ganges bath waters oṃ I bow to the Consciousness of Infinite Goodness.

bracelets

ॐ माणिक्यमुक्ताखण्डयुक्ते सुवर्णकारेण च संस्कृते ये ।
ते किङ्किणीभिः स्वरिते सुवर्णे मयाऽर्पिते देव गृहाण कङ्कणे ॥

ॐ नमः शिवाय कङ्कणे समर्पयामि

oṃ māṇikya muktā khaṇḍayukte
suvarṇakāreṇa ca saṃskṛte ye
te kiṅkiṇībhiḥ svarite suvarṇe
mayā-rpite deva gṛhāṇa kaṅkaṇe
oṃ namaḥ śivāya kaṅkaṇe samarpayāmi

oṃ United with gems and pearls, excellent gold and the alphabets of Saṃskṛta, this bracelet is yours and radiance I am offering. Oh God, accept this bracelet. With the offering of a bracelet oṃ I bow to the Consciousness of Infinite Goodness.

conch ornaments

ॐ शङ्खञ्च विविधं चित्रं बाहूनाञ्च विभूषणम् ।
मया निवेदितं भक्त्या गृहाण परमेश्वर ॥

ॐ नमः शिवाय शङ्खालङ्कारं समर्पयामि

oṃ śaṅkhañca vividhaṃ citraṃ
bāhūnāñca vibhūṣaṇam
mayā niveditaṃ bhaktyā gṛhāṇa parameśvara
oṃ namaḥ śivāya śaṅkhālaṅkāraṃ samarpayāmi

I am offering you with devotion ornaments worn upon the arms made of various qualities of conch shell. Please accept, oh Supreme Divinity. With the offering of ornaments made of conch shell oṃ I bow to the Consciousness of Infinite Goodness.

ornaments

ॐ दिव्यरत्नसमायुक्ता वह्निभानुसमप्रभाः ।
गात्राणि शोभयिष्यन्ति अलङ्काराः सुरेश्वर ॥
ॐ नमः शिवाय अलङ्कारान् समर्पयामि

oṃ divyaratnasamāyuktā vahnibhānusamaprabhāḥ
gātrāṇi śobhayiṣyanti alaṅkārāḥ sureśvara
oṃ namaḥ śivāya alaṅkārān samarpayāmi

oṃ United with divine jewels which are radiant like fire, and stones which are shining, please accept these ornaments, oh Supreme among the Gods. With the offering of ornaments oṃ I bow to the Consciousness of Infinite Goodness.

rice

अक्षतान् निर्मलान् शुद्धान् मुक्ताफलसमन्वितान् ।
गृहाणेमान् महादेव देहि मे निर्मलां धियम् ॥
ॐ नमः शिवाय अक्षतान् समर्पयामि

akṣatān nirmalān śuddhān muktāphalasamanvitān
gṛhāṇemān mahādeva dehi me nirmalāṃ dhiyam
oṃ namaḥ śivāya akṣatān samarpayāmi

Oh Great Lord, please accept these grains of rice, spotlessly clean, bestowing the fruit of liberation, and give us a spotlessly clean mind. With the offering of grains of rice oṃ I bow to the Consciousness of Infinite Goodness.

food offering

ॐ सत्पात्रं शुद्धसुहविर्व्विविधानेकभक्षणम् ।
निवेदयामि देवेश सर्वतृप्तिकरं परम् ॥

oṃ satpātraṃ śuddhasuhavirv vividhānekabhakṣaṇam
nivedayāmi deveśa sarvatṛptikaraṃ param

This ever-present platter containing varieties of the purest offerings of food we are presenting to the Lord of Gods to cause all satisfaction most excellent and transcendental.

ॐ अन्नपूर्णे सदा पूर्णे शङ्करप्राणवल्लभे ।
ज्ञानवैराग्यसिद्ध्यर्थं भिक्षां देहि नमोऽस्तु ते ॥

oṃ annapūrṇe sadā pūrṇe śaṅkara prāṇavallabhe
jñānavairāgyasiddhyarthaṃ
bhikṣāṃ dehi namo-stu te

oṃ Goddess who is full, complete and perfect with food and grains, always full, complete and perfect, the strength of the life force of Śiva, the Cause of Peace. For the attainment of perfection in wisdom and renunciation, please give us offerings. We bow down to you.

माता च पार्वती देवी पिता देवो महेश्वरः ।
बान्धवाः शिवभक्ताश्च स्वदेशो भुवनत्रयम् ॥

mātā ca pārvatī devī pitā devo maheśvaraḥ
bāndhavāḥ śivabhaktāśca svadeśo bhuvanatrayam
Our Mother is the Goddess, Pārvatī, and our Father is the Supreme Lord, Maheśvara. The Consciousness of Infinite Goodness, Śiva, Lord of the three worlds, is being extolled by his devotees.

ॐ नमः शिवाय भोगनैवेद्यम् समर्पयामि

oṃ namaḥ śivāya bhog-naivedyam samarpayāmi
With this presentation of food oṃ I bow to the Consciousness of Infinite Goodness.

drinking water

ॐ समस्तदेवदेवेश सर्वतृप्तिकरं परम् ।

अखण्डानन्दसम्पूर्णं गृहाण जलमुत्तमम् ॥

ॐ नमः शिवाय पानार्थं जलम् समर्पयामि

oṃ samasta devadeveśa sarvatṛptikaraṃ param
akhaṇḍānanda sampūrṇaṃ gṛhāṇa jalamuttamam
oṃ namaḥ śivāya pānārthaṃ jalam samarpayāmi
Lord of All the Gods and the fullness of Infinite Bliss, please accept this excellent drinking water. With this offering of drinking water oṃ I bow to the Consciousness of Infinite Goodness.

betel-nuts

पूगीफलं महद्दिव्यं नागवल्ली दलैर्युतम् ।

एलादिचूर्णसंयुक्तं ताम्बूलं प्रतिगृह्यताम् ॥

ॐ नमः शिवाय ताम्बूलं समर्पयामि

pūgīphalaṃ mahaddivyaṃ nāgavallī dalairyutam
elādicūrṇasaṃyuktaṃ tāmbūlaṃ pratigṛhyatām
oṃ namaḥ śivāya tāmbūlaṃ samarpayāmi

These betel-nuts, which are great and divine, come from vines that creep like a snake. United with cardamom ground to a powder, please accept this offering of mouth freshening betel nuts. With this offering of mouth freshening betel-nuts oṃ I bow to the Consciousness of Infinite Goodness.

dakṣiṇā

ॐ पूजाफलसमृद्ध्यर्थं तवाग्रे स्वर्णमीश्वरि ।
स्थापितं तेन मे प्रीता पूर्णान् कुरु मनोरथान् ॥

oṃ pūjāphalasmṛddhyarthaṃ tavāgre svarṇamīśvari
sthāpitaṃ tena me prītā pūrṇān kuru manorathān

oṃ For the purpose of increasing the fruits of worship, Oh Supreme Goddess of all Wealth, we establish this offering of that which is dear to me. Bring to perfection the journey of my mind.

हिरण्यगर्भगर्भस्थं हेमबीजं विभावसोः ।
अनन्तपुण्यफलदमतः शान्तिं प्रयच्छ मे ॥

hiraṅyagarbhagarbhasthaṃ hemabījaṃ vibhāvasoḥ
anantapuṇyaphaladamataḥ śāntiṃ prayaccha me

Oh Golden Womb, in whom all wombs are situated, shining brightly with the golden seed. Give infinite merits as fruits, we are wanting for Peace.

ॐ नमः शिवाय दक्षिणां समर्पयामि

oṃ namaḥ śivāya dakṣiṇāṃ samarpayāmi

With this offering of wealth oṃ I bow to the Consciousness of Infinite Goodness.

umbrella

छत्रं देव जगद्धातर ! घर्मवातप्रणाशनम् ।

गृहाण हे महामाये ! सौभाग्यं सर्वदा कुरु ॥

ॐ नमः शिवाय छत्रं समर्पयामि

chatraṃ deva jagaddhātar !
gharma vāta praṇāśanam
gṛhāṇa he mahāmāye ! saubhāgyaṃ sarvadā kuru
oṃ namaḥ śivāya chatraṃ samarpayāmi

Oh God, Creator of the Universe! This umbrella will protect you from heat and wind. Please accept it, oh Great Māyā, and remain always beautiful. With this offering of an umbrella oṃ I bow to the Consciousness of Infinite Goodness.

fly whisk

चामरं हे महादेव ! चमरीपुच्छनिर्मितम् ।

गृहीत्वा पापराशीनां खण्डनं सर्वदा कुरु ॥

ॐ नमः शिवाय चामरं समर्पयामि

cāmaraṃ he mahādeva ! camarīpucchanirmitam
gṛhītvā pāparāśīnāṃ khaṇḍanaṃ sarvadā kuru
oṃ namaḥ śivāya cāmaraṃ samarpayāmi

Oh Great God, this fly whisk is made of yak's tail. Please accept it, and always whisk away all sin. With this offering of a fly whisk oṃ I bow to the Consciousness of Infinite Goodness.

fan

बर्हिर्बर्हकृताकारं मध्यदण्डसमन्वितम् ।
गृह्यतां व्यजनं देव देहस्वेदापनुत्तये ॥
ॐ नमः शिवाय तालवृन्तं समर्पयामि

barhirbarhakṛtākāraṃ madhyadaṇḍa samanvitam
gṛhyatāṃ vyajanaṃ deva dehasvedāpanuttaye
oṃ namaḥ śivāya tālavṛntaṃ samarpayāmi

It moves back and forth with equanimity and has a stick in the middle. Please accept this fan, oh God, to keep the perspiration from your body. With this offering of a fan oṃ I bow to the Consciousness of Infinite Goodness.

mirror

दर्पणं विमलं रम्यं शुद्धबिम्बप्रदायकम् ।
आत्मबिम्बप्रदर्शनार्थर्पयामि महेश्वर ! ॥
ॐ नमः शिवाय दर्पणं समर्पयामि

darpaṇaṃ vimalaṃ ramyaṃ
śuddhabimbapradāyakam
ātmabimbapradarśanārtharpayāmi maheśvara !
oṃ namaḥ śivāya darpaṇaṃ samarpayāmi

This beautiful mirror will give a pure reflection. In order to reflect my soul, I am offering it to you, oh Great Seer of all. With this offering of a mirror oṃ I bow to the Consciousness of Infinite Goodness.

ārātrikam

ॐ चन्द्रादित्यौ च धरणी विद्युदग्निस्तथैव च ।
त्वमेव सर्वज्योतीषिं आरात्रिकं प्रतिगृह्यताम् ॥
ॐ नमः शिवाय आरात्रिकं समर्पयामि

oṃ candrādityau ca dharaṇī vidyudagnistathaiva ca
tvameva sarvajyotīṣiṃ ārātrikaṃ pratigṛhyatām
oṃ namaḥ śivāya ārātrikaṃ samarpayāmi

All knowing as the Moon, the Sun and the Divine Fire, you alone are all light, and this light we request you to accept. With the offering of light oṃ I bow to the Consciousness of Infinite Goodness.

flower

मल्लिकादि सुगन्धीनि मालित्यादीनि वै प्रभो ।
मयाऽहृतानि पूजार्थं पुष्पाणि प्रतिगृह्यताम् ॥
ॐ नमः शिवाय पुष्पम् समर्पयामि

mallikādi sugandhīni mālityādīni vai prabho
mayā-hṛtāni pūjārthaṃ puṣpāṇi pratigṛhyatām
oṃ namaḥ śivāya puṣpam samarpayāmi

Various flowers such as mallikā and others of excellent scent, are being offered to you, Our Lord. All these flowers have come from the devotion of our hearts for your worship. Be pleased to accept them. With the offering of flowers oṃ I bow to the Consciousness of Infinite Goodness.

अथ शिव कवचं

atha śiva kavacaṃ

श‍ृणु देवि प्रवक्ष्यामि कवचं सर्वसिद्धिदं ।
त्रैलोक्यरक्षणं नाम सर्वपद्विनिवारणं ॥

śṛṇu devi pravakṣyāmi kavacaṃ sarvasiddhidaṃ
trailokyarakṣaṇaṃ nāma sarvapadvinivāraṇaṃ

Listen, Oh Goddess, as I elucidate the armor of all perfection, the name which protects the three worlds, restraining all negativity.

वक्त्रकोटिसहस्रैस्तु देवकोटिशतैरपि ।
कवचस्य गुणान् वक्त्रुं नैव शक्तो महेश्वरः ॥

vaktrakoṭisahasraistu devakoṭiśtairapi
kavacasya guṇān vaktruṃ naiva śakto maheśvaraḥ

Not even hundreds or thousands of mouths, nor the Gods, nor even Maheśvara, the Great Lord (or Great Seer of All) Himself, possess the capacity to proclaim the qualities of this armor.

ॐकारो मे मुखं पातु नकारः कर्णदेशके ।
मकारः पातु शिरसि शिकारो हृदये मम ॥

oṃkāro me mukhaṃ pātu nakāraḥ karṇadeśake
makāraḥ pātu śirasi śikāro hṛdaye mama

May the letter Oṃ protect me in the face (or mouth), the letter Na in the area of the ears. May the letter Ma protect the crown of the head, while the letter Śi will protect in my heart.

वाकारोनेत्रयुग्मे च यकारो बाहु युग्मक ।
अकारस्तु मुखे पातु उकारो हृदये मम ॥

vākāronetrayugme ca yakāro bāhu yugmaka
akārastu mukhe pātu ukāro hṛdaye mama

And the letter Va in the two eyes, while the letter Ya will protect in the two arms. Let the letter A protect in the face, while the letter U in my heart.

मकारः पृष्ठदेशे च पञ्चार्णः पातु सर्वतः ।
इति ते कथितं देवि कवचं सर्वसिद्धिदं ॥

makāraḥ pṛṣṭhadeśe ca pañcārṇaḥ pātu sarvataḥ
iti te kathitaṃ devi kavacaṃ sarvasiddhidaṃ

May the letter M protect on the back side, and the five letters protect all over. This, Oh Goddess, is the explanation of all perfection,

त्रैलोक्य रक्षणं नाम सर्वसिद्धिप्रदायकं ।
कण्ठ वा दक्षिणे बाहौ कवचस्य च धारणात् ॥

trailokya rakṣaṇaṃ nāma sarvasiddhipradāyakaṃ
kaṇṭha vā dakṣiṇe bāhau kavacasya ca dhāraṇāt

the name which protects the three worlds, grantor of all perfection. If one wears such an armor at the base of the throat or on the right arm,

सर्वपापविनिर्म्मुक्तः स भवेन्नात्र संशयः ॥

sarvapāpavinirmuktaḥ sa bhavennātra saṃśayaḥ

he will be released from the bonds all sin, of this there is no doubt.

शिव शतनाम

one hundred eight names of śiva

- 1 -

ॐ शिवाय नमः

oṃ śivāya namaḥ

oṃ we bow to the Consciousness of Infinite Goodness.

- 2 -

ॐ महेश्वराय नमः

oṃ maheśvarāya namaḥ

oṃ we bow to the great seer of all.

- 3 -

ॐ शम्भवे नमः

oṃ śambhave namaḥ

oṃ we bow to he whose reality is peace.

- 4 -

ॐ पिनाकिने नमः

oṃ pinākine namaḥ

oṃ we bow to he who holds the trident.

- 5 -

ॐ शशिशेखराय नमः

oṃ śaśiśekharāya namaḥ

oṃ we bow to he upon whose head resides the moon.

- 6 -

ॐ वामदेवाय नमः

oṃ vāmadevāya namaḥ

oṃ we bow the beautiful god of love.

-7 -

ॐ विरूपाक्षाय नमः

oṃ virūpākṣāya namaḥ

oṃ we bow to he whose eyes see beyond form.

- 8 -

ॐ कपर्दिने नमः

oṃ kapardine namaḥ

oṃ we bow to he who holds a head.

- 9 -

ॐ नीलल्लोहिताय नमः

oṃ nīlalohitāya namaḥ

oṃ we bow to he who is red and blue.

- 10 -

ॐ शङ्कराय नमः

oṃ śaṅkarāya namaḥ

oṃ we bow to the cause of peace.

- 11 -

ॐ शूलपाणये नमः

oṃ śūlapāṇaye namaḥ

oṃ we bow to he with spear in hand.

- 12 -

ॐ खट्वांगिने नमः

oṃ khaṭvāṃgine namaḥ

oṃ we bow to he who holds a staff (or missiles of consciousness).

- 13 -

ॐ विष्णुबल्लभाय नमः

oṃ visṇuballabhāya namaḥ

oṃ we bow to the strength of Vishnu.

- 14 -

ॐ शिपिविष्टाय नमः

oṃ śipiviṣṭāya namaḥ

oṃ we bow to he who is present again and again.

- 15 -

ॐ अम्बिकानाथाय नमः

oṃ ambikānāthāya namaḥ

oṃ we bow to the lord of the mother of the universe.

- 16 -

ॐ श्रीकण्ठाय नमः

oṃ śrīkaṇṭhāya namaḥ

oṃ we bow to he within whose throat the Goddess of Respect dwells.

- 17 -

ॐ भक्तवत्सलाय नमः

oṃ bhaktavatsalāya namaḥ

oṃ we bow to he who loves his devotees.

- 18 -

ॐ भवाय नमः

oṃ bhavāya namaḥ

oṃ we bow to he who is the intensity of reality.

- 19 -

ॐ शर्वाय नमः

oṃ śarvāya namaḥ

oṃ we bow to he who is all.

- 20 -

ॐ त्रिलोकेशाय नमः

oṃ trilokeśāya namaḥ

oṃ we bow to the ruler of the three worlds.

- 21 -

ॐ शितिकण्ठाय नमः

oṃ śitikaṇṭhāya namaḥ

oṃ we bow to he who has a blue neck.

- 22 -

ॐ शिवाप्रियाय नमः

oṃ śivāpriyāya namaḥ

oṃ we bow to the beloved of the mother of the universe.

- 23 -

ॐ उग्राय नमः

oṃ ugrāya namaḥ

oṃ we bow to he who is fierce.

- 24 -

ॐ कपालिने नमः

oṃ kapāline namaḥ

oṃ we bow to he who bears skulls.

- 25 -

ॐ कामरये नमः

oṃ kāmaraye namaḥ

oṃ we bow to he who controls desire.

-26 -

ॐ महारूपाय नमः

oṃ mahārūpāya namaḥ

oṃ we bow to he who is the great form.

-27 -

ॐ गङ्गाधराय नमः

oṃ gaṅgādharāya namaḥ

oṃ we bow to he who supports the Ganges.

-28 -

ॐ ललाटाक्षाय नमः

oṃ lalāṭākṣāya namaḥ

oṃ we bow to he whose third eye is visible on his forehead.

-29 -

ॐ कालकालाय नमः

oṃ kālakālāya namaḥ

oṃ we bow to he who is time after time.

- 30 -

ॐ कृपानिधये नमः

oṃ kṛpānidhaye namaḥ

oṃ we bow to the giver of grace.

- 31 -

ॐ परशुहस्ताय नमः

oṃ paraśuhastāya namaḥ

oṃ we bow to he who has an axe in his hand.

- 32 -

ॐ मृगपाणये नमः

oṃ mṛgapāṇaye namaḥ

oṃ we bow to he whose hand shows the mṛga mudrā.

- 33 -

ॐ जटाधराय नमः

oṃ jaṭādharāya namaḥ

oṃ we bow to he who wears matted hair.

- 34 -

ॐ कैलासवासिने नमः

oṃ kailāsavāsine namaḥ

oṃ we bow to he who resides on Mount Kailash.

- 35 -

ॐ भीमाय नमः

oṃ bhīmāya namaḥ

oṃ we bow to he who is fearless.

- 36 -

ॐ कवचिने नमः

oṃ kavacine namaḥ

oṃ we bow to he who is an armor for protection.

- 37 -

ॐ कठोराय नमः

oṃ kaṭhorāya namaḥ

oṃ we bow to he who is solid.

- 38 -

ॐ त्रिपूरान्तकाय नमः

oṃ tripūrāntakāya namaḥ

oṃ we bow to he who is the limit of the three cities.

- 39 -

ॐ वृषाङ्काय नमः

oṃ vṛṣāṅkāya namaḥ

oṃ we bow to he who travels with a bull.

- 40 -

ॐ वृषभारुढाय नमः

oṃ vṛṣabhāruḍhāya namaḥ

oṃ we bow to he who sits on a bull.

- 41 -

ॐ सर्वकर्मणे नमः

oṃ sarvakarmaṇe namaḥ

oṃ we bow to he who is all karma.

- 42 -

ॐ सामप्रियाय नमः

oṃ sāmapriyāya namaḥ

oṃ we bow to he who loves all songs.

- 43 -

ॐ स्वरम्याय नमः

oṃ svaramyāya namaḥ

oṃ we bow to he whose praises are sung.

- 44 -

ॐ त्रिमूर्त्तये नमः

oṃ trimūrttaye namaḥ

oṃ we bow to he who is three images of being.

- 45 -

ॐ सिद्धर्थाय नमः

oṃ siddharthāya namaḥ

oṃ we bow to he who is the object of perfection.

- 46 -

ॐ सर्वज्ञाय नमः

oṃ sarvajñāya namaḥ

oṃ we bow to he who is all wisdom.

- 47 -

ॐ परमात्मने नमः

oṃ paramātmane namaḥ

oṃ we bow to he who is the supreme soul.

- 48 -

ॐ मन्त्राये नमः

oṃ mantrāye namaḥ

oṃ we bow to he who is all mantras.

- 49 -

ॐ हविषे नमः

oṃ haviṣe namaḥ

oṃ we bow to he who is all offerings.

- 50 -

ॐ यज्ञाय नमः

oṃ yajñāya namaḥ

oṃ we bow to he who is all sacrifice.

- 51 -

ॐ पञ्चवक्त्राय नमः

oṃ pañcavaktrāya namaḥ

oṃ we bow to he who has five faces.

- 52 -

ॐ सदाशिवाय नमः

oṃ sadāśivāya namaḥ

oṃ we bow to he who is always the Consciousness of Infinite Goodness.

- 53 -

ॐ विश्वेश्वराय नमः

oṃ viśveśvarāya namaḥ

oṃ we bow to he who is the supreme lord of the universe.

- 54 -

ॐ वीरभद्राय नमः

oṃ vīrabhadrāya namaḥ

oṃ we bow to he who is the excellent warrior.

- 55 -

ॐ गणनाथाय नमः

oṃ gaṇanāthāya namaḥ

oṃ we bow to he who is the lord of the multitudes.

- 56 -

ॐ प्रजापतये नमः

oṃ prajāpataye namaḥ

oṃ we bow to he who is the lord of life.

- 57 -

ॐ हिरण्यरेतसे नमः

oṃ hiraṇyaretase namaḥ

oṃ we bow to he who has golden semen.

- 58 -

ॐ दुर्धर्षाय नमः

oṃ durdharṣāya namaḥ

oṃ we bow to he who is difficult to be seen.

- 59 -

ॐ गिरिशाय नमः

oṃ giriśāya namaḥ

oṃ we bow to he who is of the mountains.

- 60 -

ॐ गिरीशाय नमः

oṃ girīśāya namaḥ

oṃ we bow to he who is lord of the mountains.

- 61 -

ॐ अनघाय नमः

oṃ anaghāya namaḥ

oṃ we bow to he who is sinless.

- 62 -

ॐ भुजङ्गभूषणाय नमः

oṃ bhujaṅga bhūṣaṇāya namaḥ

oṃ we bow to he who shines like a cobra.

- 63 -

ॐ भर्गाय नमः

oṃ bhargāya namaḥ

oṃ we bow to he who is wealth.

\- 64 -

ॐ गिरिधन्विने नमः

oṃ giridhanvine namaḥ

oṃ we bow to he who is the wealth of the mountains.

\- 65 -

ॐ गिरिप्रियाय नमः

oṃ giripriyāya namaḥ

oṃ we bow to he who is the beloved of the mountains.

\- 66 -

ॐ अष्टमूर्त्तये नमः

oṃ aṣṭamūrttaye namaḥ

oṃ we bow to he who is eight images of divinity.

\- 67 -

ॐ अनेकात्मने नमः

oṃ anekātmane namaḥ

oṃ we bow to he who is all souls.

\- 68 -

ॐ सात्वकाय नमः

oṃ sātvakāya namaḥ

oṃ we bow to he who is truth.

\- 69 -

ॐ कालाय नमः

oṃ kālāya namaḥ

oṃ we bow to he who is time.

\- 70 -

ॐ शाश्वताय नमः

oṃ śāśvatāya namaḥ

oṃ we bow to he who is eternal.

- 71 -

ॐ खण्डपरशवे नमः

oṃ khaṇḍaparaśave namaḥ

oṃ we bow to he who binds divisions in his net.

- 72 -

ॐ अजाय नमः

oṃ ajāya namaḥ

oṃ we bow to he who is unborn.

- 73 -

ॐ रुद्राय नमः

oṃ rudrāya namaḥ

oṃ we bow to he who relieves suffering.

- 74 -

ॐ कृत्तिवाससे नमः

oṃ kṛttivāsase namaḥ

oṃ we bow to he who resides in all action.

- 75 -

ॐ पुराण्टये नमः

oṃ purāṇṭaye namaḥ

oṃ we bow to he who is old.

- 76 -

ॐ भगवते नमः

oṃ bhagavate namaḥ

oṃ we bow to he who is the supreme divinity.

- 77 -

ॐ प्रमथाधिपाय नमः

oṃ pramathādhipāya namaḥ

oṃ we bow to he who associates with ghosts and goblins.

- 78 -

ॐ मृत्युञ्जयाय नमः

oṃ mṛtyuñjayāya namaḥ

oṃ we bow to he who conquers over death.

- 79 -

ॐ शुक्ष्मतनवे नमः

oṃ śuksmatanave namaḥ

oṃ we bow to he who is the subtle body.

- 80 -

ॐ जगद्व्यापिने नमः

oṃ jagadvyāpine namaḥ

oṃ we bow to he who distinguishes individuals of the world.

- 81 -

ॐ जगद्गुरवे नमः

oṃ jagadgurave namaḥ

oṃ we bow to he who is the guru of the universe.

- 82 -

ॐ सहस्रपदे नमः

oṃ sahasrapade namaḥ

oṃ we bow to he who has thousands of feet.

- 83 -

ॐ व्योमकेशाय नमः

oṃ vyomakeśāya namaḥ

oṃ we bow to he whose hair fills the atmosphere.

- 84 -

ॐ महासेनाय नमः

oṃ mahāsenāya namaḥ

oṃ we bow to he who is the great general.

- 85 -

ॐ जनकाय नमः

oṃ janakāya namaḥ

oṃ we bow to he who is father.

- 86 -

ॐ चारुविक्रमाय नमः

oṃ cāruvikramāya namaḥ

oṃ we bow to he whose motion is pleasing.

- 87 -

ॐ उग्राय नमः

oṃ ugrāya namaḥ

oṃ we bow to he who is terrible.

- 88 -

ॐ भूपतये नमः

oṃ bhūpataye namaḥ

oṃ we bow to he who is the lord of the earth.

- 89 -

ॐ स्थाणवे नमः

oṃ sthāṇave namaḥ

oṃ we bow to he who is the residence of all.

- 90 -

ॐ ब्रह्मणे नमः

oṃ brahmaṇe namaḥ

oṃ we bow to he who is creative consciousness.

- 91 -

ॐ दिगम्बराय नमः

oṃ digambarāya namaḥ

oṃ we bow to he who is clothed in space.

- 92 -

ॐ मृडाय नमः

oṃ mṛḍāya namaḥ

oṃ we bow to he who is the object of search.

- 93 -

ॐ पशुपतये नमः

oṃ paśupataye namaḥ

oṃ we bow to he who is the lord of animals.

- 94 -

ॐ देवाय नमः

oṃ devāya namaḥ

oṃ we bow to he who is god.

- 95 -

ॐ महादेवाय नमः

oṃ mahādevāya namaḥ

oṃ we bow to he who is the great god.

- 96 -

ॐ अव्ययाय नमः

oṃ avyayāya namaḥ

oṃ we bow to he who is the imperishable.

- 97 -

ॐ हरये नमः

oṃ haraye namaḥ

oṃ we bow to he who takes away all.

- 98 -

ॐ महातेजसे नमः

oṃ mahātejase namaḥ

oṃ we bow to he who is the great light.

- 99 -

ॐ भगनेत्रभिदे नमः

oṃ bhaganetrabhide namaḥ

oṃ we bow to he whose eyes sparkle like a tiger.

- 100 -

ॐ देवदेवाय नमः

oṃ devadevāya namaḥ

oṃ we bow to he who is the god of gods.

- 101 -

ॐ अव्यग्राय नमः

oṃ avyagrāya namaḥ

oṃ we bow to he who is indifferent.

- 102 -

ॐ अव्यक्ताय नमः

oṃ avyaktāya namaḥ

oṃ we bow to he who is indivisible.

- 103 -

ॐ अनन्ताय नमः

oṃ anantāya namaḥ

oṃ we bow to he who is infinite.

- 104 -

ॐ सहस्राक्षाय नमः

oṃ sahasrākṣāya namaḥ

oṃ we bow to he who has a thousand eyes.

- 105 -

ॐ मूर्त्तिजाय नमः

oṃ mūrttijāya namaḥ

oṃ we bow to he who is the image of victory.

- 106 -

ॐ तारकाय नमः

oṃ tārakāya namaḥ

oṃ we bow to he who is the illuminator.

- 107 -

ॐ हराय नमः

oṃ harāya namaḥ

oṃ we bow to he within whom all dissolves.

- 108 -

ॐ परमेश्वराय नमः

oṃ parameśvarāya namaḥ

oṃ we bow to the supreme consciousness.

ॐ नापेश्वराय नमः

oṃ nāpeśvarāya namaḥ

oṃ we bow to the residence of Dharma.

ॐ नमः इति

oṃ namaḥ iti

oṃ we bow to the completion.

शिवाष्टकम्

śivāṣṭakam

\- 1 -

प्रभुमीशमनीशमशेषगुणं
गुणहीनमहीशगराभरणम् ।
रणनिर्जितदुर्जयदैत्यपुरं
प्रणमामि शिवं शिवकल्पतरुम् ॥

prabhumīśamanīśamaśeṣaguṇaṃ
guṇahīnamahīśagarābharaṇam
raṇanirjitadurjayadaityapuraṃ
praṇamāmi śivaṃ śivakalpatarum

The Lord, who resides in the mind with infinite qualties, is also without qualities, the Lord who digested poison. It is impossible to defeat Him in battle. He vanquished the most formidable beings of duality. We bow down to Śiva, the Consciousness of Infinite Goodness, who is as a tree which gives forth the fruit of all desires.

\- 2 -

गिरिराजसुतान्वितवामतनुं
तनुनिन्दितराजितकोटिविधुम् ।
विधिविष्णुशिरोधृतपादयुगं
प्रणमामि शिवं शिवकल्पतरुम् ॥

girirājasutānvitavāmatunuṃ
tanuninditarājitakoṭividhum
vidhiviṣṇuśirodhṛtapādayugaṃ
praṇamāmi śivaṃ śivakalpatarum

Seated at His left side is the daughter of the mountains, He embodies infinite manifestations which can be known.

Brahma and Viṣṇu bow their heads to His feet. We bow down to Śiva, the Consciousness of Infinite Goodness, who is as a tree which gives forth the fruit of all desires.

- 3 -

शशलञ्छितरञ्जितसन्मुकुटं
कटिलम्बितसुन्दरकृत्तिपटम् ।
सुरशैवलिनीकृतपूतजटं
प्रणमामि शिवं शिवकल्पतरुम् ॥

śaśalañchitarañjitasanmukuṭaṃ
kaṭilambitasundarakṛttipaṭam
surśaivalinīkṛtapūtajaṭaṃ
praṇamāmi śivaṃ śivakalpatarum

Wearing the Moon of Devotion as an ornament on His crown, He wears infinite manifestations of beautiful creation. The Gods and worshipers of Śiva see Him with matted hair down to His buttocks. We bow down to Śiva, the Consciousness of Infinite Goodness, who is as a tree which gives forth the fruit of all desires.

- 4 -

नयनत्रयभूषितचारुमुखं
मुखपद्मपराजितकोटिविधुम् ।
विधुखण्डविमण्डितभालतटं
प्रणमामि शिवं शिवकल्पतरुम् ॥

nayanatraya bhūṣitacārumukhaṃ
mukhapadmaparājitakoṭividhum
vidhukhaṇḍavimaṇḍitabhālataṭaṃ
praṇamāmi śivaṃ śivakalpatarum

The three eyes are shining from that handsome face, and His lotus face defeats all with the infinity of knowledge it conveys. That knowledge is distinguished by the marks on His forehead. We bow down to Śiva, the Consciousness of Infinite Goodness, who is as a tree which gives forth the fruit of all desires.

- 5 -

वृषराजनिकेतनमादिगुरुं

गरलाशनमाजिविषाणधरम् ।

प्रमथाधिपसेवकरञ्जनकं

प्रणमामि शिवं शिवकल्पतरुम् ॥

vṛṣrājaniketanamādigurum
garalāśanamājiviṣaṇadharam
pramathādhipasevakarañjanakaṃ
praṇamāmi śivaṃ śivakalpatarum

We bow to the Supreme Teacher who is sitting on a bull, who saved all that lives by drinking poison. He is served with great delight by disembodied spirits. We bow down to Śiva, the Consciousness of Infinite Goodness, who is as a tree which gives forth the fruit of all desires.

- 6 -

मकरध्वजमत्तमतङ्गहरं

करिचर्मगनागविबोधकरम् ।

वरमार्गणशूलविषाणधरं

प्रणमामि शिवं शिवकल्पतरुम् ॥

makaradhvajamattamataṅgaharaṃ
karicarmaganāgavibodhakaram
varamārgaṇaśūlaviṣāṇadharaṃ
praṇamāmi śivaṃ śivakalpatarum

Who took away the foolish thoughts of the one with a crocodile on his flag (Kāmadeva, the Lord of Love), He is known to wear an elephant's skin and a cobra snake around His neck. He gives boons and holds a spear in His hand. We bow down to Śiva, the Consciousness of Infinite Goodness, who is as a tree which gives forth the fruit of all desires.

- 7 -

जगदुद्भवपालननाशकरं
त्रिदिवेशशिरोमणिघृष्टपदम् ।
प्रियमानवसाधुजनैकगतिं
प्रणमामि शिवं शिवकल्पतरुम् ॥

jagadudbhavapālananāśakaraṃ
tridiveśaśiromaṇighṛṣṭapadam
priyamānavasādhujanaikagatiṃ
praṇamāmi śivaṃ śivakalpatarum

He creates the perceiveable world, protects and destroys it, all place the crest jewels of their crowns at the feet of the Lord of the three worlds. He is beloved by mankind and sādhus, for all beings born there is only one refuge. We bow down to Śiva, the Consciousness of Infinite Goodness, who is as a tree which gives forth the fruit of all desires.

- 8 -

न दत्तं पुष्पं सदा पापचित्तं
पुनर्जन्मदुःखात् परित्राहि शम्भो ।
भजतोऽखिलदुःखसमिद्धहरं
प्रणमामि शिवं शिवकल्पतरुम् ॥

na dattaṃ puṣpaṃ sadā pāpacittaṃ
punarjanmaduḥkhāt paritrāhi śambho
bhajato-khiladuḥkhasamiddhaharaṃ
praṇamāmi śivaṃ śivakalpatarum

These flowers are always the ambassador offering my evil thoughts, so that Śambho, Who Radiates Peace, will take away the pain from my future lives. We celebrate He who Takes Away all pain as the offering of worship. We bow down to Śiva, the Consciousness of Infinite Goodness, who is as a tree which gives forth the fruit of all desires.

शिव यज्ञ पद्धोति

Śiva Yajña Paddhoti

The System of Worship of the Sacred Fire

एते गन्धपुष्पे वह्नेर्योगपीठाय नमः

ete gandhapuṣpe vahneryogapīṭhāya namaḥ

With these scented flowers we bow to the place of union with the divine fire.

एते गन्धपुष्पे वह्निचैतन्याय नमः

ete gandhapuṣpe vāhnicaitanyāya namaḥ

With these scented flowers we bow to the Consciousness of the Divine Fire.

एते गन्धपुष्पे ॐ अग्नि मूर्त्तये नमः

ete gandhapuṣpe oṃ agni mūrttaye namaḥ

With these scented flowers we bow to deified image of the Divine Fire.

सोभयस्यास्य देवस्य विग्रहो यन्त्र कल्पणा ।
विना यन्त्रेण चेत्पूजा देवता न प्रसीदति ॥

sobhayasyāsya devasya vigraho yantra kalpaṇā
vinā yantreṇa cetpūjā devatā na prasīdati

We contemplate the form of the yantra which depicts the radiance of the Gods. Without using the yantra in the worship of consciousness the Gods are not as pleased.

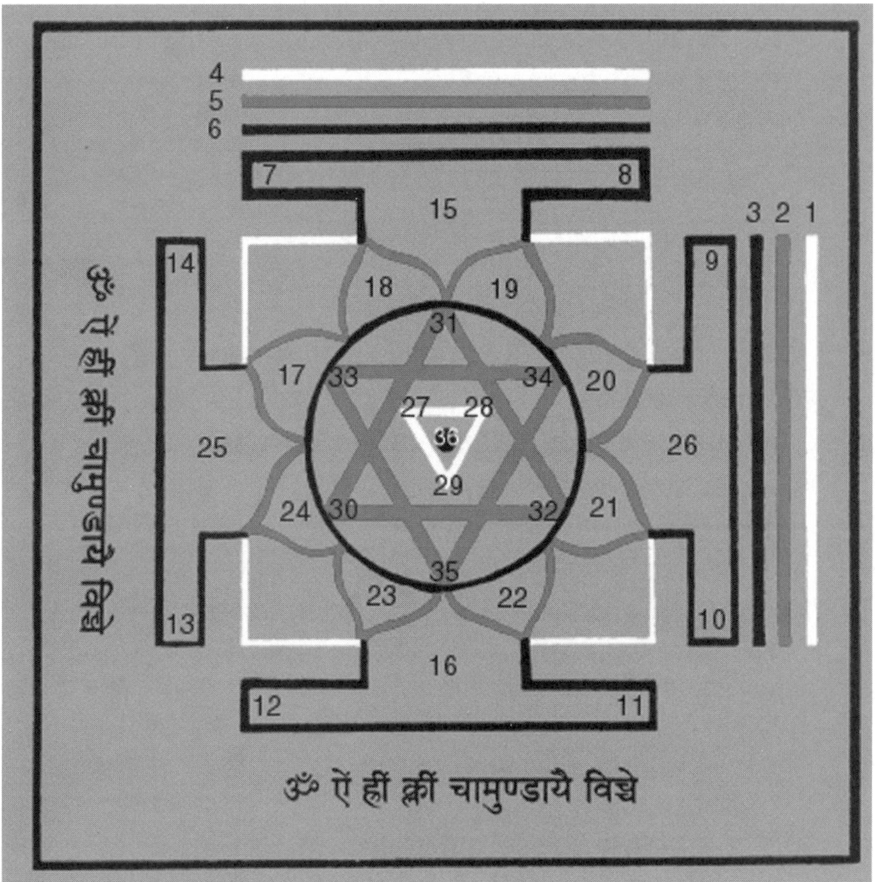

यन्त्र मन्त्रमयं प्रहुर्देवता मन्त्ररूपिणी ।
यन्त्रेणापूजितो देवः सहसा न प्रसीदति ।
सर्वेषामपि मन्त्रणां यन्त्र पूजा प्रशस्यते ॥

yantra mantramayaṃ prahurdevatā mantrarūpiṇī
yantreṇāpūjito devaḥ sahasā na prasīdati
sarveṣāmapi mantraṇāṃ yantra pūjā praśasyate

The yantra conveys the objective meaning of the mantra, while the deity is the form of the mantra. By worshiping the deity by means of the yantra, the deity is completely satisfied. To attain all the bliss of the mantra, the worship of the yantra is highly recommended.

ततः स्थण्डिलमध्ये तु हसौःगर्भं त्रिकोणकम् ।
षट्कोणं तद्वहिर्वृत्तां ततोऽष्टदलपङ्कजम् ।
भूपुरं तद्वहिर्विद्वान् विलिखेद्यन्त्रमुत्तमम् ॥

tataḥ sthaṇḍilamadhye tu hasauḥgarbhaṃ trikoṇakam
ṣaṭkoṇaṃ tadvahirvṛttāṃ tato-ṣṭadalapaṅkajam
bhūpuraṃ tadvahirvidvān vilikhedhyantramuttamam

In the center of the place of worship is the single point which contains ha and sauḥ, Śiva and Śakti without distinction. Thereafter comes the three cornered equalateral triangle. Then six angles, outside of which is a circle, followed by eight lotus petals. The four doors are outside, and in this way the wise will draw the most excellent yantra.

ॐ यन्त्रराजाय विद्महे महायन्त्राय धीमहे ।
तन्नो यन्त्रः प्रचोदयात् ॥

oṃ yantrarājāya vidmahe mahāyantrāya dhīmahe
tanno yantraḥ pracodayāt

oṃ we meditate upon the King of Yantras, contemplate the greatest yantra. May that yantra grant us increase.

ॐ परमेश्वराय विद्महे परातत्त्वाय धीमहे ।
तन्नो ब्रह्माः प्रचोदयात् ॥

oṃ parameśvarāya vidmahe parātattvāya dhīmahe tanno brahmāḥ pracodayāt

oṃ we meditate upon the Highest Supreme Divinity, contemplate the Highest Principle. May that Supreme Divinity grant us increase.

- 1 -

ॐ मुकुन्दाय नमः

oṃ mukundāya namaḥ

oṃ I bow to the Giver of Liberation.

- 2 -

ॐ ईशनाय नमः

oṃ īśanāya namaḥ

oṃ I bow to the Ruler of All.

- 3 -

ॐ पुरन्दराय नमः

oṃ purandarāya namaḥ

oṃ I bow to the Giver of Completeness.

- 4 -

ॐ ब्रह्मणे नमः

oṃ brahmaṇe namaḥ

oṃ I bow to the Creative Consciousness.

- 5 -

ॐ वैवस्वताय नमः

oṃ vaivasvatāya namaḥ

oṃ I bow to the Universal Radiance.

- 6 -

ॐ इन्दवे नमः

oṃ indave namaḥ

oṃ I bow to the Ruler of Devotion.

- 7 -

ॐ आधारशक्तये नमः

oṃ ādhāraśaktaye namaḥ

oṃ I bow to the primal energy which sustains existence.

- 8 -

ॐ कुर्म्माय नमः

oṃ kurmmāya namaḥ

oṃ I bow to the Tortoise which supports creation.

- 9 -

ॐ अनन्ताय नमः

oṃ anantāya namaḥ

oṃ I bow to Infinity (personified as a thousand hooded snake who stands upon the Tortoise holding aloft the worlds).

- 10 -

ॐ पृथिव्यै नमः

oṃ pṛthivyai namaḥ

oṃ I bow to the Earth.

- 11 -

ॐ क्षीरसमूद्राय नमः

oṃ kṣīrasamūdrāya namaḥ

oṃ I bow to the milk ocean, or ocean of nectar, the infinite expanse of existence from which all manifested.

- 12 -

ॐ श्वेतद्वीपाय नमः

oṃ śvetadvīpāya namaḥ

oṃ I bow to the Island of Purity, which is in the ocean.

- 13 -

ॐ मणिमन्दपाय नमः

oṃ maṇimandapāya namaḥ
oṃ I bow to the Palace of Gems, which is on the island, the home of the Divine Mother.

- 14 -

ॐ कल्पवृक्षाय नमः

oṃ kalpavṛkṣāya namaḥ
oṃ I bow to the Tree of Fulfillment, which satisfies all desires, growing in the palace courtyard.

- 15 -

ॐ मणिवेदिकायै नमः

oṃ maṇivedikāyai namaḥ
oṃ I bow to the altar containing the gems of wisdom.

- 16 -

ॐ रत्नसिंहासनाय नमः

oṃ ratnasiṃhāsanāya namaḥ
oṃ I bow to the throne of the jewel.

- 17 -

ॐ धर्म्माय नमः

oṃ dharmmāya namaḥ
oṃ I bow to the Way of Truth and Harmony.

- 18 -

ॐ ज्ञानाय नमः

oṃ jñānāya namaḥ
oṃ I bow to Wisdom.

- 19 -

ॐ वैराग्याय नमः

oṃ vairāgyāya namaḥ
oṃ I bow to Detachment.

- 20 -

ॐ ईश्वर्ज्याय नमः

oṃ īśvarjyāya namaḥ

oṃ I bow to the Imperishable Qualities.

- 21 -

ॐ अधर्म्माय नमः

oṃ adharmmāya namaḥ

oṃ I bow to Disharmony.

- 22 -

ॐ अज्ञानाय नमः

oṃ ajñānāya namaḥ

oṃ I bow to Ignorance.

- 23 -

ॐ अवैराग्याय नमः

oṃ avairāgyāya namaḥ

oṃ I bow to Attachment.

- 24 -

ॐ अनीश्वर्ज्याय नमः

oṃ anīśvarjyāya namaḥ

oṃ I bow to the Transient.

- 25 -

ॐ अनन्ताय नमः

oṃ anantāya namaḥ

oṃ I bow to the Infinite.

- 26 -

ॐ पद्माय नमः

oṃ padmāya namaḥ

oṃ I bow to the Lotus.

- 27 -

अं अर्कमण्डलाय द्वादशकलात्मने नमः

aṃ arkamaṇḍalāya dvādaśakalātmane namaḥ

"A" we bow to the twelve aspects of the realm of the sun. Tapinī, Tāpinī, Dhūmrā, Marīci, Jvālinī, Ruci, Sudhūmrā, Bhoga-dā, Viśvā, Bodhinī, Dhārinī, Kṣamā; Containing heat, Emanating heat, Smoky, Ray-producing, Burning, Lustrous, Purple or Smoky-red, Granting enjoyment, Universal, Which makes known, Productive of Consciousness, Which supports, Which forgives.

- 28 -

उं सोममण्डलाय षोडशकलात्मने नमः

uṃ somamaṇḍalāya ṣoḍaśakalātmane namaḥ

"U" we bow to the sixteen aspects of the realm of the moon. Amṛtā, Prāṇadā, Puṣā, Tuṣṭi, Puṣṭi, Rati, Dhṛti, Śaśinī, Candrikā, Kānti, Jyotsnā, Śrī, Prīti, Aṅgadā, Pūrṇā, Pūrṇāmṛtā; Nectar, Which sustains life, Which supports, Satisfying, Nourishing, Playful, Constancy, Unfailing, Producer of Joy, Beauty enhanced by love, Light, Grantor of Prosperity, Affectionate, Purifying the body, Complete, Full of Bliss.

- 29 -

मं वह्निमण्डलाय दशकलात्मने नमः

maṃ vahnimaṇḍalāya daśakalātmane namaḥ

"M" we bow to the ten aspects of the realm of fire: Dhūmrā, Arciḥ, Jvalinī, Śūkṣmā, Jvālinī, Visphuliṅginī, Suśrī, Surūpā, Kapilā, Havya-Kavya-Vahā; Smoky Red, Flaming, Shining, Subtle, Burning, Sparkling, Beautiful, Well-formed, Tawny, The Messenger to Gods and Ancestors.

- 30 -

ॐ सं सत्त्वाय नमः

oṃ saṃ sattvāya namaḥ

oṃ I bow to activity, execution, light, knowledge, being.

- 31 -

ॐ रं रजसे नमः

oṃ raṃ rajase namaḥ

oṃ I bow to desire, inspiration, becoming.

- 32 -

ॐ तं तमसे नमः

oṃ taṃ tamase namaḥ

oṃ I bow to wisdom, to the darkness which exposes light, to rest.

- 33 -

ॐ आं आत्मने नमः

oṃ āṃ ātmane namaḥ

oṃ I bow to the Soul.

- 34 -

ॐ अं अन्तरात्मने नमः

oṃ aṃ antarātmane namaḥ

oṃ I bow to the Innermost Soul.

- 35 -

ॐ पं परमात्मने नमः

oṃ paṃ paramātmane namaḥ

oṃ I bow to the Universal Soul, or the Consciousness which exceeds manifestation.

- 36 -

ॐ ह्रीं ज्ञानात्मने नमः

oṃ hrīṃ jñānātmane namaḥ

oṃ I bow to the Soul of Infinite Wisdom.

सर्वतो भद्रमण्डल देवता स्थापनम्

sarvato bhadramaṇḍala devatā sthāpanam

Establishment of the Excellent Circle of Deities

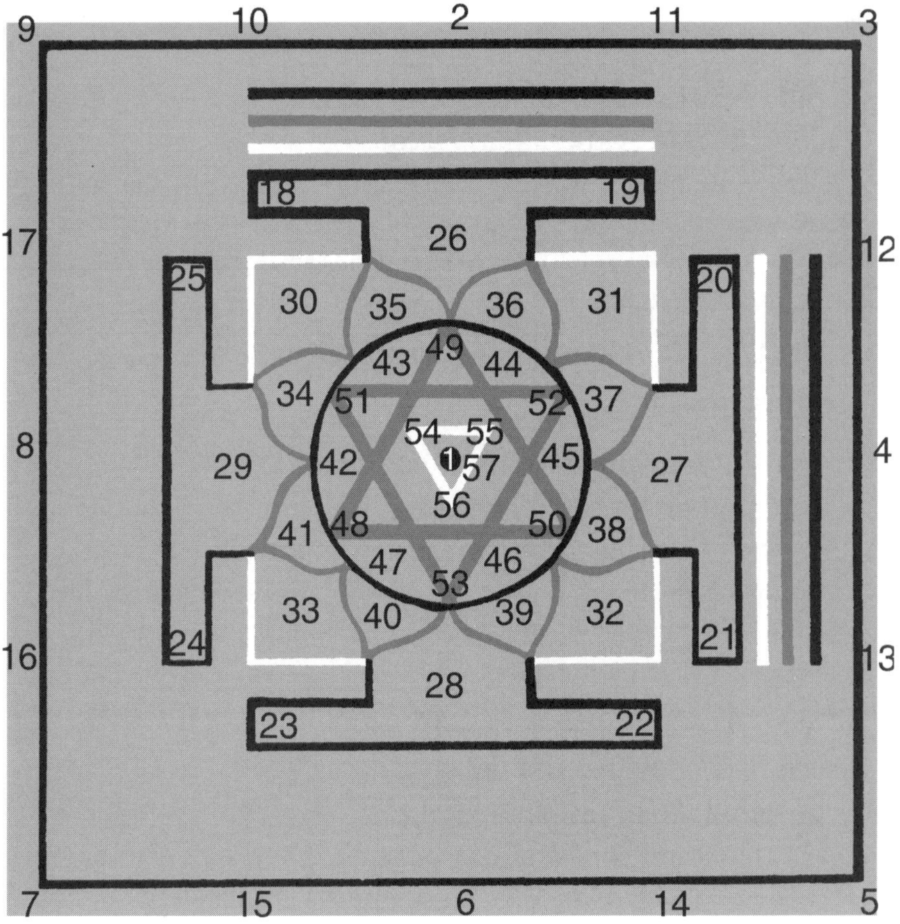

- 1 -

ॐ भूर्भुवः स्वः ब्रह्मणे नमः ब्रह्मणमावाहयामि स्थापयामि

oṃ bhūrbhuvaḥ svaḥ brahmaṇe namaḥ
brahmaṇamāvāhayāmi sthāpayāmi

oṃ the Infinite Beyond Conception, the gross body, the subtle body and the causal body, we bow to the Creative Consciousness (Center). We invoke you, invite you and establish your presence.

- 2 -

ॐ भूर्भुवः स्वः सोमाय नमः सोममावाहयामि स्थापयामि

oṃ bhūrbhuvaḥ svaḥ somāya namaḥ somamāvāhayāmi sthāpayāmi

oṃ the Infinite Beyond Conception, the gross body, the subtle body and the causal body, we bow to the Lord of Devotion (N). We invoke you, invite you and establish your presence.

- 3 -

ॐ भूर्भुवः स्वः ईशानाय नमः ईशानमावाहयामि स्थापयामि

oṃ bhūrbhuvaḥ svaḥ īśānāya namaḥ īśānamāvāhayāmi sthāpayāmi

oṃ the Infinite Beyond Conception, the gross body, the subtle body and the causal body, we bow to the Ruler of All (NE). We invoke you, invite you and establish your presence.

- 4 -

ॐ भूर्भुवः स्वः इन्द्राय नमः इन्द्रमावाहयामि स्थापयामि

oṃ bhūrbhuvaḥ svaḥ indrāya namaḥ indramāvāhayāmi sthāpayāmi

oṃ the Infinite Beyond Conception, the gross body, the subtle body and the causal body, we bow to the Rule of the Pure (E). We invoke you, invite you and establish your presence.

- 5 -

ॐ भूर्भुवः स्वः अग्नये नमः अग्निमावाहयामि स्थापयामि

oṃ bhūrbhuvaḥ svaḥ agnaye namaḥ agnimāvāhayāmi sthāpayāmi

oṃ the Infinite Beyond Conception, the gross body, the subtle body and the causal body, we bow to the Divine Fire (SE). We invoke you, invite you and establish your presence.

- 6 -

ॐ भूर्भुवः स्वः यमाय नमः यममावाहयामि स्थापयामि

oṃ bhūrbhuvaḥ svaḥ yamāya namaḥ yamamāvāhayāmi sthāpayāmi

oṃ the Infinite Beyond Conception, the gross body, the subtle body and the causal body, we bow to the Supreme Controller (S). We invoke you, invite you and establish your presence.

- 7 -

ॐ भूर्भुवः स्वः निर्ऋतये नमः निर्ऋतिमावाहयामि स्थापयामि

oṃ bhūrbhuvaḥ svaḥ nirṛtaye namaḥ nirṛtimāvāhayāmi sthāpayāmi

oṃ the Infinite Beyond Conception, the gross body, the subtle body and the causal body, we bow to the Destroyer (SW). We invoke you, invite you and establish your presence.

- 8 -

ॐ भूर्भुवः स्वः वरुणाय नमः वरुणमावाहयामि स्थापयामि

oṃ bhūrbhuvaḥ svaḥ varuṇāya namaḥ varuṇamāvāhayāmi sthāpayāmi

oṃ the Infinite Beyond Conception, the gross body, the subtle body and the causal body, we bow to the Lord of Equilibrium (W). We invoke you, invite you and establish your presence.

- 9 -

ॐ भूर्भुवः स्वः वायवे नमः वायुमावाहयामि स्थापयामि

oṃ bhūrbhuvaḥ svaḥ vāyave namaḥ vāyumāvāhayāmi sthāpayāmi

oṃ the Infinite Beyond Conception, the gross body, the subtle body and the causal body, we bow to the Lord of Liberation (NW). We invoke you, invite you and establish your presence.

- 10 -

ॐ भूर्भुवः स्वः अष्टवसुभ्यो नमः अष्टवसुन् आवाहयामि स्थापयामि

oṃ bhūrbhuvaḥ svaḥ aṣṭavasubhyo namaḥ aṣṭavasun āvāhayāmi sthāpayāmi

oṃ the Infinite Beyond Conception, the gross body, the subtle body and the causal body, we bow to the Eight Lords of Benificence. We invoke you, invite you and establish your presence.

- 11 -

ॐ भूर्भुवः स्वः एकादशरुद्रेभ्यो नमः एकादशरुद्रानावाहयामि स्थापयामि

oṃ bhūrbhuvaḥ svaḥ ekādaśarudrebhyo namaḥ ekādaśarudrānāvāhayāmi sthāpayāmi

oṃ the Infinite Beyond Conception, the gross body, the subtle body and the causal body, we bow to the Eleven Relievers from Sufferings. We invoke you, invite you and establish your presence.

- 12 -

ॐ भूर्भुवः स्वः द्वादशादित्येभ्यो नमः द्वादशादित्यानावाहयामि स्थापयामि

oṃ bhūrbhuvaḥ svaḥ dvādaśādityebhyo namaḥ dvādaśādityānāvāhayāmi sthāpayāmi

oṃ the Infinite Beyond Conception, the gross body, the subtle body and the causal body, we bow to the Twelve Sons of Light. We invoke you, invite you and establish your presence.

- 13 -

ॐ भूर्भुवः स्वः अश्विभ्यां नमः अश्विनौ आवाहयामि स्थापयामि

oṃ bhūrbhuvaḥ svaḥ aśvibhyāṃ namaḥ aśvinau āvāhayāmi sthāpayāmi

oṃ the Infinite Beyond Conception, the gross body, the subtle body and the causal body, we bow to the Two Horses of Pure Desire. We invoke you, invite you and establish your presence.

- 14 -

ॐ भूर्भुवः स्वः सपैतृकविश्वेभ्यो देवेभ्यो नमः सपैतृकविश्वान् देवानावाहयामि स्थापयामि

oṃ bhūrbhuvaḥ svaḥ sapaitṛkaviśvebhyo devebhyo namaḥ sapaitṛkaviśvān devānāvāhayāmi sthāpayāmi

oṃ the Infinite Beyond Conception, the gross body, the subtle body and the causal body, we bow to the Ancestors along with the Shining Ones of the Universe. We invoke you, invite you and establish your presence.

- 15 -

ॐ भूर्भुवः स्वः सप्तयक्षेभ्यो नमः सप्तयक्षानावाहयामि स्थापयामि

oṃ bhūrbhuvaḥ svaḥ saptayakṣebhyo namaḥ saptayakṣānāvāhayāmi sthāpayāmi

oṃ the Infinite Beyond Conception, the gross body, the subtle body and the causal body, we bow to the Energy which brings the good and bad of wealth. We invoke you, invite you and establish your presence.

- 16 -

ॐ भूर्भुवः स्वः अष्टकुलनागेभ्यो नमः

अष्टकुलनागानावाहयामि स्थापयामि

oṃ bhūrbhuvaḥ svaḥ aṣṭakulanāgebhyo namaḥ aṣṭakulanāgānāvāhayāmi sthāpayāmi

oṃ the Infinite Beyond Conception, the gross body, the subtle body and the causal body, we bow to the Family of eight snakes. We invoke you, invite you and establish your presence.

- 17 -

ॐ भूर्भुवः स्वः गन्धर्वाऽप्सरोभ्यो नमः गन्धर्वाऽप्सरसः

आवाहयामि स्थापयामि

oṃ bhūrbhuvaḥ svaḥ gandharvā-psarobhyo namaḥ gandharvā-psarasaḥ āvāhayāmi sthāpayāmi

oṃ the Infinite Beyond Conception, the gross body, the subtle body and the causal body, we bow to the celestial musicians and heavenly maidens. We invoke you, invite you and establish your presence.

- 18 -

ॐ भूर्भुवः स्वः स्कन्दाय नमः स्कन्दमावाहयामि

स्थापयामि

oṃ bhūrbhuvaḥ svaḥ skandāya namaḥ skandamāvāhayāmi sthāpayāmi

oṃ the Infinite Beyond Conception, the gross body, the subtle body and the causal body, we bow to the God of War. We invoke you, invite you and establish your presence.

- 19 -

ॐ भूर्भुवः स्वः वृषभाय नमः वृषभमावाहयामि स्थापयामि

oṃ bhūrbhuvaḥ svaḥ vṛṣabhāya namaḥ vṛṣabhamāvāhayāmi sthāpayāmi

oṃ the Infinite Beyond Conception, the gross body, the subtle body and the causal body, we bow to the Bull of Discipline, Conveyance of Śiva - Nandi. We invoke you, invite you and establish your presence.

- 20 -

ॐ भूर्भुवः स्वः शूलाय नमः शूलमावाहयामि स्थापयामि

oṃ bhūrbhuvaḥ svaḥ śūlāya namaḥ
śūlamāvāhayāmi sthāpayāmi

oṃ the Infinite Beyond Conception, the gross body, the subtle body and the causal body, we bow to the Spear of Concentration. We invoke you, invite you and establish your presence.

- 21 -

ॐ भूर्भुवः स्वः महाकालाय नमः महाकालमावाहयामि स्थापयामि

oṃ bhūrbhuvaḥ svaḥ mahākālāya namaḥ
mahākālamāvāhayāmi sthāpayāmi

oṃ the Infinite Beyond Conception, the gross body, the subtle body and the causal body, we bow to the Great Time. We invoke you, invite you and establish your presence.

- 22 -

ॐ भूर्भुवः स्वः दक्षादि सप्तगणेभ्यो नमः दक्षादि सप्तगणानावाहयामि स्थापयामि

oṃ bhūrbhuvaḥ svaḥ dakṣādi saptagaṇebhyo
namaḥ dakṣādi
saptagaṇānāvāhayāmi sthāpayāmi

oṃ the Infinite Beyond Conception, the gross body, the subtle body and the causal body, we bow to Ability and the other seven qualities. We invoke you, invite you and establish your presence.

- 23 -

ॐ भूर्भुवः स्वः दुर्गायै नमः दुर्गामावाहयामि स्थापयामि

oṃ bhūrbhuvaḥ svaḥ durgāyai namaḥ durgāmāvāhayāmi sthāpayāmi

oṃ the Infinite Beyond Conception, the gross body, the subtle body and the causal body, we bow to the Reliever of Difficulties. We invoke you, invite you and establish your presence.

- 24 -

ॐ भूर्भुवः स्वः विष्णवे नमः विष्णुमावाहयामि स्थापयामि

oṃ bhūrbhuvaḥ svaḥ viṣṇave namaḥ viṣṇumāvāhayāmi sthāpayāmi

oṃ the Infinite Beyond Conception, the gross body, the subtle body and the causal body, we bow to the All-Pervading Consciousness. We invoke you, invite you and establish your presence.

- 25 -

ॐ भूर्भुवः स्वः स्वधायै नमः स्वधामावाहयामि स्थापयामि

oṃ bhūrbhuvaḥ svaḥ svadhāyai namaḥ svadhāmāvāhayāmi sthāpayāmi

oṃ the Infinite Beyond Conception, the gross body, the subtle body and the causal body, we bow to the Ancestors. We invoke you, invite you and establish your presence.

- 26 -

ॐ भूर्भुवः स्वः मृत्युरोगेभ्यो नमः मृत्युरोगानावाहयामि स्थापयामि

oṃ bhūrbhuvaḥ svaḥ mṛtyurogebhyo namaḥ mṛtyurogānāvāhayāmi sthāpayāmi

oṃ the Infinite Beyond Conception, the gross body, the subtle body and the causal body, we bow to the Spirit of deadly illnesses. We invoke you, invite you and establish your presence.

- 27 -

ॐ भूर्भुवः स्वः गणपतये नमः गणपतिमावाहयामि स्थापयामि

oṃ bhūrbhuvaḥ svaḥ gaṇapataye namaḥ gaṇapatimāvāhayāmi sthāpayāmi

oṃ the Infinite Beyond Conception, the gross body, the subtle body and the causal body, we bow to the Lord of the Multitudes. We invoke you, invite you and establish your presence.

- 28 -

ॐ भूर्भुवः स्वः अद्भ्यो नमः अपः आवाहयामि स्थापयामि

oṃ bhūrbhuvaḥ svaḥ adbhyo namaḥ apaḥ āvāhayāmi sthāpayāmi

oṃ the Infinite Beyond Conception, the gross body, the subtle body and the causal body, we bow to Acts of Sacrifice. We invoke you, invite you and establish your presence.

- 29 -

ॐ भूर्भुवः स्वः मरुद्भ्यो नमः मरुतः आवाहयामि स्थापयामि

oṃ bhūrbhuvaḥ svaḥ marudbhyo namaḥ marutaḥ āvāhayāmi sthāpayāmi

oṃ the Infinite Beyond Conception, the gross body, the subtle body and the causal body, we bow to the Shining Ones. We invoke you, invite you and establish your presence.

- 30 -

ॐ भूर्भुवः स्वः पृथिव्यै नमः पृथ्वीमावाहयामि स्थापयामि

oṃ bhūrbhuvaḥ svaḥ pṛthivyai namaḥ pṛthvīmāvāhayāmi sthāpayāmi

oṃ the Infinite Beyond Conception, the gross body, the subtle body and the causal body, we bow to the Earth. We invoke you, invite you and establish your presence.

- 31 -

ॐ भूर्भुवः स्वः गङ्गादिनदीभ्यो नमः गङ्गादिनदीः आवाहयामि स्थापयामि

oṃ bhūrbhuvaḥ svaḥ gaṅgādinadībhyo namaḥ gaṅgādinadīḥ āvāhayāmi sthāpayāmi

oṃ the Infinite Beyond Conception, the gross body, the subtle body and the causal body, we bow to the Ganges and other rivers. We invoke you, invite you and establish your presence.

- 32 -

ॐ भूर्भुवः स्वः सप्तसागरेभ्यो नमः सप्तसागरानावाहयामि स्थापयामि

oṃ bhūrbhuvaḥ svaḥ saptasāgarebhyo namaḥ saptasāgarānāvāhayāmi sthāpayāmi

oṃ the Infinite Beyond Conception, the gross body, the subtle body and the causal body, we bow to the Seven Seas. We invoke you, invite you and establish your presence.

- 33 -

ॐ भूर्भुवः स्वः मेरवे नमः मेरुमावाहयामि स्थापयामि

oṃ bhūrbhuvaḥ svaḥ merave namaḥ merumāvāhayāmi sthāpayāmi

oṃ the Infinite Beyond Conception, the gross body, the subtle body and the causal body, we bow to Mount Meru. We invoke you, invite you and establish your presence.

- 34 -

ॐ भूर्भुवः स्वः गदाय नमः गदामावाहयामि स्थापयामि

oṃ bhūrbhuvaḥ svaḥ gadāya namaḥ gadāmāvāhayāmi sthāpayāmi

oṃ the Infinite Beyond Conception, the gross body, the subtle body and the causal body, we bow to the Club. We invoke you, invite you and establish your presence.

- 35 -

ॐ भूर्भुवः स्वः त्रिशूलाय नमः त्रिशूलमावाहयामि स्थापयामि

oṃ bhūrbhuvaḥ svaḥ triśūlāya namaḥ triśūlamāvāhayāmi sthāpayāmi

oṃ the Infinite Beyond Conception, the gross body, the subtle body and the causal body, we bow to the Trident. We invoke you, invite you and establish your presence.

- 36 -

ॐ भूर्भुवः स्वः वज्राय नमः वज्रमावाहयामि स्थापयामि

oṃ bhūrbhuvaḥ svaḥ vajrāya namaḥ vajramāvāhayāmi sthāpayāmi

oṃ the Infinite Beyond Conception, the gross body, the subtle body and the causal body, we bow to the Thunderbolt. We invoke you, invite you and establish your presence.

- 37 -

ॐ भूर्भुवः स्वः शक्तये नमः शक्तिमावाहयामि स्थापयामि

oṃ bhūrbhuvaḥ svaḥ śaktaye namaḥ śaktimāvāhayāmi sthāpayāmi

oṃ the Infinite Beyond Conception, the gross body, the subtle body and the causal body, we bow to Energy. We invoke you, invite you and establish your presence.

- 38 -

ॐ भूर्भुवः स्वः दण्डाय नमः दण्डमावाहयामि स्थापयामि

oṃ bhūrbhuvaḥ svaḥ daṇḍāya namaḥ daṇḍamāvāhayāmi sthāpayāmi

oṃ the Infinite Beyond Conception, the gross body, the subtle body and the causal body, we bow to the Staff. We invoke you, invite you and establish your presence.

- 39 -

ॐ भूर्भुवः स्वः खड्गाय नमः खड्गमावाहयामि स्थापयामि

oṃ bhūrbhuvaḥ svaḥ khaḍgāya namaḥ khaḍgamāvāhayāmi sthāpayāmi

oṃ the Infinite Beyond Conception, the gross body, the subtle body and the causal body, we bow to the Sword. We invoke you, invite you and establish your presence.

- 40 -

ॐ भूर्भुवः स्वः पाशाय नमः पाशमावाहयामि स्थापयामि

oṃ bhūrbhuvaḥ svaḥ pāśāya namaḥ pāśamāvāhayāmi sthāpayāmi

oṃ the Infinite Beyond Conception, the gross body, the subtle body and the causal body, we bow to the Net. We invoke you, invite you and establish your presence.

- 41 -

ॐ भूर्भुवः स्वः अङ्कुशाय नमः अङ्कुशमावाहयामि स्थापयामि

oṃ bhūrbhuvaḥ svaḥ aṅkuśāya namaḥ aṅkuśamāvāhayāmi sthāpayāmi

oṃ the Infinite Beyond Conception, the gross body, the subtle body and the causal body, we bow to the Goad. We invoke you, invite you and establish your presence.

- 42 -

ॐ भूर्भुवः स्वः गौतमाय नमः गौतममावाहयामि स्थापयामि

oṃ bhūrbhuvaḥ svaḥ gautamāya namaḥ gautamamāvāhayāmi sthāpayāmi

oṃ the Infinite Beyond Conception, the gross body, the subtle body and the causal body, we bow to Ṛṣi Gautam. We invoke you, invite you and establish your presence.

- 43 -

ॐ भूर्भुवः स्वः भरद्वाजाय नमः भरद्वाजमावाहयामि स्थापयामि

oṃ bhūrbhuvaḥ svaḥ bharadvājāya namaḥ bharadvājamāvāhayāmi sthāpayāmi

oṃ the Infinite Beyond Conception, the gross body, the subtle body and the causal body, we bow to Ṛṣi Bharadvāj. We invoke you, invite you and establish your presence.

- 44 -

ॐ भूर्भुवः स्वः विश्वामित्राय नमः विश्वामित्रमावाहयामि स्थापयामि

oṃ bhūrbhuvaḥ svaḥ viśvāmitrāya namaḥ viśvāmitramāvāhayāmi sthāpayāmi

oṃ the Infinite Beyond Conception, the gross body, the subtle body and the causal body, we bow to Ṛṣi Viśvāmitra we invoke you, invite you and establish your presence.

- 45 -

ॐ भूर्भुवः स्वः कश्यपाय नमः कश्यपमावाहयामि स्थापयामि

oṃ bhūrbhuvaḥ svaḥ kaśyapāya namaḥ kaśyapamāvāhayāmi sthāpayāmi

oṃ the Infinite Beyond Conception, the gross body, the subtle body and the causal body, we bow to Ṛṣi Kaśyapa. We invoke you, invite you and establish your presence.

- 46 -

ॐ भूर्भुवः स्वः जमदग्नये नमः जमदग्निमावाहयामि स्थापयामि

oṃ bhūrbhuvaḥ svaḥ jamadagnaye namaḥ jamadagnimāvāhayāmi sthāpayāmi

oṃ the Infinite Beyond Conception, the gross body, the subtle body and the causal body, we bow to Ṛṣi Jamadagni. We invoke you, invite you and establish your presence.

- 47 -

ॐ भूर्भुवः स्वः वसिष्ठाय नमः वसिष्ठमावाहयामि स्थापयामि

oṃ bhūrbhuvaḥ svaḥ vasiṣṭhāya namaḥ vasiṣṭhamāvāhayāmi sthāpayāmi

oṃ the Infinite Beyond Conception, the gross body, the subtle body and the causal body, we bow to Ṛṣi Vaṣiṣṭha. We invoke you, invite you and establish your presence.

- 48 -

ॐ भूर्भुवः स्वः अत्रये नमः अत्रिमावाहयामि स्थापयामि

oṃ bhūrbhuvaḥ svaḥ atraye namaḥ atrimāvāhayāmi sthāpayāmi

oṃ the Infinite Beyond Conception, the gross body, the subtle body and the causal body, we bow to Ṛṣi Atri. We invoke you, invite you and establish your presence.

- 49 -

ॐ भूर्भुवः स्वः अरुन्धत्यै नमः अरुन्धतीमावाहयामि स्थापयामि

oṃ bhūrbhuvaḥ svaḥ arundhatyai namaḥ arundhatīmāvāhayāmi sthāpayāmi

oṃ the Infinite Beyond Conception, the gross body, the subtle body and the causal body, we bow to Devi Arundati, wife of Vaṣiṣṭha, example of purity. We invoke you, invite you and establish your presence.

- 50 -

ॐ भूर्भुवः स्वः ऐन्द्र्यै नमः ऐन्द्रीमावाहयामि स्थापयामि

oṃ bhūrbhuvaḥ svaḥ aindryai namaḥ aindrīmāvāhayāmi sthāpayāmi

oṃ the Infinite Beyond Conception, the gross body, the subtle body and the causal body, we bow to Aindri, the energy of the Rule of the Pure. We invoke you, invite you and establish your presence.

- 51 -

ॐ भूर्भुवः स्वः कौमार्य्यै नमः कौमारीमावाहयामि स्थापयामि

oṃ bhūrbhuvaḥ svaḥ kaumāryyai namaḥ kaumārīmāvāhayāmi sthāpayāmi

oṃ the Infinite Beyond Conception, the gross body, the subtle body and the causal body, we bow to Kumari, the energy of the ever pure one. We invoke you, invite you and establish your presence.

- 52 -

ॐ भूर्भुवः स्वः ब्राह्म्यै नमः ब्राह्मीमावाहयामि स्थापयामि

oṃ bhūrbhuvaḥ svaḥ brāhmyai namaḥ brāhmīmāvāhayāmi sthāpayāmi

oṃ the Infinite Beyond Conception, the gross body, the subtle body and the causal body, we bow to Brahmi, the energy of Creative Consciousness. We invoke you, invite you and establish your presence.

- 53 -

ॐ भूर्भुवः स्वः वाराह्यै नमः वाराहीमावाहयामि स्थापयामि

oṃ bhūrbhuvaḥ svaḥ vārāhyai namaḥ vārāhīmāvāhayāmi sthāpayāmi

oṃ the Infinite Beyond Conception, the gross body, the subtle body and the causal body, we bow to Varāhi, the energy of the Boar of Sacrifice. We invoke you, invite you and establish your presence.

- 54-

ॐ भूर्भुवः स्वः चामुण्डायै नमः चामुण्डामावाहयामि स्थापयामि

oṃ bhūrbhuvaḥ svaḥ cāmuṇḍāyai namaḥ cāmuṇḍāmāvāhayāmi sthāpayāmi

oṃ the Infinite Beyond Conception, the gross body, the subtle body and the causal body, we bow to Camuṇḍa, the Conquerer of Passion and Meaness. We invoke you, invite you and establish your presence.

- 55 -

ॐ भूर्भुवः स्वः वैष्णव्यै नमः वैष्णवीमावाहयामि स्थापयामि

oṃ bhūrbhuvaḥ svaḥ vaiṣṇavyai namaḥ vaiṣṇavīmāvāhayāmi sthāpayāmi

oṃ the Infinite Beyond Conception, the gross body, the subtle body and the causal body, we bow to Vaiṣṇāvi, the energy of All-Pervading Consciousness. We invoke you, invite you and establish your presence.

- 56 -

ॐ भूर्भुवः स्वः माहेश्वर्यै नमः माहेश्वरीमावाहयामि स्थापयामि

oṃ bhūrbhuvaḥ svaḥ māheśvaryai namaḥ māheśvarīmāvāhayāmi sthāpayāmi

oṃ the Infinite Beyond Conception, the gross body, the subtle body and the causal body, we bow to Maheśvarī, the energy of the Supreme Sovereign. We invoke you, invite you and establish your presence.

- 57 -

ॐ भूर्भुवः स्वः वैनायक्यै नमः वैनायकीमावाहयामि स्थापयामि

oṃ bhūrbhuvaḥ svaḥ vaināyakyai namaḥ vaināyakīmāvāhayāmi sthāpayāmi

oṃ the Infinite Beyond Conception, the gross body, the subtle body and the causal body, we bow to Vainākī, the energy of excellent conduct. We invoke you, invite you and establish your presence.

सं गच्छध्वं

sam gacchadhvaṃ

ॐ सं गच्छध्वं सं वदध्वं सं वो मनांसि जानताम्
देवा भागं यथा पूर्वे संजानाना उपासते

oṃ saṃ gacchadhvaṃ saṃ vadadhvaṃ
saṃ vo manāṃsi jānatām
devā bhāgaṃ yathā pūrve saṃjānānā upāsate

Let all assemble together. Let all speak together. Let all minds be in harmony. The Shining Ones of ancient times all proceeded by this worship.

समानो मन्त्रः समितिः समानी समानं मनः सह चित्तमेषाम्
समानं मन्त्रमभि मन्त्रये वः समानेन वो हविषा जुहोमि

samāno mantraḥ samitiḥ samānī samānaṃ manaḥ saha cittameṣām
samānaṃ mantramabhi mantraye vaḥ samānena vo haviṣā juhomi

When all thoughts are absorbed in mantra, then consciousness becomes fixed in the recollection most glorious. When all thoughts become absorbed in mantra, then by means of mantra all thoughts are poured as oblations into the divine fire.

समानी व आकूतिः समाना हृदयानि वः
समानमस्तु वो मनो यथा वः सुसहासति

samānī va ākūtiḥ samānā hṛdayāni vaḥ
samānamastu vo mano yathā vaḥ susahāsati

This place is common. These thoughts are common. So let our hearts be shared as well. Let all thoughts, all minds, be united so that all may enjoy peace and contentment.

Set Wood
Light torches with Gayatri
Encircle howan kuṇḍa three times, and set fire on right side.

वौषाट्

vauṣāṭ open hands face up
Ultimate Purity!

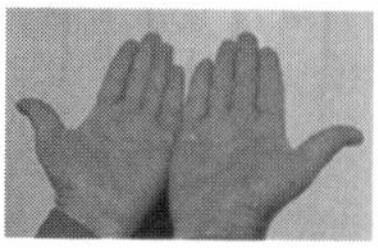

फट् फट् फट्

phaṭ phaṭ phaṭ **abhishek** - sprinkle water
Purify! Purify! Purify!

फट् फट् फट्

phaṭ phaṭ phaṭ clap
Purify! Purify! Purify!

हूं

hūṃ  aṅkuśa mudrā
Cut the Ego!

वं

vaṃ dhenu mudrā

Liberate!

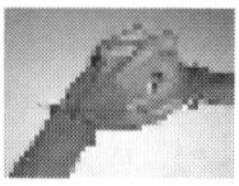

रं

raṃ yoni mudrā

Purifying Consciousness!

नमः

namaḥ prakṣan

I bow!

हुं फट् क्रव्यादिभ्यो नमः

huṃ phaṭ krayādibhyo namaḥ one stick to side

Cut the Ego! Purify all evil beings!

three times encircle howan kund:

सर्वमङ्गलमङ्गल्ये शिवे सर्वार्थसाधिके ।

शरण्ये त्र्यम्बके गौरि नारायणि नमोऽस्तु ते ॥

sarvamaṅgala maṅgalye śive sarvārtha sādhike
śaraṇye tryambake gauri nārāyaṇi namo-stu te

To the Auspicious of all Auspiciousness, to the Good, to the Accomplisher of all Objectives, to the Source of Refuge, to the Mother of the three worlds, to the Goddess Who is Rays of Light, Exposer of Consciousness, we bow to you.

सृष्टिस्थितिविनाशानां शक्तिभूते सनातनि ।

गुणाश्रये गुणमये नारायणि नमोऽस्तु ते ॥

sṛṣṭisthitivināśānāṃ śaktibhūte sanātani
guṇāśraye guṇamaye nārāyaṇi namo-stu te

You are the Eternal Energy of Creation, Preservation and Destruction in all existence; that upon which all qualities depend, that which limits all qualities, Exposer of Consciousness, we bow to you.

शरणागतदीनार्तपरित्राणपरायणे ।
सर्वस्यार्तिहरे देवि नारायणि नमोऽस्तु ते ॥

śaraṇāgatadīnārta paritrāṇa parāyaṇe
sarvasyārti hare devi nārāyaṇi namo-stu te

For those who are devoted to you and take refuge in you, you save from all discomfort and unhappiness. All worry you take away, Oh Goddess, Exposer of Consciousness, we bow to you.

return to asan:

ॐ वैश्वानराय विध्महे लालिलय धीमहे ।
तन्नो अग्निः प्रचोदयात् ॐ ॥

oṃ vaisvānarāya vidhmahe lālilaya dhīmahe
tanno agniḥ pracodayāt oṃ

We meditate upon the All-Pervading Being, contemplate the Luminous One who is the final resting place of all. May that Divine Fire, the Light of Meditation, grant us increase.

upasaṃhara mudrā

ह्वयाम्यग्निं प्रथमं स्वस्तये ।
ह्वयामि मित्रावरुणाविहावसे ।
ह्वयामि रात्रीं जगतो निवेशनीं ।
ह्वयामिदेवं सवितारमूतये ॥

hvayāmyagnim̥ prathamam̥ svastaye
hvayāmi mitrā varuṇā vihāvase
hvayāmi rātrīm̥ jagato niveṣanīm̥
hvayāmi devam̥ savitāramūtaye

I am calling you, Agni, the Divine Fire, the Light of Meditation, first to grant success. I am calling you Friendship and the Continuous Flow of Equilibrium also to receive this offering. I am calling the Night of Duality who covers the universe. I am calling the Light of Wisdom, the Divine Being, to rise up within us.

हिरण्यगर्भः समवर्तताग्रे भूतस्य जातः पतिरेक आसीत् ।
स दाधार पृथिवीं द्यामुतेमां कस्मै देवाय हविषा विधेम ॥

hiranyagarbhaḥ samavartatāgre bhūtasya jātaḥ patireka āsīt
sa dādhāra pṛthivīm̥ dyāmutemām̥ kasmai devāya haviṣā vidhema

Oh Golden Womb, You are the One Eternal Existence from which all beings born on the earth have come forth. You always bear the earth and all that rises upon it. (You tell us) to which God shall we offer our knowledge and attention?

यथा विद्वां अरंकरद् विश्वेभ्यो यजतेभ्यः ।
अयमग्ने त्वे अपि यं यज्ञं चकृमा वयम् ॥

yathā vidvām̥ aram̥karad viśvebhyoḥ yajatebhyaḥ
ayamagne tve api yam̥ yajñam̥ cakṛmā vayam

Through knowledge of this Eternal Cause, all beings born in the universe have come forth. It is in you, Oh Agni, Oh Light of Meditation, in the flame of sacrifice, that this constant movement will find rest.

त्वमग्ने प्रथमो अङ्गिरा ऋषिर्देवो देवानामभवः शिवः सखा ।
तव व्रते कवयो विद्मनापसोऽजायन्त मरुतो भ्राजदृष्टयः ॥

tvamagne prathamo aṇgirā ṛṣirdevo
devānāmabhavaḥ śivaḥ sakhā
tava vrate kavayo vidmanāpaso-
jāyanta maruto bhrājadṛṣṭayaḥ

You, Oh Divine Light of Meditation, are the first among the performers of spiritual discipline, a Seer, a God; your name became one with all the Gods. You are the friend of Śiva, the Consciousness of Infinite Goodness. Through devotion to you, all the inspired poets (Ṛṣis who propound Vedic Knowledge, or Wisdom of Universality) come to Divine Knowledge, as did the Maruts (the 49 Gods of severe penance) did come forth from your worship.

त्वं मुखं सर्वदेवनां सप्तचिर्हविद्मते ।
आगच्छ भगवनग्ने यज्ञेऽस्मिन् सन्निधा भव ॥

tvaṃ mukhaṃ sarvadevanāṃ saptacirhavidmate
āgaccha bhagavanagne yajñe-smin sannidhā bhava

You are the mouth of all the Gods, with your seven tongues you accept the offerings. Come here, Oh Lord Divine Fire, and take your seat in the midst of our sacrifice.

ॐ वैश्वानर जातवेद इहावह लोहिताक्ष सर्व कर्माणि
साधय स्वाहा ॥

oṃ vaiśvānara jātaveda ihāvaha lohitākṣa sarva
karmāṇi sādhaya svāhā

oṃ Oh Universal Being, Knower of All, come here with your red eyes. All of our Karma burn it! I AM ONE WITH GOD!

ॐ अग्नीमिळे पुरोहितं यज्ञस्य देवमृत्विजम् ।
होतारं रत्न धातमम् ॥

oṃ agnīmiḷe purohitaṃ yajñasya devamṛtvijam hotāraṃ ratna dhātamam

Oh Agni, Light of Meditation, you are the Priest of Sacrifice, serving the offering of the divine nectar of Immortality. You give jewels to those who offer.

ॐ अग्नि प्रज्वलितं वन्दे जातवेदं हुताशनम् ।
सुवर्णवर्णममलं समिद्धं विश्वतो मुखम्

oṃ agni prajvalitaṃ vande jātavedaṃ hutāśanam suvarṇavarṇamamalaṃ samiddhaṃ viśvato mukham

We lovingly adore the Divine Fire, Light of Meditation, sparkling, flaming brightly, knower of all, recipient of our offerings. With His excellent golden color, everywhere His omnipresent mouths are devouring oblations.

ॐ अग्नये नमः

oṃ agnaye namaḥ

oṃ We bow to the Divine Fire.

अग्ने त्वं शिवकनामसि

agne tvaṃ śivakanāmasi

Oh Divine Fire, we are now calling you by the name Śiva, the Consciousness of Infinite Goodness.

ॐ वागीश्वरी मृतुस्नातां नीलेन्दीवरलोचनाम् ।
वागीश्वरेण संयुक्तां कृराभव समन्वितम्

oṃ vāgīśvarī mṛtu-snātāṃ nīlendīvaralocanām
vāgīśvareṇa saṃyuktaṃ kṛrābhava samanvitam

The Supreme Goddess of Speech, dear Mother Saraswati, has just completed Her bath following Her monthly course of menstruation. With eyes of blue, bestowing boons, She moves into union with Vāgīṣvara, Brahma, the Lord of All Vibrations, and together they create the bhāva or intensity of reality, the attitude which unites all.

एते गन्धपुष्पे ॐ ह्रीं वागीश्वर्यै नमः

ete gandhapuṣpe oṃ hrīṃ vāgīśvaryai namaḥ

With these scented flowers oṃ we bow to the Supreme Goddess of Speech, or all Vibrations.

एते गन्धपुष्पे ॐ ह्रीं वागीश्वराय नमः

ete gandhapuṣpe oṃ hrīṃ vāgīśvarāya namaḥ

With these scented flowers oṃ we bow to the Supreme Lord of Speech, or all Vibrations.

एते गन्धपुष्पे ॐ अग्नेर्हिरण्यादि सप्तजिह्वाभ्यो नमः

ete gandhapuṣpe oṃ agnerhiraṇyādi
saptajihvābhyo namaḥ

With these scented flowers oṃ we bow to the seven tongues of the Divine Fire, like golden, etc.

1. Kālī	Black
2. Karālī	Increasing, formidable
3. Mano-javā	Swift as thought
4. Su-Lohitā	Excellent shine
5. Sudhūmra-Varnā	Purple
6. Ugrā or Sphulingīnī	Fearful
7. Pradīptā	Giving light

एते गन्धपुष्पे ॐ सहस्रार्चिषे हृदयाय नमः

ete gandhapuṣpe oṃ sahasrārciṣe hṛdayāya namaḥ

With these scented flowers oṃ we bow to the heart from which emanates a thousand rays.

इत्याद्यग्ने षदङ्गेभ्यो नमः

ityādyagne ṣadaṅgebhyo namaḥ

In this way establish the Divine Fire in the six centers of the body.

एते गन्धपुष्पे ॐ अग्नये जातवेदसे इत्यद्यष्टमूर्त्तिभ्यो नमः

ete gandhapuṣpe oṃ agnaye jātavedase ityadyaṣṭa mūrttibhyo namaḥ

With these scented flowers oṃ we bow to the Divine Fire, the Knower of All, etc, in His eight forms for worship.

1. Jāta-Veda	Knower of All
2. Sapta-Jihva	Seven tongued
3. Vaiśvānara	Universal Being
4. Havyā-Vāhana	Carrier of Oblations
5. Aśwodara-Ja	Fire of Stomach, lower areas
6. Kaumāra Tejaḥ	From which the son of Śiva is born
7. Viśva-Mukha	Which can devour the universe
8. Deva-Mukha	The mouth of the Gods

एते गन्धपुष्पे ॐ ब्राह्म्यद्यष्टशक्तिभ्यो नमः

ete gandhapuṣpe oṃ brāhmyadyaṣṭaśaktibhyo namaḥ

With these scented flowers oṃ we bow to the eight Śaktis or Energies, like Brāhmī, etc.

1. Brāhmī	Creative Energy
2. Nārāyaṇī	Exposer of Consciousness
3. Māheśvarī	Energy of the Seer of All
4. Cāmuṇḍā	Slayer of Passion & Meanness
5. Kaumārī	The Ever Pure One
6. Aparājitā	The Unconquerable
7. Vārāhī	The Boar of Sacrifice
8. Nārasiṃhī	The Man-lion of Courage

एते गन्धपुष्पे ॐ पद्माद्यष्टनिधिभ्यो नमः

ete gandhapuṣpe oṃ padmādyaṣṭa nidhibhyo namaḥ

With these scented flowers oṃ we bow to the eight Treasures of the Lord of Wealth, like Padma, etc.

1. Padma	The lotus of Peace
2. Mahā-Padma	The great lotus of universal Peace
3. Śaṅkha	The conch of all vibrations
4. Makara	The emblem of Love
5. Kacchapa	Tortoise, the emblem of support
6. Mukunda	The Crest gem
7. Nanda	Bliss
8. Nīla	The blue light within like a Sapphire

एते गन्धपुष्पे ॐ इन्द्रादि लोकपालेभ्यो नमः

ete gandhapuṣpe oṃ indrādi lokapālebhyo namaḥ

With these scented flowers oṃ we bow to Indra and the Protectors of the Ten Directions.

1. Indra	East
2. Agni	South-East
3. Yama	South
4. Nairrita	South-West
5. Varuṇa	West

6. Vāyu	North-West
7. Kuvera (Soma)	North
8. Īśāna	North-East
9. Brahmā	Above
10. Viṣṇu (Ananta)	Below

एते गन्धपुष्पे ॐ वज्राद्यस्त्रेभ्यो नमः

ete gandhapuṣpe oṃ vajrādyastrebhyo namaḥ

With these scented flowers oṃ we bow to the Thunderbolt and other weapons.

1. Vajra	Indra's thunderbolt
2. Śakti	Agni's spear, dart, energy
3. Daṇḍa	Yama's staff
4. Khaḍga	Nairrita's sword
5. Pāśa	Varuṇa's net or noose
6. Aṅkuśa	Vāyu's hook
7. Gadā	Kuvera's mace
8. Triśūla	Īśāna's trident
9. Padma or Kamaṇḍelu	Brahma's lotus or begging bowl
10. Cakra	Viṣṇu's discus

एते गन्धपुष्पे ॐ वह्निर्चैतन्याय नमः

ete gandhapuṣpe oṃ vahnir caintanyāya namaḥ

With these scented flowers oṃ we bow to the Consciousness of the Divine Fire.

एते गन्धपुष्पे ॐ अग्नि मूर्त्तये नमः

ete gandhapuṣpe oṃ agni mūrttaye namaḥ

With these scented flowers oṃ we bow to the Image of the Divine Fire, the Light of Meditation.

ॐ अग्नये नमः

oṃ agnaye namaḥ
oṃ we bow to the Divine Fire.

रं रं रं रं रं

raṃ raṃ raṃ raṃ raṃ
R The Subtle Body; **a** Consciousness ; **ṃ** Perfection
Raṃ The manifestation of Perfection in the Subtle Body of Consciousness.

ॐ चित् पिङ्गल हन हन दह दह पच पच सर्व ज्ञापय ज्ञापय स्वाहा

oṃ cit piṅgala hana hana daha daha paca paca sarva jñāpaya jñāpaya svāhā
The Infinite Beyond Conception, Consciousness, the subtle canal which rises, purify, purify, burn, burn, bring to perfection, bring to perfection all wisdom, all wisdom, I am One with God!

establishment within

āvāhaṇi mudrā (I invite you, please come.)

ॐ नमः शिवाय इहागच्छ

oṃ namaḥ śivāya ihāgaccha
oṃ I bow to the Consciousness of Infinite Goodness, I invite you, please come.

sthāpanī mudrā (I establish you within.)

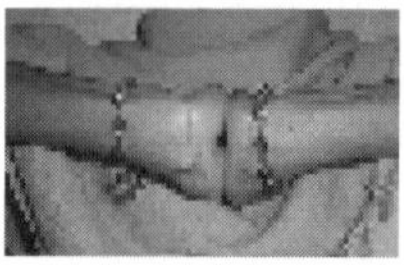

इह तिष्ठ

iha tiṣṭha
I establish you within.

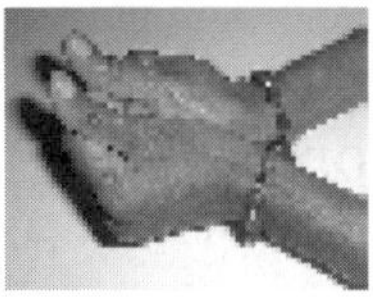

sannidhāpanī mudrā (I know you have many devotees who are requesting your attention, but I request that you pay special attention to me.)

इह सन्निरुध्यस्व

iha sannirudhyasva

I am binding you to remain here.

saṃrodhanī mudrā (I am sorry for any inconvenience caused.)

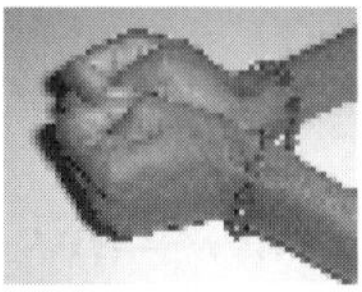

इह सनिहित भव

iha sanihita bhava

You bestow abundant wealth.

atmā samarpaṇa mudrā (I surrender my soul to you.)

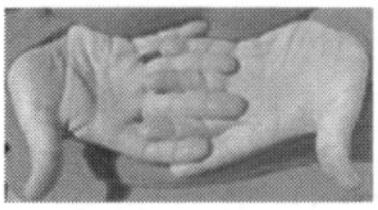

अत्राधिष्ठानं कुरु

atrādhiṣṭhānaṃ kuru

I am depending upon you to forgive me in this matter.

prakṣan (I bow to you with devotion.)

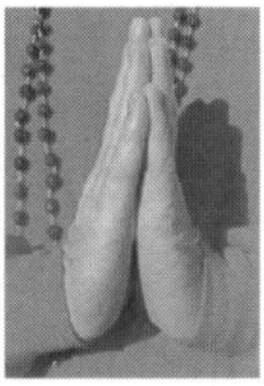

देव मम पूजां गृहाण

देव बक्तशूलवे परित्राण करायिते ।

जावोट् त्वं पूजैषामि तावोट् त्वं सुस्थिरा भव ॥

deva mama pūjāṃ gṛhāṇa
deva baktaśūlave paritrāṇa karāyite
jāvoṭ tvaṃ pūjaiṣāmi tāvoṭ tvaṃ susthirā bhava

Oh God, please accept my worship. Oh God, remove all pain from your devotees. For so long as I worship you, please remain sitting still.

prāṇa pratiṣṭhā

establishment of life

ॐ अं आं ह्रीं क्रों यं रं लं वं शं षं सं हों हं सः

oṃ aṃ āṃ hrīṃ kroṃ yaṃ raṃ laṃ vaṃ śaṃ ṣaṃ saṃ hoṃ haṃ saḥ

oṃ The Infinite Beyond Conception, Creation (the first letter), Consciousness, Māyā, the cause of the movement of the subtle body to perfection and beyond; the path of fulfillment: control, subtle illumination, one with the earth, emancipation, the soul of peace, the soul of delight, the soul of unity (all this is I), perfection, Infinite Consciousness, this is I.

ॐ नमः शिवाय प्राणा इह प्राणाः

oṃ namaḥ śivāya prāṇā iha prāṇāḥ

oṃ I bow to the Consciousness of Infinite Goodness. You are the life of this life!

ॐ अं आं ह्रीं क्रों यं रं लं वं शं षं सं हों हं सः

oṃ aṃ āṃ hrīṃ kroṃ yaṃ raṃ laṃ vaṃ śaṃ ṣaṃ saṃ hoṃ haṃ saḥ

oṃ The Infinite Beyond Conception, Creation (the first letter), Consciousness, Māyā, the cause of the movement of the subtle body to perfection and beyond; the path of fulfillment: control, subtle illumination, one with the earth, emancipation, the soul of peace, the soul of delight, the soul of unity (all this is I), perfection, Infinite Consciousness, this is I.

ॐ नमः शिवाय जीव इह स्थितः

oṃ namaḥ śivāya jīva iha sthitaḥ

oṃ I bow to the Consciousness of Infinite Goodness. You are situated in this life (or individual consciousness).

ॐ अं आं ह्रीं क्रों यं रं लं वं शं षं सं हों हं सः

oṃ aṃ āṃ hrīṃ kroṃ yaṃ raṃ laṃ vaṃ śaṃ ṣaṃ saṃ hoṃ haṃ saḥ

oṃ The Infinite Beyond Conception, Creation (the first letter), Consciousness, Māyā, the cause of the movement of the subtle body to perfection and beyond; the path of fulfillment: control, subtle illumination, one with the earth, emancipation, the soul of peace, the soul of delight, the soul of unity (all this is I), perfection, Infinite Consciousness, this is I.

ॐ नमः शिवाय सर्वेन्द्रियाणि

oṃ namaḥ śivāya sarvendriyāṇi

oṃ I bow to the Consciousness of Infinite Goodness. You are all these organs (of action and knowledge).

ॐ अं आं ह्रीं क्रों यं रं लं वं शं षं सं हों हं सः

oṃ aṃ āṃ hrīṃ kroṃ yaṃ raṃ laṃ vaṃ śaṃ ṣaṃ saṃ hoṃ haṃ saḥ

oṃ The Infinite Beyond Conception, Creation (the first letter), Consciousness, Māyā, the cause of the movement of the subtle body to perfection and beyond; the path of fulfillment: control, subtle illumination, one with the earth, emancipation, the soul of peace, the soul of delight, the soul of unity (all this is I), perfection, Infinite Consciousness, this is I.

ॐ नमः शिवाय वाग् मनस्त्वक्चक्षुः-श्रोत्र-घ्राण-प्राणा इहागत्य सुखं चिरं तिष्ठन्तु स्वाहा

oṃ namaḥ śivāya vāg manastvakcakṣuḥ śrotra ghrāṇa prāṇā ihāgatya sukhaṃ ciraṃ tiṣṭhantu svāhā

oṃ I bow to the Consciousness of Infinite Goodness. You are all these vibrations, mind, sound, eyes, ears, tongue, nose and life force. Bring forth infinite peace and establish it forever, I am One with God!

kara nyāsa

establishment in the hands

ॐ नं अंगुष्ठाभ्यां नमः

oṃ naṃ aṇguṣṭhābhyāṃ namaḥ thumb forefinger

oṃ naṃ in the thumb I bow.

ॐ मः तर्जनीभ्यां स्वाहा

oṃ maḥ tarjanībhyāṃ svāhā thumb forefinger

oṃ maḥ in the forefinger, I am One with God!

ॐ शिं मध्यमाभ्यां वषट्

oṃ śiṃ madhyamābhyāṃ vaṣaṭ thumb middlefinger

oṃ śiṃ in the middle finger, Purify!

ॐ वां अनामिकाभ्यां हुं

oṃ vāṃ anāmikābhyāṃ huṃ thumb ringfinger

oṃ vāṃ in the ring finger, Cut the Ego!

ॐ यः कनिष्ठिकाभ्यां बौषट्

oṃ yaḥ kaniṣṭhikābhyāṃ vauṣaṭ thumb littlefinger

oṃ yaḥ in the little finger, Ultimate Purity!

Roll hand over hand forwards while reciting *karatala kara* and backwards while chanting *pṛṣṭhābhyāṃ*, then clap hands when chanting *astrāya phaṭ.*

ॐ नमः शिवाय करतल कर पृष्ठाभ्यां अस्त्राय फट् ॥

oṃ namaḥ śivāya karatala kara pṛṣṭhābhyāṃ astrāya phaṭ

oṃ I bow to the Consciousness of Infinite Goodness with the weapon of Virtue.

ॐ नमः शिवाय

oṃ namaḥ śivāya

I bow to the Consciousness of Infinite Goodness.

aṅga nyāsa

establishment in the body

Holding tattva mudrā, touch heart.

ॐ नं हृदयाय नमः

oṃ naṃ hṛdayāya namaḥ touch heart

oṃ naṃ in the heart, I bow.

Holding tattva mudrā, touch top of head.

ॐ मः शिरसे स्वाहा

oṃ maḥ śirase svāhā top of head

oṃ maḥ on the top of the head, I am One with God!

With thumb extended, touch back of head.

ॐ शिं शिखायै वषट्

oṃ śiṃ śikhāyai vaṣaṭ back of head

oṃ śiṃ on the back of the head, Purify!

Holding tattva mudrā, cross both arms.

ॐ वां कवचाय हुं

oṃ vāṃ kavacāya huṃ cross both arms

oṃ vāṃ crossing both arms, Cut the Ego!

Holding tattva mudrā, touch three
eyes at once with three middle fingers.

ॐ यः नेत्रत्रयाय वौषट्

oṃ yaḥ netratrayāya vauṣaṭ touch three eyes
oṃ yaḥ in the three eyes, Ultimate Purity!

Roll hand over hand forwards while reciting *karatala kara* and backwards while chanting *pṛṣṭhābhyāṃ*, then clap hands when chanting *astrāya phaṭ*.

ॐ नमः शिवाय करतल कर पृष्ठाभ्यां अस्त्राय फट् ॥

oṃ namaḥ śivāya karatala kara pṛṣṭhābhyāṃ astrāya phaṭ

oṃ I bow to the Consciousness of Infinite Goodness with the weapon of Virtue.

ॐ नमः शिवाय

oṃ namaḥ śivāya

I bow to the Consciousness of Infinite Goodness.

japa
stapana
establishment in the fire

ॐ नमः शिवाय शान्ताय कारणत्रय हेतवे ।
निवेदयामि चात्मानं त्वं गतिः परमेश्वर ॥

oṃ namaḥ śivāya śāntāya kāraṇatraya hetave
nivedayāmi cātmānaṃ tvaṃ gatiḥ parameśvara

oṃ I bow to the Consciousness of Infinite Goodness, to Peace, to the Cause of the three worlds, I offer to you the fullness of my soul, Oh Supreme Lord.

āvāhaṇi mudrā (I invite you, please come.)

ॐ नमः शिवाय इहागच्छ

oṃ namaḥ śivāya ihāgaccha

oṃ I bow to the Consciousness of Infinite Goodness, I invite you, please come.

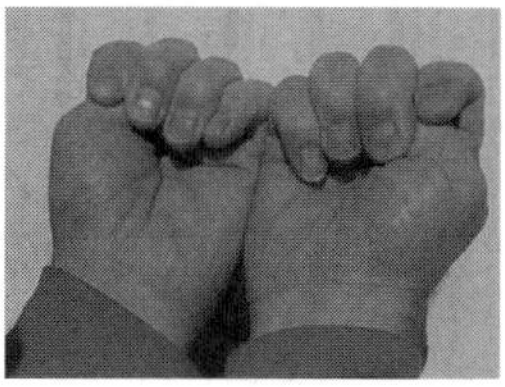

sthāpanī mudrā (I establish you within.)

इह तिष्ठ

iha tiṣṭha

I establish you within.

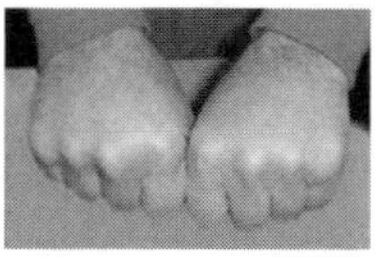

sannidhāpanī mudrā (I know you have many devotees who are requesting your attention, but I request that you pay special attention to me.)

इह सन्निदेहि

iha sannidehi

I am binding you to remain here.

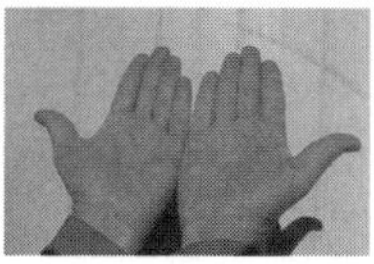

saṃrodhanī mudrā (I am sorry for any inconvenience caused.)

इह सनिहित भव

iha sanihita bhava

You bestow abundant wealth.

atmā samarpaṇa mudrā (I surrender my soul to you.)

अत्राधिष्ठानं कुरु

atrādhiṣṭhānaṃ kuru

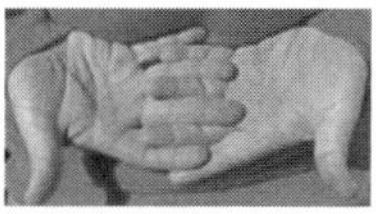

I am depending upon you to forgive me in this matter.

prakṣan (I bow to you with devotion.)

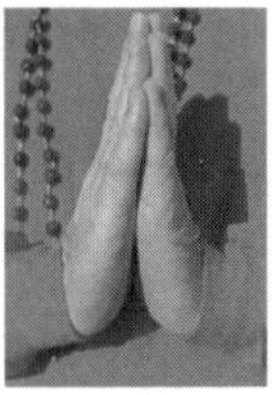

देव मम पूजां गृहाण

देव बक्तशूल्वे परित्राण करायिते ।

जावोट् त्वं पूजैषामि तावोट् त्वं सुस्थिरा भव ॥

deva mama pūjāṃ gṛhāṇa
deva baktaśūlave paritrāṇa karāyite
jāvoṭ tvaṃ pūjaiṣāmi tāvoṭ tvaṃ susthirā bhava

Oh God, please accept my worship. Oh God, remove all pain from your devotees. For so long as I worship you, please remain sitting still.

Pūjā

Worship of fire

ॐ वैश्वानर जातवेद इहावह लोहिताक्ष सर्व कर्माणि

साधय स्वाहा ॥

oṃ vaiśvānara jātaveda ihāvaha lohitākṣa sarva karmāṇi sādhaya svāhā

Oh Universal Being, Knower of All, come here with your red eyes. All of our Karma burn it! I AM ONE WITH GOD!

dhūpam
dhīpam
arghyam
puṣpam
naivedyam
taṃbūlam

ghee oblations:

ॐ अग्नये स्वाहा

oṃ agnaye svāhā

oṃ To the Divine Fire, I am One with God!

ॐ सोमाय स्वाहा

oṃ somāya svāhā
oṃ To the Moon, emblem of Devotion, I am One with God!

ॐ अग्नीषोमाभ्यां स्वाहा

oṃ agnīṣomābhyāṃ svāhā
oṃ To the Divine Fire and to the Moon, emblem of Devotion, I am One with God!

ॐ अग्नये स्विष्टकृते स्वाहा

oṃ agnaye sviṣṭakṛte svāhā
oṃ To the Divine Fire, to whom excellent honor is given, I am One with God!

ॐ भूः स्वाहा

oṃ bhūḥ svāhā
oṃ Gross Perception, I am One with God!

ॐ भुवः स्वाहा

oṃ bhuvaḥ svāhā
oṃ Subtle Perception, I am One with God!

ॐ स्वः स्वाहा

oṃ svaḥ svāhā
oṃ Intuitive Perception, I am One with God!

ॐ भूर्भुवः स्वः स्वाहा

oṃ bhūrbhuvaḥ svaḥ svāhā
oṃ Gross Perception; oṃ Subtle Perception; oṃ Intuitive Perception, I am One with God!

ॐ वैश्वानर जातवेद इहावह लोहिताक्ष सर्व कर्माणि साधय स्वाहा ॥

oṃ vaiśvānara jātaveda ihāvaha lohitākṣa sarva karmāṇi sādhaya svāhā

Oh Universal Being, Knower of All, come here with your red eyes. All of our Karma burn it! I AM ONE WITH GOD!

ॐ चित् पिङ्गल हन हन दह दह पच पच सर्व ज्ञापय ज्ञापय स्वाहा

oṃ cit piṅgala hana hana daha daha paca paca sarva jñāpaya jñāpaya svāhā

The Infinite Beyond Conception, Consciousness, the subtle canal which rises, purify, purify, burn, burn, bring to perfection, bring to perfection all wisdom, all wisdom, I am One with God!

Perform Homa of Sankalpa

Ganeśa

ॐ गं गणपतये स्वाहा

oṃ gaṃ gaṇapataye svāhā

oṃ to the Lord of Wisdom, Lord of the Multitudes, I am One with God!

शिव सहस्रनाम

śiva sahasranāma

OneThousand Names of Śiva

\- 1 -

ॐ स्थिराय स्वाहा

oṃ sthirāya svāhā

oṃ we bow to He Who Is Still, I am One with God.

\- 2 -

ॐ स्थाणवे स्वाहा

oṃ sthāṇave svāhā

oṃ we bow to the Residence, I am One with God.

\- 3 -

ॐ प्रभवे स्वाहा

oṃ prabhave svāhā

oṃ we bow to the Lord, I am One with God.

\- 4 -

ॐ भीमाय स्वाहा

oṃ bhīmāya svāhā

oṃ we bow to He Who Is Terrible, I am One with God.

\- 5 -

ॐ प्रवराय स्वाहा

oṃ pravarāya svāhā

oṃ we bow to the Foremost Boon, I am One with God.

\- 6 -

ॐ वरदाय स्वाहा

oṃ varadāya svāhā

oṃ we bow to the Giver of Boons, I am One with God.

\- 7 -

ॐ वराय स्वाहा

oṃ varāya svāhā

oṃ we bow to the Boon, I am One with God.

\- 8 -

ॐ सर्वात्मने स्वाहा

oṃ sarvātmane svāhā

oṃ we bow to the Soul of All, I am One with God.

\- 9 -

ॐ सर्वविख्यातायं स्वाहा

oṃ sarvavikhyātāya svāhā

oṃ we bow to the Substance of All, I am One with God.

\- 10 -

ॐ सर्वस्मै स्वाहा

oṃ sarvasmai svāhā

oṃ we bow to He Who Is Within All, I am One with God.

\- 11 -

ॐ सर्वकराय स्वाहा

oṃ saravakarāya svāhā

oṃ we bow to the Cause of All, I am One with God.

\- 12 -

ॐ भवाय स्वाहा

oṃ bhavāya svāhā

oṃ we bow to All Existence, I am One with God.

\- 13 -

ॐ जटिने स्वाहा

oṃ jaṭine svāhā

oṃ we bow to He Who Has Matted Hair, I am One with God.

- 14 -

ॐ चर्मिणे स्वाहा

oṃ carmiṇe svāhā

oṃ we bow to He Who Wears A Skin, I am One with God.

-15 -

ॐ शिखण्डिने स्वाहा

oṃ śikhaṇḍine svāhā

oṃ we bow to the Ultimate, I am One with God.

- 16 -

ॐ सर्वाङ्गाय स्वाहा

oṃ sarvāṅgāya svāhā

oṃ we bow to All Limbs, I am One with God.

- 17 -

ॐ सर्वभावनाय स्वाहा

oṃ sarvabhāvanāya svāhā

oṃ we bow to All Attitudes, I am One with God.

- 18 -

ॐ हराय स्वाहा

oṃ harāya svāhā

oṃ we bow to He Who Takes Away, I am One with God.

- 19 -

ॐ हरिणाक्षाय स्वाहा

oṃ hariṇākṣāya svāhā

oṃ we bow to He Who Has the Eyes of A Deer, I am One with God.

- 20 -

ॐ सर्वभूतहराय स्वाहा

oṃ sarvabhūtaharāya svāhā

oṃ we bow to He Who Takes Away All, I am One with God.

- 21 -

ॐ वृत्तये स्वाहा

oṃ vṛttaye svāhā

oṃ we bow to He Who is All Change, I am One with God.

- 22 -

ॐ प्रभवे स्वाहा

oṃ prabhave svāhā

oṃ we bow to the Lord, I am One with God.

- 23 -

ॐ निवृत्तये स्वाहा

oṃ nivṛttaye svāhā

oṃ we bow to He Who is Involution, I am One with God.

- 24 -

ॐ नियताय स्वाहा

oṃ niyatāya svāhā

oṃ we bow to He Who is Space, I am One with God.

- 25 -

ॐ शाश्वताय स्वाहा

oṃ śāśvatāya svāhā

oṃ we bow to He Who is Eternal, I am One with God.

- 26 -

ॐ ध्रुवाय स्वाहा

oṃ dhruvāya svāhā

oṃ we bow to He Who is Eternally Young, I am One with God.

- 27 -

ॐ श्मशानवासिने स्वाहा

oṃ śmaśānavāsine svāhā

oṃ we bow to He Who Dwells in the Cremation Grounds, I am One with God.

- 28 -

ॐ भगवते स्वाहा

oṃ bhagavate svāhā

oṃ we bow to He Who is All Parts, I am One with God.

- 29 -

ॐ खेचराय स्वाहा

oṃ khecarāya svāhā

oṃ we bow to He Who Levitates, I am One with God.

- 30 -

ॐ गोचराय स्वाहा

oṃ gocarāya svāhā

oṃ we bow to He Who Moves With Light, I am One with God.

- 31 -

ॐ आनन्दाय स्वाहा

oṃ ānandāya svāhā

oṃ we bow to He Who is Bliss, I am One with God.

- 32 -

ॐ अभिवाद्याय स्वाहा

oṃ abhivādyāya svāhā

oṃ we bow to He Who is Worshiped by All, I am One with God.

- 33 -

ॐ महाकर्मणे स्वाहा

oṃ mahākarmaṇe svāhā

oṃ we bow to He of Great Activity, I am One with God.

- 34 -

ॐ तपस्विने स्वाहा

oṃ tapasvine svāhā

oṃ we bow to the Performer of Purifying Austerities, I am One with God.

- 35 -

ॐ भूतभावनाय स्वाहा

oṃ bhūtabhāvanāya svāhā

oṃ we bow to the Attitudes of Existence, I am One with God.

- 36 -

ॐ उन्मत्तवेषप्रच्छन्नाय स्वाहा

oṃ unmattaveṣapracchannāya svāhā

oṃ we bow to He Who is Distinguished by the Appearance of Madness, I am One with God.

- 37 -

ॐ सर्वलोकप्रजापतये स्वाहा

oṃ sarvalokaprajāpataye svāhā

oṃ we bow to the Lord of All Beings Born in All Worlds, I am One with God.

- 38 -

ॐ महारूपाय स्वाहा

oṃ mahārūpāya svāhā

oṃ we bow to He Who Has a Great Form, I am One with God.

- 39 -

ॐ महाकयाय स्वाहा

oṃ mahākayāya svāhā

oṃ we bow to He Who Has Great Body, I am One with God.

- 40 -

ॐ वृषरूपाय स्वाहा

oṃ vṛṣarūpāya svāhā

oṃ we bow to He Who is the Form of a Bull, I am One with God.

- 41 -

ॐ महायशसे स्वाहा

oṃ mahāyaśase svāhā

oṃ we bow to He of Great Fame or Welfare, I am One with God.

- 42 -

ॐ महात्मने स्वाहा

oṃ mahātmane svāhā

oṃ we bow to He Who is a Great Soul, I am One with God.

- 43 -

ॐ सर्वभूतात्मने स्वाहा

oṃ sarvabhūtātmane svāhā

oṃ we bow to He Who is the Soul of All Existence, I am One with God.

- 44 -

ॐ विश्वरूपाय स्वाहा

oṃ viśvārūpāyā svāhā

oṃ we bow to He Who is the Form of the Universe, I am One with God.

- 45 -

ॐ महाहनवे स्वाहा

oṃ mahāhanave svāhā

oṃ we bow to He Who Has a Great Chin, I am One with God.

- 46 -

ॐ लोकपालाय स्वाहा

oṃ lokapālāya svāhā

oṃ we bow to He Who is the Protector of the World, I am One with God.

- 47 -

ॐ अन्तर्हितात्मने स्वाहा

oṃ antarhitātmane svāhā

oṃ we bow to He Who is the Inner Soul of All, I am One with God.

- 48 -

ॐ प्रसादाय स्वाहा

oṃ prasādaya svāhā

oṃ we bow to He Who is the Consecrated Offering, I am One with God.

- 49 -

ॐ हयगर्दभये स्वाहा

oṃ hayagardabhaye svāhā

oṃ we bow to He Whose Chariot is Pulled by Horses, I am One with God.

- 50 -

ॐ पवित्राय स्वाहा

oṃ pavitrāya svāhā

oṃ we bow to He Who is Pure, I am One with God.

- 51 -

ॐ महते स्वाहा

oṃ mahate svāhā

oṃ we bow to He Who is All Manifested Existence, I am One with God.

- 52 -

ॐ नियमाय स्वाहा

oṃ niyamāya svāhā

oṃ we bow to He Who is Discipline, I am One with God.

- 53 -

ॐ नियमाश्रिताय स्वाहा

oṃ niyamāśritāya svāhā

oṃ we bow to He Who is the Refuge of Discipline, I am One with God.

- 54 -

ॐ सर्वकर्मणे स्वाहा

oṃ sarvakarmaṇe svāhā

oṃ we bow to He Who is All Action, I am One with God.

- 55 -

ॐ स्वयम्भूताय स्वाहा

oṃ svayambhūtāya svāhā

oṃ we bow to He From Whom All Elements Have Come Forth, I am One with God.

- 56 -

ॐ आदये स्वाहा

oṃ ādaye svāhā

oṃ we bow to He Who is the Very First, I am One with God.

- 57 -

ॐ आदिकराय स्वाहा

oṃ ādikarāya svāhā

oṃ we bow to He Who has Authority, I am One with God.

- 58 -

ॐ निधये स्वाहा

oṃ nidhaye svāhā

oṃ we bow to He Who has the Treasure, I am One with God.

- 59 -

ॐ सहस्राक्षाय स्वाहा

oṃ sahasrākṣāya svāhā

oṃ we bow to He Who Has a Thousand Eyes, I am One with God.

- 60 -

ॐ विशालाक्षाय स्वाहा

oṃ viśālākṣāya svāhā

oṃ we bow to He Who Has Immense Eyes, I am One with God.

- 61 -

ॐ सोमाय स्वाहा

oṃ somāya svāhā

oṃ we bow to He Who is the Moon of Devotion, I am One with God.

- 62 -

ॐ नक्षत्रसाधकाय स्वाहा

oṃ nakṣatrasādhakāya svāhā

oṃ we bow to He Who Puts the Stars in their Places, I am One with God.

- 63 -

ॐ चन्द्राय स्वाहा

oṃ candrāya svāhā

oṃ we bow to He Who is the Light of the Moon, I am One with God.

- 64 -

ॐ सूर्याय स्वाहा

oṃ sūryāya svāhā

oṃ we bow to He Who is the Light of the Sun, I am One with God.

- 65 -

ॐ शनये स्वाहा

oṃ śanaye svāhā

oṃ we bow to He Who is the Discipline of Saturn, I am One with God.

- 66 -

ॐ केतवे स्वाहा

oṃ ketave svāhā

oṃ we bow to He Who Restricts as the South Node, I am One with God.

- 67 -

ॐ ग्रहाय स्वाहा

oṃ grahāya svāhā

oṃ we bow to He Who is All the Planets, I am One with God.

- 68 -

ॐ ग्रहपतये स्वाहा

oṃ grahapataye svāhā

oṃ we bow to He Who is the Lord of All Planets, I am One with God.

- 69 -

ॐ वराय स्वाहा

oṃ varāya svāhā

oṃ we bow to the Giver of Boons, I am One with God.

- 70 -

ॐ अत्रये स्वाहा

oṃ atraye svāhā

oṃ we bow to He Who is Before the Three, I am One with God.

- 71 -

ॐ अत्र्यानमस्कर्त्रे स्वाहा

oṃ atryānamaskartre svāhā

oṃ we bow to He Who Receives Respect From the One Beyond the Three, I am One with God.

- 72 -

ॐ मृगवाणार्पणाय स्वाहा

oṃ mṛgavāṇārpaṇāya svāhā

oṃ we bow to He Who Offers Arrows As Swift As a Deer, I am One with God.

- 73 -

ॐ अनघाय स्वाहा

oṃ anaghāya svāhā

oṃ we bow to He Who is without Sin, I am One with God.

- 74 -

ॐ महातपसे स्वाहा

oṃ mahātapase svāhā

oṃ we bow to He Who is A Great Ascetic, I am One with God.

- 75 -

ॐ घोरतपसे स्वाहा

oṃ ghoratapase svāhā

oṃ we bow to He Who Practices Frightening Asceticism, I am One with God.

- 76 -

ॐ अदीनाय स्वाहा

oṃ adīnāya svāhā

oṃ we bow to He Who is Never Lowly, I am One with God.

- 77 -

ॐ दीनसाधकाय स्वाहा

oṃ dīnasādhakāya svāhā

oṃ we bow to He Who Raises the Lowly, I am One with God.

- 78 -

ॐ संवत्सराय स्वाहा

oṃ saṃvatsarāya svāhā

oṃ we bow to He Who is the Years, I am One with God.

- 79 -

ॐ मम्त्राय स्वाहा

oṃ mamtrāya svāhā

oṃ we bow to He Who is the Mantra, I am One with God.

- 80 -

ॐ प्रमाणाय स्वाहा

oṃ pramāṇāya svāhā

oṃ we bow to He Who is the Proof, I am One with God.

- 81 -

ॐ परमतपसे स्वाहा

oṃ paramatapase svāhā

oṃ we bow to He Who is the Supreme Ascetic, I am One with God.

- 82 -

ॐ योगिने स्वाहा

oṃ yogine svāhā

oṃ we bow to the He Who is the One of Union, I am One with God.

- 83 -

ॐ योज्याय स्वाहा

oṃ yojyāya svāhā

oṃ we bow to He Who is Worthy of Union, I am One with God.

- 84 -

ॐ महाबीजाय स्वाहा

oṃ mahābījāya svāhā

oṃ we bow to He Who is the Great Seed, I am One with God.

- 85 -

ॐ महारेतसे स्वाहा

oṃ mahāretase svāhā

oṃ we bow to the One of Great Seeds, I am One with God.

- 86 -

ॐ महाबलाय स्वाहा

oṃ mahābalāya svāhā

oṃ we bow to the Great Strength, I am One with God.

- 87 -

ॐ सुवर्णरेतसे स्वाहा

oṃ survarṇaretase svāhā

oṃ we bow to He Who Has Seeds of Gold, I am One with God.

- 88 -

ॐ सर्वज्ञाय स्वाहा

oṃ sarvajñāya svāhā

oṃ we bow to He Who is All Knowing, I am One with God.

- 89 -

ॐ सुबीजाय स्वाहा

oṃ subījāya svāhā

oṃ we bow to He Who is the Seed of Excellence, I am One with God.

- 90 -

ॐ बीजवाहनाय स्वाहा

oṃ bījavāhanāya svāhā

oṃ we bow to He Who is the Conveyance of Seeds, I am One with God.

- 91 -

ॐ दशबाहवे स्वाहा

oṃ daśabāhave svāhā

oṃ we bow to He Who Has Ten Arms, I am One with God.

- 92 -

ॐ अनिमिषाय

oṃ animiṣāya

oṃ we bow to He Who Doesn't Blink, I am One with God.

- 93 -

ॐ नीलकण्ठाय स्वाहा

oṃ nīlakaṇṭhāyā svāhā

oṃ we bow to He Who Has A Blue Throat, I am One with God.

- 94 -

ॐ उमापतये स्वाहा

oṃ umāpataye svāhā

oṃ we bow to the Lord of Umā, I am One with God.

- 95 -

ॐ विश्वरूपाय स्वाहा

oṃ viśvarūpāya svāhā

oṃ we bow to the Form of the Universe, I am One with God.

- 96 -

ॐ स्वयंश्रेष्ठाय स्वाहा

oṃ svayaṃśreṣṭāya svāhā

oṃ we bow to He Himself is Most Excellent, I am One with God.

- 97 -

ॐ बलबीराय स्वाहा

oṃ balabīrāya svāhā

oṃ we bow to He Who is A Strong Warrior, I am One with God.

- 98 -

ॐ अबलाय स्वाहा

oṃ abalāya svāhā

oṃ we bow to He Who Protects the Weak, I am One with God.

- 99 -

ॐ गणाय स्वाहा

oṃ gaṇāya svāhā

oṃ we bow to the Multitudes, I am One with God.

- 100 -

ॐ गणकर्त्रे स्वाहा

oṃ gaṇakartre svāhā

oṃ we bow to the Maker of the Multitudes, I am One with God.

- 101 -

ॐ गणपतये स्वाहा

oṃ gaṇapataye svāhā

oṃ we bow to the Lord of the Multitudes, I am One with God.

- 102 -

ॐ दिग्वाससे स्वाहा

oṃ digvāsase svāhā

oṃ we bow to He Who Resides in All Directions, I am One with God.

- 103 -

ॐ कामाय स्वाहा

oṃ kāmāya svāhā

oṃ we bow to He Who is Desire, I am One with God.

- 104 -

ॐ मन्त्रविदे स्वाहा

oṃ mantravide svāhā

oṃ we bow to the Knower of Mantras, I am One with God.

- 105 -

ॐ परमाय स्वाहा

oṃ paramāya svāhā

oṃ we bow to He Who is Supreme, I am One with God.

- 106 -

ॐ मन्त्राय स्वाहा

oṃ mantrāya svāhā

oṃ we bow to He Who is Mantra, I am One with God.

- 107 -

ॐ सर्वभावकराय स्वाहा

oṃ sarvabhāvakarāya svāhā

oṃ we bow to the Giver of All Attitudes, I am One with God.

- 108 -

ॐ हराय स्वाहा

oṃ harāya svāhā

oṃ we bow to He Who Takes Away, I am One with God.

- 109 -

ॐ कमण्डलुधराय स्वाहा

oṃ kamaṇḍaludharāya svāhā

oṃ we bow to He Who Holds a Begging Bowl, I am One with God.

- 110 -

ॐ धन्विने स्वाहा

oṃ dhanvine svāhā

oṃ we bow to He Who Has All Wealth, I am One with God.

- 111 -

ॐ बाणहस्ताय स्वाहा

oṃ bāṇahastāya svāhā

oṃ we bow to He Who Has a Bow in His Hand, I am One with God.

- 112 -

ॐ कपालवते स्वाहा

oṃ kapālavate svāhā

oṃ we bow to He Who Carries a Skull, I am One with God.

- 113 -

ॐ अशनिने स्वाहा

oṃ aśanine svāhā

oṃ we bow to He Who Wields a Thunderbolt, I am One with God.

- 114 -

ॐ शतघ्निंने स्वाहा

oṃ śatarghnimṃne svāhā

oṃ we bow to He Who Kills Hundreds, I am One with God.

- 115 -

ॐ खड्गिने स्वाहा

oṃ khaḍgine svāhā

oṃ we bow to He Who Holds a Sword, I am One with God.

- 116 -

ॐ पट्टिशिने स्वाहा

oṃ paṭṭiśine svāhā

oṃ we bow to He Who Holds a Battle-axe, I am One with God.

- 117 -

ॐ आयुधिने स्वाहा

oṃ āyudhine svāhā

oṃ we bow to He Who Holds a Trident, I am One with God.

- 118 -

ॐ महते स्वाहा

oṃ mahate svāhā

oṃ we bow to He Who is Adorable, I am One with God.

- 119 -

ॐ स्रुवहस्ताय स्वाहा

oṃ sruvahastāya svāhā

oṃ we bow to He Who Holds the Yajña Spoon in His Hand, I am One with God.

- 120 -

ॐ सुरूपाय स्वाहा

oṃ surūpāya svāhā

oṃ we bow to He Who Has an Excellent Form, I am One with God.

- 121 -

ॐ तेजसे स्वाहा

oṃ tejase svāhā

oṃ we bow to He Who is Light, I am One with God.

- 122 -

ॐ तेजस्करनिधये स्वाहा

oṃ tejaskaranidhaye svāhā

oṃ we bow to He Who Gives Light, I am One with God.

- 123 -

ॐ उष्णीषिणे स्वाहा

oṃ uṣṇīṣiṇe svāhā

oṃ we bow to He Who Gives Heat, I am One with God.

- 124 -

ॐ सुवक्त्राय स्वाहा

oṃ suvaktrāya svāhā

oṃ we bow to He of Excellent Speech, I am One with God.

- 125 -

ॐ उदग्राय स्वाहा

oṃ udagrāya svāhā

oṃ we bow to He Who is Fierce, I am One with God.

- 126 -

ॐ विनताय स्वाहा

oṃ vinatāya svāhā

oṃ we bow to He Who is Humble, I am One with God.

- 127 -

ॐ दीर्घाय स्वाहा

oṃ dīrghāya svāhā

oṃ we bow to He Who is Tall, I am One with God.

- 128 -

ॐ हरिकेशाय स्वाहा

oṃ harikeśāya svāhā

oṃ we bow to He Who Cognizes Existence, I am One with God.

- 129 -

ॐ सुतीर्थाय स्वाहा

oṃ sutīrthāya svāhā

oṃ we bow to He Who is the Excellent Place of Pilgrimage, I am One with God.

- 130 -

ॐ कृष्णाय स्वाहा

oṃ kṛṣṇāya svāhā

oṃ we bow to He Who is the Doer of All, I am One with God.

- 131 -

ॐ शृगालरूपाय स्वाहा

oṃ śṛgālarūpāya svāhā

oṃ we bow to He Who Takes the Form of a Jackal, I am One with God.

- 132 -

ॐ सिद्धार्थाय स्वाहा

oṃ siddhārthāya svāhā

oṃ we bow to He Who is the Object of Attainment, I am One with God.

- 133 -

ॐ मुण्डाय स्वाहा

oṃ muṇḍāya svāhā

oṃ we bow to He Who is the Head, I am One with God.

- 134 -

ॐ सर्वशुभकराय स्वाहा

oṃ sarvaśubhakarāya svāhā

oṃ we bow to He Who is the Cause of All Purity, I am One with God.

- 135 -

ॐ अजाय स्वाहा

oṃ ajāya svāhā

oṃ we bow to He Who is Without Birth, I am One with God.

- 136 -

ॐ बहुरूपाय स्वाहा

oṃ bahurūpāya svāhā

oṃ we bow to He Who Has Many Forms, I am One with God.

- 137 -

ॐ गन्धधारिणे स्वाहा

oṃ gandhadhāriṇe svāhā

oṃ we bow to He Who Wears All Scents, I am One with God.

- 138 -

ॐ कपर्दिने स्वाहा

oṃ kapardine svāhā

oṃ we bow to He Who Has Matted Hair, I am One with God.

- 139 -

ॐ ऊर्ध्वरेतसे स्वाहा

oṃ ūrdhvaretase svāhā

oṃ we bow to He Whose Seed Flows Up, I am One with God.

- 140 -

ॐ ऊर्ध्वलिङ्गाय स्वाहा

oṃ ūrdhvaliṅgāya svāhā

oṃ we bow to He Whose Subtlety is Above, I am One with God.

- 141 -

ॐ ऊर्ध्वशायिने स्वाहा

oṃ ūrdhvaśāyine svāhā

oṃ we bow to He Who Rests Above, I am One with God.

- 142 -

ॐ नभस्थलाय स्वाहा

oṃ nabhasthalāya svāhā

oṃ we bow to He Who Dwells in Space, I am One with God.

- 143 -

ॐ त्रिजटाय स्वाहा

oṃ trijaṭāya svāhā

oṃ we bow to He Who Has Three Locks of Matted Hair, I am One with God.

- 144 -

ॐ चीरवाससे स्वाहा

oṃ cīravāsase svāhā

oṃ we bow to He Who Resides in the Infinite, I am One with God.

- 145 -

ॐ रुद्राय स्वाहा

oṃ rudrāya svāhā

oṃ we bow to He Who Takes Away the Tears, I am One with God.

- 146 -

ॐ सेनापतये स्वाहा

oṃ senāpataye svāhā

oṃ we bow to He Who is the Commander of the Army, I am One with God.

- 147 -

ॐ विभवे स्वाहा

oṃ vibhave svāhā

oṃ we bow to He Who is Present Everywhere, I am One with God.

- 148 -

ॐ अहश्चराय स्वाहा

oṃ ahaścarāya svāhā

oṃ we bow to He Who Moves During Daylight, I am One with God.

- 149 -

ॐ नक्तञ्चराय स्वाहा

oṃ naktañcarāya svāhā

oṃ we bow to He Who Moves During the Night, I am One with God.

- 150 -

ॐ तिग्ममन्यवे स्वाहा

oṃ tigmamanyave svāhā

oṃ we bow to He Whose Anger is Fierce, I am One with God.

- 151 -

ॐ सुवर्चसे स्वाहा

oṃ suvarcase svāhā

oṃ we bow to He Who Has Illumination, I am One with God.

- 152 -

ॐ गजघ्ने स्वाहा

oṃ gajaghne svāhā

oṃ we bow to He Who Killed An Elephant, I am One with God.

- 153 -

ॐ दैत्यघ्ने स्वाहा

oṃ daityaghne svāhā

oṃ we bow to He Who Slays Duality, I am One with God.

- 154 -

ॐ कालाय स्वाहा

oṃ kālāya svāhā

oṃ we bow to He Who is Time, I am One with God.

- 155 -

ॐ लोकधात्रे स्वाहा

oṃ lokadhātre svāhā

oṃ we bow to He Who Supports the World, I am One with God.

- 156 -

ॐ गुणाकराय स्वाहा

oṃ guṇākarāya svāhā

oṃ we bow to He Who is the Cause of All Qualities, I am One with God.

- 157 -

ॐ सिंहशार्दूलरूपाय स्वाहा

oṃ siṃhaśārdūlarūpāya svāhā

oṃ we bow to He Who is the Form of a Lion and Tiger, I am One with God.

- 158 -

ॐ आर्द्रंचर्माम्बरावृताय स्वाहा

oṃ ārdraṃcarmāmbarāvṛtāya svāhā

oṃ we bow to He Who Wears the Skin of an Elephant, I am One with God.

- 159 -

ॐ कालयोगिने स्वाहा

oṃ kālayogine svāhā

oṃ we bow to He Who is United With Time, I am One with God.

- 160 -

ॐ महानादाय स्वाहा

oṃ mahānādāya svāhā

oṃ we bow to He Who is Great Sound, I am One with God.

- 161 -

ॐ सर्वकामाय स्वाहा

oṃ sarvakāmāya svāhā

oṃ we bow to He Who is All Desires, I am One with God.

- 162 -

ॐ चतुष्पथाय स्वाहा

oṃ catuṣpathāya svāhā

oṃ we bow to He Who Manifests the Fourfold Path, I am One with God.

- 163 -

ॐ निशाचराय स्वाहा

oṃ niśācarāya svāhā

oṃ we bow to He Who Moves in the Night, I am One with God.

- 164 -

ॐ प्रेतचारिणे स्वाहा

oṃ pretacāriṇe svāhā

oṃ we bow to He Who Moves With Disembodied Spirits, I am One with God.

- 165 -

ॐ भूतचारिणे स्वाहा

oṃ bhūtacāriṇe svāhā

oṃ we bow to He Who Moves With All Elements, I am One with God.

- 166 -

ॐ महेश्वराय स्वाहा

oṃ maheśvarāya svāhā

oṃ we bow to He Who is the Great Seer of All, I am One with God.

- 167 -

ॐ बहुभूताय स्वाहा

oṃ bahubhūtāya svāhā

oṃ we bow to He Who Has Many Elements, I am One with God.

- 168 -

ॐ बहुधाराय स्वाहा

oṃ bahudhārāya svāhā

oṃ we bow to He Who Supports Many, I am One with God.

- 169 -

ॐ स्वर्भानवे स्वाहा

oṃ svarbhānave svāhā

oṃ we bow to He Who is His Own Light, I am One with God.

- 170 -

ॐ अमिताय स्वाहा

oṃ amitāya svāhā

oṃ we bow to He Who is Without Measure, I am One with God.

- 171 -

ॐ गतये स्वाहा

oṃ gataye svāhā

oṃ we bow to He Who is the Refuge, I am One with God.

- 172 -

ॐ नृत्यप्रियाय स्वाहा

oṃ nṛtyapriyāya svāhā

oṃ we bow to He Who Loves Dance, I am One with God.

- 173 -

ॐ नित्यनर्ताय स्वाहा

oṃ nityanartāya svāhā

oṃ we bow to He Who is Always Dancing, I am One with God.

- 174 -

ॐ नर्तकाय स्वाहा

oṃ nartakāya svāhā

oṃ we bow to He Who Causes Others to Dance, I am One with God.

- 175 -

ॐ सर्वलालसाय स्वाहा

oṃ sarvalālasāya svāhā

oṃ we bow to He Who is All Desires, I am One with God.

- 176 -

ॐ घोराय स्वाहा

oṃ ghorāya svāhā

oṃ we bow to He Who is Fierce, I am One with God.

- 177 -

ॐ महातपसे स्वाहा

oṃ mahātapase svāhā

oṃ we bow to He Who is the Great Ascetic, I am One with God.

- 178 -

ॐ पाशाय स्वाहा

oṃ pāśāya svāhā

oṃ we bow to He Who Holds the Noose, I am One with God.

- 179 -

ॐ नित्याय स्वाहा

oṃ nityāya svāhā

oṃ we bow to He Who is Eternal, I am One with God.

- 180 -

ॐ गिरिरुहाय स्वाहा

oṃ giriruhāya svāhā

oṃ we bow to He Who is Situated Upon a Mountain, I am One with God.

- 181 -

ॐ नभसे स्वाहा

oṃ nabhase svāhā

oṃ we bow to He Who is as Vast as the Sky, I am One with God.

- 182 -

ॐ सहस्रहस्ताय स्वाहा

oṃ sahasrahastāya svāhā

oṃ we bow to He Who Has A Thousand Arms, I am One with God.

- 183 -

ॐ विजयाय स्वाहा

oṃ bijayāya svāhā

oṃ we bow to He Who is Victorious, I am One with God.

- 184 -

ॐ व्यवसायाय स्वाहा

oṃ vyavasāyāya svāhā

oṃ we bow to He Who is Great Effort, I am One with God.

- 185 -

ॐ अतन्द्रिताय स्वाहा

oṃ atandritāya svāhā

oṃ we bow to He Who is Always Active, I am One with God.

- 186 -

ॐ अघर्षणाय स्वाहा

oṃ agharṣaṇāya svāhā

oṃ we bow to He Who cannot be Confronted, I am One with God.

- 187 -

ॐ धर्षणात्मने स्वाहा

oṃ dharṣaṇātmane svāhā

oṃ we bow to He Who is Aggressive, I am One with God.

- 188 -

ॐ यज्ञघ्ने स्वाहा

oṃ yajñaghne svāhā

oṃ we bow to He Who Destroyed the Yajña, I am One with God.

- 189 -

ॐ कामनाशकाय स्वाहा

oṃ kāmanāśakāya svāhā

oṃ we bow to He Who Destroyed Love, I am One with God.

- 190 -

ॐ दक्षयागापहारिणे स्वाहा

oṃ dakṣayāgāpahāriṇe svāhā

oṃ we bow to He Who Destroyed Dakṣa's Yajña, I am One with God.

- 191 -

ॐ सुमहाय्याय स्वाहा

oṃ sumahāyyāya svāhā

oṃ we bow to He Who Conceals the Light, I am One with God.

- 192 -

ॐ मध्यमाय स्वाहा

oṃ madhyamāya svāhā

oṃ we bow to He Who is in the Middle, I am One with God.

- 193 -

ॐ तेजापहारिणे स्वाहा

oṃ tejāpahāriṇe svāhā

oṃ we bow to He Who Moves With Light, I am One with God.

- 194 -

ॐ बलघ्ने स्वाहा

oṃ balaghne svāhā

oṃ we bow to He Who Destroys Haughtiness, I am One with God.

- 195 -

ॐ मुदिताय स्वाहा

oṃ muditāya svāhā

oṃ we bow to He Who is Delighted, I am One with God.

- 196 -

ॐ अर्थाय स्वाहा

oṃ arthāya svāhā

oṃ we bow to He Who is the Object or Meaning, I am One with God.

- 197 -

ॐ अजिताय स्वाहा

oṃ ajitāya svāhā

oṃ we bow to He Who is Undefeatable, I am One with God.

- 198 -

ॐ अवराय स्वाहा

oṃ avarāya svāhā

oṃ we bow to He Who is Most Beloved, I am One with God.

- 199 -

ॐ गम्भीराय स्वाहा

oṃ gambhīrāya svāhā

oṃ we bow to He Who is Serious, I am One with God.

- 200 -

ॐ गम्भीरघोषाय स्वाहा

oṃ gambhīraghoṣāya svāhā

oṃ we bow to He Who is Extremely Serious, I am One with God.

- 201 -

ॐ गंभीरबलवाहनाय स्वाहा

oṃ gaṃbhīrabalavāhanāya svāhā

oṃ we bow to He Who is the Conveyance of the Strength of Seriousness, I am One with God.

- 202 -

ॐ न्यग्रोधरूपाय स्वाहा

oṃ nyagrodharūpāya svāhā

oṃ we bow to He Who is the Form of a Banyan Tree, I am One with God.

- 203 -

ॐ न्यग्रोधाय स्वाहा

oṃ nyagrodhāya svāhā

oṃ we bow to He Who is a Banyan Tree, I am One with God.

- 204 -

ॐ वृक्षकर्णस्थितये स्वाहा

oṃ vṛkṣakarṇasthitaye svāhā

oṃ we bow to He Who Resides in the Senses of Trees, I am One with God.

- 205 -

ॐ विभवे स्वाहा

oṃ vibhave svāhā

oṃ we bow to He Who is Always Present, I am One with God.

- 206 -

ॐ सुतीक्ष्णदशनाय स्वाहा

oṃ sutīkṣṇadaśanāya svāhā

oṃ we bow to He Who Has Vision With Excellent Clarity, I am One with God.

- 207 -

ॐ महाकायाय स्वाहा

oṃ mahākāyāya svāhā

oṃ we bow to He Who Has a Great Body, I am One with God.

- 208 -

ॐ महाननाय स्वाहा

oṃ mahānanāya svāhā

oṃ we bow to He Who Has a Great Face, I am One with God.

- 209 -

ॐ विष्वक्सेनाय स्वाहा

oṃ viṣvaksenāya svāhā

oṃ we bow to He Who Has an Undefeatable Army, I am One with God.

- 210 -

ॐ हरये स्वाहा

oṃ haraye svāhā

oṃ we bow to He Who Presides over the Gross, Subtle and Causal Bodies, I am One with God.

- 211 -

ॐ यज्ञाय स्वाहा

oṃ yajñāya svāhā

oṃ we bow to He Who is Sacrifice, I am One with God.

- 212 -

ॐ संयुगापीडवाहनाय स्वाहा

oṃ saṃyugāpīḍavāhanāya svāhā

oṃ we bow to He Who is the Conveyance of the Pain of the Ages, I am One with God.

- 213 -

ॐ तिक्ष्णतापाय स्वाहा

oṃ tikṣṇatāpāya svāhā

oṃ we bow to He Who is Intensive Light, I am One with God.

- 214 -

ॐ हर्यश्वाय स्वाहा

oṃ haryaśvāya svāhā

oṃ we bow to He Who is the Form of a Horse, I am One with God.

- 215 -

ॐ सहाय स्वाहा

oṃ sahāya svāhā

oṃ we bow to He Who is a Friend, I am One with God.

- 216 -

ॐ कर्मकालविदे स्वाहा

oṃ karmakālavide svāhā

oṃ we bow to He Who Knows the Time of Action, I am One with God.

- 217 -

ॐ विष्णुप्रसादिताय स्वाहा

oṃ viṣṇuprāsāditāyā svāhā

oṃ we bow to He Who Receives the Consecrated Offering of Viṣṇu, I am One with God.

- 218 -

ॐ यज्ञाय स्वाहा

oṃ yajñāya svāhā

oṃ we bow to He Who is Sacrifice, I am One with God.

- 219 -

ॐ समुद्राय स्वाहा

oṃ samudrāya svāhā

oṃ we bow to He Who is the Ocean, I am One with God.

- 220 -

ॐ वडवामुखाय स्वाहा

oṃ vaḍavāmukhāya svāhā

oṃ we bow to He Who is the Heat in the Ocean, I am One with God.

- 221 -

ॐ हुताशनसहाय स्वाहा

oṃ hutāśanasahāya svāhā

oṃ we bow to He Who is the Friend of Fire, I am One with God.

- 222 -

ॐ प्रशन्तात्मने स्वाहा

oṃ praśantātmane svāhā

oṃ we bow to He Who Has a Peaceful Soul, I am One with God.

- 223 -

ॐ हुताशनाय स्वाहा

oṃ hutāśanāya svāhā

oṃ we bow to He Who is the Fire, I am One with God.

- 224 -

ॐ उग्रतेजसे स्वाहा

oṃ ugratejase svāhā

oṃ we bow to He Who is Fierce Light, I am One with God.

- 225 -

ॐ महातेजसे स्वाहा

oṃ mahātejase svāhā

oṃ we bow to He Who is the Great Light, I am One with God.

- 226 -

ॐ जन्याय स्वाहा

oṃ janyāya svāhā

oṃ we bow to He Who is All Beings Born, I am One with God.

- 227 -

ॐ बिजयकालविदे स्वाहा

oṃ bijayakālavide svāhā

oṃ we bow to He Who Knows the Time of Victory, I am One with God.

- 228 -

ॐ ज्योतिषामयनाय स्वाहा

oṃ jyotiṣāmayanāya svāhā

oṃ we bow to He Who Manifests the Bliss of Light, I am One with God.

- 229 -

ॐ सिद्धये स्वाहा

oṃ siddhaye svāhā

oṃ we bow to He Who Has Attained, I am One with God.

- 230 -

ॐ सर्वविग्रहाय स्वाहा

oṃ sarvavigrahāya svāhā

oṃ we bow to He Who is Every Form, I am One with God.

- 231 -

ॐ शिखिने स्वाहा

oṃ śikhine svāhā

oṃ we bow to He Who is the Summit or Ultimate, I am One with God.

- 232 -

ॐ मुण्डिने स्वाहा

oṃ muṇḍine svāhā

oṃ we bow to He Who is the Head, I am One with God.

- 233 -

ॐ जटिने स्वाहा

oṃ jaṭine svāhā

oṃ we bow to He Who Has Matted Hair, I am One with God.

- 234 -

ॐ ज्वालिने स्वाहा

oṃ jvāline svāhā

oṃ we bow to He Who is Light, I am One with God.

- 235 -

ॐ मूर्तिजाय स्वाहा

oṃ mūrtijāya svāhā

oṃ we bow to He Who Gives Birth to the Symbol of Divinity, I am One with God.

- 236 -

ॐ मूर्द्धगाय स्वाहा

oṃ mūrddhagāya svāhā

oṃ we bow to He Who Resides in the Head, I am One with God.

- 237 -

ॐ बलिने स्वाहा

oṃ baline svāhā

oṃ we bow to He Who is the Sacrificial Offering, I am One with God.

- 238 -

ॐ वेणविने स्वाहा

oṃ veṇavine svāhā

oṃ we bow to He Who Holds a Flute, I am One with God.

- 239 -

ॐ पणविने स्वाहा

oṃ paṇavine svāhā

oṃ we bow to He Who Holds a Drum, I am One with God.

- 240 -

ॐ तालिने स्वाहा

oṃ tāline svāhā

oṃ we bow to He Who Holds Cymbals, I am One with God.

- 241 -

ॐ खलिने स्वाहा

oṃ khaline svāhā

oṃ we bow to He Who Has the Threshing Floor, I am One with God.

- 242 -

ॐ कालकटकटाय स्वाहा

oṃ kālakaṭakaṭāya svāhā

oṃ we bow to He Who Conceals Time, I am One with God.

- 243 -

ॐ नक्षत्रविग्रहमतये स्वाहा

oṃ nakṣatravigrahamataye svāhā

oṃ we bow to He Who Orders the Stars and Planets, I am One with God.

- 244 -

ॐ गुणबुद्धये स्वाहा

oṃ guṇabuddhaye svāhā

oṃ we bow to He Who Knows All Qualities, I am One with God.

- 245 -

ॐ लगाय स्वाहा

oṃ lagāya svāhā

oṃ we bow to He Who is Handsome, I am One with God.

- 246 -

ॐ अग्माय स्वाहा

oṃ agmāya svāhā

oṃ we bow to He Who Does Not Move, I am One with God.

- 247 -

ॐ प्रजापतये स्वाहा

oṃ prajāpataye svāhā

oṃ we bow to the Lord of All Beings Born, I am One with God.

- 248 -

ॐ विश्ववाहवे स्वाहा

oṃ viśvavāhave svāhā

oṃ we bow to the Arms of the Universe, I am One with God.

- 249 -

ॐ विभागाय स्वाहा

oṃ vibhāgāya svāhā

oṃ we bow to He Who Doesn't Allow Divisions, I am One with God.

- 250 -

ॐ सर्वगाय स्वाहा

oṃ sarvagāya svāhā

oṃ we bow to He Who Present Everywhere, I am One with God.

- 251 -

ॐ अमुखाय स्वाहा

oṃ amukhāya svāhā

oṃ we bow to He Who Has No Face, I am One with God.

- 252 -

ॐ विमोचनाय स्वाहा

oṃ vimocanāya svāhā

oṃ we bow to He Who Erases, I am One with God.

- 253 -

ॐ सुसरणाय स्वाहा

oṃ susarṇāya svāhā

oṃ we bow to He Who Has Excellent Memory, I am One with God.

- 254 -

ॐ हिरण्यकवचोद्भवाय स्वाहा

oṃ hiraṇyakavacodbhavāya svāhā

oṃ we bow to He Who Raises the Golden Shield, I am One with God.

- 255 -

ॐ मेढजाय स्वाहा

oṃ meḍhajāya svāhā

oṃ we bow to He Who Manifests From the Male Organ, I am One with God.

- 256 -

ॐ ललचारिणे स्वाहा

oṃ lalacāriṇe svāhā

oṃ we bow to He Who Continues to Play, I am One with God.

- 257 -

ॐ महीचारिणे स्वाहा

oṃ mahīcāriṇe svāhā

oṃ we bow to He Who Moves the World, I am One with God.

- 258 -

ॐ स्तुताय स्वाहा

oṃ stutāya svāhā

oṃ we bow to He Who is Song, I am One with God.

- 259 -

ॐ सर्वतूर्यनिनादिने स्वाहा

oṃ sarvatūryaninādine svāhā

oṃ we bow to He Who Contains all Vibrations of the Beyond, I am One with God.

- 260 -

ॐ सर्वातोद्यषरिग्रहाय स्वाहा

oṃ sarvātodyaṣarigrahāya svāhā

oṃ we bow to Lord of All Beings Born, I am One with God.

- 261 -

ॐ व्यालरूपाय स्वाहा

oṃ vyālarūpāya svāhā

oṃ we bow to He Who Has a Strange Form, I am One with God.

- 262 -

ॐ गुहावासिने स्वाहा

oṃ guhāvāsine svāhā

oṃ we bow to He Who Resides in a Cave, I am One with God.

- 263 -

ॐ गुहाय स्वाहा

oṃ guhāya svāhā

oṃ we bow to He Who is a Cave, I am One with God.

- 264 -

ॐ मालिने स्वाहा

oṃ māline svāhā

oṃ we bow to He Who Wears a Garland, I am One with God.

- 265 -

ॐ तरङ्गबिदे स्वाहा

oṃ taraṅgābide svāhā

oṃ we bow to He Who Knows Waves, I am One with God.

- 266 -

ॐ त्रिदशाय स्वाहा

oṃ tridaśāya svāhā

oṃ we bow to He Who is the Three Circumstances, I am One with God.

- 267 -

ॐ त्रिकालधृषे स्वाहा

oṃ trikāladhṛṣe svāhā

oṃ we bow to He Who Sees the Three Times, I am One with God.

- 268 -

ॐ कर्मसर्वबन्धविमोचनाय स्वाहा

oṃ karmasarvabandhavimocanāya svāhā

oṃ we bow to He Who Removes the Bonds of All Karma, I am One with God.

- 269 -

ॐ असुरेन्द्राणां बन्धनाय स्वाहा

oṃ asurendrāṇāṃ bandhanāya svāhā

oṃ we bow to He Who Binds the Lord of Duality, I am One with God.

- 270 -

ॐ युधिशत्रुविनाशिने स्वाहा

oṃ yudhiśatruvināśine svāhā

oṃ we bow to He Who Destroys Enemies, I am One with God.

- 271 -

ॐ सांख्यप्रसादाय स्वाहा

oṃ sāṃkhyaprasādāya svāhā

oṃ we bow to He Who is the Consecration of the Enumeration of Principles, I am One with God.

- 272 -

ॐ दुर्वाससे स्वाहा

oṃ durvāsase svāhā

oṃ we bow to He Who is Difficult to be Controlled, I am One with God.

- 273 -

ॐ सर्वसाधुनिषेविताय स्वाहा

oṃ sarvasādhuniṣevitāya svāhā

oṃ we bow to He Who is Served by all Sādhus, I am One with God.

- 274 -

ॐ प्रस्कन्दनाय स्वाहा

oṃ praskandanāya svāhā

oṃ we bow to He Who Eradicates, I am One with God.

- 275 -

ॐ बिभागज्ञाय स्वाहा

oṃ bibhāgajñāya svāhā

oṃ we bow to He Who Knows Divisions, I am One with God.

- 276 -

ॐ अतुल्याय स्वाहा

oṃ atulyāya svāhā

oṃ we bow to He Who is Incomparable, I am One with God.

-277 -

ॐ यज्ञभागविदे स्वाहा

oṃ yajñabhāgavide svāhā

oṃ we bow to He Who Knows the Divisions of Sacrifice, I am One with God.

- 278 -

ॐ सर्वचारिणे स्वाहा

oṃ sarvacāriṇe svāhā

oṃ we bow to He Who Moves All, I am One with God.

- 279 -

ॐ सर्ववासाय स्वाहा

oṃ sarvavāsāya svāhā

oṃ we bow to He Who is the Residence of All, I am One with God.

- 280 -

ॐ दुर्वासिसे स्वाहा

oṃ durvāsase svāhā

oṃ we bow to He Who is Difficult to be Controlled, I am One with God.

- 281 -

ॐ वासवाय स्वाहा

oṃ vāsavāya svāhā

oṃ we bow to He Who is the Resident, I am One with God.

- 282 -

ॐ अमराय स्वाहा

oṃ amarāya svāhā

oṃ we bow to He Who is Immortal, I am One with God.

- 283 -

ॐ हेमाय स्वाहा

oṃ hemāya svāhā

oṃ we bow to He Who Dwells in Cold, I am One with God.

- 284 -

ॐ हेमकराय स्वाहा

oṃ hemakarāya svāhā

oṃ we bow to He Who Causes Cold, I am One with God.

- 285 -

ॐ अयज्ञसर्वधारिणे स्वाहा

oṃ ayajñasarvadhāriṇe svāhā

oṃ we bow to He Who Supports All Who Sacrifice, I am One with God.

- 286 -

ॐ धरोत्तमाय स्वाहा

oṃ dharottamāya svāhā

oṃ we bow to He Who Supports Excellence, I am One with God.

- 287 -

ॐ लोहिताक्षाय स्वाया

oṃ lohitākṣāya svāyā

oṃ we bow to He Who Has Red Eyes, I am One with God.

- 288 -

ॐ महाक्षाय स्वाहा

oṃ mahākṣāya svāhā

oṃ we bow to He Who Has Great Eyes, I am One with God.

- 289 -

ॐ विजयाक्षाय स्वाहा

oṃ vijayākṣāya svāhā

oṃ we bow to He Whose Eyes Are Victorious, I am One with God.

- 290 -

ॐ विशारदाय स्वाहा

oṃ viśāradāya svāhā

oṃ we bow to He Who is Intelligent, I am One with God.

- 291 -

ॐ सर्वकामदाय स्वाहा

oṃ sarvakāmadāya svāhā

oṃ we bow to He Who Gives All Desires, I am One with God.

- 292 -

ॐ सर्वकालप्रसादाय स्वाहा

oṃ sarvakālaprasādāya svāhā

oṃ we bow to He Who is the Consecration of All Time, I am One with God.

- 293 -

ॐ सुबलाय स्वाहा

oṃ subalāya svāhā

oṃ we bow to He Who Has Excellent Strength, I am One with God.

- 294 -

ॐ बलरूपधृषे स्वाहा

oṃ balarūpadhṛṣe svāhā

oṃ we bow to He Who Perceives the Form of All Strength, I am One with God.

- 295 -

ॐ संग्रहाय स्वाहा

oṃ saṃgrahāya svāhā

oṃ we bow to He Who Protects Devotees, I am One with God.

- 296 -

ॐ निग्रहाय स्वाहा

oṃ nigrahāya svāhā

oṃ we bow to He Who is Controls His Senses, I am One with God.

- 297 -

ॐ कर्त्रे स्वाहा

oṃ kartre svāhā

oṃ we bow to He Who is the Doer, I am One with God.

- 298 -

ॐ सर्पचीरनिवासाय स्वाहा

oṃ sarpacīranivāsāya svāhā

oṃ we bow to He Who Resides on the Infinite Snake, I am One with God.

- 299 -

ॐ मुख्याय स्वाहा

oṃ mukhyāya svāhā

oṃ we bow to He Who is Foremost, I am One with God.

- 300 -

ॐ अमुख्याय स्वाहा

oṃ amukhyāya svāhā

oṃ we bow to He Who is Less, I am One with God.

- 301 -

ॐ देहाय स्वाहा

oṃ dehāya svāhā

oṃ we bow to He Who is the Body, I am One with God.

- 302 -

ॐ काहलये स्वाहा

oṃ kāhalaye svāhā

oṃ we bow to He Who Plays a Drum, I am One with God.

- 303 -

ॐ सर्वकामवराय स्वाहा

oṃ sarvakāmavarāya svāhā

oṃ we bow to He Who Bestows All Desires, I am One with God.

- 304 -

ॐ सर्वदाय स्वाहा

oṃ sarvadāya svāhā

oṃ we bow to He Who is the Giver of All, I am One with God.

- 305 -

ॐ सर्वतोमुखाय स्वाहा

oṃ sarvatomukhāya svāhā

oṃ we bow to He Who is the Face of All, I am One with God.

- 306 -

ॐ आकाशनिर्विरूपाय स्वाहा

oṃ ākāśanirvirūpāya svāhā

oṃ we bow to He Who is the Form of the Formless Ether, I am One with God.

- 307 -

ॐ निपातिने स्वाहा

oṃ nipātine svāhā

oṃ we bow to He Who is Not Lowly, I am One with God.

- 308 -

ॐ अवशाय स्वाहा

oṃ avaśāya svāhā

oṃ we bow to He Who cannot be Controled, I am One with God.

- 309 -

ॐ खगाय स्वाहा

oṃ khagāya svāhā

oṃ we bow to He Who is Free as a Bird, I am One with God.

- 310 -

ॐ रौद्ररूपाय स्वाहा

oṃ raudrarūpāya svāhā

oṃ we bow to He Who has a Terrible Form, I am One with God.

- 311 -

ॐ अंशवे स्वाहा

oṃ aṃśave svāhā

oṃ we bow to He Who is a Ray of Light, I am One with God.

- 312 -

ॐ आदित्याय स्वाहा

oṃ ādityāya svāhā

oṃ we bow to He Who is Without Duality, I am One with God.

- 313 -

ॐ बहुरश्मये स्वाहा

oṃ bahuraśmaye svāhā

oṃ we bow to He Who has Many Rays, I am One with God.

- 314 -

ॐ सुवर्चसिने स्वाहा

oṃ suvarcasine svāhā

oṃ we bow to He Who has Excellent Radiance, I am One with God.

- 315 -

ॐ वसुवेगाय स्वाहा

oṃ vasuvegāya svāhā

oṃ we bow to He Who has the Speed of the Wind, I am One with God.

- 316 -

ॐ महावेगाय स्वाहा

oṃ mahāvegāya svāhā

oṃ we bow to He Who has Great Speed, I am One with God.

- 317 -

ॐ मनोवेगाय स्वाहा

oṃ manovegāya svāhā

oṃ we bow to He Who has the Speed of the Mind, I am One with God.

- 318 -

ॐ निशाचराय स्वाहा

oṃ niśācarāya svāhā

oṃ we bow to He Who Moves At Night, I am One with God.

- 319 -

ॐ सर्ववासिने स्वाहा

oṃ sarvavāsine svāhā

oṃ we bow to He Who Resides in All, I am One with God.

- 320 -

ॐ श्रियावासिने स्वाहा

oṃ śriyāvāsine svāhā

oṃ we bow to He Who Resides in Respect, I am One with God.

- 321 -

ॐ उपदेशकराय स्वाहा

oṃ upadeśakarāya svāhā

oṃ we bow to He Who is the Cause of Advice, I am One with God.

- 322 -

ॐ अकराय स्वाहा

oṃ akarāya svāhā

oṃ we bow to He Who is Uncaused, I am One with God.

- 323 -

ॐ मुनये स्वाहा

oṃ munaye svāhā

oṃ we bow to the Wise Being, I am One with God.

- 324 -

ॐ आत्मनिरालोकाय स्वाहा

oṃ ātmanirālokāya svāhā

oṃ we bow to the Soul Beyond the Worlds, I am One with God.

- 325 -

ॐ सम्भग्नाय स्वाहा

oṃ sambhagnāya svāhā

oṃ we bow to He Who is Adored, I am One with God.

- 326 -

ॐ सहस्रदाय स्वाहा

oṃ sahasradāya svāhā

oṃ we bow to the Giver of Thousands, I am One with God.

- 327 -

ॐ पक्षिणे स्वाहा

oṃ pakṣiṇe svāhā

oṃ we bow to He Who is a Bird, I am One with God.

- 328 -

ॐ पक्षरूपाय स्वाहा

oṃ pakṣarūpāya svāh

oṃ we bow to He Who is the Form of a Friend, I am One with God.

- 329 -

ॐ अतिदीप्ताय स्वाहा

oṃ atidīptāya svāhā

oṃ we bow to He Who is Expansive Light, I am One with God.

- 330 -

ॐ विशाम्पतये स्वाहा

oṃ viśāmpataye svāhā

oṃ we bow to He Who is the Lord of Beings, I am One with God.

- 331 -

ॐ उन्मादाय स्वाहा

oṃ unmādāya svāhā

oṃ we bow to He Who is Crazy, I am One with God.

- 332 -

ॐ मदनाय स्वाहा

oṃ madanāya svāhā

oṃ we bow to He Who is Intoxicated, I am One with God.

- 333 -

ॐ कामाय स्वाहा

oṃ kāmāya svāhā

oṃ we bow to He Who is Desire, I am One with God.

- 334 -

ॐ अश्वत्थाय स्वाहा

oṃ aśvatthāya svāhā

oṃ we bow to He Who is the Pipal Tree, I am One with God.

- 335 -

ॐ अर्थकराय स्वाहा

oṃ arthakarāya svāhā

oṃ we bow to He Who is the Cause of Wealth, I am One with God.

- 336 -

ॐ यशसे स्वाहा

oṃ yaśase svāhā

oṃ we bow to He Who is Welfare or Fame, I am One with God.

- 337 -

ॐ वामदेवाय स्वाहा

oṃ vāmadevāya svāhā

oṃ we bow to He Who is the God of Love, I am One with God.

- 338 -

ॐ वामाय स्वाहा

oṃ vāmāya svāhā

oṃ we bow to He Who is the Beloved, I am One with God.

- 339 -

ॐ प्राचे स्वाहा

oṃ prāce svāhā

oṃ we bow to He Who is Oldest, I am One with God.

- 340 -

ॐ दक्षिणाय स्वाहा

oṃ dakṣiṇāya svāhā

oṃ we bow to He Who is the Gift to Gods and Priests, I am One with God.

- 341 -

ॐ वामनाय स्वाहा

oṃ vāmanāya svāhā

oṃ we bow to He Who has the Appearance of a Dwarf, I am One with God.

- 342 -

ॐ सिद्धयोगिने स्वाहा

oṃ siddhayogine svāhā

oṃ we bow to He Who Has Attained to Union, I am One with God.

- 343 -

ॐ महर्षये स्वाहा

oṃ maharṣaye svāhā

oṃ we bow to He Who is a Great Seer, I am One with God.

- 344 -

ॐ शिद्धर्थाय स्वाहा

oṃ śiddharthāya svāhā

oṃ we bow to He Who is the Object of Attainment, I am One with God.

- 345 -

ॐ सिद्धसाधकाय स्वाहा

oṃ siddhasādhakāya svāhā

oṃ we bow to He Who is the Sādhu of Attainment, I am One with God.

- 346 -

ॐ भिक्षवे स्वाहा

oṃ bhikṣave svāhā

oṃ we bow to He Who is an Ascetic, I am One with God.

- 347 -

ॐ भिक्षरूपाय स्वाहा

oṃ bhikṣarūpāya svāhā

oṃ we bow to He Who is the Form of a Begging Ascetic, I am One with God.

- 348 -

ॐ विपणाय स्वाहा

oṃ vipaṇāya svāhā

oṃ we bow to He Who Wears no Sectarian Marks, I am One with God.

- 349 -

ॐ मृदवे स्वाहा

oṃ mṛdave svāhā

oṃ we bow to He Whose Heart is Soft, I am One with God.

- 350 -

ॐ अव्ययाय स्वाहा

oṃ avyayāya svāhā

oṃ we bow to He Who is Immortal, I am One with God.

- 351 -

ॐ महासेनाय स्वाहा

oṃ mahāsenāya svāhā

oṃ we bow to He Who is a Great Warrior, I am One with God.

- 352 -

ॐ विशाखाय स्वाहा

oṃ viśākhāya svāhā

oṃ we bow to He Who is Without Branches, I am One with God.

- 353 -

ॐ षष्टिभागाय स्वाहा

oṃ ṣaṣṭibhāgāya svāhā

oṃ we bow to He Who Has Sixty Parts, I am One with God.

- 354 -

ॐ गवाम्पतये स्वाहा

oṃ gavāmpataye svāhā

oṃ we bow to He Who is Lord of His Senses, I am One with God.

- 355 -

ॐ वज्रहस्ताय स्वाहा

oṃ vajrahastāya svāhā

oṃ we bow to He Who Has a Thunderbolt in His Hand, I am One with God.

- 356 -

ॐ विष्कम्भिने स्वाहा

oṃ viṣkambhine svāhā

oṃ we bow to He Who is the Support, I am One with God.

- 357 -

ॐ चमूस्तम्भनाय स्वाहा

oṃ camūstambhanāya svāhā

oṃ we bow to He Who Mesmerizes Enemies, I am One with God.

- 358 -

ॐ वृत्तवृत्तकराय स्वाहा

oṃ vṛttavṛttakarāya svāhā

oṃ we bow to He Who Causes the Changing and the Changeless, I am One with God.

- 359 -

ॐ तालाय स्वाहा

oṃ tālāya svāhā

oṃ we bow to He Who is the Base, I am One with God.

- 360 -

ॐ मधवे स्वाहा

oṃ madhave svāhā

oṃ we bow to He Who is Sweet, I am One with God.

- 361 -

ॐ मधुकलोचनाय स्वाहा

oṃ madhukalocanāya svāhā

oṃ we bow to He Who Has Sweet Eyes, I am One with God.

- 362 -

ॐ वाचस्पत्याय स्वाहा

oṃ vācaspatyāya svāhā

oṃ we bow to He Who is the Lord of All Vibrations, I am One with God.

- 363 -

ॐ वाजसनाय स्वाहा

oṃ vājasanāya svāhā

oṃ we bow to He Who Knows the Vedas, I am One with God.

- 364 -

ॐ अश्रमपूजिताय स्वाहा

oṃ aśramapūjitāya svāhā

oṃ we bow to He Who is Worshiped in Ashrams, I am One with God.

- 365 -

ॐ ब्रह्मचारिणे स्वाहा

oṃ brahmacāriṇe svāhā

oṃ we bow to He Who Moves With God, I am One with God.

- 366 -

ॐ लाकचारिणे स्वाहा

oṃ lākacāriṇe svāhā

oṃ we bow to He Who Moves in the Manifested Existence, I am One with God.

- 367 -

ॐ सर्वचारिणे स्वाहा

oṃ sarvacāriṇe svāhā

oṃ we bow to He Who Moves With All, I am One with God.

- 368 -

ॐ विचारविदे स्वाहा

oṃ vicāravide svāhā

oṃ we bow to He Who Knows What Does Not Move, I am One with God.

- 369 -

ॐ ईशानाय स्वाहा

oṃ īśānāya svāhā

oṃ we bow to the Seer of All, I am One with God.

- 370 -

ॐ ईश्वराय स्वाहा

oṃ īśvarāya svāhā

oṃ we bow to the Seer of All, I am One with God.

- 371 -

ॐ कालाय स्वाहा

oṃ kālāya svāhā

oṃ we bow to He Who is Time, I am One with God.

- 372 -

ॐ निशाचारिणे स्वाहा

oṃ niśācāriṇe svāhā

oṃ we bow to He Who Moves in the Night, I am One with God.

- 373 -

ॐ पिनाकधृगे स्वाहा

oṃ pinākadhṛge svāhā

oṃ we bow to He Who Holds a Bow, I am One with God.

- 374 -

ॐ निमित्तस्थाय स्वाहा

oṃ nimittasthāya svāhā

oṃ we bow to He Who is the Target

- 375 -

ॐ निमित्ताय स्वाहा

oṃ nimittāya svāhā

oṃ we bow to He Who is the Cause, I am One with God.

- 376 -

ॐ नन्दये स्वाहा

oṃ nandaye svāhā

oṃ we bow to He Who is Bliss, I am One with God.

- 377 -

ॐ नन्दिकराय स्वाहा

oṃ nandikarāya svāhā

oṃ we bow to the Cause of Bliss, I am One with God.

- 378 -

ॐ हरये स्वाहा

oṃ haraye svāhā

oṃ we bow to He Who Presides over the Gross, Subtle and Causal Bodies, I am One with God.

- 379 -

ॐ नन्दीश्वराय स्वाहा

oṃ nandīśvarāya svāhā

oṃ we bow to the Supreme Lord of Bliss, I am One with God.

- 380 -

ॐ नन्दिने स्वाहा

oṃ nandine svāhā

oṃ we bow to He Who is Filled With Bliss, I am One with God.

- 381 -

ॐ नन्दनाय स्वाहा

oṃ nandanāya svāhā

oṃ we bow to He Who Projects Bliss, I am One with God.

- 382 -

ॐ नन्दिवर्धनाय स्वाहा

oṃ nindivardhanāya svāhā

oṃ we bow to He Who Radiates Bliss, I am One with God.

- 383 -

ॐ भगहारिणे स्वाहा

oṃ bhagahāriṇe svāhā

oṃ we bow to He Who Takes Away the Parts, I am One with God.

- 384 -

ॐ निहन्त्रे स्वाहा

oṃ nihantre svāhā

oṃ we bow to He Who Conquers, I am One with God.

- 385 -

ॐ कालाय स्वाहा

oṃ kālāya svāhā

oṃ we bow to He Who is Art, I am One with God.

- 386 -

ॐ ब्रह्मणे स्वाहा

oṃ brahmaṇe svāhā

oṃ we bow to He Who is Creative Consciousness, I am One with God.

- 387 -

ॐ पितामहाय स्वाहा

oṃ pitāmahāya svāhā

oṃ we bow to He Who is the Great Grandfather of Creation, I am One with God.

- 388 -

ॐ चतुर्मुखाय स्वाहा

oṃ caturmukhāya svāhā

oṃ we bow to He Who Has Four Faces, I am One with God.

- 389 -

ॐ महालिङ्गाय स्वाहा

oṃ mahāliṅgāya svāhā

oṃ we bow to He Who is the Great Subtle Symbol, I am One with God.

- 390 -

ॐ चारुलिङ्गाय स्वाहा

oṃ cāruliṅgāya svāhā

oṃ we bow to He Who is the Manifested Symbol, I am One with God.

- 391 -

ॐ लिङ्गाध्यक्षाय स्वाहा

oṃ liṅgādhyakṣāya svāhā

oṃ we bow to He Who is the Leader of Symbols, I am One with God.

- 392 -

ॐ सुराध्यक्षाय स्वाहा

oṃ surādhyakṣāya svāhā

oṃ we bow to He Who is the Leader of Gods, I am One with God.

- 393 -

ॐ योगाध्यक्षाय स्वाहा

oṃ yogādhakṣāya svāhā

oṃ we bow to He Who is the Leader of Union, I am One with God.

- 394 -

ॐ युगावहाय स्वाहा

oṃ yugāvahāya svāhā

oṃ we bow to He Who is the Conveyor of Ages, I am One with God.

- 395 -

ॐ वीजाध्यक्षाय स्वाहा

oṃ vījādhyakṣāya svāhā

oṃ we bow to He Who is the Leader of Seeds, I am One with God.

- 396 -

ॐ बीजकर्त्रे स्वाहा

oṃ bījakartre svāhā

oṃ we bow to He Who is the Maker of Seeds, I am One with God.

- 397 -

ॐ अध्यात्मानुगताय स्वाहा

oṃ adhyātmānugatāya svāhā

oṃ we bow to He Who Follows Spirituality, I am One with God.

- 398 -

ॐ बलाय स्वाहा

oṃ balāya svāhā

oṃ we bow to He Who is Strong, I am One with God.

- 399 -

ॐ इतिहासाय स्वाहा

oṃ itihāsāya svāhā

oṃ we bow to He Who is History, I am One with God.

- 400 -

ॐ सङ्कल्पाय स्वाहा

oṃ saṅkalpāya svāhā

oṃ we bow to He Who is a Spiritual Vow, I am One with God.

- 401 -

ॐ गौतमाय स्वाहा

oṃ gautamāya svāhā

oṃ we bow to He Who Radiates Light, I am One with God.

- 402 -

ॐ निशाकराय स्वाहा

oṃ niśākarāya svāhā

oṃ we bow to He Who is the Cause of Night, I am One with God.

- 403 -

ॐ दम्भाय स्वाहा

oṃ dambhāya svāhā

oṃ we bow to He Who Subdues All, I am One with God.

- 404 -

ॐ अदम्भाय स्वाहा

oṃ adambhāya svāhā

oṃ we bow to He Who Cannot be Subdued, I am One with God.

- 405 -

ॐ वैदम्भाय स्वाहा

oṃ vaidambhāya svāhā

oṃ we bow to He Who is Humble, I am One with God.

- 406 -

ॐ वश्याय स्वाहा

oṃ vaśyāya svāhā

oṃ we bow to He Who is Controlled by Devotion, I am One with God.

- 407 -

ॐ वशकराय स्वाहा

oṃ vaśakāraya svāhā

oṃ we bow to He Who is the Cause of Control, I am One with God.

- 408 -

ॐ कल्ये स्वाहा

oṃ kalaye svāhā

oṃ we bow to He Who is Darkness, I am One with God.

- 409 -

ॐ लोककर्त्रे स्वाहा

oṃ lokakartre svāhā

oṃ we bow to He Who is the Maker of Worlds, I am One with God.

- 410 -

ॐ पशुपतये स्वाहा

oṃ paśupataye svāhā

oṃ we bow to He Who is the Lord of Animals, I am One with God.

- 411 -

ॐ महाकर्त्रे स्वाहा

oṃ mahākartre svāhā

oṃ we bow to He Who is Maker of the Great, I am One with God.

- 412 -

ॐ अनौषधाय स्वाहा

oṃ anauṣadhāya svāhā

oṃ we bow to He Who is Without Medicinal Plants, I am One with God.

- 413 -

ॐ अक्षराय स्वाहा

oṃ akṣarāya svāhā

oṃ we bow to He Who is Imperishable, I am One with God.

- 414 -

ॐ परब्रह्मणे स्वाहा

oṃ parabrahmaṇe svāhā

oṃ we bow to He Who is the Supreme Divinity, I am One with God.

- 415 -

ॐ बलवते स्वाहा

oṃ balavate svāhā

oṃ we bow to He Who is the Spirit of Strength, I am One with God.

- 416 -

ॐ शक्राय स्वाहा

oṃ śakrāya svāhā

oṃ we bow to He Who is the Lord of Gods, I am One with God.

- 417 -

ॐ नीतये स्वाहा

oṃ nītaye svāhā

oṃ we bow to He Who is Organization, I am One with God.

- 418 -

ॐ अनीतये स्वाहा

oṃ anītaye svāhā

oṃ we bow to He Who is Without Order, I am One with God.

- 419 -

ॐ शुद्धात्मने स्वाहा

oṃ śuddhātmane svāhā

oṃ we bow to He Who is a Pure Soul, I am One with God.

- 420 -

ॐ मान्याय स्वाहा

oṃ mānyāya svāhā

oṃ we bow to He Who is Adored, I am One with God.

- 421 -

ॐ शुद्धाय स्वाहा

oṃ śuddhāya svāhā

oṃ we bow to He Who is Pure, I am One with God.

- 422 -

ॐ गतागताय स्वाहा

oṃ gatāgatāya svāhā

oṃ we bow to He Who Moves and Moves Not, I am One with God.

- 423 -

ॐ बहुप्रसादाय स्वाहा

oṃ bahuprasādāya svāhā

oṃ we bow to He Who is Many Consecrated Offerings, I am One with God.

- 424 -

ॐ सुस्वप्नाय स्वाहा

oṃ susvapnāya svāhā

oṃ we bow to He Who is the Excellent Dream, I am One with God.

- 425 -

ॐ दर्पणाय स्वाहा

oṃ darpaṇāya svāhā

oṃ we bow to He Who is the Mirror, I am One with God.

- 426 -

ॐ अमित्रजिते स्वाहा

oṃ amitrajite svāhā

oṃ we bow to He Who Conquers Those Who are not Friends, I am One with God.

- 427 -

ॐ वेदकराय स्वाहा

oṃ vedakarāya svāhā

oṃ we bow to He Who is the Cause of Wisdom, I am One with God.

- 428 -

ॐ मन्त्रकराय स्वाहा

oṃ mantrakarāya svāhā

oṃ we bow to He Who is the Cause of Mantras, I am One with God.

- 429 -

ॐ विदुषे स्वाहा

oṃ viduṣe svāhā

oṃ we bow to He Who is the Learned One, I am One with God.

- 430 -

ॐ समरमर्दनाय स्वाहा

oṃ samaramardanāya svāhā

oṃ we bow to He Who Destroys Enmity, I am One with God.

- 431 -

ॐ महामेघनिवासिने स्वाहा

oṃ mahāmeghanivāsine svāhā

oṃ we bow to He Who Resides in a Great Cloud, I am One with God.

- 432 -

ॐ महाघोराय स्वाहा

oṃ mahāghorāya svāhā

oṃ we bow to He Who is Greatly Frightful, I am One with God.

- 433 -

ॐ वंशिने स्वाहा

oṃ vaṃśine svāhā

oṃ we bow to He Who is a Family, I am One with God.

- 434 -

ॐ कराय स्वाहा

oṃ karāya svāhā

oṃ we bow to He Who is the Hand of God, I am One with God.

- 435 -

ॐ अग्निज्वालाय स्वाहा

oṃ agnijvālāya svāhā

oṃ we bow to He Who is the Light of Fire, I am One with God.

- 436 -

ॐ महाज्वालाय स्वाहा

oṃ mahājvālāya svāhā

oṃ we bow to He Who is Great Light, I am One with God.

- 437 -

ॐ अतिधूम्राय स्वाहा

oṃ atidhūmrāya svāhā

oṃ we bow to He Who is Great Smoke, I am One with God.

- 438 -

ॐ हुताय स्वाहा

oṃ hutāya svāhā

oṃ we bow to He Who is the Offering in Sacrifice, I am One with God.

- 439 -

ॐ हविषे स्वाहा

oṃ haviṣe svāhā

oṃ we bow to He Who is the Sacrificial Offering to the Divine Fire, I am One with God.

- 440 -

ॐ वृषणाय स्वाहा

oṃ vṛṣaṇāya svāhā

oṃ we bow to He Who is a Bull, I am One with God.

- 441 -

ॐ शङ्कराय स्वाहा

oṃ śaṅkarāya svāhā

oṃ we bow to He Who is the Cause of Peace, I am One with God.

- 442 -

ॐ वर्चस्विने स्वाहा

oṃ varcasvine svāhā

oṃ we bow to He Who is Full of Energy, I am One with God.

- 443 -

ॐ धूमकेतनाय स्वाहा

oṃ dhūmaketanāya svāhā

oṃ we bow to He Who is a Smoky Fire, I am One with God.

- 444 -

ॐ नीलाय स्वाहा

oṃ nīlāya svāhā

oṃ we bow to He Who is Blue Like an Emerald, I am One with God.

- 445 -

ॐ अङ्गलुब्धाय स्वाहा

oṃ aṅgalubdhāya svāhā

oṃ we bow to He Who Has Obtained a Body, I am One with God.

- 446 -

ॐ शोभनाय स्वाहा

oṃ śobhanāya svāhā

oṃ we bow to He Who Shines with Purity, I am One with God.

- 447 -

ॐ निखग्रहाय स्वाहा

oṃ nikhagrahāya svāhā

oṃ we bow to He Who is a Giver, I am One with God.

- 448 -

ॐ स्वस्तिदाय स्वाहा

oṃ svastidāya svāhā

oṃ we bow to He Who is the Giver of Blessings, I am One with God.

- 449 -

ॐ स्वस्तिभावाय स्वाहा

oṃ svastibhāvāya svāhā

oṃ we bow to He Who is the Attitude of Blessings, I am One with God.

- 450 -

ॐ भागिने स्वाहा

oṃ bhāgine svāhā

oṃ we bow to He Who Shares the Wealth, I am One with God.

- 451 -

ॐ भागकराय स्वाहा

oṃ bhāgakarāya svāhā

oṃ we bow to He Who is the Cause of Wealth, I am One with God.

- 452 -

ॐ लघवे स्वाहा

oṃ laghave svāhā

oṃ we bow to He Who is Light, I am One with God.

- 453 -

ॐ उत्सङ्गाय स्वाहा

oṃ utsaṅgāya svāhā

oṃ we bow to He Who is Excellent Association, I am One with God.

- 454 -

ॐ महाङ्गाय स्वाहा

oṃ mahāṅgāya svāhā

oṃ we bow to He Who Has a Great Body, I am One with God.

- 455 -

ॐ महागर्भपरायणाय स्वाहा

oṃ mahāgarbhaparāyaṇāya svāhā

oṃ we bow to He Who Carries the Great Womb, I am One with God.

- 456 -

ॐ कृष्णवर्णाय स्वाहा

oṃ kṛṣṇavarṇāya svāhā

oṃ we bow to He Who is of Black Color

- 457 -

ॐ सुवर्णाय स्वाहा

oṃ suvarṇāya svāhā

oṃ we bow to He Who is Excellent Color

- 458 -

ॐ सर्वदेहिनामिन्द्रियाय स्वाहा

oṃ sarvadehināmindriyāya svāhā

oṃ we bow to He Who Presides over the Senses of All Beings in a Body, I am One with God.

- 459 -

ॐ महापादाय स्वाहा

oṃ mahāpādāya svāhā

oṃ we bow to He Who Has Great Feet, I am One with God.

- 460 -

ॐ महाहस्ताय स्वाहा

oṃ mahāhastāya svāhā

oṃ we bow to He Who Has Great Hands, I am One with God.

- 461 -

ॐ महाकायाय स्वाहा

oṃ mahākāyāya svāhā

oṃ we bow to He Who Has a Great Body, I am One with God.

- 462 -

ॐ महायशसे स्वाहा

oṃ mahāyaśase svāhā

oṃ we bow to He Who is Great Welfare, I am One with God.

- 463 -

ॐ महामूर्घ्ने स्वाहा

oṃ mahāmūrghne svāhā

oṃ we bow to He Who Has a Great Head, I am One with God.

- 464 -

ॐ महामात्राय स्वाहा

oṃ mahāmātrāya svāhā

oṃ we bow to He Who Has Great Size, I am One with God.

- 465 -

ॐ महानेत्राय स्वाहा

oṃ mahānetrāya svāhā

oṃ we bow to He Who Has Great Eyes, I am One with God.

- 466 -

ॐ निशालयाय स्वाहा

oṃ niśālayāya svāhā

oṃ we bow to He Who Dissolves into Darkness, I am One with God.

- 467 -

ॐ महान्तकाय स्वाहा

oṃ mahāntakāya svāhā

oṃ we bow to He Who is the Cause of the Great End, I am One with God.

- 468 -

ॐ महाकर्णाय स्वाहा

oṃ mahākarṇāya svāhā

oṃ we bow to He Who Has Great Ears, I am One with God.

- 469 -

ॐ महोष्ठाय स्वाहा

oṃ mahoṣṭhāya svāhā

oṃ we bow to He Who Has Great Lips, I am One with God.

- 470 -

ॐ महाहनवे स्वाहा

oṃ mahāhanave svāhā

oṃ we bow to He Who Has a Great Chin, I am One with God.

- 471 -

ॐ महानाशाय स्वाहा

oṃ mahānāśāya svāhā

oṃ we bow to He Who Has a Great Nose, I am One with God.

- 472 -

ॐ महाकम्बवे स्वाहा

oṃ mahākambave svāhā

oṃ we bow to He Who Has a Great Throat, I am One with God.

- 473 -

ॐ महाग्रीवाय स्वाहा

oṃ mahāgrīvāya svāhā

oṃ we bow to He Who Has a Great Neck, I am One with God.

- 474 -

ॐ श्मशानभाजे स्वाहा

oṃ śmaśānabhāje svāhā

oṃ we bow to He Who Plays in the Cremation Grounds, I am One with God.

- 475 -

ॐ महावक्षसे स्वाहा

oṃ mahāvakṣase svāhā

oṃ we bow to He Who Has a Great Chest, I am One with God.

- 476 -

ॐ महोरस्काय स्वाहा

oṃ mahoraskāya svāhā

oṃ we bow to He Who Has a Great Breast, I am One with God.

- 477 -

ॐ अन्तरात्मने स्वाहा

oṃ antarātmane svāhā

oṃ we bow to He Who is the Inner Soul of All, I am One with God.

- 478 -

ॐ मृगालयाय स्वाहा

oṃ mṛgālayāya svāhā

oṃ we bow to He Who Dissolves with the Speed of a Deer, I am One with God.

- 479 -

ॐ लम्बनाय स्वाहा

oṃ lambanāya svāhā

oṃ we bow to He Who Wears Existence, I am One with God.

- 480 -

ॐ लम्बितोष्ठाय स्वाहा

oṃ lambitoṣṭhāya svāhā

oṃ we bow to He Who has Big Lips, I am One with God.

- 481 -

ॐ महामायाय स्वाहा

oṃ mahāmāyāya svāhā

oṃ we bow to He Who is the Great Measurement of Consciousness, I am One with God.

- 482 -

ॐ पयोनिधये स्वाहा

oṃ payonidhaye svāhā

oṃ we bow to He Who is Organized with Clarity, I am One with God.

- 483 -

ॐ महादन्ताय स्वाहा

oṃ mahādantāya svāhā

oṃ we bow to He Who Has Great Teeth, I am One with God.

- 484 -

ॐ महादंष्ट्राय स्वाहा

oṃ mahādaṃṣṭrāya svāhā

oṃ we bow to He Who Has Great Tusks, I am One with God.

- 485 -

ॐ महाजिह्वाय स्वाहा

oṃ mahājihvāya svāhā

oṃ we bow to He Who Has a Great Tongue, I am One with God.

- 486 -

ॐ महामुखाय स्वाहा

oṃ mahāmukhāya svāhā

oṃ we bow to He with a Great Face, I am One with God.

- 487 -

ॐ महानखाय स्वाहा

oṃ mahānakhāya svāhā

oṃ we bow to He with Great Nails, I am One with God.

- 488 -

ॐ महारोम्णे स्वाहा

oṃ mahāromṇe svāhā

oṃ we bow to He with Great Body Hair, I am One with God.

- 489 -

ॐ महाकेशाय स्वाहा

oṃ mahākeśāya svāhā

oṃ we bow to He with Great Hair on His Head, I am One with God.

- 490 -

ॐ महाजटाय स्वाहा

oṃ mahājaṭāya svāhā

oṃ we bow to He with Great Matted Hair, I am One with God.

- 491 -

ॐ प्रसन्नाय स्वाहा

oṃ prasannāya svāhā

oṃ we bow to He Who is Happy, I am One with God.

- 492 -

ॐ प्रसादाय स्वाहा

oṃ prasādāya svāhā

oṃ we bow to He Who is the Consecrated Offering, I am One with God.

- 493 -

ॐ प्रत्ययाय स्वाहा

oṃ pratyayāya svāhā

oṃ we bow to He Who Has a Firm Conviction, I am One with God.

- 494 -

ॐ गिरिसाधनाय स्वाहा

oṃ girisādhanāya svāhā

oṃ we bow to He Who Performs Discipline in the Mountains, I am One with God.

- 495 -

ॐ स्नेहनाय स्वाहा

oṃ snehanāya svāhā

oṃ we bow to He Who is Beloved, I am One with God.

- 496 -

ॐ अस्नेहनाय स्वाहा

oṃ asnehanāya svāhā

oṃ we bow to He Who is Beyond Love, I am One with God.

- 497 -

ॐ अजिताय स्वाहा

oṃ ajitāya svāhā

oṃ we bow to He Who is Invincible, I am One with God.

- 498 -

ॐ महामुनये स्वाहा

oṃ mahāmunaye svāhā

oṃ we bow to He Who is the Great Wise One, I am One with God.

- 499 -

ॐ वृक्षाकाराय स्वाहा

oṃ vṛkṣākārāya svāhā

oṃ we bow to He Who is the Cause of the Tree of Life, I am One with God.

- 500 -

ॐ वृक्षकेतवे स्वाहा

oṃ vṛkṣaketave svāhā

oṃ we bow to He Who is the Limitations of the Tree of Life, I am One with God.

- 501 -

ॐ अनलाय स्वाहा

oṃ analāya svāhā

oṃ we bow to He Who is Fire, I am One with God.

- 502 -

ॐ वायुवाहनाय स्वाहा

oṃ vāyuvahanāya svāhā

oṃ we bow to He Who is the Conveyance of the Wind, I am One with God.

- 503 -

ॐ गण्डनिले स्वाहा

oṃ gaṇḍanile svāhā

oṃ we bow to He Who is the Repository of Scent, I am One with God.

- 504 -

ॐ मेरुधाम्ने स्वाहा

oṃ merudhāmne svāhā

oṃ we bow to He Who is the Backbone of Existence, I am One with God.

- 505 -

ॐ देवाधिपतये स्वाहा

oṃ devādhipataye svāhā

oṃ we bow to He Who is the Supreme Lord of the Gods, I am One with God.

- 506 -

ॐ अथर्वशीर्षाय स्वाहा

oṃ atharvaśīrṣāya svāhā

oṃ we bow to He Who is the Highest Meaning, I am One with God.

- 507 -

ॐ सामास्याय स्वाहा

oṃ sāmāsyāya svāhā

oṃ we bow to He Who is Derived From Songs, I am One with God.

- 508 -

ॐ ऋक्सहस्रामितेक्षणाय स्वाहा

oṃ ṛksahasrāmitekṣaṇāya svāhā

oṃ we bow to He Who is the Thousands of Injunctions of the Ṛg Veda, I am One with God.

- 509 -

ॐ यजुःपादभुजाय स्वाहा

oṃ yajuḥpādabhujāya svāhā

oṃ we bow to He Who is the Feet and the Arms of the Yajur Veda, I am One with God.

- 510 -

ॐ गुह्याय स्वाहा

oṃ guhyāya svāhā

oṃ we bow to He Who is the Secret Place, I am One with God.

- 511 -

ॐ प्रकाशाय स्वाहा

oṃ prakāśāya svāhā

oṃ we bow to He Who is Illumination, I am One with God.

- 512 -

ॐ जङ्गमाय स्वाहा

oṃ jaṅgamāya svāhā

oṃ we bow to He Who is the Beings that Move, I am One with God.

- 513 -

ॐ अमोघार्थाय स्वाहा

oṃ amoghārthāya svāhā

oṃ we bow to He Who is the Object of Infallibility, I am One with God.

- 514 -

ॐ प्रसादाय स्वाहा

oṃ prasādāya svāhā

oṃ we bow to He Who is the Consecrated Offering, I am One with God.

- 515 -

ॐ आभिगम्याय स्वाहा

oṃ ābhigamyāya svāhā

oṃ we bow to He Who is Easily Attainable, I am One with God.

- 516 -

ॐ सुदर्शनाय स्वाहा

oṃ sudarśanāya svāhā

oṃ we bow to He Who is Excellent Intuitive Vision, I am One with God.

- 517 -

ॐ उपकाराय स्वाहा

oṃ upakārāya svāhā

oṃ we bow to He Who is the Benefactor, I am One with God.

- 518 -

ॐ प्रियाय स्वाहा

oṃ priyāya svāhā

oṃ we bow to He Who is the Beloved, I am One with God.

- 519 -

ॐ सर्वाय स्वाहा

oṃ sarvāya svāhā

oṃ we bow to He Who is All, I am One with God.

- 520 -

ॐ कनकाय स्वाहा

oṃ kanakāya svāhā

oṃ we bow to He Who is Gold, I am One with God.

- 521 -

ॐ काञ्चनच्छवये स्वाहा

oṃ kāñcanacchavaye svāhā

oṃ we bow to He Who is of Golden Color, I am One with God.

- 522 -

ॐ नाभये स्वाहा

oṃ nābhaye svāhā

oṃ we bow to He Who is the Navel, I am One with God.

- 523 -

ॐ नन्दिकराय स्वाहा

oṃ nandikarāya svāhā

oṃ we bow to He Who is the Cause of Bliss, I am One with God.

- 524 -

ॐ भावाय स्वाहा

oṃ bhāvāya svāhā

oṃ we bow to He Who is the Attitude, I am One with God.

- 525 -

ॐ पुष्करस्थपतये स्वाहा

oṃ puṣkarasthapataye svāhā

oṃ we bow to He Who Established the Pilgrimage Place of Puṣkar, I am One with God.

- 526 -

ॐ स्थिराय स्वाहा

oṃ sthirāya svāhā

oṃ we bow to He Who is Still, I am One with God.

- 527 -

ॐ द्वादशाय स्वाहा

oṃ dvādaśāya svāhā

oṃ we bow to He Who is the Twelve, I am One with God.

- 528 -

ॐ त्रासनाय स्वाहा

oṃ trāsanāya svāhā

oṃ we bow to He Who Creates Fear of Evil, I am One with God.

- 529 -

ॐ आद्याय स्वाहा

oṃ ādyāya svāhā

oṃ we bow to He Who is Foremost, I am One with God.

- 530 -

ॐ यज्ञाय स्वाहा

oṃ yajñāya svāhā

oṃ we bow to He Who is Sacrifice, I am One with God.

- 531 -

ॐ यज्ञसमाहिताय स्वाहा

oṃ yajñasamāhitāya svāhā

oṃ we bow to He Who is the Benefit Conferred by Sacrifice, I am One with God.

- 532 -

ॐ नक्ताय स्वाहा

oṃ naktāya svāhā

oṃ we bow to He Who is the Night, I am One with God.

- 533 -

ॐ कलये स्वाहा

oṃ kalaye svāhā

oṃ we bow to He Who is Darkness, I am One with God.

- 534 -

ॐ कालाय स्वाहा

oṃ kālāya svāhā

oṃ we bow to He Who is Time, I am One with God.

- 535 -

ॐ मकराय स्वाहा

oṃ makarāya svāhā

oṃ we bow to He Who is Known by the Letter M, the Culmination, I am One with God.

- 536 -

ॐ कलपूजिताय स्वाहा

oṃ kalapūjitāya svāhā

oṃ we bow to He Who is Worshiped By Darkness, I am One with God.

- 537 -

ॐ सगणाय स्वाहा

oṃ sagaṇāya svāhā

oṃ we bow to He Who is with the Multitudes, I am One with God.

- 538 -

ॐ गणकराय स्वाहा

oṃ gaṇakarāya svāhā

oṃ we bow to He Who is the Cause of the Multitudes, I am One with God.

- 539 -

ॐ भूतवाहनसारथये स्वाहा

oṃ bhūtavāhanasārathaye svāhā

oṃ we bow to He Who Drives the Conveyance of All Elements, I am One with God.

- 540 -

ॐ भस्मशयाय स्वाहा

oṃ bhasmaśayāya svāhā

oṃ we bow to He Who Rests in Ashes, I am One with God.

- 541 -

ॐ भस्मगोप्त्रे स्वाहा

oṃ bhasmagoptre svāhā

oṃ we bow to He Who Hides in Ashes, I am One with God.

- 542 -

ॐ भस्मभूताय स्वाहा

oṃ bhasmabhūtāya svāhā

oṃ we bow to He Who is the Element in Ashes, I am One with God.

- 543 -

ॐ तरवे स्वाहा

oṃ tarave svāhā

oṃ we bow to He Who Takes Across, I am One with God.

- 544 -

ॐ गणाय स्वाहा

oṃ gaṇāya svāhā

oṃ we bow to He Who is the Multitude, I am One with God.

- 545 -

ॐ लोकपालाय स्वाहा

oṃ lokapālāya svāhā

oṃ we bow to He Who is Protector of the Worlds, I am One with God.

- 546 -

ॐ अलोकाय स्वाहा

oṃ alokāya svāhā

oṃ we bow to He Who is Beyond Worlds, I am One with God.

- 547 -

ॐ महात्मने स्वाहा

oṃ mahātmane svāhā

oṃ we bow to He Who is the Great Soul, I am One with God.

- 548 -

ॐ सर्वपूजिताय स्वाहा

oṃ sarvapūjitāya svāhā

oṃ we bow to He Who is Worshiped by All, I am One with God.

- 549 -

ॐ शुक्लाय स्वाहा

oṃ śuklāya svāhā

oṃ we bow to He Who is Bright, I am One with God.

- 550 -

ॐ त्रिशुक्लाय स्वाहा

oṃ triśuklāya svāhā

oṃ we bow to He Who is Brighter Than the Three, I am One with God.

- 551 -

ॐ सम्पन्नाय स्वाहा

oṃ sampannāya svāhā

oṃ we bow to He Who is Totally Free, I am One with God.

- 552 -

ॐ शुचये स्वाहा

oṃ śucaye svāhā

oṃ we bow to He Who is Shining with Purity, I am One with God.

- 553 -

ॐ भूतनिषेविताय स्वाहा

oṃ bhūtaniṣevitāya svāhā

oṃ we bow to He Who is Served by the Elements, I am One with God.

- 554 -

ॐ आश्रमस्थाय स्वाहा

oṃ āśramasthāya svāhā

oṃ we bow to He Who is Established in Ashrams, I am One with God.

- 555 -

ॐ क्रियावस्थाय स्वाहा

oṃ kriyāvasthāya svāhā

oṃ we bow to He Who is Situated in Actions, I am One with God.

- 556 -

ॐ विश्वकर्मपतये स्वाहा

oṃ viśvakarmapataye svāhā

oṃ we bow to He Who is the Lord of the Universe of Actions, I am One with God.

- 557 -

ॐ वराय स्वाहा

oṃ varāya svāhā

oṃ we bow to He Who is the Boon, I am One with God.

- 558 -

ॐ विशालशाखाय स्वाहा

oṃ viśālaśākhāya svāhā

oṃ we bow to He Who Has Enormous Branches, I am One with God.

- 559 -

ॐ ताम्रोष्ठाय स्वाहा

ṃ tāmroṣṭhāya svāhā

oṃ we bow to He Who Has Copper Lips, I am One with God.

- 560 -

ॐ अम्बुजाय स्वाहा

oṃ ambujāya svāhā

oṃ we bow to He Who is the Ocean, I am One with God.

- 561 -

ॐ सुनिश्चलाय स्वाहा

oṃ suniścalāya svāhā

oṃ we bow to He Who is Excellent Without Movement, I am One with God.

- 562 -

ॐ कपिलाय स्वाहा

oṃ kapilāya svāhā

oṃ we bow to He Who is Tawny Color, I am One with God.

- 563 -

ॐ कपिशाय स्वाहा

oṃ kapiśāya svāhā

oṃ we bow to He Who is the Lord of Monkeys, I am One with God.

- 564 -

ॐ शुक्लाय स्वाहा

oṃ śuklāya svāhā

oṃ we bow to He Who is Bright, I am One with God.

- 565 -

ॐ आयुषे स्वाहा

oṃ āyuṣe svāhā

oṃ we bow to He Who is Life, I am One with God.

- 566 -

ॐ पराय स्वाहा

oṃ parāya svāhā

oṃ we bow to He Who is Supreme, I am One with God.

- 567 -

ॐ अपराय स्वाहा

oṃ aparāya svāhā

oṃ we bow to He Who is Beyond, I am One with God.

- 568 -

ॐ गन्धर्वाय स्वाहा

oṃ gandharvāya svāhā

oṃ we bow to He Who is a Celestial Singer, I am One with God.

- 569 -

ॐ अदितये स्वाहा

oṃ aditaye svāhā

oṃ we bow to He Who is Beyond Duality, I am One with God.

- 570 -

ॐ तार्क्ष्याय स्वाहा

oṃ tārkṣyāya svāhā

oṃ we bow to He Who is King of the Birds, I am One with God.

- 571 -

ॐ सुविज्ञेयाय स्वाहा

oṃ suvijñeyāya svāhā

oṃ we bow to He Who is Excellent Knowledge, I am One with God.

- 572 -

ॐ सुशारदाय स्वाहा

oṃ suśāradāya svāhā

oṃ we bow to He Who is the Giver of Knowledge, I am One with God.

- 573 -

ॐ परश्वधायुधाय स्वाहा

oṃ paraśvadhāyudhāya svāhā

oṃ we bow to He Who Holds the Battle-axe of Good Actions, I am One with God.

- 574 -

ॐ देवाय स्वाहा

oṃ devāya svāhā

oṃ we bow to He Who is God, I am One with God.

- 575 -

ॐ अनुकारिणे स्वाहा

oṃ anukāriṇe svāhā

oṃ we bow to He Who Helps Others, I am One with God.

- 576 -

ॐ सुवान्धवाय स्वाहा

oṃ suvāndhavāya svāhā

oṃ we bow to He Who is Excellent Attachments, I am One with God.

- 577 -

ॐ तुम्बवीणाय स्वाहा

oṃ tumbavīṇāya svāhā

oṃ we bow to He Who is the Viṇa Instrument, I am One with God.

- 578 -

ॐ महाक्रोधाय स्वाहा

oṃ mahākrodhāya svāhā

oṃ we bow to He Who is Great Anger, I am One with God.

- 579 -

ॐ ऊर्ध्वरेतसे स्वाहा

oṃ ūrdhvaretase svāhā

oṃ we bow to He Whose Seed Flows Up, I am One with God.

- 580 -

ॐ जल्लेशयाय स्वाहा

oṃ jaleśayāya svāhā

oṃ we bow to He Who is a Body of Water, I am One with God.

- 581 -

ॐ उग्राय स्वाहा

oṃ ugrāya svāhā

oṃ we bow to He Who is Fierce, I am One with God.

- 582 -

ॐ वंशकराय स्वाहा

oṃ vaṃśakarāya svāhā

oṃ we bow to He Who is All Victorious, I am One with God.

- 583 -

ॐ वंशाय स्वाहा

oṃ vaṃśāya svāhā

oṃ we bow to He Who is a Flute, I am One with God.

- 584 -

ॐ वंशनादाय स्वाहा

oṃ vaṃśanādāya svāhā

oṃ we bow to He Who is the Vibration of the Flute, I am One with God.

- 585 -

ॐ आनन्दिताय स्वाहा

oṃ ānanditāya svāhā

oṃ we bow to He Who is Without Fault, I am One with God.

- 586 -

ॐ सर्वाङ्गरूपाय स्वाहा

oṃ sarvāṅgarūpāya svāhā

oṃ we bow to He Who is the Form of All Limbs, I am One with God.

- 587 -

ॐ मायाविने स्वाहा

oṃ māyāvine svāhā

oṃ we bow to He Who Spreads Illusion, I am One with God.

- 588 -

ॐ सुहृदाय स्वाहा

oṃ suhṛdāya svāhā

oṃ we bow to He Who Has an Excellent Heart, I am One with God.

- 589 -

ॐ अनिलाय स्वाहा

oṃ anilāya svāhā

oṃ we bow to He Who is Wind, I am One with God.

- 590 -

ॐ अनलाय स्वाहा

oṃ analāya svāhā

oṃ we bow to He Who is Fire, I am One with God.

- 591 -

ॐ बन्धनाय स्वाहा

oṃ bandhanāya svāhā

oṃ we bow to He Who is Bound, I am One with God.

- 592 -

ॐ बन्धकर्त्रे स्वाहा

oṃ bandhakartre svāhā

oṃ we bow to He Who Creates Bondage, I am One with God.

- 593 -

ॐ सुबन्धनविमोचनाय स्वाहा

oṃ subandhanavimocanāya svāhā

oṃ we bow to He Who is the Excellent One That Destroys Bonds, I am One with God.

- 594 -

ॐ सयज्ञारये स्वाहा

oṃ sayajñāraye svāhā

oṃ we bow to He Who is with Those Who Sacrifice, I am One with God.

- 595 -

ॐ सकामारये स्वाहा

oṃ sakāmāraye svāhā

oṃ we bow to He Who is with Those Who So Desire, I am One with God.

- 596 -

ॐ महादंष्ट्राय स्वाहा

oṃ mahādaṃṣṭrāya svāhā

oṃ we bow to He Who Has Great Tusks, I am One with God.

- 597 -

ॐ महायुधाय स्वाहा

oṃ mahāyudhāya svāhā

oṃ we bow to He Who is a Great Warrior, I am One with God.

- 598 -

ॐ बहुधानिन्दिताय स्वाहा

oṃ bahudhāninditāya svāhā

oṃ we bow to He Who is Often Ridiculed, I am One with God.

- 599 -

ॐ शर्वाय स्वाहा

oṃ śarvāya svāhā

oṃ we bow to He Who is an Archer, I am One with God.

- 600 -

ॐ शङ्कराय स्वाहा

oṃ śaṅkarāya svāhā

oṃ we bow to He Who is the Cause of Peace, I am One with God.

- 601 -

ॐ शङ्कराय स्वाहा

oṃ śaṅkarāya svāhā

oṃ we bow to He Who is the Cause of Peace, I am One with God.

- 602 -

ॐ अधनाय स्वाहा

oṃ adhanāya svāhā

oṃ we bow to He Who is Without Wealth, I am One with God.

- 603 -

ॐ अमरेशाय स्वाहा

oṃ amareśāya svāhā

oṃ we bow to He Who is the Eternal Lord, I am One with God.

- 604 -

ॐ महादेवाय स्वाहा

oṃ mahādevāya svāhā

oṃ we bow to He Who is the Great God, I am One with God.

- 605 -

ॐ विश्वदेवाय स्वाहा

oṃ viśvadevāya svāhā

oṃ we bow to He Who is the Universal God, I am One with God.

- 606 -

ॐ सुरारिघ्ने स्वाहा

oṃ surārighne svāhā

oṃ we bow to He Who is the Destroyer of Enemies of Gods, I am One with God.

- 607 -

ॐ अहिर्बुध्न्याय स्वाहा

oṃ ahirbudhnyāya svāhā

oṃ we bow to He Who Resides in the Regions Below, I am One with God.

- 608 -

ॐ अनिलाभाय स्वाहा

oṃ anilābhāya svāhā

oṃ we bow to He Who is Imperceptible Like the Wind, I am One with God.

- 609 -

ॐ चेकिताय स्वाहा

oṃ cekitāya svāhā

oṃ we bow to He Who Has One Pointed Consciousness, I am One with God.

- 610 -

ॐ हविषे स्वाहा

oṃ haviṣe svāhā

oṃ we bow to He Who is the Offering to the Sacrificial Fire, I am One with God.

- 611 -

ॐ अजैकपादे स्वाहा

oṃ ajaikapāde svāhā

oṃ we bow to He Who is Born with One Foot, I am One with God.

- 612 -

ॐ कपालिने स्वाहा

oṃ kapāline svāhā

oṃ we bow to He Who Bears a Skull, I am One with God.

- 613 -

ॐ त्रिशङ्कवे स्वाहा

oṃ triśaṅkave svāhā

oṃ we bow to He Who Has Three Marks on His Forehead, I am One with God.

- 614 -

ॐ अजिताय स्वाहा

oṃ ajitāya svāhā

oṃ we bow to He Who is Undefeatable

- 615 -

ॐ शिवाय स्वाहा

oṃ śivāya svāhā

oṃ we bow to He Who is the Consciousness of Infinite Goodness

- 616 -

ॐ धन्वन्तरये स्वाहा

oṃ dhanvantaraye svāhā

oṃ we bow to He Who is the Lord of Medicines, I am One with God.

- 617 -

ॐ धूमकेतवे स्वाहा

oṃ dhūmaketave svāhā

oṃ we bow to He Who Restricts Unclarity, I am One with God.

- 618 -

ॐ स्कन्दाय स्वाहा

oṃ skandāya svāhā

oṃ we bow to He Who is the Warrior of the Gods, I am One with God.

- 619 -

ॐ वैश्रवणाय स्वाहा

oṃ vaiśravaṇāya svāhā

oṃ we bow to He Who is the Universal Being, I am One with God.

- 620 -

ॐ धात्रे स्वाहा

oṃ dhātre svāhā

oṃ we bow to He Who is the Creator, I am One with God.

- 621 -

ॐ शक्राय स्वाहा

oṃ śakrāya svāhā

oṃ we bow to He Who is Lord of Gods, I am One with God.

- 622 -

ॐ विष्णवे स्वाहा

oṃ viṣṇave svāhā

oṃ we bow to He Who Pervades the Universe, I am One with God.

- 623 -

ॐ भिन्नाय स्वाहा

oṃ bhinnāya svāhā

oṃ we bow to He Who is Different, I am One with God.

- 624 -

ॐ त्वष्ट्रे स्वाहा

oṃ tvaṣṭre svāhā

oṃ we bow to He Who Makes New, I am One with God.

- 625 -

ॐ ध्रुवाय स्वाहा

oṃ dhruvāya svāhā

oṃ we bow to He Who is Eternally Young, I am One with God.

- 626 -

ॐ धराय स्वाहा

oṃ dharāya svāhā

oṃ we bow to He Who Supports, I am One with God.

- 627 -

ॐ प्रभावाय स्वाहा

oṃ prabhāvāya svāhā

oṃ we bow to He Who Shines, I am One with God.

- 628 -

ॐ सर्वगर्वाय स्वाहा

oṃ sarvagarvāya svāhā

oṃ we bow to He Who is the All-pervading Wind, I am One with God.

- 629 -

ॐ अर्यम्णे स्वाहा

oṃ aryamṇe svāhā

oṃ we bow to He Who is Respected For His Knowledge, I am One with God.

- 630 -

ॐ सवित्रे स्वाहा

oṃ savitre svāhā

oṃ we bow to He Who is the Light of Wisdom, I am One with God.

- 631 -

ॐ रवये स्वाहा

oṃ ravaye svāhā

oṃ we bow to He Who is the Light of the Sun, I am One with God.

- 632 -

ॐ उषङ्गवे स्वाहा

oṃ uṣaṅgave svāhā

oṃ we bow to He Whose Rays are Hot, I am One with God.

- 633 -

ॐ विधात्रे स्वाहा

oṃ vidātre svāhā

oṃ we bow to He Who is Creator, I am One with God.

- 634 -

ॐ मान्धात्रे स्वाहा

oṃ māndhātre svāhā

oṃ we bow to He Who Creates Thoughts, I am One with God.

-635 -

ॐ भूतभावनाय स्वाहा

oṃ bhūtabhāvanāya svāhā

oṃ we bow to He Who is the Attitude of Existence, I am One with God.

- 636 -

ॐ विभवे स्वाहा

oṃ vibhave svāhā

oṃ we bow to He Who is Present Everywhere, I am One with God.

- 637 -

ॐ वर्णविभाविने स्वाहा

oṃ varṇavibhāvine svāhā

oṃ we bow to He Who is with Different Colors, Castes, and Creeds, I am One with God.

- 638 -

ॐ सर्वकामगुणावहाय स्वाहा

oṃ sarvakāmaguṇāvahāya svāhā

oṃ we bow to He Who is the Conveyor of All Desirable Qualities, I am One with God.

- 639 -

ॐ पद्मनाभाय स्वाहा

oṃ padmanābhāya svāhā

oṃ we bow to He Who Has A Lotus in His Navel, I am One with God.

- 640 -

ॐ महागर्भाय स्वाहा

oṃ mahāgarbhāya svāhā

oṃ we bow to He Who is the Great Womb, I am One with God.

- 641 -

ॐ चन्द्रवक्त्राय स्वाहा

oṃ candravaktrāya svāhā

oṃ we bow to He Who is the Face of the Moon, I am One with God.

- 642 -

ॐ अनिलाय स्वाहा

oṃ anilāya svāhā

oṃ we bow to He Who is Independant, I am One with God.

- 643 -

ॐ अनलाय स्वाहा

oṃ analāya svāhā

oṃ we bow to He Whose Power Increases, I am One with God.

- 644 -

ॐ बलवते स्वाहा

oṃ balavate svāhā

oṃ we bow to He Who is Strong, I am One with God.

- 645 -

ॐ उपशान्ताय स्वाहा

oṃ upaśāntāya svāhā

oṃ we bow to He Who Has the Highest Peace, I am One with God.

- 646 -

ॐ पुराणाय स्वाहा

oṃ purāṇāya svāhā

oṃ we bow to He Who is Old, I am One with God.

- 647 -

ॐ पुण्यचञ्चवे स्वाहा

oṃ puṇyacañcave svāhā

oṃ we bow to He Who Moves With Merit, I am One with God.

- 648 -

ॐ इत्यै स्वाहा

oṃ ityai svāhā

oṃ we bow to He Who is the End, I am One with God.

- 649 -

ॐ कुरुकर्त्रे स्वाहा

oṃ kurukartre svāhā

oṃ we bow to He Who is the Doer of All Actions, I am One with God.

- 650 -

ॐ कुरुवासिने स्वाहा

oṃ kuruvāsine svāhā

oṃ we bow to He Who Resides in All Actions, I am One with God.

- 651 -

ॐ पुरुहूताय स्वाहा

oṃ puruhūtāya svāhā

oṃ we bow to He Who is the Performer of Worship, I am One with God.

- 652 -

ॐ गुणौषधाय स्वाहा

oṃ guṇauśadhāya svāhā

oṃ we bow to He Who is the Qualities of Vegetation, I am One with God.

- 653 -

ॐ सर्वाशयाय स्वाहा

oṃ sarvāśayāya svāhā

oṃ we bow to He Who Allows Rest to All Beings, I am One with God.

- 654 -

ॐ दर्भचारिणे स्वाहा

oṃ darbhacāriṇe svāhā

oṃ we bow to He Who is Pleased by the Offering of Darbha Grass, I am One with God.

- 655 -

ॐ सर्वप्राणिपतये स्वाहा

oṃ sarvaprāṇipataye svāhā

oṃ we bow to He Who is the Lord of All Beings, I am One with God.

- 656 -

ॐ देवदेवाय स्वाहा

oṃ devadevāya svāhā

oṃ we bow to He Who is the God of Gods, I am One with God.

- 657 -

ॐ सुखासक्ताय स्वाहा

oṃ sukhāsaktāya svāhā

oṃ we bow to He Who is Unattached to Happiness, I am One with God.

- 658 -

ॐ सदसते स्वाहा

oṃ sadasate svāhā

oṃ we bow to He Who is Pure Truth, I am One with God.

- 659 -

ॐ सर्वरत्नविदे स्वाहा

oṃ sarvaratnavide svāhā

oṃ we bow to He Who Knows All Jewels, I am One with God.

- 660 -

ॐ कैलाशगिरिवासिने स्वाहा

oṃ kailāśagirivāsine svāhā

oṃ we bow to He Who Resides on the Kailaśa Mountain, I am One with God.

- 661 -

ॐ हिमवद्गिरिशंश्रयाय स्वाहा

oṃ himavadgiriśaṃśrayāya svāhā

oṃ we bow to He Who Reposes in the Himalayan Mountains, I am One with God.

- 662 -

ॐ कूलहारिणे स्वाहा

oṃ kūlahāriṇe svāhā

oṃ we bow to He Who Destroys the Banks of Rivers, I am One with God.

- 663 -

ॐ कूलकर्त्रे स्वाहा

oṃ kūlakartre svāhā

oṃ we bow to He Who Makes the Banks of Rivers, I am One with God.

- 664 -

ॐ बहुविद्याय स्वाहा

oṃ bahuvidyāya svāhā

oṃ we bow to He Who Has Much Knowledge, I am One with God.

- 665 -

ॐ बहुप्रदाय स्वाहा

oṃ bahupradāya svāhā

oṃ we bow to He Who Gives Much, I am One with God.

- 666 -

ॐ वणिजाय स्वाहा

oṃ vaṇijāya svāhā

oṃ we bow to He Who Trades for Wealth, I am One with God.

- 667 -

ॐ वर्धकिने स्वाहा

oṃ vardhakine svāhā

oṃ we bow to He Who Works with Wood, I am One with God.

- 668 -

ॐ वृक्षाय स्वाहा

oṃ vṛkṣāya svāhā

oṃ we bow to He Who is a Tree, I am One with God.

- 669 -

ॐ वकुलाय स्वाहा

oṃ vakulāya svāhā

oṃ we bow to He Who is the Vakula Tree, I am One with God.

- 670 -

ॐ चन्दनाय स्वाहा

oṃ candanāya svāhā

oṃ we bow to He Who is Sandalwood, I am One with God.

- 671 -

ॐ छन्दाय स्वाहा

oṃ chandāya svāhā

oṃ we bow to He Who is the Wish Fulfilling Tree, I am One with God.

- 672 -

ॐ सारग्रीवाय स्वाहा

oṃ sāragrīvāya svāhā

oṃ we bow to He Who Has a Mighty Neck, I am One with God.

- 673 -

ॐ महाजत्रवे स्वाहा

oṃ mahājatrave svāhā

oṃ we bow to He Who Has Strong Shoulders, I am One with God.

- 674 -

ॐ अलोलाय स्वाहा

oṃ alolāya svāhā

oṃ we bow to He Who is Steady, I am One with God.

- 675 -

ॐ महौषधाय स्वाहा

oṃ mahauṣadhāya svāhā

oṃ we bow to He Who is Great Vegetation, I am One with God.

- 676 -

ॐ सिद्धार्थकारिणे स्वाहा

oṃ siddhārthakāriṇe svāhā

oṃ we bow to He Who is the Cause of All Objects of Attainment, I am One with God.

- 677 -

ॐ छन्दोव्याकरणोत्तर सिद्धार्थाय स्वाहा

oṃ chandovyākaraṇottarasiddhārthāya svāhā

oṃ we bow to He Who is Adept in the Scriptures, I am One with God.

- 678 -

ॐ सिंहनादाय स्वाहा

oṃ siṃhanādāya svāhā

oṃ we bow to He Who is the Roar of a Lion, I am One with God.

- 679 -

ॐ सिंहदंष्ट्राय स्वाहा

oṃ siṃhadaṃṣṭrāya svāhā

oṃ we bow to He Who Has the Teeth of a Lion, I am One with God.

- 680 -

ॐ सिंहगाय स्वाहा

oṃ siṃhagāya svāhā

oṃ we bow to He Who Has the Body of a Lion, I am One with God.

- 681 -

ॐ सिंहवाहनाय स्वाहा

oṃ siṃhavāhanāya svāhā

oṃ we bow to He Who Has the Conveyance of a Lion, I am One with God.

- 682 -

ॐ प्रभावात्मने स्वाहा

oṃ prabhāvātmane svāhā

oṃ we bow to He Who is the Radiant Soul, I am One with God.

- 683 -

ॐ जगत्कालस्थानाय स्वाहा

oṃ jagatkālasthānāya svāhā

oṃ we bow to He Who is the Residence of Manifested Time, I am One with God.

- 684 -

ॐ लोकहिताय स्वाहा

oṃ lokahitāya svāhā

oṃ we bow to He Who is the Welfare of the People, I am One with God.

- 685 -

ॐ तरवे स्वाहा

oṃ tarave svāhā

oṃ we bow to He Who Takes Across, I am One with God.

- 686 -

ॐ सारङ्गाय स्वाहा

oṃ sāraṅgāya svāhā

oṃ we bow to He Who is a Bird, I am One with God.

- 687 -

ॐ नवचक्राङ्गाय स्वाहा

oṃ navacakrāṅgāya svāhā

oṃ we bow to He Who Embodies Nine Centers of Energy, I am One with God.

- 688 -

ॐ केतुमालिने स्वाहा

oṃ ketumāline svāhā

oṃ we bow to He Who Cultivates Restriction, I am One with God.

- 689 -

ॐ सभायनाय स्वाहा

oṃ sabhāyanāya svāhā

oṃ we bow to He Who Heads the Association, I am One with God.

- 690 -

ॐ भूतालयाय स्वाहा

oṃ bhūtālayāya svāhā

oṃ we bow to He Who Reposes at the Base of Existence, I am One with God.

- 691 -

ॐ भूतपतये स्वाहा

oṃ bhūtapataye svāhā

oṃ we bow to He Who is the Lord of Existence, I am One with God.

- 692 -

ॐ अहोरात्राय स्वाहा

oṃ ahorātrāya svāhā

oṃ we bow to He Who is the Entire Night, I am One with God.

- 693 -

ॐ अनिन्दिताय स्वाहा

oṃ aninditāya svāhā

oṃ we bow to He Who Cannot Be Slandered, I am One with God.

- 694 -

ॐ सर्वभूतवाहवे स्वाहा

oṃ sarvabhūtavāhave svāhā

oṃ we bow to He Who Conveys All Existence, I am One with God.

- 695 -

ॐ सर्वभूतनिलयाय स्वाहा

oṃ sarvabhūtanilayāya svāhā

oṃ we bow to He Who Reposes Within All Existence, I am One with God.

- 696 -

ॐ विभवे स्वाहा

oṃ vibhave svāhā

oṃ we bow to He Who is Unborn, I am One with God.

- 697 -

ॐ भवाय स्वाहा

oṃ bhavāya svāhā

oṃ we bow to He Who is Existence, I am One with God.

- 698 -

ॐ अमोघाय स्वाहा

oṃ amoghāya svāhā

oṃ we bow to He Who is Infallible, I am One with God.

- 699 -

ॐ संयताय स्वाहा

oṃ saṃyatāya svāhā

oṃ we bow to He Who Controls All, I am One with God.

- 700 -

ॐ अश्वाय स्वाहा

oṃ aśvāya svāhā

oṃ we bow to He Who is the Desire for Wisdom, I am One with God.

- 701 -

ॐ भोजनाय स्वाहा

oṃ bhojanāya svāhā

oṃ we bow to He Who is Food, I am One with God.

- 702 -

ॐ प्राणधारणाय स्वाहा

oṃ prāṇadhāraṇāya svāhā

oṃ we bow to He Who Supports All Life, I am One with God.

- 703 -

ॐ धृतिमते स्वाहा

oṃ dhṛtimate svāhā

oṃ we bow to He Whose Mind is Constant, I am One with God.

- 704 -

ॐ मतिमते स्वाहा

oṃ matimate svāhā

oṃ we bow to He Whose Mind is Thoughtful, I am One with God.

- 705 -

ॐ दक्षाय स्वाहा

oṃ dakṣāya svāhā

oṃ we bow to He Who Has Ability, I am One with God.

- 706 -

ॐ सत्कृताय स्वाहा

oṃ satkṛtāya svāhā

oṃ we bow to He Who Performs True Action, I am One with God.

- 707 -

ॐ युगाधिपाय स्वाहा

oṃ yugādhipāya svāhā

oṃ we bow to He Who is the Lord of Ages, I am One with God.

- 708 -

ॐ गोपालाय स्वाहा

oṃ gopālāya svāhā

oṃ we bow to He Who is the Protector of Light, I am One with God.

- 709 -

ॐ गोपतये स्वाहा

oṃ gopataye svāhā

oṃ we bow to He Who is the Lord of Light, I am One with God.

- 710 -

ॐ ग्रामाय स्वाहा

oṃ grāmāya svāhā

oṃ we bow to He Who is the Community, I am One with God.

- 711 -

ॐ गोचर्मवसनाय स्वाहा

oṃ gocarmavasanāya svāhā

oṃ we bow to He Who is Clothed in Light, I am One with God.

- 712 -

ॐ हरये स्वाहा

oṃ haraye svāhā

oṃ we bow to He Who Presides over the Gross, Subtle and Causal Bodies, I am One with God.

- 713 -

ॐ हिरण्यबाहवे स्वाहा

oṃ hiraṇyabāhave svāhā

oṃ we bow to He Who Has Golden Arms, I am One with God.

- 714 -

ॐ प्रवेशिनां गुहापालाय स्वाहा

oṃ praveśināṃ guhāpālāya svāhā

oṃ we bow to He Who Protects the Entrance to the Cave, I am One with God.

- 715 -

ॐ प्रकृष्टारये स्वाहा

oṃ prakṛṣṭāraye svāhā

oṃ we bow to He Who Has Vanquished the Enemy Within, I am One with God.

- 716 -

ॐ महाहर्षाय स्वाहा

oṃ mahāharṣāya svāhā

oṃ we bow to He Who Has Great Joy, I am One with God.

- 717 -

ॐ जितकामाय स्वाहा

oṃ jitakāmāya svāhā

oṃ we bow to He Who Has Conquered Desire, I am One with God.

- 718 -

ॐ जितेन्द्रियाय स्वाहा

oṃ jitendriyāya svāhā

oṃ we bow to He Who Has Controlled His Senses, I am One with God.

- 719 -

ॐ गान्धाराय स्वाहा

oṃ gāndhārāya svāhā

oṃ we bow to He Who is Music, I am One with God.

- 720 -

ॐ सुवासाय स्वाहा

oṃ suvāsāya svāhā

oṃ we bow to He Who Dwells in Excellence, I am One with God.

- 721 -

ॐ तपःसक्ताय स्वाहा

oṃ tapaḥsaktāya svāhā

oṃ we bow to He Who is Firm in Austerities, I am One with God.

- 722 -

ॐ रतये स्वाहा

oṃ rataye svāhā

oṃ we bow to He Who is the Spring, I am One with God.

- 723 -

ॐ नराय स्वाहा

oṃ narāya svāhā

oṃ we bow to He Who is Mankind, I am One with God.

- 724 -

ॐ महागीताय स्वाहा

oṃ mahāgītāya svāhā

oṃ we bow to He Who is the Great Song, I am One with God.

- 725 -

ॐ महानृत्याय स्वाहा

oṃ mahānṛtyāya svāhā

oṃ we bow to He Who is Great Dance, I am One with God.

- 726 -

ॐ अप्सरोगणसेविताय स्वाहा

oṃ apsarogaṇasevitāya svāhā

oṃ we bow to He Who is Served by Multitudes of Heavenly Damsels, I am One with God.

- 727 -

ॐ महाकेतवे स्वाहा

oṃ mahāketave svāhā

oṃ we bow to He Who is the Great Restriction, I am One with God.

- 728 -

ॐ महाधातवे स्वाहा

oṃ mahādhātave svāhā

oṃ we bow to He Who is the Great Creator, I am One with God.

- 729 -

ॐ नैकसानुचराय स्वाहा

oṃ naikasānucarāya svāhā

oṃ we bow to He Who Wanders Over the Summit, I am One with God.

- 730 -

ॐ चलाय स्वाहा

oṃ calāya svāhā

oṃ we bow to He Who Moves, I am One with God.

- 731 -

ॐ आवेदनीयाय स्वाहा

oṃ āvedanīyāya svāhā

oṃ we bow to He Who Cannot Be Studied, I am One with God.

- 732 -

ॐ आदेशाय स्वाहा

oṃ ādeśāya svāhā

oṃ we bow to He Who Has No Particular Place, I am One with God.

- 733 -

ॐ सर्वगन्धसुखाबहाय स्वाहा

oṃ sarvagandhasukhābahāya svāhā

oṃ we bow to He Who is the Conveyor of All Enjoyable Scents, I am One with God.

- 734 -

ॐ तोरणाय स्वाहा

oṃ toraṇāya svāhā

oṃ we bow to He Who is the Decorated Doorway, I am One with God.

- 735 -

ॐ तारणाय स्वाहा

oṃ tāraṇāya svāhā

oṃ we bow to He Who Takes Across, I am One with God.

- 736 -

ॐ वाताय स्वाहा

oṃ vātāya svāhā

oṃ we bow to He Who is the Wind, I am One with God.

- 737 -

ॐ परिधिने स्वाहा

oṃ paridhine svāhā

oṃ we bow to He Who is the Protective Boundary, I am One with God.

-738 -

ॐ पतिखेचराय स्वाहा

oṃ patikhecarāya svāhā

oṃ we bow to He Who is the Lord Who Levitates, I am One with God.

- 739 -

ॐ संयोगवर्धनाय स्वाहा

oṃ saṃyogavardhanāya svāhā

oṃ we bow to He Who Has Conquered the Fullest Union, I am One with God.

- 740 -

ॐ गुणाधिकवृद्धाय स्वाहा

oṃ guṇādhikavṛddhāya svāhā

oṃ we bow to He Who is Older Than Qualities, I am One with God.

- 741 -

ॐ अधिकवृद्धाय स्वाहा

oṃ adhikavṛddhāya svāhā

oṃ we bow to He Who is Oldest, I am One with God.

- 742 -

ॐ नित्यात्मसहाय स्वाहा

oṃ nityātmasahāya svāhā

oṃ we bow to He Who is with the Eternal Soul, I am One with God.

- 743 -

ॐ देवासुरपतये स्वाहा

oṃ devāsurapataye svāhā

oṃ we bow to He Who is the Lord of Gods and Asuras, I am One with God.

- 744 -

ॐ पत्ये स्वाहा

oṃ patye svāhā

oṃ we bow to He Who is the Lord, I am One with God.

- 745 -

ॐ युक्ताय स्वाहा

oṃ yuktāya svāhā

oṃ we bow to He Who is in Union, I am One with God.

- 746 -

ॐ युक्तबाहवे स्वाहा

oṃ yuktabāhave svāhā

oṃ we bow to He Who Embraces All with His Arms, I am One with God.

- 747 -

ॐ दिविसुपर्वदेवाय स्वाहा

oṃ divisuparvadevāya svāhā

oṃ we bow to He Who is the Lord of the King of Heaven, I am One with God.

- 748 -

ॐ आषाढाय स्वाहा

oṃ āśāḍhāya svāhā

oṃ we bow to He Who Grants Endurance, I am One with God.

- 749 -

ॐ सुषाढाय स्वाहा

oṃ suṣāḍhāya svāhā

oṃ we bow to He Who Has Excellent Endurance, I am One with God.

- 750 -

ॐ ध्रुवाय स्वाहा

oṃ dhruvāya svāhā

oṃ we bow to He Who is Eternally Young, I am One with God.

- 751 -

ॐ हरिणाय स्वाहा

oṃ hariṇāya svāhā

oṃ we bow to He Who is Like a Deer, I am One with God.

- 752 -

ॐ हराय स्वाहा

oṃ harāya svāhā

oṃ we bow to He Who Takes Away, I am One with God.

- 753 -

ॐ आवर्तमानवपुषे स्वाहा

oṃ āvartamānavapuṣe svāhā

oṃ we bow to He Who Grants Bodies to Those Who Take Birth, I am One with God.

- 754 -

ॐ वसुश्रेष्ठाय स्वाहा

oṃ vasuśreṣṭhāya svāhā

oṃ we bow to He Who is the Foremost Wealth, I am One with God.

- 755 -

ॐ महापथाय स्वाहा

oṃ mahāpathāya svāhā

oṃ we bow to He Who is the Great Path, I am One with God.

- 756 -

ॐ विमर्षशिरोहारिणये स्वाहा

oṃ vimarṣaśirohāriṇaye svāhā

oṃ we bow to He Who Takes to the Highest Experience, I am One with God.

- 757 -

ॐ सर्वलक्षणलक्षिताय स्वाहा

oṃ sarvalakṣaṇalakṣitāya svāhā

oṃ we bow to He Who is the Goal of All Goals, I am One with God.

- 758 -

ॐ अक्षरयोगिने स्वाहा

oṃ akṣarayogine svāhā

oṃ we bow to He Who is in Union With the Eternal, I am One with God.

- 759 -

ॐ सर्वयोगिने स्वाहा

oṃ sarvayogine svāhā

oṃ we bow to He Who is in Union With All, I am One with God.

- 760 -

ॐ महाबलाय स्वाहा

oṃ mahābalāya svāhā

oṃ we bow to He Who is Great Strength, I am One with God.

- 761 -

ॐ समाम्नायाय स्वाहा

oṃ samāmnāyāya svāhā

oṃ we bow to He Who Shares the Wisdom of the Vedas, I am One with God.

- 762 -

ॐ असभाम्नायाय स्वाहा

oṃ asabhāmnāyāya svāhā

oṃ we bow to He Who is Beyond the Wisdom of the Vedas, I am One with God.

- 763 -

ॐ तीर्थदेवाय स्वाहा

oṃ tīrthadevāya svāhā

oṃ we bow to He Who is the Lord of Pilgrimage, I am One with God.

- 764 -

ॐ महारथाय स्वाहा

oṃ mahārathāya svāhā

oṃ we bow to He Who is the Great Conveyance, I am One with God.

- 765 -

ॐ निर्जीवाय स्वाहा

oṃ nirjīvāya svāhā

oṃ we bow to He Who is Without Life, I am One with God.

- 766 -

ॐ जीवनाय स्वाहा

oṃ jīvanāya svāhā

oṃ we bow to He Who is All Life, I am One with God.

- 767 -

ॐ मन्त्राय स्वाहा

oṃ mantrāya svāhā

oṃ we bow to He Who is Mantra, I am One with God.

- 768 -

ॐ शुभाक्षाय स्वाहा

oṃ śubhākṣāya svāhā

oṃ we bow to He Who is the Eye of Purity, I am One with God.

- 769 -

ॐ बहुकर्कशाय स्वाहा

oṃ bahukarkaśāya svāhā

oṃ we bow to He Who Has Stern Discipline, I am One with God.

- 770 -

ॐ रत्नप्रभूताय स्वाहा

oṃ ratnaprabhūtāya svāhā

oṃ we bow to He Who is the Lord of Jewels, I am One with God.

- 771 -

ॐ रत्नाङ्गाय स्वाहा

oṃ ratnāṅgāya svāhā

oṃ we bow to He Who is the Embodiment of Jewels, I am One with God.

- 772 -

ॐ महार्णवनिपानविदे स्वाहा

oṃ mahārṇavanipānavide svāhā

oṃ we bow to He Who Consumes the Great Waves of the Ocean, I am One with God.

- 773 -

ॐ मूलाय स्वाहा

oṃ mūlāya svāhā

oṃ we bow to He Who is the Root, I am One with God.

- 774 -

ॐ त्रिशूलाय स्वाहा

oṃ triśūlāya svāhā

oṃ we bow to He Who is the Trident, I am One with God.

- 775 -

ॐ अमृताय स्वाहा

oṃ amṛtāya svāhā

oṃ we bow to He Who is the Nectar of Immortality, I am One with God.

- 776 -

ॐ व्यक्ताव्यक्ताय स्वाहा

oṃ vyaktāvyaktāya svāhā

oṃ we bow to He Who Is Manifest and Unmanifest, I am One with God.

- 777 -

ॐ तपोनिधये स्वाहा

oṃ taponidhaye svāhā

oṃ we bow to He Who is the Lord of Purifying Austerities, I am One with God.

- 778 -

ॐ आरोहणाय स्वाहा

oṃ ārohaṇāya svāhā

oṃ we bow to He Who Does Not Cry, I am One with God.

- 779 -

ॐ अधिरोधाय स्वाहा

oṃ adhirodhāya svāhā

oṃ we bow to He Who is Before Those That Cry, I am One with God.

- 780 -

ॐ शीलधारिणे स्वाहा

oṃ śīladhāriṇe svāhā

oṃ we bow to He Who Stands Like a Stone, I am One with God.

- 781 -

ॐ महायशसे स्वाहा

oṃ mahāyaśase svāhā

oṃ we bow to He Who is Great Welfare, I am One with God.

- 782 -

ॐ सेनाकल्पाय स्वाहा

oṃ senākalpāya svāhā

oṃ we bow to He Who is the Conquering Idea, I am One with God.

- 783 -

ॐ महाकल्पाय स्वाहा

oṃ mahākalpāya svāhā

oṃ we bow to He Who is the Great Idea, I am One with God.

- 784 -

ॐ योगाय स्वाहा

oṃ yogāya svāhā

oṃ we bow to He Who is Union, I am One with God.

- 785 -

ॐ युगकराय स्वाहा

oṃ yugakarāya svāhā

oṃ we bow to He Who is the Cause of Ages, I am One with God.

- 786 -

ॐ हरये स्वाहा

oṃ haraye svāhā

oṃ we bow to He Who Presides over the Gross, Subtle and Causal Bodies, I am One with God.

- 787 -

ॐ युगरूपाय स्वाहा

oṃ yugarūpāya svāhā

oṃ we bow to He Who is the Form of Ages, I am One with God.

- 788 -

ॐ महारूपाय स्वाहा

oṃ mahārūpāya svāhā

oṃ we bow to He Who is the Great Form, I am One with God.

- 789 -

ॐ महागहनाय स्वाहा

oṃ mahāgahanāya svāhā

oṃ we bow to He Who Killed the Elephant, I am One with God.

- 790 -

ॐ वधाय स्वाहा

oṃ vadhāya svāhā

oṃ we bow to He Who Dissolves, I am One with God.

- 791 -

ॐ न्यायनिर्वपणाय स्वाहा

oṃ nyāyanirvapaṇāya svāhā

oṃ we bow to He Who Ditributes According to Merit, I am One with God.

- 792 -

ॐ पादाय स्वाहा

oṃ pādāya svāhā

oṃ we bow to He Who Supports, I am One with God.

- 793 -

ॐ पण्डिताय स्वाहा

oṃ paṇḍitāya svāhā

oṃ we bow to He Who is Knowledgeable, I am One with God.

- 794 -

ॐ अचलोपमाय स्वाहा

oṃ acalopamāya svāhā

oṃ we bow to He Who is Without Movement, I am One with God.

- 795 -

ॐ बहुमालाय स्वाहा

oṃ bahumālāya svāhā

oṃ we bow to He Who Has Various Manifestations, I am One with God.

- 796 -

ॐ महामालाय स्वाहा

oṃ mahāmālāya svāhā

oṃ we bow to He Who Has a Great Manifestation, I am One with God.

- 797 -

ॐ शशिहरसुलोचनाय स्वाहा

oṃ śaśiharasulocanāya svāhā

oṃ we bow to He Whose Excellent Eyes Shine Like the Moon, I am One with God.

- 798 -

ॐ विस्तारलवणाकूपाय स्वाहा

oṃ vistāralavaṇākūpāya svāhā

oṃ we bow to He Who Has the Ocean as His Water Source, I am One with God.

- 799 -

ॐ त्रियुगाय स्वाहा

oṃ triyugāya svāhā

oṃ we bow to He Who is the Three Ages, I am One with God.

- 800 -

ॐ सफलोदयाय स्वाहा

oṃ saphalodayāya svāhā

oṃ we bow to He Who Gives Rise to Excellent Fruit, I am One with God.

- 801 -

ॐ त्रिनेत्राय स्वाहा

oṃ trinetrāya svāhā

oṃ we bow to He Who Has Three Eyes, I am One with God.

- 802 -

ॐ विषाणाङ्गाय स्वाहा

oṃ vipāṇāṅgāya svāhā

oṃ we bow to He Who Has Eight Forms, I am One with God.

- 803 -

ॐ मणिविद्धाय स्वाहा

oṃ maṇividdhāya svāhā

oṃ we bow to He Who Knows Gems, I am One with God.

- 804 -

ॐ जटाधराय स्वाहा

oṃ jaṭādharāya svāhā

oṃ we bow to He Who Wears Matted Hair, I am One with God.

- 805 -

ॐ विन्दवे स्वाहा

oṃ vindave svāhā

oṃ we bow to He Who Knows the One Point of Origin, I am One with God.

- 806 -

ॐ विसर्गाय स्वाहा

oṃ visargāya svāhā

oṃ we bow to He Who is Heavenly, I am One with God.

- 807 -

ॐ सुमुखाय स्वाहा

oṃ sumukhāya svāhā

oṃ we bow to He Who Has an Excellent Face, I am One with God.

- 808 -

ॐ शराय स्वाहा

oṃ śarāya svāhā

oṃ we bow to He Who Has an Arrow, I am One with God.

- 809 -

ॐ सर्वायुधाय स्वाहा

oṃ sarvāyudhāya svāhā

oṃ we bow to He Who Has All Weapons, I am One with God.

- 810 -

ॐ सहाय स्वाहा

oṃ sahāya svāhā

oṃ we bow to He Who is the Helper, I am One with God.

- 811 -

ॐ निवेदनाय स्वाहा

oṃ nivedanāya svāhā

oṃ we bow to He Who is Dedicated, I am One with God.

- 812 -

ॐ सुखजाताय स्वाहा

oṃ sukhajātāya svāhā

oṃ we bow to He Who Gives Birth to Comfort, I am One with God.

- 813 -

ॐ सुगन्धाराय स्वाहा

oṃ sugandhārāya svāhā

oṃ we bow to He Who Has Excellent Music, I am One with God.

- 814 -

ॐ महाधनुषे स्वाहा

oṃ mahādanuṣe svāhā

oṃ we bow to He Who is the Great Bow, I am One with God.

- 815 -

ॐ गन्धषालिभगवते स्वाहा

oṃ gandhaṣālibhagavate svāhā

oṃ we bow to He Who is Divine Scent, I am One with God.

- 816 -

ॐ सर्वकर्मोत्थानाय स्वाहा

oṃ sarvakarmotthānāya svāhā

oṃ we bow to He Who Gives Rise to All Action, I am One with God.

- 817 -

ॐ मन्थानबहुलबाहवे स्वाहा

oṃ manthānabahulabāhave svāhā

oṃ we bow to He Whose Arms Churn Like the Wind, I am One with God.

- 818 -

ॐ सकलाय स्वाहा

oṃ sakalāya svāhā

oṃ we bow to He Who is Whole, I am One with God.

- 819 -

ॐ सर्वलोचनाय स्वाहा

oṃ sarvalocanāya svāhā

oṃ we bow to He Who Sees with All Eyes, I am One with God.

- 820 -

ॐ तलस्तालाय स्वाहा

oṃ talastālāya svāhā

oṃ we bow to He Who Has Cymbals in His Hands, I am One with God.

- 821 -

ॐ करस्थालिने स्वाहा

oṃ karasthāline svāhā

oṃ we bow to He Who Eats from His Hands, I am One with God.

- 822 -

ॐ ऊर्ध्वसंहननाय स्वाहा

oṃ ūrdhvasaṃhananāya svāhā

oṃ we bow to He Who Has a Robust Body, I am One with God.

- 823 -

ॐ महते स्वाहा

oṃ mahate svāhā

oṃ we bow to He Who is a Great Thinker, I am One with God.

- 824 -

ॐ छत्राय स्वाहा

oṃ chatrāya svāhā

oṃ we bow to He Who is the Refuge, I am One with God.

- 825 -

ॐ सुच्छत्राय स्वाहा

oṃ succhatrāya svāhā

oṃ we bow to He Who is the Excellent Refuge, I am One with God.

- 826 -

ॐ विख्यातलोकाय स्वाहा

oṃ vikhyātalokāya svāhā

oṃ we bow to He Who Enumerates All Beings, I am One with God.

- 827 -

ॐ सर्वाश्रयक्रमाय स्वाहा

oṃ sarvāśrayakramāya svāhā

oṃ we bow to He Who is Order of Refuge, I am One with God.

- 828 -

ॐ मुण्डाय स्वाहा

oṃ muṇḍāya svāhā

oṃ we bow to He Who Has a Shaven Head, I am One with God.

- 829 -

ॐ विरूपाय स्वाहा

oṃ virūpāya svāhā

oṃ we bow to He Who Has No Form, I am One with God.

- 830 -

ॐ विकृताय स्वाहा

oṃ vikṛtāya svāhā

oṃ we bow to He Who Has a Strange Form, I am One with God.

- 831 -

ॐ दण्डिने स्वाहा

oṃ daṇḍine svāhā

oṃ we bow to He Who is Punishment, I am One with God.

- 832 -

ॐ कुण्डिने स्वाहा

oṃ kuṇḍine svāhā

oṃ we bow to He Who is the Container, I am One with God.

- 833 -

ॐ विकुर्वाणाय स्वाहा

oṃ vikurvāṇāya svāhā

oṃ we bow to He Who Cannot Be Attained Through Action, I am One with God.

- 834 -

ॐ हर्यक्षाय स्वाहा

oṃ haryakṣāya svāhā

oṃ we bow to He Who Has Eyes Like a Deer, I am One with God.

- 835 -

ॐ ककुभाय स्वाहा

oṃ kakubhāya svāhā

oṃ we bow to He Who Fills the Quarters, I am One with God.

- 836 -

ॐ वज्रिणे स्वाहा

oṃ vajriṇe svāhā

oṃ we bow to He Who is Lightning, I am One with God.

- 837 -

ॐ शतजिह्वाय स्वाहा

oṃ śatajihvāya svāhā

oṃ we bow to He Who Has a Hundred Tongues, I am One with God.

- 838 -

ॐ सहस्रपदे स्वाहा

oṃ sahasrapade svāhā

oṃ we bow to He Who a Thousand Feet, I am One with God.

- 839 -

ॐ सहस्रमूर्ध्ने स्वाहा

oṃ sahasramurdhne svāhā

oṃ we bow to He Who Has a Thousand Heads, I am One with God.

- 840 -

ॐ देवेन्द्राय स्वाहा

oṃ devendrāya svāhā

oṃ we bow to He Who is the Lord of Gods, I am One with God.

- 841 -

ॐ सर्वदेवमयाय स्वाहा

oṃ sarvadevamayāya svāhā

oṃ we bow to He Who is the Manifestation of All Gods, I am One with God.

- 842 -

ॐ गुरवे स्वाहा

oṃ gurave svāhā

oṃ we bow to He Who is the Guru, I am One with God.

- 843 -

ॐ सहस्रबाहवे स्वाहा

oṃ sahasrabāhave svāhā

oṃ we bow to He Who Has a Thousand Arms, I am One with God.

- 844 -

ॐ सर्वाङ्गाय स्वाहा

oṃ sarvāṅgāya svāhā

oṃ we bow to He Who Embodies All, I am One with God.

- 845 -

ॐ शरण्याय स्वाहा

oṃ śaraṇyāya svāhā

oṃ we bow to He Who Gives Refuge, I am One with God.

- 846 -

ॐ सर्वलोककृते स्वाहा

oṃ sarvalokakṛte svāhā

oṃ we bow to He Who is the Maker of All Worlds, I am One with God.

- 847 -

ॐ पवित्राय स्वाहा

oṃ pavitrāya svāhā

oṃ we bow to He Who is Pure, I am One with God.

- 848 -

ॐ त्रिककुन्मन्त्राय स्वाहा

oṃ trikakunmantrāya svāhā

oṃ we bow to He Who is the Threefold Mantra, I am One with God.

- 849 -

ॐ कनिष्ठाय स्वाहा

oṃ kaniṣṭhāya svāhā

oṃ we bow to He Who is the Youngest Son, I am One with God.

- 850 -

ॐ कृष्णपिंगलाय स्वाहा

oṃ kṛṣṇapiṃgalāya svāhā

oṃ we bow to He Who is Dark and Light, I am One with God.

- 851 -

ॐ ब्रह्मदण्डविनिर्मात्रे स्वाहा

oṃ brahmadaṇḍavinirmātre svāhā

oṃ we bow to He Who is the Author of Divine Punishment, I am One with God.

- 852 -

ॐ सतघ्नीपाशशक्तिमते स्वाहा

oṃ sataghnīpāśaśaktimate svāhā

oṃ we bow to He Who Has the Energy to Slay Hundreds at a Time, I am One with God.

- 853 -

ॐ पद्मगर्भाय स्वाहा

oṃ padmagarbhāya svāhā

oṃ we bow to He Who is a Lotus Womb, I am One with God.

- 854 -

ॐ महागर्भाय स्वाहा

oṃ mahāgarbhāya svāhā

oṃ we bow to He Who is the Great Womb, I am One with God.

- 855 -

ॐ ब्रह्मगर्भाय स्वाहा

oṃ brahmagarbhāya svāhā

oṃ we bow to He Who is the Divine Womb, I am One with God.

- 856 -

ॐ जलजोद्भवाय स्वाहा

oṃ jalajodbhavāya svāhā

oṃ we bow to He Who Creates Life from Water, I am One with God.

- 857 -

ॐ गभस्तये स्वाहा

oṃ gabhastaye svāhā

oṃ we bow to He Who is Rays of Light, I am One with God.

- 858 -

ॐ ब्रह्मकृते स्वाहा

oṃ brahmakṛte svāhā

oṃ we bow to He Who is the Supreme Maker, I am One with God.

- 859 -

ॐ ब्रह्मिणे स्वाहा

oṃ brahmiṇe svāhā

oṃ we bow to He Who is the Seeker of God, I am One with God.

- 860 -

ॐ ब्रह्मविदे स्वाहा

oṃ brahmavide svāhā

oṃ we bow to He Who is Known by God, I am One with God.

- 861 -

ॐ ब्रह्मणाय स्वाहा

oṃ brahmaṇāya svāhā

oṃ we bow to He Who is the Knowledge of God, I am One with God.

- 862 -

ॐ गतये स्वाहा

oṃ gataye svāhā

oṃ we bow to He Who is the Refuge, I am One with God.

- 863 -

ॐ अनन्तरूपाय स्वाहा

oṃ anantarūpāya svāhā

oṃ we bow to He Who is the Form of the Infinite, I am One with God.

- 864 -

ॐ नैकात्मने स्वाहा

oṃ naikātmane svāhā

oṃ we bow to He Who is One Soul, I am One with God.

- 865 -

ॐ स्वयम्भुवतिग्मतेजसे स्वाहा

oṃ svayambhuvatigmatejase svāhā

oṃ we bow to He Who is Himself the Light of the World, I am One with God.

- 866 -

ॐ ऊर्ध्वगात्मने स्वाहा

oṃ ūrdhvagātmane svāhā

oṃ we bow to He Who is the Rise of the Soul

- 867 -

ॐ पशुपतये स्वाहा

oṃ paśupataye svāhā

oṃ we bow to He Who is the Lord of Animals

- 868 -

ॐ घातरंहसे स्वाहा

oṃ ghātaraṃhase svāhā

oṃ we bow to He Who Slays Swiftly, I am One with God.

- 869 -

ॐ मनोजवाय स्वाहा

oṃ manojavāya svāhā

oṃ we bow to He Who is as Swift as the Mind, I am One with God.

- 870 -

ॐ चन्दनिने स्वाहा

oṃ candanine svāhā

oṃ we bow to He Who is Sandal, I am One with God.

- 871 -

ॐ पद्मनालाग्राय स्वाहा

oṃ padmanālāgrāya svāhā

oṃ we bow to He Who Cannot be Measured Even by the Lotus One, I am One with God.

- 872 -

ॐ सुरभ्युत्तारणाय स्वाहा

oṃ surabhyuttāraṇāya svāhā

oṃ we bow to He Who Raises the Cow Who Gives All, I am One with God.

- 873 -

ॐ नराय स्वाहा

oṃ narāya svāhā

oṃ we bow to He Who is Mankind, I am One with God.

- 874 -

ॐ कर्णिकारमहास्रग्विणे स्वाहा

oṃ karṇikāramahāsragviṇe svāhā

oṃ we bow to He Who Has Mantras in His Hands and Ears, I am One with God.

- 875 -

ॐ नीलमौलये स्वाहा

oṃ nīlamaulaye svāhā

oṃ we bow to He Who is Crowned by Blue Gems, I am One with God.

- 876 -

ॐ पिनाकधृषे स्वाहा

oṃ pinākadhṛṣe svāhā

oṃ we bow to He Who Wields a Spear, I am One with God.

- 877 -

ॐ उमापतये स्वाहा

oṃ umāpataye svāhā

oṃ we bow to He Who is the Lord of Umā, I am One with God.

- 878 -

ॐ उमाकान्ताय स्वाहा

oṃ umākāntāya svāhā

oṃ we bow to He Who is the Inner Essence of Umā, I am One with God.

- 879 -

ॐ जाह्नवीधृषे स्वाहा

oṃ jānavīdhṛṣe svāhā

oṃ we bow to He Who Supports the Ganges, I am One with God.

- 880 -

ॐ उमाधवाय स्वाहा

oṃ umādhavāya svāhā

oṃ we bow to He Who is the Lord of Umā, I am One with God.

- 881 -

ॐ वरवराहाय स्वाहा

oṃ varavarāhāya svāhā

oṃ we bow to He Who is the Boon of Boons, I am One with God.

- 882 -

ॐ वरदाय स्वाहा

oṃ varadāya svāhā

oṃ we bow to He Who is the Giver of Boons, I am One with God.

- 883 -

ॐ वरेण्याय स्वाहा

oṃ vareṇyāya svāhā

oṃ we bow to He Who is the Highest, I am One with God.

- 884 -

ॐ सुमहास्वनाय स्वाहा

oṃ sumahāsvanāya svāhā

oṃ we bow to He Who Has the Most Excellent Great Sound, I am One with God.

- 885 -

ॐ महाप्रसादाय स्वाहा

oṃ mahāprasādāya svāhā

oṃ we bow to He Who is the Great Consecrated Offering, I am One with God.

- 886 -

ॐ दमनाय स्वाहा

oṃ damanāya svāhā

oṃ we bow to He Who Extinguishes Evil, I am One with God.

- 887 -

ॐ शत्रुघ्ने स्वाहा

oṃ satrughne svāhā

oṃ we bow to He Who is the Slayer of Enemies, I am One with God.

- 888 -

ॐ श्वेतपिङ्गलाय स्वाहा

oṃ svetapiṅgalāya svāhā

oṃ we bow to He Who is White and Yellow, I am One with God.

- 889 -

ॐ पीतात्मने स्वाहा

oṃ pītātmane svāhā

oṃ we bow to He Who Has a Golden Soul, I am One with God.

- 890 -

ॐ परमात्मने स्वाहा

oṃ paramātmane svāhā

oṃ we bow to He Who is the Supreme Soul, I am One with God.

- 891 -

ॐ प्रयतात्मने स्वाहा

oṃ prayatātmane svāhā

oṃ we bow to He Whose Soul Makes Efforts, I am One with God.

- 892 -

ॐ प्रधानधृषे स्वाहा

oṃ pradhānadhṛṣe svāhā

oṃ we bow to He Who is Perceived as the Foremost, I am One with God.

- 893 -

ॐ सर्वपार्श्वमुखाय स्वाहा

oṃ sarvapārśvamukhāya svāhā

oṃ we bow to He Whose Face is on Every Side, I am One with God.

- 894 -

ॐ त्र्यक्षाय स्वाहा

oṃ tryakṣāya svāhā

oṃ we bow to He Who Has Three Eyes, I am One with God.

- 895 -

ॐ सर्वधारणवराय स्वाहा

oṃ sarvadhāraṇavarāya svāhā

oṃ we bow to He Who Gives the Boon of All Contemplation, I am One with God.

- 896 -

ॐ चराचरात्मने स्वाहा

oṃ carācarātmane svāhā

oṃ we bow to He Who is the Soul of What Moves and What Does Not Move, I am One with God.

- 897 -

ॐ सूक्ष्मात्मने स्वाहा

oṃ sūkṣmātmane svāhā

oṃ we bow to He Who is the Soul of All Subtlety, I am One with God.

- 898 -

ॐ अमृतगोवृषेश्वराय स्वाहा

oṃ amṛtagovṛṣeśvarāya svāhā

oṃ we bow to He Who is the Supreme Lord Who Rides a Bull and Illuminates the Light of Immortal Bliss, I am One with God.

- 899 -

ॐ साध्यर्षये स्वाहा

oṃ sādhyarṣaye svāhā

oṃ we bow to He Who is the True Ṛṣi, I am One with God.

- 900 -

ॐ आदित्यवसवे स्वाहा

oṃ ādityavasave svāhā

oṃ we bow to He Who Resides in the Sons of Non-Duality, I am One with God.

- 901 -

ॐ विवस्वत्सवित्रमृताय स्वाहा

oṃ vivasvatsavitramṛtāya svāhā

oṃ we bow to He Who is the Nectar of Immortal Bliss of the Light of Wisdom, I am One with God.

- 902 -

ॐ व्यासाय स्वाहा

oṃ vyāsāya svāhā

oṃ we bow to He Who Tells Stories and Explains Dharma, I am One with God.

- 903 -

ॐ सर्वसुसंक्षेपविस्तराय स्वाहा

oṃ sarvasusaṃkṣepavistarāya svāhā

oṃ we bow to He Who is the Excellent Explanation of All Hidden Meanings, I am One with God.

- 904 -

ॐ पर्ययनराय स्वाहा

oṃ paryayanarāya svāhā

oṃ we bow to He Who is All Humanity, I am One with God.

- 905 -

ॐ क्रतवे स्वाहा

oṃ kratave svāhā

oṃ we bow to He Who Does, I am One with God.

- 906 -

ॐ संवत्सराय स्वाहा

oṃ saṃvatsarāya svāhā

oṃ we bow to He Who is Years, I am One with God.

- 907 -

ॐ मासाय स्वाहा

oṃ māsāya svāhā

oṃ we bow to He Who is Months, I am One with God.

- 908 -

ॐ पक्षाय स्वाहा

oṃ pakṣāya svāhā

oṃ we bow to He Who is a Fortnight, I am One with God.

- 909 -

ॐ संख्यासमापनाय स्वाहा

oṃ saṃkhyāsamāpanāya svāhā

oṃ we bow to He Who is the End of the Enumeration of Principles, I am One with God.

- 910 -

ॐ कलायै स्वाहा

oṃ kalāyai svāhā

oṃ we bow to He Who is Darkness, I am One with God.

- 911 -

ॐ काष्ठायै स्वाहा

oṃ kāṣṭhāyai svāhā

oṃ we bow to He Who is Moments, I am One with God.

- 912 -

ॐ लवेभ्यः स्वाहा

oṃ lavebhyaḥ svāhā

oṃ we bow to He Who is Particles of Time, I am One with God.

- 913 -

ॐ मात्राभ्यः स्वाहा

oṃ mātrābhyaḥ svāhā

oṃ we bow to He Who is Even Smaller Still, I am One with God.

- 914 -

ॐ मुहूर्ताहःक्षपाभ्यः स्वाहा

oṃ muhūrtāhaḥkṣapābhyaḥ svāhā

oṃ we bow to He Who is Auspicious Times, I am One with God.

- 915 -

ॐ क्षणेभ्यः स्वाहा

oṃ kṣaṇebhyaḥ svāhā

oṃ we bow to He Who is an Instant, I am One with God.

- 916 -

ॐ विश्वक्षेत्राय स्वाहा

oṃ viśvakṣetrāya svāhā

oṃ we bow to He Who is the Universal Field, I am One with God.

- 917 -

ॐ प्रजाबीजाय स्वाहा

oṃ prajābījāya svāhā

oṃ we bow to He Who is the Seed of All Beings Born, I am One with God.

- 918 -

ॐ लिङ्गाय स्वाहा

oṃ liṅgāya svāhā

oṃ we bow to He Who is the Symbol, I am One with God.

- 919 -

ॐ आद्यनिर्गमाय स्वाहा

oṃ ādyanirgamāya svāhā

oṃ we bow to He Who is the Foremost Which Cannot Be Surpassed, I am One with God.

- 920 -

ॐ सते स्वाहा

oṃ sate svāhā

oṃ we bow to He Who is True Existence, I am One with God.

- 921 -

ॐ असते स्वाहा

oṃ asate svāhā

oṃ we bow to He Who is Untrue Existence, I am One with God.

- 922 -

ॐ व्यक्ताय स्वाहा

oṃ vyaktāya svāhā

oṃ we bow to He Who is an Individual, I am One with God.

- 923 -

ॐ अव्यक्ताय स्वाहा

oṃ avyaktāya svāhā

oṃ we bow to He Who is Undividable, I am One with God.

- 924 -

ॐ पित्रे स्वाहा

oṃ pitre svāhā

oṃ we bow to He Who is a Father, I am One with God.

- 925 -

ॐ मात्रे स्वाहा

oṃ mātre svāhā

oṃ we bow to He Who is a Mother, I am One with God.

- 926 -

ॐ पितामहाय स्वाहा

oṃ pitāmahāya svāhā

oṃ we bow to He Who is a Grandfather, I am One with God.

- 927 -

ॐ स्वर्गद्वाराय स्वाहा

oṃ svargadvārāya svāhā

oṃ we bow to He Who is the Door to Heaven, I am One with God.

- 928 -

ॐ प्रजाद्वाराय स्वाहा

oṃ prajādvārāya svāhā

oṃ we bow to He Who is the Door to All Beings Born, I am One with God.

- 929 -

ॐ मोक्षद्वाराय स्वाहा

oṃ mokṣadvārāya svāhā

oṃ we bow to He Who is the Door to Liberation, I am One with God.

- 930 -

ॐ त्रिविष्टपाय स्वाहा

oṃ triviṣṭapāya svāhā

oṃ we bow to He Who is the Behavior Which Leads to Heaven, I am One with God.

- 931 -

ॐ निर्वाणाय स्वाहा

oṃ nirvāṇāya svāhā

oṃ we bow to He Who is the Ultimate Realization of Silence, I am One with God.

- 932 -

ॐ हादनाय स्वाहा

oṃ hādanāya svāhā

oṃ we bow to He Who Shares Delight, I am One with God.

- 933 -

ॐ ब्रह्मलोकाय स्वाहा

oṃ brahmalokāya svāhā

oṃ we bow to He Who is the Residence of Supreme Divinity, I am One with God.

- 934 -

ॐ परागतये स्वाहा

oṃ parāgataye svāhā

oṃ we bow to He Who is the Supreme Mover, I am One with God.

- 935 -

ॐ देवासुरविनिमत्रि स्वाहा

oṃ devāsuravinirmātre svāhā

oṃ we bow to He Who is the Author of All Actions of Gods and Asuras, I am One with God.

- 936 -

ॐ देवासुरपरायणाय स्वाहा

oṃ devāsuraparāyaṇāya svāhā

oṃ we bow to He Who is the Mover of Gods and Asuras, I am One with God.

- 937 -

ॐ देवासुरगुरवे स्वाहा

oṃ devāsuragurave svāhā

oṃ we bow to He Who is the Guru of Gods and Asuras, I am One with God.

- 938 -

ॐ देवाय स्वाहा

oṃ devāya svāhā

oṃ we bow to He Who is God, I am One with God.

- 939 -

ॐ देवासुरनमस्कृताय स्वाहा

oṃ devāsuranamaskṛtāya svāhā

oṃ we bow to He Who is Respected by Gods and Asuras, I am One with God.

- 940 -

ॐ देवासुरमहामात्राय स्वाहा

oṃ devāsuramahāmātrāya svāhā

oṃ we bow to He Who is the Great Definition of Gods and Asuras, I am One with God.

- 941 -

ॐ देवासुरगणाश्रयाय स्वाहा

oṃ devāsuragaṇāśrayāya svāhā

oṃ we bow to He Who is the Refuge of Gods and Asuras, I am One with God.

- 942 -

ॐ देवासुरगणाध्यक्षाय स्वाहा

oṃ devāsuragaṇādhyakṣāya svāhā

oṃ we bow to He Who is the Leader of the Multitudes of Gods and Asuras, I am One with God.

- 943 -

ॐ देवासुरगणाग्रण्ये स्वाहा

oṃ devāsuragaṇāgraṅye svāhā

oṃ we bow to He Who is the Leader of the Multitudes of Gods and Asuras, I am One with God.

- 944 -

ॐ देवातिदेवाय स्वाहा

oṃ devātidevāya svāhā

oṃ we bow to He Who is the God of Gods, I am One with God.

- 945 -

ॐ देवर्षये स्वाहा

oṃ devarṣaye svāhā

oṃ we bow to He Who is the Ṛṣi of the Gods, I am One with God.

- 946 -

ॐ देवासुरवरप्रदाय स्वाहा

oṃ devāsuravarapradāya svāhā

oṃ we bow to He Who is the Grantor of Boons to Gods and Asuras, I am One with God.

- 947 -

ॐ देवासुरेश्वराय स्वाहा

oṃ devāsureśvarāya svāhā

oṃ we bow to He Who is the Supreme Lord of Gods and Asuras, I am One with God.

- 948 -

ॐ विश्वाय स्वाहा

oṃ viśvāya svāhā

oṃ we bow to He Who is the Universe, I am One with God.

- 949 -

ॐ देवासुरमहेश्वराय स्वाहा

oṃ devāsuramaheśvarāya svāhā

oṃ we bow to He Who is the Great Supreme Lord of Gods and Asuras, I am One with God.

- 950 -

ॐ सर्वदेवमयाय स्वाहा

oṃ sarvadevamayāya svāhā

oṃ we bow to He Who is the Manifestation of All Gods, I am One with God.

- 951 -

ॐ अचिन्त्याय स्वाहा

oṃ acintyāya svāhā

oṃ we bow to He Who is Unthinkable, I am One with God.

- 952 -

ॐ देवात्मने स्वाहा

oṃ devātmane svāhā

oṃ we bow to He Who is the Soul of Gods, I am One with God.

- 953 -

ॐ आत्मसम्भवाय स्वाहा

oṃ ātmasambhavāya svāhā

oṃ we bow to He Who is the Possibilities of the Soul, I am One with God.

- 954 -

ॐ उद्भिदे स्वाहा

oṃ udbhide svāhā

oṃ we bow to He Who Destroys Ignorance, I am One with God.

- 955 -

ॐ त्रिविक्रमाय स्वाहा

oṃ trivikramāya svāhā

oṃ we bow to He Who Works on Three Levels, I am One with God.

- 956 -

ॐ वैद्याय स्वाहा

oṃ vaidyāya svāhā

oṃ we bow to He Who Cures Disease, I am One with God.

- 957 -

ॐ विरजाय स्वाहा

oṃ virajāya svāhā

oṃ we bow to He Who is Sinless, I am One with God.

- 958 -

ॐ नीरजाय स्वाहा

oṃ nīrajāya svāhā

oṃ we bow to He Who is Free From Passion, I am One with God.

- 959 -

ॐ अमराय स्वाहा

oṃ amarāya svāhā

oṃ we bow to He Who is Immortal, I am One with God.

- 960 -

ॐ ईड्याय स्वाहा

oṃ īḍyāya svāhā

oṃ we bow to He Who is Praiseworthy, I am One with God.

- 961 -

ॐ हस्तीश्वराय स्वाहा

oṃ hastīśvarāya svāhā

oṃ we bow to He Who is the Lord of Elephants, I am One with God.

- 962 -

ॐ व्याघ्राय स्वाहा

oṃ vyāghrāya svāhā

oṃ we bow to He Who is a Tiger, I am One with God.

- 963 -

ॐ देवसिंहाय स्वाहा

oṃ devasiṃhāya svāhā

oṃ we bow to He Who is a Lion Amongst Gods, I am One with God.

- 964 -

ॐ नरर्षभाय स्वाहा

oṃ nararṣabhāya svāhā

oṃ we bow to He Who is Best Among Men, I am One with God.

- 965 -

ॐ विबुधाय स्वाहा

oṃ vibudhāya svāhā

oṃ we bow to He Who is Known, I am One with God.

- 966 -

ॐ अग्रवराय स्वाहा

oṃ agravarāya svāhā

oṃ we bow to He Who is Honored in Sacrifice, I am One with God.

- 967 -

ॐ सूक्ष्माय स्वाहा

oṃ sūkṣmāya svāhā

oṃ we bow to He Who is Subtle, I am One with God.

- 968 -

ॐ सर्वदेवाय स्वाहा

oṃ sarvadevāya svāhā

oṃ we bow to He Who is All Gods, I am One with God.

- 969 -

ॐ तपोमयाय स्वाहा

oṃ tapomayāya svāhā

oṃ we bow to He Who is the Manifestation of Purifying Austerities, I am One with God.

- 970 -

ॐ सुयुक्ताय स्वाहा

oṃ suyuktāya svāhā

oṃ we bow to He Who is Excellent Union, I am One with God.

- 971 -

ॐ शोभनाय स्वाहा

oṃ śobhanāya svāhā

oṃ we bow to He Who Shines, I am One with God.

- 972 -

ॐ वज्रिणे स्वाहा

oṃ vajriṇe svāhā

oṃ we bow to He Who Has Lightning, I am One with God.

- 973 -

ॐ प्रासानांप्रभवाय स्वाहा

oṃ prāsānāṃprabhavāya svāhā

oṃ we bow to He Who Radiates Contentment, I am One with God.

- 974 -

ॐ अव्याय स्वाहा

oṃ avyāya svāhā

oṃ we bow to He Who is Attained Through Devotion, I am One with God.

- 975 -

ॐ गुहाय स्वाहा

oṃ guhāya svāhā

oṃ we bow to He Who is Secret, I am One with God.

- 976 -

ॐ कान्ताय स्वाहा

oṃ kāntāya svāhā

oṃ we bow to He Who is Beauty Enhanced By Love, I am One with God.

- 977 -

ॐ निजसर्गाय स्वाहा

oṃ nijasargāya svāhā

oṃ we bow to He Who Himself is Heaven, I am One with God.

- 978 -

ॐ पवित्राय स्वाहा

oṃ pavitrāya svāhā

oṃ we bow to He Who is Pure, I am One with God.

- 979 -

ॐ सर्वपावनाय स्वाहा

oṃ sārvapāvanāya svāhā

oṃ we bow to He Who is the Refreshing Breeze of All, I am One with God.

- 980 -

ॐ शृङ्गिणे स्वाहा

oṃ śṛṇgiṇe svāhā

oṃ we bow to He Who Dwells at the Summit, I am One with God.

- 981 -

ॐ शृङ्गप्रियाय स्वाहा

oṃ sṛṇgapriyāya svāhā

oṃ we bow to He Who is Beloved of the One Who Dwells at the Summit, I am One with God.

- 982 -

ॐ बभ्रवे स्वाहा

oṃ babhrave svāhā

oṃ we bow to He Who is of Redish Hue, I am One with God.

- 983 -

ॐ राजराजाय स्वाहा

oṃ rājarājāya svāhā

oṃ we bow to He Who is the King of Kings, I am One with God.

- 984 -

ॐ निरानयाय स्वाहा

oṃ nirānayāya svāhā

oṃ we bow to He Who is Free From Blemish, I am One with God.

- 985 -

ॐ अभिरामाय स्वाहा

oṃ abhirāmāya svāhā

oṃ we bow to He Who is the Supreme Manifestation of the Subtle Body of Consciousness, I am One with God.

- 986 -

ॐ सुरगणाय स्वाहा

oṃ suragaṇāya svāhā

oṃ we bow to He Who is the Multitude of Gods, I am One with God.

- 987 -

ॐ विरामाय स्वाहा

oṃ virāmāya svāhā

oṃ we bow to He Who is With the Manifestation of the Subtle Body of Consciousness, I am One with God.

- 988 -

ॐ सर्वसाधनाय स्वाहा

oṃ sarvasādhanāya svāhā

oṃ we bow to He Who is All Discipline, I am One with God.

- 989 -

ॐ ललाटाक्षाय स्वाहा

oṃ lalāṭākṣāya svāhā

oṃ we bow to He Who Has a Third Eye in the Forehead, I am One with God.

- 990 -

ॐ विश्वदेवाय स्वाहा

oṃ viśvadevāya svāhā

oṃ we bow to He Who is the Universal God, I am One with God.

- 991 -

ॐ हरिणाय स्वाहा

oṃ hariṇāya svāhā

oṃ we bow to He Who is Swift Like a Deer, I am One with God.

- 992 -

ॐ ब्रह्मवर्चसे स्वाहा

oṃ brahmavarcase svāhā

oṃ we bow to He Who Has Spiritual Brilliance, I am One with God.

- 993 -

ॐ स्थावरपतये स्वाहा

oṃ sthāvarapataye svāhā

oṃ we bow to He Who is the Lord of All Established, I am One with God.

- 994 -

ॐ नियमेन्द्रियवर्धनाय स्वाहा

oṃ niyamendriyavardhanāya svāhā

oṃ we bow to He Who Controls His Senses According to a Discipline, I am One with God.

- 995 -

ॐ सिद्धार्थाय स्वाहा

oṃ siddhārthāya svāhā

oṃ we bow to He Who is the Object of Attainment, I am One with God.

- 996 -

ॐ सिद्धभूतार्थाय स्वाहा

oṃ siddhabhūtārthāya svāhā

oṃ we bow to He Who is the Object of Attainment of Existence, I am One with God.

- 997 -

ॐ अचिन्त्याय स्वाहा

oṃ acintyāya svāhā

oṃ we bow to He Who is Unthinkable, I am One with God.

- 998 -

ॐ सत्यव्रताय स्वाहा

oṃ satyavratāya svāhā

oṃ we bow to He Who is True to His Vows, I am One with God.

- 999 -

ॐ शुचये स्वाहा

oṃ śucaye svāhā

oṃ we bow to He Who is Purity, I am One with God.

- 1000 -

ॐ व्रताधिपाय स्वाहा

oṃ vratādhipāya svāhā

oṃ we bow to He Who is the Supreme Vow, I am One with God.

- 1001 -

ॐ पराय स्वाहा

oṃ parāya svāhā

oṃ we bow to He Who is Supreme, I am One with God.

- 1002 -

ॐ ब्रह्मणे स्वाहा

oṃ brahmaṇe svāhā

oṃ we bow to He Who is Supreme Divinity, I am One with God.

- 1003 -

ॐ भक्तानां परमगतये स्वाहा

oṃ bhaktānāṃ paramagataye svāhā

oṃ we bow to He Who is the Supreme Refuge of Devotees, I am One with God.

- 1004 -

ॐ विमुक्ताय स्वाहा

oṃ vimuktāya svāhā

oṃ we bow to He Who is Liberated, I am One with God.

- 1005 -

ॐ मुक्ततेजसे स्वाहा

oṃ muktatejase svāhā

oṃ we bow to He Who is the Light of Liberation, I am One with God.

- 1006 -

ॐ श्रीमते स्वाहा

oṃ śrīmate svāhā

oṃ we bow to He Who is the Mind of Respect, I am One with God.

- 1007 -

ॐ श्रीवर्धनाय स्वाहा

oṃ śrīvardhanāya svāhā

oṃ we bow to He Who Bestows Spiritual Wealth, I am One with God.

- 1008 -

ॐ जगते स्वाहा

oṃ jagate svāhā

oṃ we bow to He Who is the Entire Perceivable Universe, I am One with God.

ॐ नमः इति

oṃ namaḥ iti

And that is the end.

Any other mantras that you choose to perform
At end of Homa:

ॐ नमः शिवाय स्वाहा

oṃ namaḥ śivāya svāhā

oṃ I bow to the Consciousness of Infinite Goodness, I am One with God.

सर्वतो भद्रमण्डल देवता होम

sarvato bhadramaṅḍala devatā homa

Sacrificial Fire Offerings to the
Excellent Circle of all the Gods

- 1 -

ॐ ब्रह्मणे नमः स्वाहा

oṃ brahmaṇe namaḥ svāhā

We bow to Creative Consciousness (Center), I am One with God.

- 2 -

ॐ सोमाय नमः स्वाहा

oṃ somāya namaḥ svāhā

We bow to Lord of Devotion (N), I am One with God.

- 3 -

ॐ ईशानाय नमः स्वाहा

oṃ īśānāya namaḥ svāhā

We bow to Ruler of All (NE), I am One with God.

- 4 -

ॐ इन्द्राय नमः स्वाहा

oṃ indrāya namaḥ svāhā

We bow to Rule of the Pure (E), I am One with God.

- 5 -

ॐ अग्नये नमः स्वाहा

oṃ agnaye namaḥ svāhā

We bow to Divine Fire (SE), I am One with God.

- 6 -

ॐ यमाय नमः स्वाहा

oṃ yamāya namaḥ svāhā

We bow to Supreme Controller (S), I am One with God.

- 7 -

ॐ निर्ऋतये नमः स्वाहा

oṃ nirṛtaye namaḥ svāhā

We bow to Destroyer (SW), I am One with God.

- 8 -

ॐ वरुणाय नमः स्वाहा

oṃ varuṇāya namaḥ svāhā

We bow to Lord of Equilibrium (W), I am One with God.

- 9 -

ॐ वायवे नमः स्वाहा

oṃ vāyave namaḥ svāhā

We bow to Lord of Liberation (NW), I am One with God.

- 10 -

ॐ अष्टवसुभ्यो नमः स्वाहा

oṃ aṣṭavasubhyo namaḥ svāhā

We bow to the Eight Lords of Benificence, I am One with God.

- 11 -

ॐ एकादशरुद्रेभ्यो नमः स्वाहा

oṃ ekādaśarudrebhyo namaḥ svāhā

We bow to the Eleven Relievers from Sufferings, I am One with God.

- 12 -

ॐ द्वादशादित्येभ्यो नमः स्वाहा

oṃ dvādaśādityebhyo namaḥ svāhā

We bow to the Twelve Sons of Light, I am One with God.

- 13 -

ॐ अश्विभ्यां नमः स्वाहा

oṃ aśvibhyāṃ namaḥ svāhā

We bow to the Two Horses of Pure Desire, I am One with God.

- 14 -

ॐ सपैतृकविश्वेभ्यो देवेभ्यो नमः स्वाहा

oṃ sapaitṛkaviśvebhyo devebhyo namaḥ svāhā

We bow to the Ancestors along with the Shining Ones of the Universe, I am One with God.

- 15 -

ॐ सप्तयक्षेभ्यो नमः स्वाहा

oṃ saptayakṣebhyo namaḥ svāhā

We bow to the Energy which brings the good and bad of wealth, I am One with God.

- 16 -

ॐ अष्टकुलनागेभ्यो नमः स्वाहा

oṃ aṣṭakulanāgebhyo namaḥ svāhā

We bow to the Family of eight snakes, I am One with God.

- 17 -

ॐ गन्धर्वाऽप्सरोभ्यो नमः स्वाहा

oṃ gandharvā-psarobhyo namaḥ svāhā

We bow to the celestial musicians and heavenly maidens, I am One with God.

- 18 -

ॐ स्कन्दाय नमः स्वाहा

oṃ skandāya namaḥ svāhā

We bow to the God of War, I am One with God.

- 19 -

ॐ वृषभाय नमः स्वाहा

oṃ vṛṣabhāya namaḥ svāhā

We bow to the Bull of Discipline, Conveyance of Śiva -- Nandi, I am One with God.

- 20 -

ॐ शूलाय नमः स्वाहा

oṃ śūlāya namaḥ svāhā

We bow to the Spear of Concentration, I am One with God.

- 21 -

ॐ महाकालाय नमः स्वाहा

oṃ mahākālāya namaḥ svāhā

We bow to the Great Time, I am One with God.

- 22 -

ॐ दक्षादि सप्तगणेभ्यो नमः स्वाहा

oṃ dakṣādi saptagaṇebhyo namaḥ svāhā

We bow to to Ability and the other seven qualities, I am One with God.

- 23 -

ॐ दुर्गायै नमः स्वाहा

oṃ durgāyai namaḥ svāhā

We bow to the Reliever of Difficulties, I am One with God.

- 24 -

ॐ विष्णवे नमः स्वाहा

oṃ viṣṇave namaḥ svāhā

We bow to the All-Pervading Consciousness, I am One with God.

- 25 -

ॐ स्वधायै नमः स्वाहा

oṃ svadhāyai namaḥ svāhā

We bow to the Ancestors, I am One with God.

- 26 -

ॐ मृतयुरोगेभ्यो नमः स्वाहा

oṃ mṛtyurogebhyo namaḥ svāhā

We bow to the Spirit of deadly illnesses, I am One with God.

- 27 -

ॐ गणपतये नमः स्वाहा

oṃ gaṇapataye namaḥ svāhā

We bow to the Lord of the Multitudes, I am One with God.

- 28 -

ॐ अद्भ्यो नमः स्वाहा

oṃ adbhyo namaḥ svāhā

We bow to to Acts of Sacrifice, I am One with God.

- 29 -

ॐ मरुद्भ्यो नमः स्वाहा

oṃ marudbhyo namaḥ svāhā

We bow to the Shining Ones, I am One with God.

- 30 -

ॐ पृथिव्यै नमः स्वाहा

oṃ pṛthivyai namaḥ svāhā

We bow to the Earth, I am One with God.

- 31 -

ॐ गङ्गादिनदीभ्यो नमः स्वाहा

oṃ gaṅgādinadībhyo namaḥ svāhā

We bow to the Ganges and other rivers, I am One with God.

- 32 -

ॐ सप्तसागरेभ्यो नमः स्वाहा

oṃ saptasāgarebhyo namaḥ svāhā

We bow to the Seven Seas, I am One with God.

- 33 -

ॐ मेरवे नमः स्वाहा

oṃ merave namaḥ svāhā

We bow to Mount Meru, I am One with God.

- 34 -

ॐ गदाय नमः स्वाहा

oṃ gadāya namaḥ svāhā

We bow to the Club, I am One with God.

- 35 -

ॐ त्रिशूलाय नमः स्वाहा

oṃ triśūlāya namaḥ svāhā

We bow to the Trident, I am One with God.

- 36 -

ॐ वज्राय नमः स्वाहा

oṃ vajrāya namaḥ svāhā

We bow to the thunderbolt, I am One with God.

- 37 -

ॐ शक्तये नमः स्वाहा

oṃ śaktaye namaḥ svāhā

We bow to Energy, I am One with God.

- 38 -

ॐ दण्डाय नमः स्वाहा

oṃ daṇḍāya namaḥ svāhā

We bow to the Staff, I am One with God.

- 39 -

ॐ खड्गाय नमः स्वाहा

oṃ khaḍgāya namaḥ svāhā

We bow to the Sword, I am One with God.

- 40 -

ॐ पाशाय नमः स्वाहा

oṃ pāśāya namaḥ svāhā

We bow to the Net, I am One with God.

- 41 -

ॐ अङ्कुशाय नमः स्वाहा

oṃ aṅkuśāya namaḥ svāhā

We bow to the Goad, I am One with God.

- 42 -

ॐ गौतमाय नमः स्वाहा

oṃ gautamāya namaḥ svāhā

We bow to Ṛṣi Gautam, I am One with God.

- 43 -

ॐ भरद्वाजाय नमः स्वाहा

oṃ bharadvājāya namaḥ svāhā

We bow to Ṛṣi Bharadvāj, I am One with God.

- 44 -

ॐ विश्वामित्राय नमः स्वाहा

oṃ viśvāmitrāya namaḥ svāhā

We bow to Ṛṣi Viśvāmitra, I am One with God.

- 45 -

ॐ कश्यपाय नमः स्वाहा

oṃ kaśyapāya namaḥ svāhā

We bow to Ṛṣi Kaśyapa, I am One with God.

- 46 -

ॐ जमदग्नये नमः स्वाहा

oṃ jamadagnaye namaḥ svāhā

We bow to Ṛṣi Jamadagni, I am One with God.

- 47 -

ॐ वसिष्ठाय नमः स्वाहा

oṃ vasiṣṭāya namaḥ svāhā

We bow to Ṛṣi Vaṣisṭha, I am One with God.

- 48 -

ॐ अत्रये नमः स्वाहा

oṃ atraye namaḥ svāhā

We bow to Ṛṣi Atri, I am One with God.

- 49 -

ॐ अरुन्धत्यै नमः स्वाहा

oṃ arundhatyai namaḥ svāhā

We bow to Devi Arundati, wife of Vaṣisṭha, example of purity, I am One with God.

- 50 -

ॐ ऐन्द्र्यै नमः स्वाहा

oṃ aindryai namaḥ svāhā

We bow to Aindri, the energy of the Rule of the Pure, I am One with God.

- 51 -

ॐ कौमार्य्यै नमः स्वाहा

oṃ kaumāryyai namaḥ svāhā

We bow to Kumarī, the energy of the Ever Pure One, I am One with God.

- 52 -

ॐ ब्राह्म्यै नमः स्वाहा

oṃ brāhmyai namaḥ svāhā

We bow to Brahmi, the energy of Creative Consciousness, I am One with God.

- 53 -

ॐ वाराह्यै नमः स्वाहा

oṃ vārāhyai namaḥ svāhā

We bow to Varāhi, the energy of the Boar of Sacrifice, I am One with God.

- 54 -

ॐ चामुण्डायै नमः स्वाहा

oṃ cāmuṅḍāyai namaḥ svāhā

We bow to Cāmuṇḍa, the Conquerer of Passion and Meaness, I am One with God.

- 55 -

ॐ वैष्णव्यै नमः स्वाहा

oṃ vaiṣṇavyai namaḥ svāhā

We bow to Vaiṣṇāvi, the energy of All-Pervading Consciousness, I am One with God.

- 56 -

ॐ माहेश्वर्यै नमः स्वाहा

oṃ māheśvaryai namaḥ svāhā

We bow to Maheśvarī, the energy of the Supreme Sovereign, I am One with God.

- 57 -

ॐ वैनायक्यै नमः स्वाहा

oṃ vaināyakyai namaḥ svāhā

We bow to Vainākī, the energy of excellent conduct, I am One with God.

सर्वमङ्गलमङ्गल्ये शिवे सर्वार्थसाधिके ।
शरण्ये त्र्यम्बके गौरि नारायणि नमोऽस्तु ते स्वाहा ॥

**sarvamaṅgala maṅgalye śive sarvārtha sādhike
śaraṇye tryambake gauri nārāyaṇi namo-stu te svāhā**

To the Auspicious of all Auspiciousness, to the Good, to the Accomplisher of all Objectives, to the Source of Refuge, to the Mother of the three worlds, to the Goddess Who is Rays of Light, Exposer of Consciousness, we bow to you, I am One with God.

सृष्टिस्थितिविनाशानां शक्तिभूते सनातनि ।
गुणाश्रये गुणमये नारायणि नमोऽस्तु ते स्वाहा ॥

**sṛṣṭisthitivināśānāṃ śaktibhūte sanātani
guṇāśraye guṇamaye nārāyaṇi namo-stu te svāhā**

You are the Eternal Energy of Creation, Preservation and Destruction in all existence; that upon which all qualities depend, that which limits all qualities, Exposer of Consciousness, we bow to you, I am One with God.

शरणागतदीनार्तपरित्राणपरायणे ।
सर्वस्यार्तिहरे देवि नारायणि नमोऽस्तु ते स्वाहा ॥

**śaraṇāgatadīnārta paritrāṇa parāyaṇe
sarvasyārti hare devi nārāyaṇi namo-stu te svāhā**

For those who are devoted to you and take refuge in you, you save from all discomfort and unhappiness. All worry you take away, Oh Goddess, Exposer of Consciousness, we bow to you, I am One with God.

पूर्णहुति
Pūrṇahuti

ॐ इतः पूर्व प्राणबुद्धिदेह धर्माधिकारतो ।
जाग्रत् स्वप्नशुषुप्तयवस्थाशु मनसा ॥

oṃ itaḥ pūrva prāṇabuddhideha dharmādhikārato
jāgrat svapnaśuṣuptayavasthāśu manasā

oṃ Thus the full and complete intelligence of the Life Force, the Cause of Dharma, the Way of Truth to Perfection, has been given. Waking Consciousness, dreaming (or thinking) Consciousness, and Consciousness in dreamless sleep (intuitive Consciousness) in which all thoughts are situated.

वाचा कर्मणा हस्ताभ्यां पध्भ्यामूदरेण शिश्ना ।
यत् कृतं तद्युक्तं यत् स्मृतं तत् सर्वं ब्रह्मार्पणं भवतु स्वाहा ॥

vācā karmaṇā hastābhyāṃ padhbhyāmūdareṇa śiśnā
yatkṛtaṃ tadyuktaṃ yat smṛtaṃ tatsarvaṃ brahmārpaṇaṃ bhavatu svāhā

All speech has been offered with folded hands raised in respect while bowing to the lotus feet. That activity, that union, that memory, all of that has been offered to the Supreme Divinity, I am One with God.

मां मदीयञ्च सकलं श्री चण्डिका चरणे समर्पये ।
ॐ तत् सत् ॥

māṃ madīyañca sakalaṃ
śrī caṇḍikā caraṇe samarpaye
oṃ tat sat

All of me and all that belongs to me entirely, I surrender to the feet of the respected Caṇḍikā, She Who Tears Apart Thought. Oṃ the Infinite, That is Truth.

ॐ ब्रह्मार्पणं ब्रह्म हविर्ब्रह्माग्नौ ब्रह्मणा हुतम् ।
ब्रह्मैव तेन गन्तव्यं ब्रह्मकर्मसमाधिना ॥

oṃ brahmārpaṇaṃ brahma havir
brahmāgnau brahmaṇā hutam
brahmaiva tena gantavyaṃ
brahmakarmasamādhinā

oṃ The Supreme Divinity makes the offering; the Supreme Divinity is the offering; offered by the Supreme Divinity, in the fire of the Supreme Divinity. By seeing the Supreme Divinity in all actions, one realizes that Supreme Divinity.

ॐ पूर्णमदः पूर्णमिदं पूर्णात् पूर्णमुदुच्यते ।
पूर्णस्य पूर्णमादाय पूर्णमेवावशिश्यते ॥

oṃ pūrṇamadaḥ pūrṇamidaṃ
pūrṇāt pūrṇamuducyate
pūrṇasya pūrṇamādāya pūrṇamevāva śiṣyate

oṃ That is whole and perfect; this is whole and perfect. From the whole and perfect, the whole and perfect becomes manifest. If the whole and perfect issue forth from the whole and perfect, even still only the whole and perfect will remain.

क्षमास्य

kṣamāsya

Please forgive me.

visarjana mudrā

tilak

त्र्यायुषञ्जमदग्ने कश्यपस्यत्त्र्यायुषम् ।

यद्देवेषुत्त्र्यायुषन्तन्नोऽअस्तुत्त्र्यायुषम् ॥

tryāyuṣañjamadagne kaśyapasyattryāyuṣam
yaddeveṣuttryāyuṣantanno-astuttryāyuṣam

Three lifetimes filled with Peace is the blessing of Jamadagni (Literally, He who gives birth to Fire). From the muni, Kaśyapa, three lifetimes filled with Peace. From all the Gods three lifetimes filled with Peace, so let that be unto you, three lifetimes filled with Peace!

आरति

ārati

Dance in Celebration

जय शिव ॐकार । (बोलो) जय शिव ॐकार ।

ब्रह्म विष्णु सदा शिव । अर्धाङ्गि धारा ॥

ॐ हर हर हर महादेव ॥

jaya śiva oṃkāra, (bolo) jaya śiva oṃkāra
brahma viṣṇu sadā śiva, ardhāṅgi dhārā
oṃ hara hara hara mahādeva

Victory to Śiva, the Consciousness of Infinite Goodness, in the form of oṃ. Let's say, Victory to Śiva, the Consciousness of Infinite Goodness, in the form of oṃ. Creative Consciousness, Preserving Consciousness, and always the Consciousness of Continuous Transformation (as well as the Consciousness of Infinite Goodness) who with only His part supports all living beings. oṃ He Who Takes Away, He Who Takes Away, He Who Takes Away, the Great God.

एकानन चरानन पञ्चानन राजे, (शिव) पञ्चानन राजे ।
हंसासन गरुडासन । वृष वाहन ते सोहे ॥
ॐ हर हर हर महादेव ॥

ekā nana carā nana pañcā nana rāje,
(śiva) pañcā nana rāje haṃs āsana garuḍāsana
vṛṣa vāhana te sohe
oṃ hara hara hara mahādeva

He shows Himself with one face, with four faces and with five faces as well, Oh Śiva, with five faces as well. Sitting upon a swan, sitting upon the King of Birds, a golden eagle, sitting upon a bull. oṃ He Who Takes Away, He Who Takes Away, He Who Takes Away, the Great God.

दोय भूज च चतुर्भूज दशभूज ते सोहे,
(शिव) दशभूज ते सोहे ।
तीन रूप निराखता । त्रिभुवन जन मोहे ॥
ॐ हर हर हर महादेव ॥

doya bhūja ca caturbhūja daśabhūja te sohe,
(śiva) daśabhūja te sohe
tīna rūpa nirākhatā, tri bhuvana jana mohe
oṃ hara hara hara mahādeva

With two arms and with four arms and with ten arms as well, Oh Śiva, with ten arms as well. These three forms revolve, these three forms revolve in the ignorance of the inhabitants of the three worlds. oṃ He Who Takes Away, He Who Takes Away, He Who Takes Away, the Great God.

अक्षर्माला वनमाला रुण्डमाला धारि,

(शिव) रुण्डमाला धारि । चन्दन मृग मद् चन्द् ।

भले शुभकारी ॥ ॐ हर हर हर महादेव ॥

ākṣarmālā vanamālā ruṇḍamālā dhāri,
(śiva) ruṇḍamālā dhāri candana mṛga mada canda,
bhale śubha kārī
oṃ hara hara hara mahādeva

With a garland of letters, with a garland of forest flowers, with a garland of skulls as well, Oh Śiva, with a garland of skulls as well. With the scent of sandle, with the scent of musk, with the scent of spiritous liquor as well, truly you are the cause of purification. oṃ He Who Takes Away, He Who Takes Away, He Who Takes Away, the Great God.

श्वेताम्बर पिताम्बर बाघम्बर अङ्गे,

(शिव) बाघम्बर अङ्गे ।

सेनतादिक प्रभु तादिक । भूतादिक ते सङ्गे ॥

ॐ हर हर हर महादेव ॥

śvetāmbara pitāmbara bāghambara aṅge,
(śiva) bāghambara aṅge
senatādika prabhu tādika, bhūtādika te saṅge
oṃ hara hara hara mahādeva

With a white colored cloth, with a yellow colored cloth, with a tiger skin aparell as well, Oh Śiva, with a tiger skin apparell as well. With an army, as Lord of the armies, with an army, as Lord of the armies, and accompanied by an army of ghosts and goblins as well. oṃ He Who Takes Away, He Who Takes Away, He Who Takes Away, the Great God.

कर मध्ये कमण्डलु चक्र त्रिशूल धरता
(शिव) चक्र त्रिशूल धरता । जगत कर्ता जगत हर्ता ।
जगत पालन कर्ता ॥ ॐ हर हर हर महादेव ॥

**kara madhye kamaṇḍalu cakra triśūla dharatā,
(śiva) cakra triśūla dharatā, jagata kartā jagata hartā
jagata pālana kartā, oṃ hara hara hara mahādeva**

In His hands He holds a water pot, a discus, and a trident as well, Oh Śiva, a discus and a trident as well. He makes the perceivable universe, and He takes away the perceivable universe, and He protects the perceivable universe as well. oṃ He Who Takes Away, He Who Takes Away, He Who Takes Away, the Great God.

ब्रह्म विष्णु सदाशिव जनत आविवेका,
(शिव) जनत आविवेका ।
प्रनव आक्षर ॐमध्ये । ये तीनो एका ॥
ॐ हर हर हर महादेव ॥

**brahma viṣṇu sadāśiva janata āvivekā, (śiva) janata āvivekā pranava ākṣara oṃ madhye, ye tīna ekā
oṃ hara hara hara mahādeva**

Creative Conciousness, Preserving Consciousness, and always the Consciousness of Continuous Transformation (as well as the Consciousness of Infinite Goodness), to those people without discrimination (appear separate). But within the holy syllable oṃ, but within the holy syllable oṃ, the three are actually ONE. oṃ He Who Takes Away, He Who Takes Away, He Who Takes Away, the Great God.

त्रिगुण स्वामि कि आरति यो कोइ नर गावे,
(शिव) यो कोइ नर गावे । बनात शिवानन्द स्वामि ।
वञ्चित फल पह्वे ॥ ॐ हर हर हर महादेव ॥

triguṇa svāmi ki ārati yo koi nara gāve,
(śiva) yo koi nara gāve, banāta śivānanda svāmi
vañcita phala pahve, oṃ hara hara hara mahādeva

Whatever man will sing this praise of the Master of the three gunas (qualities), Oh Śiva, whatever man will sing. Make him a master of the Bliss of Infinite Consciousness, make him a master of the Bliss of Infinite Consciousness, certainly that will be the fruit he receives. oṃ He Who Takes Away, He Who Takes Away, He Who Takes Away, the Great God.

जय शिव ॐकार । (बोलो) जय शिव ॐकार ।
ब्रह्म विष्णु सदा शिव । अर्धाङ्गि धारा ॥
ॐ हर हर हर महादेव ॥

jaya śiva oṃkāra, (bolo) jaya śiva oṃkāra
brahma viṣṇu sadā śiva, ardhāṅgi dhārā
oṃ hara hara hara mahādeva

Victory to Śiva, the Consciousness of Infinite Goodness, in the form of oṃ. Let's say, Victory to Śiva, the Consciousness of Infinite Goodness, in the form of oṃ. Creative Consciousness, Preserving Consciousness, and always the Consciousness of Continuous Transformation (as well as the Consciousness of Infinite Goodness) who with only His part supports all living beings. oṃ He Who Takes Away, He Who Takes Away, He Who Takes Away, the Great God.

प्रणाम्

praṇām

सर्वमङ्गलमङ्गल्ये शिवे सर्वार्थसाधिके ।
शरण्ये त्र्यम्बके गौरि नारायणि नमोऽस्तु ते ॥

sarvamaṅgala maṅgalye śive sarvārtha sādhike
śaraṇye tryambake gauri nārāyaṇi namo-stu te

To the Auspicious of all Auspiciousness, to the Good, to the Accomplisher of all Objectives, to the Source of Refuge, to the Mother of the three worlds, to the Goddess Who is Rays of Light, Exposer of Consciousness, we bow to you.

सृष्टिस्थितिविनाशानां शक्तिभूते सनातनि ।
गुणाश्रये गुणमये नारायणि नमोऽस्तु ते ॥

sṛṣṭisthitivināśānāṃ śaktibhūte sanātani
guṇāśraye guṇamaye nārāyaṇi namo-stu te

You are the Eternal Energy of Creation, Preservation and Destruction in all existence; that upon which all qualities depend, that which limits all qualities, Exposer of Consciousness, we bow to you.

शरणागतदीनार्तपरित्राणपरायणे ।
सर्वस्यार्तिहरे देवि नारायणि नमोऽस्तु ते ॥

śaraṇāgatadīnārta paritrāṇa parāyaṇe
sarvasyārti hare devi nārāyaṇi namo-stu te

For those who are devoted to you and take refuge in you, you save from all discomfort and unhappiness. All worry you take away, Oh Goddess, Exposer of Consciousness, we bow to you.

दुर्गां शिवां शान्तिकरीं ब्रह्माणीं ब्रह्मणः प्रियाम् ।
सर्वलोकप्रणेत्रीञ्च प्रणमामि सदा शिवाम् ॥

durgāṃ śivāṃ śāntikarīṃ
brahmāṇīṃ brahmaṇaḥ priyām
sarvaloka praṇetrīñca praṇamāmi sadā śivām

The Reliever of Difficulties, Exposer of Goodness, Cause of Peace, Infinite Consciousness, Beloved by Knowers of Consciousness; all the inhabitants of all the worlds always bow to Her, and I am bowing to Goodness Herself.

मङ्गलां शोभनां शुद्धां निष्कलां परमां कलाम् ।
विश्वेश्वरीं विश्वमातां चण्डिकां प्रणमाम्यहम् ॥

maṅgalāṃ śobhanāṃ śuddhāṃ
niṣkalāṃ paramāṃ kalām
viśveśvarīṃ viśvamātāṃ
caṇḍikāṃ praṇamāmyaham

Welfare, Radiant Beauty, Completely Pure, without limitations, the Ultimate Limitation, the Lord of the Universe, the Mother of the Universe, to you Caṇḍi, to the Energy which Tears Apart Thought, I bow in submission.

सर्वदेवमयीं देवीं सर्वरोगभयापहाम् ।
ब्रह्मेशविष्णुनमितां प्रणमामि सदा शिवाम् ॥

sarvadevamayīṃ devīṃ sarvarogabhayāpahām
brahmeśaviṣṇunamitāṃ praṇamāmi sadā śivām

Composed of all the Gods, removing all sickness and fear, Brahma, Maheśvara and Viṣṇu bow down to Her, and I always bow down to the Energy of Infinite Goodness.

विन्ध्यस्थां विन्ध्यनिलयां दिव्यस्थाननिवासिनीम् ।
योगिनीं योगजननीं चण्डिकां प्रणमाम्यहम् ॥

**vindhyasthāṃ vindhyanilayāṃ
divyasthānanivāsinīm
yoginīṃ yogajananīṃ caṇḍikāṃ praṇamāmyaham**

The dwelling place of Knowledge, residing in Knowledge, Resident in the place of Divine Illumination, the Cause of Union, the Knower of Union, to the Energy Which Tears Apart Thought we constantly bow.

ईशानमातरं देवीमीश्वरीमीश्वरप्रियाम् ।
प्रणतोऽस्मि सदा दुर्गां संसारार्णवतारिणीम् ॥

**īśānamātaraṃ devīmīśvarīmīśvarapriyām
praṇato-smi sadā durgāṃ saṃsārārṇavatāriṇīm**

The Mother of the Supreme Consciousness, the Goddess Who is the Supreme Consciousness, beloved by the Supreme Consciousness, we always bow to Durgā, the Reliever of Difficulties, who takes aspirants across the difficult sea of objects and their relationships.

ॐ महादेव महात्राण महायोगि महेश्वर ।
सर्वपापहरां देव मकाराय नमो नमः ॥

**oṃ mahādeva mahātrāṇa mahāyogi maheśvara
sarvapāpaharāṃ deva makārāya namo namaḥ**

oṃ The Great God, the Great Reliever, the Great Yogi, Oh Supreme Lord, Oh God who removes all Sin, in the form of the letter "M" which dissolves creation, we bow to you again and again.

ॐ नमः शिवाय शान्ताय कारणत्रय हेतवे ।
निवेदयामि चात्मानं त्वं गतिः परमेश्वर ॥

oṃ namaḥ śivāya śāntāya kāraṇatraya hetave
nivedayāmi cātmānaṃ tvaṃ gatiḥ parameśvara

oṃ I bow to the Consciousness of Infinite Goodness, to Peace, to the Cause of the three worlds, I offer to you the fullness of my soul, Oh Supreme Lord.

त्वमेव माता च पिता त्वमेव त्वमेव बन्धुश्च सखा त्वमेव ।
त्वमेव विद्या द्रविणं त्वमेव त्वमेव सर्वम् मम देवदेव ॥

tvameva mātā ca pitā tvameva
tvameva bandhuśca sakhā tvameva
tvameva vidyā draviṇaṃ tvameva
tvameva sarvam mama deva deva

You alone are Mother and Father, you alone are friend and relative. You alone are knowledge and wealth, Oh my God of Gods, you alone are everything.

कायेन वाचा मनसेन्द्रियैर्वा बुद्ध्यात्मानवप्रकृतस्वभावत् ।
करोमि यद्यत् सकल्म् परस्मै नारायणायेति समर्पयामि ॥

kāyena vācā manasendriyairvā
buddhyātmā nava prakṛta svabhavat
karomi yadyat sakalam parasmai
nārāyaṇāyeti samarpayāmi

Body, speech, mind, the five organs of knowledge (five senses) and the intellect; these nine are the natural condition of human existence. In their highest evolution, I move beyond them all, as I surrender completely to the Supreme Consciousness.

ॐ पापोऽहं पापकर्माहं पापात्मा पापसम्भव ।

त्राहि मां पुण्डरीकाक्षं सर्वपापहरो हरिः ॥

oṃ pāpo-haṃ pāpakarmāhaṃ
pāpātmā pāpasambhava
trāhi māṃ puṇḍarīkākṣaṃ sarvapāpa haro hariḥ

oṃ I am of sin, confusion, duality; my actions are of duality; this entire existence is of duality. Oh Savior and Protector, Oh Great Consciousness, take away all sin, confusion, duality.

ॐ मन्त्रहीनं क्रियाहीनं भक्तिहीनं सुरेश्वरि ।

यत्पूजितं मया देवि परिपूर्णं तदस्तु मे ॥

oṃ mantrahīnaṃ kriyāhīnaṃ
bhaktihīnaṃ sureśvari
yatpūjitaṃ mayā devi paripūrnaṃ tadastu me

oṃ I know nothing of mantras. I do not perform good conduct. I have no devotion, Oh Supreme Goddess. But Oh my God, please accept the worship that I offer.

त्वमेव प्रत्यक्षम् ब्रह्माऽसि ।

त्वामेव प्रत्यक्षम् ब्रह्म वदिष्यामि ।

ऋतम् वदिष्यामि, सत्यम् वदिष्यामि ।

तन मामवतु, तद् वक्तारमवतु ।

अवतु माम्, अवतु वक्तारम् ॥

tvameva pratyakṣam brahmā-si
tvāmeva pratyakṣam brahma vadiṣyāmi
ṛtam vadiṣyāmi, satyam vadiṣyāmi

tana māmavatu, tada vaktāramavatu
avatu mām, avatu vaktāram

You alone are the Perceivable Supreme Divinity. You alone are the Perceivable Supreme Divinity, so I shall declare. I shall speak the nectar of immortality. I shall speak Truth. May this body be your instrument. May this mouth be your instrument. May the Divine always be with us. May it be thus.

ॐ सह नाववतु सह नौ भुनक्तु । सह वीर्यं करवावहै ।
तेजस्विनावधीतमस्तु । मा विद्विषावहै ॥

oṃ saha nāvavatu, saha nau bhunaktu
saha vīryam karavāvahai tejasvināvadhītamastu
mā vidviṣāvahai

oṃ May the Lord protect us. May the Lord grant us enjoyment of all actions. May we be granted strength to work together. May our studies be thorough and faithful. May all disagreement cease.

ॐ असतो मा सद् गमय । तमसो मा ज्योतिर्गमय ।
मृत्योर्मा अमृतं गमय ॥

oṃ asatomā sad gamaya tamasomā jyotirgamaya
mṛtyormā amṛtaṃ gamaya

oṃ From untruth lead us to Truth. From darkness lead us to the Light. From death lead us to Immortality.

ॐ सर्वेषां स्वस्तिर्भवतु । सर्वेषां शान्तिर्भवतु । सर्वेषां पूर्णं भवतु । सर्वेषां मङ्गलं भवतु सर्वे भवन्तु सुखिनः । सर्वे सन्तु निरामयाः । सर्वे भद्राणि पश्यन्तु । मा कश्चिद् दुःख भाग्भवेत् ॥

oṃ sarveṣāṃ svastir bhavatu sarveṣāṃ śāntir bhavatu sarveṣāṃ pūrṇaṃ bhavatu sarveṣaṃ maṅgalaṃ bhavatu sarve bhavantu sukhinaḥ sarve santu nirāmayāḥ sarve bhadrāṇi paśyantu mā kaścid duḥkha bhāgbhavet

oṃ May all be blessed with the highest realization. May all be blessed with Peace. May all be blessed with Perfection. May all be blessed with Welfare. May all be blessed with comfort and happiness. May all be free from misery. May all perceive auspiciousness. May all be free from infirmities.

गुरुर्ब्रह्मा गुरुर्विष्णुः गुरुर्देवो महेश्वरः ।
गुरुः साक्षात् परं ब्रह्म तस्मै श्रीगुरवे नमः ॥

gurur brahmā gururviṣṇuḥ gururdevo maheśvaraḥ guruḥ sākṣāt paraṃ brahma tasmai śrīgurave namaḥ

The Guru is Brahmā, Guru is Viṣṇu, Guru is the Lord Maheśvara. The Guru is actually the Supreme Divinity, and therefore we bow down to the Guru.

ॐ ब्रह्मार्पणं ब्रह्म हविर्ब्रह्माग्नौ ब्रह्मणा हुतम् ।
ब्रह्मैव तेन गन्तव्यं ब्रह्मकर्मसमाधिना ॥

oṃ brahmārpaṇaṃ brahma havir
brahmāgnau brahmaṇā hutam
brahmaiva tena gantavyaṃ
brahmakarma samādhinā

oṃ The Supreme Divinity makes the offering; the Supreme Divinity is the offering; offered by the Supreme Divinity, in the fire of the Supreme Divinity. By seeing the Supreme Divinity in all actions, one realizes that Supreme Divinity.

ॐ पूर्णमदः पूर्णमिदं पूर्णात् पूर्णमुदच्यते ।
पूर्णस्य पूर्णमादाय पूर्णमेवावशिष्यते ॥

oṃ pūrṇamadaḥ pūrṇamidaṃ
pūrṇāt pūrṇamudacyate
pūrṇasya pūrṇamādāya pūrṇamevāva śiṣyate

oṃ That is whole and perfect; this is whole and perfect. From the whole and perfect, the whole and perfect becomes manifest. If the whole and perfect issue forth from the whole and perfect, even still only the whole and perfect will remain.

ॐ शान्तिः शान्तिः शान्तिः

oṃ śāntiḥ śāntiḥ śāntiḥ

oṃ Peace, Peace, Peace

Appendix

शिवोऽहम् शिवोऽहम्

śivo-ham śivo-ham

मनो बुद्ध्यहङ्कार चित्तानि नाहम्
न च श्रोत्र जिह्वे न च घ्राण नेत्रे
न च व्योमा भूमिर्न तेजो न वायु
चिदानन्द रूपः शिवोऽहम् शिवोऽहम्

mano buddhyahaṅkāra cittāni nāham
na ca śrotra jihve na ca ghrāṇa netre
na ca vyomā bhūmirna tejo na vāyu
cidānanda rūpaḥ śivo-ham śivo-ham

I am not the mind, nor the intellect, neither the ego nor the perceptions of Consciousness. Nor am I the ears, the tongue, nor the nose nor eyes. I am not the ether nor the earth, not fire nor wind. I am the form of the Bliss of Consciousness, I am Śiva, I am Śiva.

न च प्राणा संज्ञो न वै पञ्च वायु
न वा सप्त धा तुर्न्न वा पञ्च कोषः
न वाक् पाणि पादम् न चोपस्थ पायु
चिदानन्द रूपः शिवोऽहम् शिवोऽहम्

na ca prāṇā saṃṅo na vai pañcā vāyu
na vā sapta dhā turnna vā pañcā koṣaḥ
na vāk pāṇi pādam na copastha pāyu
cidānanda rūpaḥ śivo-ham śivo-ham

I am neither the life force nor the five forms of breath; neither the seven constituent elements of the body, nor the five sheaths or coverings. I am not speach, nor hands nor feet nor even the organs of reproduction and elimination. I am the form of the Bliss of Consciousness, I am Śiva, I am Śiva.

न मे द्वेष रागौ ना मे लोभ मोहौ
मदो नैव मे नैव मात्सर्य भावः
न धर्मो न चार्थो न कामो न मोक्ष
चिदानन्द रूपः शिवोऽहम् शिवोऽहम्

na me dveṣa rāgau nā me lobha mohau
mado naiva me naiva mātsarya bhāvaḥ
na dharmo na cārtho na kāmo na mokṣa
cidānanda rūpaḥ śivo-ham śivo-ham

I have neither attraction nor repulsion, neither greed nor delusion. Neither are the attitudes of ignorance nor jealousy present in me. Neither have I any Dharma (Ideal of Perfection) nor any wealth, no desires nor liberation. I am the form of the Bliss of Consciousness, I am Śiva, I am Śiva.

न पुण्यम् न पापम् न सौख्यम् न दुःखम्
न मन्त्रो न तीर्थम् न वेद न यज्ञः
अहम् भोजनम् नैव भोज्यम् न भोक्ता
चिदानन्द रूपः शिवोऽहम् शिवोऽहम्

na puṇyam na pāpam na saukhyam na duḥkham
na mantro na tīrtham na veda na yajñaḥ
aham bhojanam naiva bhojyam na bhoktā
cidānanda rūpaḥ śivo-ham śivo-ham

I have no merits nor do I have any sin. I have neither pleasure nor do I have pain. I have no mantras nor places of pilgrimage, neither wisdom nor sacrifice. I am not the act of eating, nor the food nor the enjoyer. I am the form of the Bliss of Consciousness, I am Śiva, I am Śiva.

न मृत्युर्न सङ्का न मे जाति भेदः
पिता नैव मे नैव माता च जन्म
न बन्दुर्न मित्रम् गुरु नैव सिश्यम्
चिदानन्द रूपः शिवोऽहम् शिवोऽहम्

na mṛtyurna saṅkā na me jāti bhedaḥ
pitā naiva me naiva mātā ca janma
na bandurna mitram guru naiva siśyam
cidānanda rūpaḥ śivo-ham śivo-ham

I have neither death nor fear, nor any distinction of caste. Neither do I have a father nor a mother, nor even have I been born. I have no friend nor any comrade, neither a guru nor a disciple. I am the form of the Bliss of Consciousness, I am Śiva, I am Śiva.

अहम् निर्विकल्पो निराकार रूपो
विभुत् वाच् सर्वात्र सर्वेन्द्रियाणाम्
न चा संगतो नैव मुक्तिर्न्न मेय
चिदानन्द रूपः शिवोऽहम् शिवोऽहम्

aham nirvikalpo nirākāra rūpo
vibhut vāc sarvātra sarvendriyāṇām
na cā saṃgato naiva muktirnna meya
cidānanda rūpaḥ śivo-ham śivo-ham

I have no concept or idea, the form of the formless. I exist everywhere, in every manifestation, within all that can be perceived. I am not united nor can I be liberated. I am the form of the Bliss of Consciousness, I am Śiva, I am Śiva.

पुरुष शुक्त

puruṣa śukta

- 1 -

ॐ सहस्रशीर्षा पुरुषः सहस्राक्षः सहस्रपात् ।
स भूमिं विश्वतो वृत्वाऽत्यतिष्ठद्दशाङ्गुलम् ॥

oṃ sahasraśīrṣā puruṣaḥ sahasrākṣaḥ sahasrapāt
sa bhūmiṃ viśvato vṛtvā-tyatiṣṭhaddaśāṅgulām

The Supreme Being has innumerable (thousands of) heads, innumerable eyes, innumerable feet. Even though He extends beyond the universe of manifested objects, He dwells in a space of ten fingers breadth (in the heart of all beings).

- 2 -

पुरुष एवेकं सर्वं यद्भूतं यच्च भाव्यम् ।
उतामृतत्वस्येशानो यदन्नेनातिरोहति ॥

puruṣa evekaṃ sarvaṃ yadbhūtaṃ yacca bhāvyam
utāmṛtatvasyeśāno yadannenātirohati

The entire universe is the Supreme Being, what has manifested past, present and furture. Above all, the immortal existence, He provides nourishment for life.

- 3 -

एतावानस्य महिमाऽतो ज्यायांश्च पूरुषः ।
पादोऽस्य विश्वा भूतानि त्रिपादस्यामृतं दिवि ॥

etāvānasya mahimā-to jyāyāṃśca pūruṣaḥ
pādo-sya viśvā bhūtāni tripādasyāmṛtaṃ divi

The entire existence manifests His Glory, which the Supreme Being transcends. The perceivable beings constitute His quarter part. Three quarters embodying immortality, remain inconceivable in the heavens.

- 4 -

त्रिपादूर्ध्व उदैत्पुरुषः पादोऽस्येहाभवत्पुनः ।
ततोविष्वं व्यक्रामत्साशनानशनेऽअभि ॥

tripādūrdhva udaitpuruṣaḥ pādo-syehābhavatpunaḥ
tatoviṣvaṃ vyakrāmatsāśanānaśane-abhi

Three parts of the Supreme Being is above birth and death, the fourth part manifested as the universe. From this came forth existence which eats and eats not.

- 5 -

ततो विराडजायत विराजोऽअधि पूरुषः ।
सजातोऽअत्यरिच्यत पश्चाद्भूमिमथो पुरः ॥

tato virāḍajāyata virājo-adhi pūruṣaḥ
sajāto-atyaricyata paścādbhūmimātho puraḥ

Then Radiance came forth, and from Radiance the Supreme Being shined. Then He gave birth to the earth, with places both high and low.

- 6 -

तस्माद्यज्ञत्सवहुतः सम्भृतं पृषदाज्यम् ।
पशूंस्तांश्चक्रे वायव्यानरण्या ग्राम्याश्च ये ॥

tāsmādyjñatsavahutaḥ sambhṛtaṃ pṛṣadājyam
paśūṃstāṃścakre vāyavyānāraṇyā grāmyāścā ye

Then from this sacrifice of great devotion came forth animals of the air, of the forests and those who live in villages.

- 7 -

तस्माद्यज्ञत्सर्वहुतऽऋचः सामानि जज्ञिरे ।
छन्दांऽसि जज्ञिरे तस्माद्यजुस्तस्मादजायत ॥

tāsmādyajñatsarvahuta-ṛcaḥ sāmāni jajñire
chandāṃ-si jajñire tasmādyajustasmādajāyata

Then from this sacrifice of great devotion came forth hymns and songs of praise, and sacrificial mantras, the various rhythms of sacrificial scripture all were born.

- 8 -

तस्मादश्वाऽअजायन्त ये के चोभयादतः ।
गावो ह जज्ञिरे तस्मात्तस्माज्ञाताऽअजावयः ॥

tasmādaśvā-ajāyanta ye ke cobhayādataḥ
gāvo ha jajñire tasmāttasmājjātā-ajāvayaḥ

Then were born horses and cows and varieties of life all came into being in that sacrifice.

- 9 -

तं यज्ञं बर्हिषि प्रौक्षन्पुरुषं जातमग्रतः ।
तेन देवाऽअयजन्त साध्याऽऋषयश्च ये ॥

taṃ yajñaṃ barhiṣi praukṣanpuruṣaṃ jātamagrataḥ
tena devā-ayajanta sādhyā-ṛṣayaśca ye

The sacrifice was blessed, which gave birth to that Supreme Being. In this way came forth the Gods and Seers of Eternal Reality.

- 10 -

यत्पुरुषं व्यदधुः कतिधा व्यकल्पयन् ।
मखं किमस्यासीत्किं बाहू किमूरू पादाऽउच्येते ॥

yatpuruṣaṃ vyadadhuḥ katidhā vyakalpayan
makhaṃ kimasyāsītkiṃ bāhū kimūrū pādā-ucyete

With great thought was that Supreme Being manifested. What became His head, what His arms, what His thighs and what His feet?

- 11 --

ब्राह्मणोऽस्य मुखमासीद् बाहू राजन्यः कृतः ।

ऊरू तदस्य यद्वैश्यः पद्भ्यां शूद्रोऽअजायत ॥

brāhmaṇo-sya mukhamāsīd bāhū rājanyaḥ kṛtaḥ

ūrū tadasya yadvaiśyaḥ padbhyāṃ śūdro-ajāyata

From His head came the Knowers of Wisdom, from His arms kings and administrators. From His thighs came forth those of circulation and distribution, and from His feet support and sustenance*.

- 12 -

चन्द्रमा मनसो जातश्चक्षोः सूर्यो ऽअजायत ।

श्रोत्राद्वायुश्च प्राणाणश्च मखादग्निरजायत ॥

candramā manaso jātaścakṣoḥ sūryo-ajāyata

śrotrādvāyuścā prāṇāṇaśca makhādagnirajāyata

His mind gave birth to the Moon, and His eyes gave birth to the Sun. From His ears and His breath came the Wind, and from His mouth came the Lord of Fire.

- 13 -

नाभ्या ऽआसीदन्तरिक्षठं शीर्ष्णो द्यौः समवर्त्तत ।

पद्भ्यां भूमिर्द्दिशः श्रोत्रात्तथा लोकांऽअकल्पयन् ॥

nābbhyā-āsīdantarikṣaṭhaṃ śīrṣṇo dyauḥ samavarttata

padbhyāṃ bhūmirddiśaḥ śrotrāttathā lokāṃ-akalpayan

*The Puruṣa, the Supreme Being, is the full and complete body of existence. Puru means full, complete, perfect; iṣa means Lord or Ruler, Seer; thus the Seer of Perfection or the Perfect Lord. He requires every function in order to sustain Himself: a Central Nervous System, or Intellect; an Administrative System, and Circulatory and Nourishments Systems. This makes Him full and Complete as an integrated whole. The verse does not mean that children born in a Brahmiṇ family are higher than others, as so often it is interpreted. Rather it shows that the Puruṣa performs every function, and any man wishing perfection, must emulate His perfect nature.

From His navel came forth the atmosphere, and from His head the heavens. From His feet came the earth, and from his ears the directions. Thus existence became manifested.

- 14 -

यत्पुरुषेण हविषा देवा यज्ञमतन्वत ।

वसन्तोऽस्यासीदाज्यं ग्रीष्मऽईध्मः शरद्धविः ॥

yatpuruṣeṇa haviṣā devā yajñamatanvata
vasanto-syāsīdājyaṃ grīṣma-īdhmaḥ śaraddhaviḥ

The Gods performed sacrifice with that Supreme Being as the offering. Spring was the clarified oil, Summer the fuel and Autumn the oblation.

- 15 -

सप्तास्यासन्परिधयस्त्रिः सप्त समिधः कृताः ।

देवा यद्यज्ञं तन्वानाऽअबध्नन्पुरुषं पशुम् ॥

saptāsyāsanparidhayastriḥ sapta samidhaḥ kṛtāḥ
devā yadyajñaṃ tanvānā-abadhnānpuruṣaṃ paśum

Seven were the limitations defined*, three times seven, the ingedients used. When the Gods offered that sacrifice, they bound that Supreme Being as an animal.

-16-

यज्ञेन यज्ञमयजन्त देवास्तानि धर्म्माणि प्रथमान्यासन् ।

ते ह नाकं महिमानः सचन्त यत्र पूर्वे

साध्याः सन्ति देवाः ॥

*There are many possibilities for the seven limitations defined. The most logical is:

ॐ भूः ॐ भुवः ॐ स्वः ॐ महः ॐ जनः ॐ तपः ॐ सत्यं ।

oṃ bhūḥ oṃ bhuvaḥ oṃ svaḥ oṃ mahaḥ oṃ janaḥ oṃ tapaḥ oṃ satyaṃ

Oṃ Gross Perception; Oṃ Subtle Perception; Oṃ Intuitive Perception; Oṃ the Cosmic Body of Nature; Oṃ the Body of Universal Knowledge; Oṃ the Body of Light; Oṃ the Ultimate Truth, Consciousness, Bliss.

Other possibile interpretations are the seven meters, seven levels of heaven and hell, or for that matter all of the various attributes classified by seven.

yajñena yajñamayajanta devāstāni dharmmāṇi prathamānyāsan
te ha nākaṃ mahimānaḥ sacanta yatra pūrve sādhyāḥ santi devāḥ

By sacrifice, the Gods gave birth to sacrifice, and the first principles of eternal Dharma were established. Those who live according to the glorious way, ultimately reach the highest abode where the Gods dwell in that ancient perfection.

रुद्राष्टकम्

rudrāṣṭakam

- 1 -

नमामीशमीशान निर्वाण रूपं
विभु व्यापकं ब्रह्म वेद स्वरूपं ।
निजं निर्गुणं निर्विकल्पं निरीहं
चिदाकाश माकाश वासं भजेऽहं ॥

namāmīśamīśāna nirvāṇa rūpaṃ
vibhu vyāpakaṃ brahma veda svarūpaṃ
nijaṃ nirguṇaṃ nirvikalpaṃ nirīhaṃ
cidākāśa mākāśa vāsaṃ bhaje-haṃ

We bow down with devotion to the Lord of Lords, the form of Infinite Realization, the all-pervading, Creative Consciousness, which creates the individual phenomena of existence, the intrinsic nature of Wisdom. That reality is without attributes, beyond conception, not admitting of distinction. We laud the consciousness as vast as space, which wears the infinity of space as a garment.

- 2 -

निराकार मोंकार मूलं तुरीयं

गिरा ग्यान गोतीत मीशं गिरीशं ।

करालं महाकाल कालं कृपालं

गुणागार संसार पारं नतोऽहं ॥

nirākāra moṃkāra mūlaṃ turīyaṃ
girā gyāna gotīta mīśaṃ girīśaṃ
karālaṃ mahākāla kālaṃ kṛpālaṃ
guṇāgāra saṃsāra pāraṃ nato-haṃ

We bow down with devotion to He who is without any particular form, the root of Oṃ, beyond empirical, conceptual or intuitive experience; beyond speech, wisdom or knowledge of the senses, Lord of the mountains; terrible, the Great Time, All Time, Giver of Grace; the repository of all qualities, and beyond the world of objects and relationships.

- 3 -

तुषाराद्रि संकाश गौरं गभीरं

मनोभूत कोटि प्रभा श्री शरीरं ।

स्फुरन्मौलि कल्लोलिनी चारु गंगा

लसद्भाल बालेन्दु कंथे भुजंगा ॥

tuṣārādri saṃkāśa gauraṃ gabhīraṃ
manobhūta koṭi prabhā śrī śarīraṃ
sphuranmauli kallolinī cāru gaṃgā
lasadbhāla bālendu kaṃthe bhujaṃgā

Who is white like the snow-clad mountains, serious; whose body shines with the beautiful light of ten million Gods of Love. Upon his head the beautiful river, Gaṅgā, is flowing. On his forehead the second day's digit of the moon resides, and showing a necklace made of a snake around his neck.

- 4 -

चलत् कुण्डलं भ्रू सुनेत्रं विशालं
प्रसन्नाननं नीलकंठं दयालं ।
मृगा धीश चर्माम्बरं मुण्डमालं
प्रियं शङ्करं सर्वनाथ भजामि ॥

calat kuṇḍalaṃ bhrū sunetraṃ viśālaṃ
prasannānanaṃ nīlakaṃṭhaṃ dayālaṃ
mṛgā dhīśa carmām baraṃ muṇḍamālaṃ
priyaṃ śaṅkaraṃ sarvanātha bhajāmi

The rings in his ears are moving to and fro. He has beautiful eyebrows and large wide eyes. He has a pleased expression on his face, a blue throat, and is the essence of compassion. He wears apparel of a lion's skin, and displays a garland of skulls. He is the beloved of all, and the Lord of all. We bow down with devotion to the Cause of Peace.

- 5 -

प्रचण्डं प्रकृष्टं प्रगल्भं परेशं
अखण्डं अजं भानु कोटि प्रकाशं ।
त्रयः शूल निर्मूलनं शूलपानिं
भजेऽहं भवानीपतिं भावगम्यं ॥

pracaṇḍaṃ prakṛṣṭaṃ pragalbhaṃ pareśaṃ
akhaṇḍaṃ ajaṃ bhānu koṭi prakāśaṃ
trayaḥ śūla nirmūlanaṃ śūlapānim
bhaje-haṃ bhavānīpatiṃ bhāvagamyaṃ

He is terrible, the ultimate, radiating light, the Supreme Lord, not admitting divisions, without birth, shining like ten million suns. He removes the three kinds of difficulties. He holds a trident in his hand, and we bow down with devotion to He who is always in bhāva (of ecstatic love), the Lord of the Divine Mother.

- 6 -

कलातीत कल्याण कल्पान्तकारी

सदा सज्जन आनन्ददाता पुरारी ।

चिदानन्द संदोह मोहापहारी

प्रसीद प्रसीद प्रभो मन्मथारी ॥

kalātīta kalyāṇa kalpāntakārī
sadā sajjan ānanda dātā purārī
cidānanda saṃdoha mohāpahārī
prasīda prasīda prabho manmathārī

He is beyond limitations, the intrinsic nature of welfare, who brings each age of time to its culmination, who always gives the bliss of infinite consciousness to true beings. He dwells in the City (of nine gates). He gives the bliss of consciousness, cuts asunder the bonds of ignorance. Oh Lord, be pleased, be pleased, you who put the mind into equilibrium.

- 7 -

न यावद् उमानाथ पादारविन्दं

भजन्तीह लोके परे वा नराणां ।

न तावत्सुखं शान्ति सन्तापनाशं

प्रसीद प्रभो सर्व भूताधिवासं ॥

na yāvad umānātha pādāra vindaṃ
bhajantīha loke pare vā narāṇāṃ
na tāvatsukhaṃ śānti santāpanāśaṃ
prasīda prabho sarva bhūtādhivāsaṃ

So long as devotees do not praise the Lord of Umā, there will be no happiness nor peace nor purifying austerities in the world. Oh Lord who resides within every being of existence, be pleased.

- 8 -

न जानामि योगं जपं नैव पूजां
नतोऽहं सदा सर्वदा शम्भु तुभ्यं ।
जरा जन्म दुःखौघ तातप्यमानं
प्रभो पाहि आपन्नमामीश शम्भो ॥

na jānāmi yogaṃ japaṃ naiva pūjāṃ
nato-haṃ sadā sarvadā śambhu tubhyaṃ
jarā janma duḥkhaugha tātap yamānaṃ
prabho pāhi āpannamāmīśa śambho

We do not know what is union, nor how to recite mantras, nor how to perform worship. But oh You who shine with Peace, again and again we are bowing down to you. Please save us from the pains of birth. Oh Lord who shines with Peace, we are bowing down to you.

- 9 -

रुद्राष्टकमिदं प्रोक्तं विप्रेण हरतोषये ।
ये पठन्ति नरा भक्त्या तेषं शम्भुः प्रसीदति ॥

rudrāṣṭakam idaṃ proktaṃ vipreṇa haratoṣaye
ye paṭhanti narā bhaktyā teṣaṃ śambhuḥ prasīdati

In this way the learned ones sing these eight verses of praise to Rudra, the Reliever of Sufferings. Whatever human being will sing these verses with devotion, the Lord who shines with Peace will be pleased.

लिंगाष्टकम्

liṅgāṣṭakam

- 1 -

ब्रह्म मुरारि सुरार्चित लिंगम्
निर्मल भासित शोभित लिंगम् ।
जन्ममज दुःख विनाशन लिंगम्
तत्प्रणमामि सदाशिव लिंगम् ॥

brahma murāri surārcita liṃgam
nirmala bhāsita śobhita liṃgam
janmamaja duhkha vināśana liṃgam
tatpraṇamāmi sadāśiva liṃgam

The liṃgam is the symbol of the eternal Lord Śiva. It is adorned by Brahma, Viṣṇu and all the gods. The liṃgam is taintless, shining and beautiful. It is the Destroyer of the miseries that follow birth. We bow down to that eternal symbol of the eternal Śiva.

- 2 -

देव मुनि प्रवरार्चित लिंगम्
काम दहन करुणाकर लिंगम् ।
रावण दर्प विनाशन लिंगम्
तत्प्रणमामि सदाशिव लिंगम् ॥

deva muni pravarārcita liṃgam
kāma dahana karuṇākara liṃgam
rāvaṇa darpa vināśana liṃgam
tatpraṇamāmi sadāśiva liṃgam

The symbol that is adored by the gods and great sages, that denotes the destruction of the God of Lust, the Ocean of

Mercy, and is the vanquisher of Rāvaṇa's pride. We bow down to that eternal symbol of the eternal Śiva.

- 3 -

सर्व सुगन्धि सुलेपित लिंगम्
बुद्धि-विवर्द्ध कारण लिंगम् ।
सिद्ध सुरासुर वन्दित लिंगम्
तत्प्रणमामि सदाशिव लिंगम् ॥

sarva sugandhi sulepita liṃgam
buddhi-vivarddha kāraṇa liṃgam
siddha surāsura vandita liṃgam
tatpraṇamāmi sadāśiva liṃgam

The symbol is annointed with fragrant unguents like sandal paste, etc. The symbol enhances the intellect and is worshiped by Siddhas, gods and asuras. We bow down to that eternal symbol of the eternal Śiva.

- 4 -

कनक महामणि भूषित लिंगम्
फणिपति-वेष्टित शोभित लिंगम् ।
दक्ष सुयज्ञ विनाशन लिंगम्
तत्प्रणमामि सदाशिव लिंगम् ॥

kanaka mahāmaṇi bhūṣita liṃgam
phaṇipati-veṣṭita śobhita liṃgam
dakṣa suyajña vināśana liṃgam
tatpraṇamāmi sadāśiva liṃgam

The symbol is adorned with jewels of gold and precious gems that shine with the Lord of Serpants that encircles it, and that obstructed the sacrifice performed by Dakṣa. We bow down to that eternal symbol of the eternal Śiva.

- 5 -

कुंकुम चन्दन लेपित लिंगम्
पंकज हार सुशोभित लिंगम् ।
संचित पाप विनाशन लिंगम्
तत्प्रणमामि सदाशिव लिंगम् ॥

kuṃkuma candana lepita liṃgam
paṃkaja hāra suśobhita liṃgam
saṃcita pāpa vināśana liṃgam
tatpraṇamāmi sadāśiva liṃgam

The symbol is annointed with vermilion and sandal paste, with a large fan shining behind it. It destroys all of the sin attained in many births. We bow down to that eternal symbol of the eternal Śiva.

- 6 -

देवगणार्चित सेवित लिंगम्
भावैर्भक्तिरेव च लिंगम् ।
दिनकर कोटि प्रभाकर लिंगम्
तत्प्रणमामि सदाशिव लिंगम् ॥

devagaṇārcita sevita liṃgam
bhāvairbhaktireva ca liṃgam
dinakara koṭi prabhākara liṃgam
tatpraṇamāmi sadāśiva liṃgam

The symbol is worshiped by gods with great devotion, and shines with the brilliance of millions of suns. We bow down to that eternal symbol of the eternal Śiva.

- 7 -

अष्टदलोपरि वेष्टित लिंगम्

सर्व समुद्भव कारण लिंगम् ।

अष्ट दरिद्र विनाशन लिंगम्

तत्प्रणमामि सदाशिव लिंगम ॥

aṣṭadalopari veṣṭita liṃgam
sarva samudbhava kāraṇa liṃgam
aṣṭa daridra vināśana liṃgam
tatpraṇamāmi sadāśiva liṃgam

The symbol is seated in the eight petalled seat, which is the cause of all creations, and destroys all kinds of destitution. We bow down to that eternal symbol of the eternal Śiva.

- 8 -

सुरगुरु सुरवर पूजित लिंगम्

सुरतरु पुष्प सदार्चित लिंगम् ।

परात्परं परमात्मक लिंगम्

तत्प्रणमामि सदाशिव लिंगम् ॥

suraguru suravara pūjita liṃgam
surataru puṣpa sadārcita liṃgam
parātparaṃ paramātmaka liṃgam
tatpraṇamāmi sadāśiva liṃgam

The liṃgam is worshiped by the Guru of the Gods, Bṛhaspati, and all of the gods offer flowers grown in the heavenly gardens to the symbol of the Supreme Soul. We bow down to that eternal symbol of the eternal Śiva.

शिवपञ्चाक्षरस्तोत्रम्

śivapañcākṣara stotram

- 1 -

नागेन्द्रहाराय त्रिलोचनाय

भस्माङ्गरागाय महेश्वराय ।

नित्याय शुद्धाय दिगम्बराय

तस्मै (न) काराय नमः शिवाय ॥

nāgendrahārāya trilocanāya
bhasmāṅgarāgāya maheśvarāya
nityāya śuddhāya digambarāya
tasmai (na) kārāya namaḥ śivāya

He is the King of Snakes, He Who Takes Away, the One with Three Eyes Who Covers His body with Ashes, the Great Supreme Lord of All. Her is Eternal, Pure, Clothed in Space. Therefore, with the letter Na we bow down to Śiva.

- 2 -

मन्दाकिनीसलिलचन्दनचर्चिताय

नन्दीश्वरप्रमथनाथमहेश्वराय ।

मन्दारपुष्पबहुपुष्पसुपूजिताय

तस्मै (म) काराय नमः शिवाय ॥

mandākinīsalilacandanacarcitāya
nandīśvara pramathanātha maheśvarāya
mandārapuṣpa bahupuṣpa supūjitāya
tasmai (ma) kārāya namaḥ śivāya

He is a stone in the midst of the Mandākinī river, covered by sandal paste, the Supreme Lord of Bliss, Lord of the Foremost, the Great Supreme Lord of All. He is worshiped with many excellent flowers from the mind. Therefore, with the letter Ma we bow down to Śiva.

- 3 -

शिवाय गौरीवदनाब्जवृन्द

सूर्याय दक्षाध्वरनाशकाय ।

श्रीनीलकण्ठाय वृषध्वजनाशकाय

तस्मै (शि) काराय नमः शिवाय ॥

śivāya gaurīvadanābjavṛnda
sūryāya dakṣādhvara nāśakāya
śrīnīlakaṇṭhāya vṛṣadhvaja nāśakāya
tasmai (śi) kārāya namaḥ śivāya

The Consciousness of Infinite Goodness, the Blissful face of Gaurī, She Who is Rays of Light, the Sun, Light of Wisdom, Who Destoyed Dakṣa's Sacrifice. The Respected One with a Blue Throat, Who Destroys while sitting on His bull. Therefore, with the letter Śi we bow down to Śiva.

- 4 -

वसिष्ठकुम्भोद्भवगौतमाय

मुनीन्द्रदेवार्चितशेखराय ।

चन्द्रार्कवैश्वानरलोचनाय

तस्मै (व) काराय नमः शिवाय ॥

vasiṣṭhakumbhodbhavagautamāya
munīndradevārcitaśekharāya
candrārkavaiśvānaralocanāya
tasmai (va) kārāya namaḥ śivāya

Vasiṣṭha and others from the family of existence, Gautam, the Lord of the wise ones, and other Gods offer to the Highest Divinity. The Moon and the Sun and the Fire are His eyes. Therefore, with the letter Va we bow down to Śiva.

- 5 -

यक्षस्वरूपाय जटाधराय
पिनकहस्ताय सनातनाय ।
दिव्याय देवाय दिगम्बराय
तस्मै (य) काराय नमः शिवाय ॥

yakṣasvarūpāya jaṭādharāya
pinakahastāya sanātanāya
divyāya devāya digambarāya
tasmai (ya) kārāya namaḥ śivāya

He is the intrinsic nature of the Lords of Wealth, who wears matted hair. He holds a spear in His hands, He is eternal. He is Divine, a God, Who is clothed in Space. Therefore, with the letter Ya we bow down to Śiva.

- 6 -

पञ्चाक्षरमिदं पुण्यं यः पठेच्छिवसन्निधौ ।
शिवलोकमवाप्नोति शिवेन सह मोदते ॥

pañcākṣarmidaṃ puṇyaṃ
yaḥ paṭhecchivasannidhau
śivalokamavāpnoti
śivena saha modate

This five letter song has such merit that whoever will read it with all their might, Śiva will be extremely pleased, and he or she will attain to His proximity.

भव सागर

bhava sāgara

भव सागर तारण कारण हे
रवि नन्दन बन्धन खण्डन हे ।
शरणागत किङ्कर भीतमने
गुरु देव दया कर दीनजने ॥

bhava sāgara tāraṇa kāraṇa he
ravi nandana bandhana khaṇḍana he
śaraṇāgata kiṅkara bhītamane
guru deva dayā kara dīnajane

You show the way of crossing over the ocean of existence, cutting asunder the bondage of the bliss of the Light of Wisdom. Granting refuge for the purity of mind, O divine Guru, be compassionate and illuminate the darkness.

हृदिकन्दर तामस भास्कर हे
तूमि विष्णु प्रजापति शङ्कर हे ।
परब्रह्म परात् पर वेद भणे
गुरु देव दया कर दीनजने ॥

hṛdi kandara tāmasa bhāskara he
tūmi viṣṇu prajāpati śaṅkara he
parabrahma parāt para veda bhaṇe
guru deva dayā kara dīnajane

In the center of the heart, your light destroys darkness. You are Viṣṇu, Prajāpati Brahma, and Śiva Śaṅkara. You are greater than the greatest, the highest knowledge, O divine Guru, be compassionate and illuminate the darkness.

मन वारण शासन अङ्कुश हे
नर त्राण तरे हरि चाक्षुष हे ।
गुण गान परायण देव गणे
गुरु देव दया कर दीनजने ॥

mana vāraṇa śāsana aṅkuśa he
nara trāṅa tare hari cākṣuṣa he
guṇa gāna parāyaṇa deva gaṇe
guru deva dayā kara dīnajane

You are a goad to discipline the changing mind, to take from man all obstacles to divine sight. You always extoll the divine qualities of the shining ones. O divine Guru, be compassionate and illuminate the darkness.

कुल कुण्डलिनी घुम भञ्जक हे
हृदि ग्रन्थि विदारण कारक हे ।
मम मानस चण्चल रत्रदिने
गुरु देव दया कर दीनजने ॥

kula kuṇḍalinī ghuma bhañjaka he
hṛdi granthi vidāraṇa kāraka he
mama mānasa caṇcala ratradine
guru deva dayā kara dīnajane

You awaken the sleeping kuṇḍalinī energy, and cut the knots which entangle the heart. Turn the night of confusion into the day of knowledge. O divine Guru, be compassionate and illuminate the darkness.

रिपुसुधन मङ्गल नायक हे
शुख शान्ति वराभय दायक हे ।
त्रयताप हरे तव नाम गुणे
गुरु देव दया कर दीनजने ॥

ripusudhana maṅgala nāyaka he
śukha śānti varābhaya dāyaka he
trayatāpa hare tava nāma guṇe
guru deva dayā kara dīnajane

Your gracious glance purifies all limitations, you are the giver of the blessings of comfort and peace. For those who recite your name you remove the three kinds of afflictions. O divine Guru, be compassionate and illuminate the darkness.

अभिमान प्रभाव विमर्द्दक हे
गति हीन जने तूमि रक्षक हे ।
चित शङ्कित बञ्चित भक्ति धने
गुरु देव दया कर दीनजने ॥

abhimāna prabhāva vimarddaka he
gati hīna jane tūmi rakṣaka he
cita śaṅkita bañcita bhakti dhane
guru deva dayā kara dīnajane

You crush the rise of possessiveness, and protect us from that which would slay the soul. You give pure devotion to free Consciousness from the bondage of the forces of doubt. O divine Guru, be compassionate and illuminate the darkness.

तव नाम सदा शुभ सादक हे
पति ताधम मानव पावक हे ।
महिमा तव गोचर शुद्ध मने
गुरु देव दया कर दीनजने ॥

tava nāma sadā śubha sādaka he
pati tādhama mānava pāvaka he
mahimā tava gocara śuddha mane
guru deva dayā kara dīnajane

Therefore the aspirants to divinity always recite your pure name, as you are like the Lord offering purity to men. Your greatness is perceivable only by minds that are pure. O divine Guru, be compassionate and illuminate the darkness.

जय सद्गुरु ईश्वर प्रापक हे
भव रोग विकार विनाशक हे ।
मन जेन रहे तव श्री चरणे
गुरु देव दया कर दीनजने ॥

jaya sadguru īśvara prāpaka he
bhava roga vikāra vināśaka he
mana jena rahe tava śrī caraṇe
guru deva dayā kara dīnajane

Victory to the true guru, who destroys the diseases of wordly bondage, leading humans to Supreme Divinity. So that our mind can remain at your respected lotus feet, O divine Guru, be compassionate and illuminate the darkness.

कौपीनपञ्चकं

kaupīnapañcakam

- 1 -

वेदान्तवाक्येषु सदा रमन्तो भिक्षान्नमात्रेण च तुष्टिमन्तः ।
अशोकवन्तः करुणैकवन्तः कौपीनवन्तः खलु
भाग्यवन्तः ॥

vedāntavākyeṣu sadā ramanto
bhikṣānnamātreṇa ca tuṣṭimantaḥ
aśokavantaḥ karuṇaikavantaḥ
kaupīnavantaḥ khalu bhāgyavantaḥ

He always contemplates Vedanta Philosophy (seeing everywhere Oneness). He is always content with the food received by begging. He is free from sorrow and grief, full of compassion. How fortunate is he who girds his loins with a Kaupīn loin cloth.

- 2 -

मूलं तरोः केवलमाश्रयन्तः पाणिद्वयं भोक्तुममत्रयन्तः ।
कन्थामपि स्त्रीमिव कुत्सयन्तः कौपीनवन्तः खलु
भाग्यवन्तः ॥

mūlaṃ taroḥ kevalamāśrayantaḥ
pāṇidvayaṃ bhoktummatrayantaḥ
kanthāmapi strīmiva kutsayantaḥ
kaupīnavantaḥ khalu bhāgyavantaḥ

He only resides at the foot of a tree, making his plate of food by his own two hands, as well as his patched blanket. He sees the absurdities of existence with intelligence. How fortunate is he who girds his loins with a Kaupīn loin cloth.

\- 3 -

देहाभिमानं परिहृत्य दूरादात्मानमात्मन्यवलोकयन्तः ।

अहिर्निशं ब्रह्मणि ये रमन्तः कौपीनवन्तः खलु

भाग्यवन्तः ॥

dehābhimānaṃ parihṛtya dūrād
ātmānamātmayavalokayantaḥ
ahirnaśaṃ brahmaṇi ye ramantaḥ
kaupīnavantaḥ khalu bhāgyavantaḥ

Discriminating between body and mind, master of his own soulṇ he delights in Infinite Consciousness day and night. How fortunate is he who girds his loins with a Kaupīn loin cloth.

\- 4 -

स्वानन्दभावे परितुष्टिमन्तः स्वशान्तसर्वेन्द्रियवृत्तिमन्तः ।

नान्तं न मध्यं न बहिः स्मरन्तः कौपीनवन्तः खलु

भाग्यवन्तः ॥

svānandabhāve parituṣṭimantaḥ
svaśāntasarvendriyavṛttimantaḥ
nāntaṃ na madhyaṃ na bahiḥ smarantaḥ
kaupīnavantaḥ khalu bhāgyavantaḥ

He resides contented in the bliss of communion with his own soul. He has silenced the changes and modifications of all the organs within him. All memories have been silenced from outside, from inside and in the middle. How fortunate is he who girds his loins with a Kaupīn loin cloth.

- 5 -

पञ्चाक्षरं पावनमुच्चरन्तः पतिं पशूनां हृदि भावयन्तः ।
भिक्षाशना दिक्षु परिभ्रमन्तः कौपीनवन्तः खलु
भाग्यवन्तः ॥

pañcākṣaraṃ pāvanamuccarantaḥ
patiṃ paśūnāṃ hṛdi bhāvayantaḥ
bhikṣāśanā dikṣu paribhramantaḥ
kaupīnavantaḥ khalu bhāgyavantaḥ

He continually recites the pure five lettered mantra (Na Ma Śi Va Ya), and maintains the attitude of highest divinity within his heart. He wanders in all the directions to receive offerings. How fortunate is he who girds his loins with a Kaupīn loin cloth.

अथ शिव चालीसा

atha śiva cālīsā

दोहा

dohā

जय गणेश गिरिजा सुवन मङ्गल मूल सुजान ।
कहत अयोद्यादास तुम देहु अभय वरदान ॥

jaya gaṇeśa girijā suvana maṅgala mūla sujāna
kahata ayodyādāsa tum dehu abhaya varadāna

Praise to Ganesha, the son of She who is born of the mountain, the excellent one, who is the root of all welfare. It is said that you are the servant of Peace (Ayodyā, the devotee who sings the song). Give to us the blessing of freedom from fear.

उमापति महादेव कि जय

umāpati mahādeva ki jaya

Victory to the Great God the Lord of Umā!

चौपाई

caupāī

जय गिरिजापति दीन दयाला । सदा करत सन्तन प्रतिपाला ॥

jaya girijāpati dīna dayālā
sadā karata santana pratipālā

Praise to the Lord of She who is born of the mountain (Śiva), who is kind and compassionate to the poor, who always protects his children.

भाला चन्द्रमा सोहत नीके । कानन कुण्डल नागफनी के ॥

bhālā candramā sohata nīke
kānana kuṅḍala nāgaphanī ke

Upon whose forehead the moon is shining elegantly, and whose ears are ornamented by rings of cobra snakes.

अङ्ग गौर शिर गङ्ग बहाये । मुण्डमाल तन छार लगाये ॥

aṅga gaura śira gaṅga bahāye
muṇḍamāla tana chāra lagāye

His body is white, and upon his head the Ganga river is flowing. He wears a garland of skulls, and covers his body with ashes.

वस्त्र खाल बाघम्बर सोहे । छवि को देख नाग मुनि मोहे ॥

vastra khāla bāghambara sohe
chavi ko dekha nāga muni mohe

He wears a tiger skin garment, and his countenance appears fascinating as a naked ascetic.

मैना मातु को हवे दुलारी । बाम अङ्ग सोहत छवि न्यारी ॥

mainā mātu ko have dulārī
bāma aṅga sohata chavi nyārī

To the mother maina bird, he is as a beloved daughter. His left side shines with a female countenance.

कर त्रिशूल बाघम्बर धारी । करत सदा शत्रुन क्षयकारी ॥

kara triśūla bāghambara dhārī
karata sadā śatruna kṣaya kārī

In his hand the tiger skin clad One (Shiva) holds a trident. Always he destroys all that is enemical.

नन्दि गणेश सोहैं तहँ कैसे । सागर मद्ये कमल हैं जैसे ॥

nandi gaṇeśa sohaiṃ tahaṁ kaise
sāgara madye kamala haiṃ jaise

How are Nandi and Ganesh always there before you? Just like the lotus is in the midst of the water.

कार्तिक श्याम और गणराऊ । या छवि को कहि जात न काऊ ॥

kārtika śyāma aur gaṇarāū
yā chavi ko kahi jāta na kāū

Kartik and the dark one and others of the multitude (of divine beings), (will not be able to see) this countenance manifested in another form or any other place.

देवन जबहीं जाय पुकारा । तबही दुःख प्रभु आप निवारा ॥

devana jabahīṃ jāya pukārā
tabahī duḥkha prabhu āpa nivārā

Whenever the Gods make a shout for victory, then, Oh Lord, you prevent all pain.

किया उपद्रव तारक भारी । देवन सब मिलि तुमहिं जुहारी ॥

kiyā upadrava tāraka bhārī
devana saba mili tumahiṃ juhārī

When that great disturbance was caused by the Asura Tāraka, all the Gods united in worship to you.

तुरत षडानन आप पठायउ । लव निमेष महँ मारि गिरायउ ॥

turata ṣaḍānana āpa paṭhāyau
lava nimeṣa mahaṁ māri girāyau

Quickly you dispatched the six faced one (Kartikeya), and between the moments of a twinkling of an eye, he was thrown down to his death.

आप जलंधर असुर संहारा । सुयश तुम्हार विदित संसारा ॥

āpa jalaṃdhar asura saṃhārā
suyaśa tumhāra vidita saṃsārā

You defeated the demon Jalandhara, making your excellent welfare know to the Sansara, the world of objects and relationships.

त्रिपुरासुर सन युद्ध मचायी । सबहिं कृपा कर लीन बचायी ॥

tripurāsura sana yuddha macāyī
sabahiṃ kṛpā kara līna bacāyī

You made war against Tripurasura, and saved everyone by the grace of your absorption.

किया तपहिं भागीरथ भारी । पुरब प्रतिज्ञा तासु पुरारी ॥

kiyā tapahiṃ bhāgīratha bhārī
puraba pratijñā tāsu purārī

Oh Purari, resident of the City (a name of Śiva), what a great spiritual discipline Bhagiratha performed to complete his promise.

दानिन महँ तुम सम कोउ नाहिं । सेवक स्तुति करत सदाहीं ॥

dānina mahaṁ tuma sama kou nāhiṃ
sevaka stuti karata sadāhīṃ

There is no other comparable to your generous nature, and your devotees always sing your praises.

वेद् नाम महिमा तव गाई । अकथ अनादि भेद् नहिं पाई ॥

veda nāma mahimā tava gāī
akatha anādi bheda nahiṃ pāī

The Vedas sing the greatness of your name, but the eternal, ever-existant, indescribable is not found in the manifestations of division.

प्रकट उद्धि मन्थन में ज्वाला । जरत सुरासुर भये विहाला ॥

prakaṭa udadhi mathana meṃ jvālā
jarata surāsura bhaye vihālā

Your light manifested in the churning of the ocean, removing the ancient fear of both Gods and asuras.

कीन्ह दया तहँ करी सहाई । नीलाकंहु तब नाम कहाई ॥

kīnha dayā tahaṁ karī sahāī
nīlākaṃhu taba nāma kahāī

With what compassion you offered assistance there, when they called the name of the Blue-necked One.

पूजन रामचन्द्र जब कीन्हां । जीत के लंक विभीषण दीन्हा ॥

pūjana rāmacandra jaba kīnhāṃ
jīta ke laṃka vibhīṣaṇa dīnhā

When Ramachandra performed worship, you gave him Vibhiṣaṇa to defeat Laṅka.

सहस कमल में हो रहे धारी । कीन्ह परीक्षा तबहिं पुरारी ॥

sahasa kamala meṃ ho rahe dhārī
kīnha parīkṣā tabahiṃ purārī

Oh Purari, you performed the test of holding a thousand lotuses.

एक कमल प्रभु राखेउ जोई । कमल नयन पूजन चहं सोई ॥

eka kamala prabhu rākheu joī
kamala nayana pūjana cahaṃ soī

Oh Lord, who placed that one lotus there? It was the same lotus-eyed one who desired the puja.

कठिन भक्ति देखी प्रभु शंकर । भये प्रसन्न दिये ईच्छित वर ॥

kaṭhina bhakti dekhī prabhu śaṃkara
bhaye prasanna diye īcchita vara

Oh Lord Śaṅkara, the Cause of Peace, seeing his difficult austerities of devotion, being pleased you gave him the desired boon.

जय जय जय अनंत अविनाशी । करत कृपा सब के घटवासी ॥

jaya jaya jaya anaṃta avināśī
karata kṛpā saba ke ghaṭavāsī

Victory, Victory, Victory to the Infinite who is Indestructible. Give your grace to all the residents of creation.

दुष्ट सकल नित मोहि सतावै । भ्रमत रहे मोहि चैन न आवे ॥

duṣṭa sakala nita mohi satāvai
bhramata rahe mohi caina na āve

Every day my evil-mind is troubled. I continue in confusion and ignorance, and consciousness does not come to me.

त्राहि त्राहि मैं नाथ पुकारो । यहि अवसर मोहि आन उबारो ॥

trāhi trāhi maiṃ nātha pukāro
yahi avasara mohi āna ubāro

Save me, save me, Oh Lord! Hear my call! Raise me up at this time.

लै त्रिशूल शत्रुन को मारो । संकट से मोहि आन उबारो ॥

lai triśūla śatruna ko māro
saṃkaṭa se mohi āna ubāro

Kill the enemies with your trident, and raise me up above all pain.

मातु पिता भ्राता सब कोई । संकट में पूछत नहिं कोई ॥

mātu pitā bhrātā saba koī
saṃkaṭa meṃ pūchata nahiṃ koī

Mother, father, brothers, nor any others, do not even ask me about my pain.

स्वामी एक है आस तुम्हारी । आय हरहु अब संकट भारी ॥

svāmī eka hai āsa tumhārī
āya harahu aba saṃkaṭa bhārī
You are the only refuge, oh Master. Now take away the great weight of my pain.

धन निरधन को देत सदाहीं । जो कोई जांचे सो फल पाहीं ॥

dhana niradhana ko deta sadāhīṃ
jo koī jāṃce so phala pāhīṃ
You give to the rich and you give to the poor. Whoever comes in want, to him it is given.

अस्तुति केहि विधि करौं तुम्हारी । क्षमहु नाथ अब चूक हमारी ॥

astuti kehi vidhi karauṃ tumhārī
kṣamahu nātha aba cūka hamārī
I have no such capacity to sing your praises. Whatever mistakes I have made, please forgive them all.

शंकर हो संकट के नाशन । मङ्गल कारण विघ्न विनाशन ॥

śaṃkara ho saṃkaṭa ke nāśan
maṅgala kāraṇa vighna vināśana
Śaṅkara, Oh Cause of Peace, you are the destroyer of all pain, the cause of welfare, and destroyer of obstacles.

योगी यति मुनि द्यान लगावैं । नारद शारद शीश नवावैं ॥

yogī yati muni dyāna lagāvaiṃ
nārada śārada śīśa navāvaiṃ
Yogis, ascetics, and great wise beings, meditate upon you, as well as Narad and Śarad bow their heads to you.

नमो नमो जय नमो शिवाय । सुर ब्रह्मादिक पार न पाय ॥

namo namo jaya namo śivāya
sura brahmādika pāra na pāya
I bow, I bow, Victory! I bow to Śiva! The Gods and Brahma and other divine beings cannot discover the end of your infinity.

जो यह पाठ करे मन लाई । ता पार होत है शम्भु सहाई ॥

jo yaha pāṭha kare mana lāī
tā pāra hota hai śambhu sahāī
Whoever will recite this song with one point of mind, Śambhu, the giver of bliss, will always protect.

ऋनिया जो कोई हो अधिकारी । पाठ करे सो पावनहारी ॥

ṛniyā jo koī ho adhikārī
pāṭha kare so pāvanahārī
Debtors or others who are in want of Śiva's blessings, if they recite this song, will certainly receive according to their desires.

पुत्र हीन करे ईच्छा कोई । निश्चय शिव प्रसाद तेहि होई ॥

putra hīna kare īcchā koī
niścaya śiva prasāda tehi hoī

Whoever is without children and desirous of a child, without a doubt, Śiva will grant fulfillment to them.

पण्डित त्रयोदशी को लावे । द्यान पूर्वक होम करावे ॥

paṇḍita trayodaśī ko lāve
dyāna pūrvaka homa karāve

The wise and learned ones perform the vow of worship on the thirteenth day, and meditate and perform the fire sacrifice for Lord Śiva.

त्रयोदशी व्रत करे हमेशा । तन नहीं ताके रहे कलेशा ॥

trayodaśī vrata kare hameśā
tana nahīṃ tāke rahe kaleśā

Who always performs the vow of worship on the thirteenth day, his body will continue to be free from pain.

धूप दीप नैवेद्य चढावे । संकर सन्मुख पाठ सुनावे ॥

dhūpa dīpa naivedya caḍhāve
saṃkara sanmukha pāṭha sunāve

Offerings of incense, lights and food will be made, and this recitation will be made in front of Lord Śiva.

जन्म जन्म के पाप नसावे । अन्तवास शिवपुर में पावे ॥

janma janma ke pāpa nasāve
antavāsa śivapura meṃ pāve

Sins of many births will be destroyed, and at last you will reside in the city of Śiva.

कहै अयोद्या आस तुम्हारी। जानि सकल दुःख हरहु हमारी॥

kahai ayodyā āsa tumhārī
jāni sakala duḥkha harahu hamārī

This is the expectation of your devotee (Ayodya name); I know you will remove all pain from me.

दोहा

dohā

नित्त नेम कर प्रातः ही पाठ करौ चालीस।
तुम मेरी मनोकामना पूर्ण करो जगदीश॥

nitta nema kara prātḥa hī pāṭha karau cālīsa
tuma merī manokāmanā pūrṇa karo jagadīśa

If one will always recite this song of praise in the early morning of every day, every desire will be fulfilled, Oh Lord of the Universe.

उमापति महादेव कि जय

umāpati mahādeva ki jaya

Victory to the Great God the Lord of Umā!

The Pronunciation of Saṃskṛta Transliteration

a	organ, sum
ā	father
ai	ai sle
au	sauerkraut
b	but
bh	abhor
c	church
ḍ	dough
d	dough (slightly toward the th sound of though)
ḍh	adh ere
dh	adhere
e	prey
g	go
gh	doghouse
ḥ	slight aspiration of preceding vowel
h	hot
i	it
ī	police
j	jump
jh	lodgehouse
k	kid
kh	workhorse
l	lug
ṃ	resonant nasalization of preceding vowe
m	mud
ṅ	sing
ṇ	under
ñ	piñata
n	no
o	no
p	pub
ph	uphill
ṛ	no English equivalent; a simple vowel r , such as appears in many Slavonic languages

r room
ś shawl (pronounced with a slight whistle; German sprechen)
ṣ shun
s sun
ṭ tomato
t water
ṭh Thailand
u push
ū rude
v vodka (midway between w and v)
y yes

Books by Shree Maa and Swami Satyananda Saraswati

Bhagavad Gītā
Chaṇḍi Pāṭh
Cosmic Pūjā
Devī Gītā
Devī Mandir Songbook
Durgā Pūjā Beginner
Ganeśa Pūjā
Gems From the Chaṇḍi
Guru Gītā
Hanumān Pūjā
Kālī Dhyānam
Kālī Pūjā
Lalitā Triśati
Sadhu Stories from the Himalayas
Shree Maa - The Guru & the Goddess
Shree Maa, The Life of a Saint
Śiva Pūjā Beginner
Śiva Pūjā & Advanced Yajña
Sundara Kāṇḍa
Swāmī Purāṇa

Cassette Tapes and CDs by Shree Maa and Swamiji

Lalitā Triśati
Navarṇa Mantra
Shree Maa at the Devi Mandir
Shree Maa in Mendocino
Śiva Pūjā Beginner
Shiva is in My Heart
The Goddess is Everywhere
The Songs of Ramprasad
The Thousand Names of Kālī

Please visit us on the
World Wide Web at http://www.shreemaa.org